EXPLORING MASCULINITIES

Gender in Law, Culture, and Society

Series Editor
Martha Albertson Fineman, Emory University School of Law, USA

Gender in Law, Culture, and Society will address key issues and theoretical debates related to gender, culture, and the law. Its titles will advance understanding of the ways in which a society's cultural and legal approaches to gender intersect, clash, and are reconciled or remain in tension. The series will further examine connections between gender and economic and political systems, as well as various other cultural and societal influences on gender construction and presentation, including social and legal consequences that men and women uniquely or differently encounter. Intended for a scholarly readership as well as for courses, its titles will be a mix of single-authored volumes and collections of original essays that will be both pragmatic and theoretical. It will draw from the perspectives of critical and feminist legal theory, as well as other schools of jurisprudence. Interdisciplinary, and international in scope, the series will offer a range of voices speaking to significant questions arising from the study of law in relation to gender, including the very nature of law itself.

Other titles in the series

Feminism, Law, and Religion
Edited by Marie A. Failinger, Elizabeth R. Schiltz and Susan J. Stabile
ISBN 9781409444190

Critical Queer Studies: Law, Film, and Fiction in Contemporary American Culture
Casey Charles
ISBN 9781409444060

Exploring Masculinities

Feminist Legal Theory Reflections

Edited by

MARTHA ALBERTSON FINEMAN
Emory University, USA

MICHAEL THOMSON
University of Leeds, UK

ASHGATE

Published by
Ashgate Publishing Limited
Wey Court East
Union Road
Farnham
Surrey, GU9 7PT
England

Ashgate Publishing Company
110 Cherry Street
Suite 3-1
Burlington, VT 05401-3818
USA

www.ashgate.com

British Library Cataloguing in Publication Data
A catalogue record for this book is available from the British Library

The Library of Congress has cataloged the printed edition as follows:
Exploring masculinities : feminist legal theory reflections / by Martha Albertson Fineman and Michael Thomson.
pages cm. — (Gender in law, culture, and society)
Includes bibliographical references and index.
ISBN 978-1-4724-1511-0 (hardback : alk. paper) — ISBN 978-1-4724-1512-7 (pbk. : alk. paper) — ISBN 978-1-4724-1513-4 (ebook) — ISBN 978-1-4724-1514-1 (epub) 1. Men. 2. Masculinity. 3. Feminist theory. 4. ex role. 5. en—Legal status, laws, etc. I. Fineman, Martha, editor of compilation. II. Thomson, Michael, 1970– editor of compilation.
HQ1090.E92 2013
305.31–dc23

2013020865

ISBN 9781472415110 (hbk)
ISBN 9781472415127 (pbk)
ISBN 9781472415134 (ebk – PDF)
ISBN 9781472415141 (ebk – ePUB)

MIX
Paper from
responsible sources
FSC
www.fsc.org
FSC® C013985

Printed in the United Kingdom by Henry Ling Limited,
at the Dorset Press, Dorchester, DT1 1HD

Contents

List of Tables

Notes on Contributors

Jamie R. Abrams is Assistant Professor at the University of Louisville Brandeis School of Law, where she teaches Torts, Domestic Relations, and Legislation. She has previously published in numerous law and gender journals, including the *Cardozo Law Review*, the *South Carolina Law Review* and the *West Virginia Law Review* on topics relating to obstetric malpractice claims, masculinities theory, sex discrimination, reproductive rights, immigrant rights, and legal education pedagogy. She received her LL.M from Columbia University and her J.D. from the American University Washington College of Law, gaining the highest academic honours from both institutions.

Fionnuala Ní Aoláin concurrently holds the Dorsey & Whitney Chair in Law at the University of Minnesota Law School and a chair in Law at the Transitional Justice Institute (Belfast). She was a Fulbright scholar at Harvard Law School and Associate-in-Law at Columbia Law School, Associate Professor of Law at the Hebrew University, and co-founder of the Transitional Justice Institute at the University of Ulster. Ní Aoláin has been active in human rights and women's rights issues in Ireland and internationally throughout her academic career. She is co-author of *On the Frontlines: Gender, War, and the Post-conflict Process* (Oxford University Press, 2011), along with Dina Haynes and Naomi Cahn.

Chris Beasley is Professor in Politics and Co-director of the Fay Gale Centre for Research on Gender at the University of Adelaide. Her books include *Heterosexuality in Theory and Practice* (with Heather Brook and Mary Holmes, Routledge, 2012), *Engaging with Carol Bacchi* (edited with Angelique Bletsas, University of Adelaide Press, 2012), *Gender & Sexuality: Critical Theories, Critical Thinkers* (Sage, 2005), *What is Feminism?* (Sage, 1999), and *Sexual Economyths* (Allen & Unwin, 1994). She is currently writing a book on contemporary popular film titled *The Cultural Politics of Popular Film: Power, Culture and Society* (with Heather Brook, Manchester University Press).

Naomi Cahn is the Harold H. Greene Professor of Law at George Washington University Law School. She has written numerous law review articles and several books in the areas of family law, international law, and feminism. Professor Cahn is a member of the executive committee of the Women in International Law Interest Group of the American Society of International Law, and a member of the Yale Cultural Cognition Project. She is co-author of *On the Frontlines: Gender, War, and the Post-conflict Process* (Oxford University Press, 2011), along with Fionnuala Ní Aoláin and Dina Haynes.

David S. Cohen is Associate Professor of Law at the Earle Mack School of Law at Drexel University. Prior to teaching, he was a staff attorney with the Women's Law Project in Philadelphia. David teaches courses in constitutional law and sex discrimination, and his scholarship focuses on gender, masculinity, and sex segregation. His recent publications include 'The Stubborn Persistence of Sex Segregation' in the *Columbia Journal of Gender and Law* and 'Keeping Men "Men" and Women Down: Sex Segregation, Anti-essentialism, and Masculinity' in the *Harvard Journal of Law and Gender*. He is currently working on a book about violence against abortion providers.

Richard Collier is Professor of Law at Newcastle University, UK. He has published widely in the area of law and gender, with a particular focus on issues surrounding men and masculinities, and his books include: *Men, Law and Gender: Essays on the 'Man' of Law* (Routledge, 2010), *Fragmenting Fatherhood: A Socio-legal Study* (with Sally Sheldon, Hart, 2008), *Masculinities, Crime and Criminology: Men, Corporeality and the Criminal(ised) Body* (Sage, 1998), *Masculinity, Law and the Family* (Routledge, 1995), and *Fathers' Rights Activism and Law Reform in Comparative Perspective* (edited with Sally Sheldon, Hart, 2006). Richard is presently conducting a research project on male lawyers, masculinities and work–life balance in the legal profession entitled *Fathers, Lawyers and Work–Life Balance*. Richard is an editorial board member of *Social and Legal Studies: An International Journal*.

Frank Rudy Cooper is Professor of Law at Suffolk University in Boston, Massachusetts. He previously taught at Villanova University School of Law. He is co-editor of *Masculinities and the Law: A Multidimensional Approach* (New York University Press, 2012) (with Ann C. McGinley). He is co-founder of the John Mercer Langston Black Male Law Faculty Writing Workshop and a past or present board member of several national law professor organizations.

Jocelyn Elise Crowley is Professor of Public Policy at Rutgers, The State University of New Jersey. Her research focuses primarily on American social policy, and she has published her work in over fifteen peer-reviewed journals. In addition, her books include *The Politics of Child Support in America* (Cambridge University Press, 2003), *Defiant Dads: Fathers' Rights Activists in America* (Cornell University Press, 2008), and *Mothers Unite! Organizing for Workplace Flexibility and the Transformation of Family Life* (Cornell University Press, 2013).

Nancy E. Dowd is Professor and David H. Levin Chair in Family Law and Director of the Center on Children and Families at the Fredric G. Levin College of Law. She is the author of *The Man Question: Male Subordination and Privilege* (New York University Press, 2010), and in addition to her scholarship on masculinities her work is currently focused on issues surrounding the juvenile justice system and fatherhood. She is the series editor for Families, Law, and Society for New York University Press.

Roja Fazaeli is Assistant Professor in Islamic Civilisation(s) at the Department of Near and Middle Eastern Studies, Trinity College Dublin. She has published numerous papers and book chapters on the topics of Islam and gender, Islamic feminism, and human rights. Roja is a global affiliate at the School of Law, Emory University and serves on the editorial board of the *Journal for Religion and Human Rights*. She is also a board member of Amnesty International, Ireland.

Martha Albertson Fineman is Robert W. Woodruff Professor of Law. She received a B.A. from Temple University in 1971 and a J.D. from the University of Chicago in 1975. Fineman is the founding director of the Feminism and Legal Theory Project, an interdisciplinary project she began at the University of Wisconsin in 1984. She directs the Vulnerability and the Human Condition Initiative. Her scholarly work focuses on various aspects of the legal regulation of intimacy and on the social, cultural and legal implications of human dependency and vulnerability. She has won numerous awards for her writing and teaching, including the prestigious Harry Kalven Prize for Distinguished Research in Law and Society.

Marie Fox is Professor of Socio-legal Studies at the University of Birmingham. Her research focuses on how law regulates human and animal bodies. Recent publications include 'Realising Social Justice in Public Health Law' (with Michael Thomson) (2013) 21(2) *Medical Law Review* 278–309, 'The New Politics of Male Circumcision: HIV/AIDS, Health Law and Social Justice' (with Michael Thomson) (2012) 32 *Legal Studies* 255–81, 'Law and Veterinary Ethics', in C. Wathes (ed.) *Veterinary and Animal Ethics* (Wiley Blackwell, 2012), 'Embryonic Hopes: Controversy, Alliance and Reproductive Entities in Law and the Social Sciences' (with M. Jacob, B. Prainsack, M. Murphy and T. Franklin) (2010) 19 *Social and Legal Studies* 497–517, and 'Legal Embodiment: Analysing the Body of Healthcare Law' (with R. Fletcher and J. McCandless) (2008) 16 *Medical Law Review* 321–45.

Dina Haynes is Professor of Law at New England Law School. She has previously taught at Georgetown University Law Center, American University's Washington College of Law, and the University of Nevada, Las Vegas. Prior to teaching, Haynes was a practising international human rights lawyer in a variety of positions and has worked on human rights, human trafficking, gender, and post-conflict reconstruction issues in Chad, Botswana, South Africa, Rwanda, Croatia, Bosnia and Herzegovina, Serbia, Macedonia and Romania. She is co-author of *On the Frontlines: Gender, War, and the Post-conflict Process* (Oxford University Press, 2011), along with Fionnuala Ní Aoláin and Naomi Cahn.

Ann C. McGinley is William S. Boyd Professor of Law at the Boyd School of Law of the University of Nevada, Las Vegas, where she has taught since 1999. An internationally known scholar on employment discrimination, Professor McGinley has published numerous articles on masculinities and employment discrimination law. She is co-editor with Frank Rudy Cooper of *Masculinities and the Law: A Multidimensional Approach* (New York University Press, 2012).

Maria Cristina Morales received a Ph.D. from Texas A&M University and is currently Associate Professor of Sociology at the University of Texas at El Paso. Dr Morales has written several articles on gender/sex. For example, she coined the term 'border sexual conquest' to describe how structural violence marginalizes women but also ignites agency, which has been applied to the feminicides in Juárez and border control measures along the U.S.–Mexico and Morocco–Spanish borders. She has also collaborated with law professor Leticia Saucedo to study how masculinity operates to mask discriminatory practices in immigrant workplaces and on how it shapes incentives for border crossing.

Camille A. Nelson is Dean and Professor of Law at Suffolk University Law School. Before joining Suffolk Law she taught at Hofstra and Saint Louis universities. She received her B.A. from the University of Toronto, her law degree from the University of Ottawa, and a Master of Laws from Columbia Law School in New York. She clerked for Justice Frank Iacobucci of the Supreme Court of Canada before working as a litigation associate at McCarthy Tétrault in Toronto, the largest law firm in Canada. Dean Nelson is an elected member of the American Law Institute and is widely recognized for her writings and lectures, which have focused on the intersection of critical race theory and cultural studies with particular emphasis on criminal law and procedure, health law and comparative law.

Clifford Rosky is Associate Professor of Law at the University of Utah's S.J. Quinney College of Law, where he teaches courses on criminal law, civil rights, and sexuality, gender and law. Before joining the faculty, he served as a research fellow for the Williams Institute on Sexual Orientation Law & Public Policy at the UCLA School of Law. His research has been published in the *Yale Journal of Law & Feminism*, the *Arizona Law Review*, the *Buffalo Law Review* and the *Connecticut Law Review*.

Leticia Saucedo is Professor of Law and Director of Clinical Legal Education at U.C. Davis School of Law. Her research interests lie in the areas of employment, labour and immigration law.

Michael Thomson is Professor of Law at the University of Leeds, UK. His research spans the fields of health law, children's rights and legal theory with a particular focus on legal embodiment. Recent work with Marie Fox has addressed legal responses to genital cutting. He is the author of *Reproducing Narrative: Gender, Reproduction and Law* (Dartmouth, 1998), *Feminist Perspectives on Health Care Law* (edited with Sally Sheldon, Cavendish, 1998), and *Endowed: Regulating the Male Sexed Body* (Routledge, 2008). His current work explores alternative decision-making frameworks and the pursuit of social justice in health and child law.

Juliet A. Williams is Associate Professor of Gender Studies at UCLA. She is the author of *Liberalism and the Limits of Power* (Palgrave Macmillan, 2005) and co-editor of *Public Affairs: Politics in the Age of Sex Scandals* (with Paul Apostolidis, Duke University Press, 2004). As a socio-legal scholar, she has published widely on contemporary gender politics, with articles appearing in such journals as *Signs* and the *Harvard Journal of Law and Gender*. Her current book project, *Making a Difference: Single-sex Public Education and the New Politics of Gender Equality*, examines recent debates over the nature and significance of gender difference in school settings.

Acknowledgements

We are grateful to the contributors for their hard work and inspiring papers. We also thank the anonymous reviewers, who gave such thorough and careful suggestions for revisions on each of the chapters. Lastly, we are grateful to Brenda Huffman and Yvana Mols of Emory Law School, both of whom helped tremendously, and with characteristic goodwill, during the final stages of readying this collection for publication.

Martha Albertson Fineman
Michael Thomson

Chapter 1
Introduction

Martha Albertson Fineman and Michael Thomson

This collection of chapters investigates the ways in which emerging masculinities theories in law could inform feminist legal theory in particular and law in general. Masculinities theories generally explore relationships of subordination between different men and how those relationships rebound in the subordination of women. A central theme of masculinities studies has been the construction of idealized and societally praised forms of masculinity. In addition to devaluing women and 'non-masculine' men, such hegemonic modes of masculinity serve to create a general sense of anxiety among men as to whether they can live up to the hyper-gendered standards.

Relations of subordinations and the process of indoctrination into hegemonic masculinity have implications for law. As many of the chapters in this collection illustrate, law is constantly in a dynamic interaction with masculinities: it has both influenced existing masculinities and has been influenced by those masculinities. Despite the integral link between law and masculinities, few feminist legal scholars have examined the implications of masculinities theories for feminist legal theorizing. The chapters in this collection are intended to focus feminist and critical theoretical attention on masculinities and to consider the implications of masculinities theories for law and legal theory.

Part I sets out the theoretical trajectory of masculinities studies as a field and its application in law. In Chapter 2, Nancy E. Dowd highlights the importance to feminist theory of 'asking the man question'. Dowd believes that by asking '[w]hat is the position of [some or all] boys and/or men in [a] situation', feminist theorists can better understand the social and psychological construction of male dominance. Also, 'asking the man question' will spur feminist theory to be attentive to harm suffered by boys and men, thus avoiding essentialism in understanding multiple and diverse forms of discrimination and inequality. Masculinity analysis, according to Dowd, can inform feminist theory by making visible gender issues embedded in situations in which one sex is dominant, regardless of whether members of the dominant sex are privileged or harmed by those gender issues. Dowd warns feminist theorists about the risks in adopting a masculinities approach of displacing the focus on women's issues or ending up blaming women for men's challenges. She cautions that masculinities scholars need to constantly challenge masculine hegemony and patriarchy and work towards creating a reoriented masculinity as an affirmative identity.

In Chapter 3, Martha Albertson Fineman raises some concerns about the use of masculinities theory that are part of a broader critique about the limitations of focusing on identity-based approaches in seeking social justice and equality. Too often identity-based arguments, theories and approaches fail to address complex institutional and structural forms of injustice. She argues that the most important task for those interested in a social justice project at this particular time in legal history (at least in the United States) is to construct a universal legal subject based on an appreciation of the human condition with which to effectively combat the exalted universal liberal subject with its attendant political mandates of personal responsibility, small government and autonomy.

In Part II, the authors use insights from a masculinities approach to study the sociopolitical construction of gender identities in specific settings. Roja Fazaeli points to evolution of notions of gender identity as a result of sociopolitical developments in the contemporary Middle Eastern context. In both Palestine and Iran, women have shown an increased willingness to participate in seeking 'martyrdom' in fighting against Israel or the United States. As a result, the historically masculine notion of martyrdom is being challenged in ways that have transformed cultural understandings of both femininity and masculinity. On the one hand, values of bravery and political militancy traditionally deemed masculine are used to explain women. Women are deemed equal to men in their duty to protect their country or faith and seeking martyrdom in that path. On the other hand, men are described with some traditionally feminine attributes such as economic and political dependence and weakness.

The role of sociopolitical factors in forming gender identities is again revisited in Camille A. Nelson's chapter. Nelson believes that the presence of misogynist and homophobic themes in recent Jamaican dancehall music has to be understood in the context of the construction of Jamaican national masculinity in colonial and post-colonial Jamaica. As a primary vehicle of national identity construction in post-colonial Jamaica, dancehall defines 'Jamaican-ness' as being not 'gay, lesbian, white or weak'. Unknown to dancehall artists, however, they are deriving their formulation of Jamaican national identity from a historical trajectory of homophobia and opposition to non-procreative sex in which British colonial impositions have been constitutive. Nelson concludes, 'in seeking to legitimize themselves post independence, Jamaicans struck a legislative bargain with their former colonizers.' She underscores the importance of understanding cultural roots of gender oppression in other parts of the world and warns against ignoring such local, historical and cultural issues in framing strategies to help gender equity activists around the world.

Frank Rudy Cooper's chapter investigates the effects of intersectional factors such as race, class or position in social institutions on the construction of gender identities. He considers how individuals perform their socially defined gender roles in real-world occurrences influenced by those intersectional factors. In explaining the 2009 confrontation between a police officer and a black male Harvard scholar, Henry Louis Gates, Jr., that led to Gates's arrest, Cooper asserts that the officer's class background and position in the police department as well as Gates's race were relevant factors in explaining the parties' behaviour. All these factors (the so-called 'penalty statuses') are markers of one's identity that may make an individual insecure in his masculinity, creating anxieties and efforts to reclaim his masculinity. What resulted in the Gates arrest was a 'masculinity contest' between the police officer and Gates that created a zero-sum game of claiming dominance over the other party.

In Part III, the authors provide insights into how understanding historical constructions of gender identities can inform more effective public policy and activism. Marie Fox and Michael Thomson discuss the notions of masculinity underlying medical recommendations for male genital cutting and warn against the continued presence of such stereotypical notions in the contemporary mobilization of male circumcision in response to HIV/AIDS in sub-Saharan Africa. Historically, medical recommendations in the United States for male circumcision were often grounded in projects aimed at controlling black masculinity, perceived as hyper-sexual and threatening. Circumcision has also been tied to concerns regarding sexually transmitted diseases and male hygiene. Against this historical background, the authors argue for a more careful examination of contemporary – largely American funded – circumcision programmes. Further, Fox and Thomson point out that the current policy encouraging male genital cutting in sub-Saharan Africa pays little attention to concerns over women's health, including risks that any protection offered by circumcision is overstated, will not be evident (if at all) for decades, and will compromise women's ability to negotiate condom use and, ultimately, their health. Given this background, Fox and Thomson express concerns over funnelling resources towards population level circumcision programmes in attempts to fight HIV/AIDS in Africa.

Chris Beasley explores the idea of reorienting masculinity towards embracing equitable gender practices. She proposes that masculinity theory needs to rethink its understanding of hetero-masculinity and heterosexuality by integrating pleasure as a key component of its understanding of heterosexual relationships. She finds that conceptions of heterosexuality in both gender and sexuality studies and preventive health literature are informed by a negative conception focused on risk, danger and prevention. Against this background, Beasley proposes a positive narrative of hetero-masculinity that embraces egalitarian sexual practices. Beasley cites the successes of campaigns based on condoms as an erotic necessity in increasing men's acceptance of condom use to support her proposition.

The theme of reorienting masculinities towards positive directions in order to prevent male aggression is the topic of the chapter by Fionnuala Ní Aoláin, Naomi Cahn and Dina Haynes. They argue that the construction of aggressive masculine identities in post-conflict eras is a result of frustrations men feel when unable to positively express their masculine roles in post-conflict periods. Aggressive masculinities harm women and the negative implications of unaddressed masculinities in causing continued gender violence means that effective post-conflict transition programmes will have to be mindful of the importance of attention to masculinities. The authors propose that post-conflict transition programmes need to make attempts at socializing men in their communities, emphasize values of gender equity to them, and address male victimization during periods of conflict. Accordingly, they criticize current Disarmament, Demobilization and Reintegration practices as not adequately addressing gender violence in post-conflict reconciliation efforts.

Jamie R. Abrams critiques the lack of attention to social construction of gender identities and their role in transformations of gender violence in the context of feminist movements' attempts at reforms in the contexts of domestic violence and military integration laws. While both areas of feminist law reform successfully challenged and led to modified visions of prevalent hegemonic masculinities, their success was to some extent tainted by the influences of existing masculinities on the law reform projects. Law reforms for protection of women in domestic violence situations resulted in reinforcing the dominant conception of men as being naturally prone to violence, as well as portraying women as weak and in need of protection. Governmental protection of female soldiers in the wake of military gender integration similarly has reproduced the image of women as weak and in need of protection. As a result, opponents of women's integration can assert that 'they find it irreconcilable to position women as "helpless victims of sexual harassment" by male service members, while contemplating women as "fearless warriors" in direct ground combat.' Abrams therefore recommends that law reform measures should incorporate masculinities theory, which will benefit them in understanding gender violence and discrimination.

In two separate chapters in Part IV, Juliet A. Williams and David S. Cohen discuss movements for single-sex education. Williams discusses the political dynamics by which proponents of single-sex education have pursued their goals. She points to the limitation of the intermediate scrutiny analysis adopted by the Supreme Court in analysing sex discrimination. She points out that, despite their questionable scientific accuracy, the recent wave of identifying biological and brain-based distinctions between boys and girls is likely to be used to justify single-sex education. These narratives appeal to the inadequacies of Supreme Court criteria for evaluating sexually discriminatory laws that emphasize 'real' and biological differences between sexes that could be grounds for constitutionally permissible discrimination. Proponents of single-sex education also claim that current co-education is responsible for the inequalities in the educational system harming poor and disadvantaged kids. Williams warns of the risk of cooptation of economic and class inequalities in order to bolster the same-sex education movement, which is rooted in assumptions about gender identity and not informed by economic or class-based concerns.

Cohen points to the construction of dominant forms of masculine and feminine gender identities in the context of the single-sex education. The masculine identity constructed in single-sex education is a hegemonic one, with traits of heteronormativity, aggression, high activity, sports obsession, competitiveness, stoicism, and rejection of things perceived as feminine. Those essentialized notions of masculine identity prevent alternative conceptions of masculinities to flourish, thus alienating both girls and boys who fail to live up to this ideal. It also creates anxieties in all boys who are cast in competition with each other to achieve this ideal masculinity. Unlike Williams, Cohen believes that current anti-discrimination jurisprudence both in United States' Supreme Court case law and concerning Title IX of the Civil Rights Act's 'anti-essentialism thread' if read properly have potentials for confronting the threat of single-sex public education.

Part V considers masculinities at work. Ann C. McGinley investigates possibilities for plaintiffs to challenge workplace structures that reward socially defined parameters of masculinity under American anti-discrimination jurisprudence. She asserts that academic tenure-track jobs that require heavy time investment during a point in the life-course where men typically have greater flexibility than women may be prone to attacks based on a disparate impact theory of discrimination. Gender-biased curricula and training programmes also could be challenged both under disparate impact and disparate treatment theories of discrimination. McGinley notes that masculinities studies could be used to show that hiring criteria, such as a preference for competitiveness or aggressiveness for car dealers, embody stereotypes that favour white males and disfavour minority men and females. She argues that establishing this fact could lead to more viable anti-discrimination challenges to such hiring criteria.

Leticia M. Saucedo and Maria Cristina Morales undertake a qualitative empirical study of immigrant construction workers employed in the Las Vegas residential construction industry and interrogate patterns of masculinity developed in that context. Due to the effect of oppressive work conditions, immigrant workers reinterpret their experiences in ways that elevate them above women in workplace hierarchy. As such, the brown-collar hyper-masculinity of immigrant workers is built around understanding their abilities and experiences as uniquely qualifying them for the work at hand. They interpret their willingness to take jobs as independent contractors (rather than employees with greater benefits) as representing their ability to take risks and showing their entrepreneurial capabilities. They also cast their withstanding of the challenges of immigration as evidence of their extraordinary toughness. Their hyper-masculine workplace culture also disdains complaints about health and safety risks as indicating weakness and fragility. The authors recommend empowering new workforce narratives that emphasize safety and health.

In Part VI on the family, Richard Collier discusses how emerging discourses on fathers' rights (especially concerning men's post-divorce child adoption and visitation rights) relate to new socially and legally constructed images of masculinity. While protests by fathers' rights groups often embody public representations of hyper-masculine modes of behaviour, they also present issues of men's emotional health that cut across traditional notions of masculinity and the kind of rational and reasonable fatherhood portrayed in law. Collier believes that exhibiting such behaviour seems to be one of the many ways in which men, while drawing upon conventional notions of male parental responsibility, respond to accumulated personal problems and the emotional trauma they are experiencing in the divorce setting. Collier urges a comprehensive understanding of how the construction of gender identity manifests itself in the divorce context, including attention to emotion, and the welfare of the disputants.

In her chapter, Jocelyn Elise Crowley describes the views of many members of fathers' rights movements and proposes ways to effectively accommodate their concerns in family law. Analysing the results of surveys she conducted, she concludes that proponents of fathers' rights movements believe they are prevented from parenting their children after divorce because the current child custody system is anti-child, excessively interventionist, and biased towards mothers. Crowley believes that a de-gendered legal standard that gives priority custodial preference to the parent who has contributed most to the child's life prior to divorce would work to lessen the influence of gender biases in custodial determinations and also encourage more egalitarian divisions of parental responsibilities.

Finally, Clifford J. Rosky investigates the role of homophobic and sexist stereotypes in custody and visitation cases involving the children of gay and lesbian parents. Because of the strength of the belief that children are more likely to be influenced by the parent of the same sex in formulating their gender identity, gay fathers of boys and lesbian mothers of girls face stereotypes more frequently than gay fathers of girls or lesbian mothers of boys. Influenced by a concern over the perceived central role of the 'masculine' father in the development of masculine boys, homophobic stereotypes are frequently found in cases of boys with both gay fathers and lesbian mothers. On the other hand, gay fathers of girls faced considerably fewer instances of stereotyping in the cases studied by the author. Rosky speculates that, because masculinity is perceived as more socially valuable than femininity, 'unmasculine' gay fathers are allowed to raise female daughters despite another social stereotype in which 'fatherless' daughters are harmed by lack of strong male role models.

Together the chapters in this collection probably raise more questions about how the relationship between feminisms and masculinities theories will unfold over the next decade than they answer. The only observation we can feel confident in making is that the interaction of masculinities scholars with those engaged in feminist legal theory work has been productive and creative, enhancing the work of both groups of scholars and activists – a pattern we would like to see continue.

PART I
Feminist Legal Theory and Masculinities and Law

Chapter 2
Asking the Man Question: Masculinities Analysis and Feminist Theory[1]

Nancy E. Dowd

Masculinities scholarship is an essential piece of feminist analysis and of critical equality analysis. It requires that we 'ask the man question' to further unravel inequalities (Dowd 2008, 2010). Asking the 'man question' means simply to ask, 'What is the position of boys and/or men in this situation?' Implicit in this question should be a second question, 'Does this apply to all boys and/or men, or only to some, or does it affect different men differently?' A decade ago Angela Harris urged legal scholars to ask the 'man question' by exposing the masculinities present in the brutal sodomization of Abner Louima, a Haitian immigrant, by white police officers while Louima was in police custody (Harris 2000). To many, race alone explained what had occurred in the Louima case. Failure to recognize how masculinities infused that incident as well, Harris argued, would ratify and condone male-on-male violence, hypermasculinity in police culture, and the racial hierarchy of masculinities present in the incident. In the decade since Harris's analysis, much work has been done in masculinities scholarship, but few legal scholars have brought this perspective into the mainstream of critical legal scholarship (Collier 2010a, McGinley 2010, 2007a, 2004, Cooper 2006a, Gavanas 2004a, Giller 2004, Howarth 2002, Kimmel 1997a, Levit 1996, 1999, Vojdik 2002). This book marks one of several movements towards examining and considering what masculinities scholarship can offer (*Harvard Journal of Law and Gender* 2010, Cooper and McGinley 2012, McGinley 2010).

In this chapter, I suggest a framework of masculinities analysis and describe its relationship to feminist theory. First, I consider why we should ask the 'man question' and how we should ask it. Second, I explore how masculinities analysis might be useful in our examination of the 'man question.' Masculinities work can be used to understand more clearly how male privilege and dominance are constructed. It can make us see harms suffered by boys and men that we have largely ignored. It may also reinforce and strengthen the commitment to antiessentialism in feminist theory. Exposing the complexities and multiplicity of masculinities leads towards understanding intersectional and multiple forms of discrimination more clearly. In this way, it is analogous to noticing that the issues

---

1 This is an edited version of an article that appeared in 33 *Harvard Journal of Law and Gender* 415–30 (2010).

and positions of all women are not the same and include instances of women subordinating women.

Masculinities analysis may also remind us to be attentive to different patterns of inequality and to our interpretation of those patterns. Where one sex is sole or dominant, dominance should be something that triggers scrutiny. This should matter both when the dominant sex benefits (as in occupying high-paid jobs) and when it is harmed (as in occupying more prison cells). We should question not only why one sex fills or dominates the pattern, but also the gendered meaning of both who is present and who is absent. Oddly, when one sex is dominant, sometimes gender issues are rendered invisible. Examples of this are male predominance in the juvenile and adult criminal justice systems, and women's predominance in the welfare system. Invisibility is fostered by gender-neutral language that covers the predominance of gender patterns, but also by the acceptance of the pattern as usual, normal and taken for granted.

On the other hand, where both sexes are present, one or both may claim bias. We tend to frame competing claims of bias as requiring prioritization or hierarchy rather than seeing how they interconnect. We tend to argue over who has the more important issues to address or the most pressing 'crisis'. Resisting this 'either/or' approach or a hierarchy of inequalities is critical. For example, in education, there are inequality issues for both girls and boys, women and men. Rather than exclusively focusing on the issues of one sex to the exclusion of the other, as if only one can claim our focus or deserve our attention, we should see and insist on addressing both. Inequalities often interlock (Ehrenreich 2002). A battle of the sexes, moreover, may only divert attention from more serious issues of race and class (Jenkins 2006). Examining subordination in isolation undermines our understanding and our attack upon the interacting dynamic, even if gender-specific problem solving is needed.

Finally, doing masculinities analysis is tricky and risky. It triggers the potential for adverse, counterproductive outcomes. Raising issues about men when so many issues about women remain generates resistance and distrust. The embrace of masculinities analysis is justifiably a cautious one due to the persistence of patriarchy's reinvention of itself, even using the language and arguments of feminists to reinscribe dominance. Masculinities analysis needs to continually challenge itself to challenge the hegemony of men and male power. The project of imagining positive, affirming, egalitarian masculinities is ongoing, but it is absolutely essential. Finally, the ultimate theoretical model remains unclear: whether masculinities scholarship and feminist theory will mutually influence each other but remain separate, or whether they will build a larger, more comprehensive gender analysis.

A Framework of Masculinities Analysis

The Man Question

Feminist theory has continually questioned, disputed and debated itself, and that self-analysis has only strengthened feminist analysis (see, e.g., Chamallas 2012, Bartlett 2000, Littleton 1987, Weisberg 1993, Higgins 2004). Incorporating masculinities scholarship continues that tradition, as well as correcting an essentialist, limited view of men. By examining the construction of identity and power, it increases our understanding and estimation of the source and functioning of subordination. At the same time, it allows us to see that the culture and structure of gender harms boys and men as well, whether it is the 'price' of privilege (for example, the stress or danger associated with certain jobs), or the result of men subordinating men as a way of performing masculinities (as when men are the victims of male violence or workplace harassment), or the harm inflicted by women on boys (who disproportionately are the target of physical forms of child abuse) (Dowd 2010). In addition, by exposing the multiplicity and hierarchy of masculinities, masculinities work delivers the powerful insight that gender does not confer privilege on all men. Because the combination of race and/or class with gender can trigger subordination (at the hands of both men and women), it reveals how race and class are feminist issues because they are intertwined with the playing out of gender power.

In my prior work I have argued that masculinities scholarship suggests a series of teachings (Dowd 2008, 2010). These are what I have identified as core propositions, presented here in summary:

1. Men are not universal or undifferentiated.
2. Men pay a price for privilege.
3. Intersections of manhood particularly with race, class, and sexual orientation are critical to the interplay of privilege and disadvantage, to hierarchies among men, and factors that may entirely trump male gender privilege.
4. Masculinity is a social construction, not a biological given.
5. Hegemonic masculinity recognizes that one masculinity norm dominates multiple masculinities.
6. The patriarchal dividend is the benefit that all men have from the dominance of men in the overall gender order.
7. The two most common pieces defining masculinity are, at all costs, to not be like a woman and not be gay.
8. Masculinity is as much about relation to other men as it is about relation to women.
9. Men, although powerful, feel powerless.
10. Masculinities study exposes how structures and cultures are gendered male.

11. The spaces and places that men and women daily inhabit and work within are remarkably different.
12. The role of men in achieving feminist goals is uncertain and unclear.
13. The asymmetry of masculinities scholarship and feminist theory reflects the differences in the general position of men and women (Dowd 2010: 73–82).

The implications of these teachings for feminist theory are that feminists should 'ask the man question' as part of the core inquiry of 'asking the other question' that Mari Matsuda so skilfully and simply has demonstrated is critical to justice (Matsuda 1993). Whether obvious or hidden, masculinities issues are frequently present in gender analysis. This does not mean shifting focus away from women, as the dynamics of gender power are asymmetrical. Because the relative position of women in general and men in general may be different, the nature of the issues and the analysis is not parallel, and gender specificity may be necessary to achieve gender equality. It is also critical to recognize the significant risk in adding masculinities analysis. Masculinities work may be hijacked to reinforce, rather than to undermine, patriarchy.

How Asking the Man Question Will Make a Difference

There are particular places and ways in which masculinities scholarship can make a difference to feminist analysis. First, and consistent with what has been the central focus of feminist analysis, it can contribute to a better understanding of male power and the process of subordination, and therefore to the goal of women's equality. For example, masculinities analysis reveals that male power is exercised over other men as well as over all (or nearly all) women. Examples of this include bullying and fighting. This underlies the seeming paradox that, although men are powerful, many men feel powerless. Masculinities analysis also uncovers male complicity in men's subordination by other men, even as it exposes hierarchies among men, particularly those of class and race. These insights are critical to designing strategic alliances as well as to understanding the complex dynamics of subordination not only of women, but also of many men by men who hold power and privilege. This might inform our view of persisting sex segregation at work, sexual harassment, income inequality, street and domestic violence, sexual assault, gender policing at school and work, and the devaluing of things associated with women as well as with men who engage in work or behaviour that is associated with women. Ultimately, then, by exposing the dynamics of male privilege and subordination, masculinities analysis exposes why men have an interest in harming women. Hierarchies of men reinforce subordination of women, as well as support hierarchies among women. Recognizing more completely these dynamics leads to feminist knowledge and self-critique, which is critical to fomenting real change.

In conjunction with this focus on further unravelling the nature of male power, masculinities analysis helps identify the *interaction of privilege and harm*. Frequently, attributes associated with men (leadership, strength, sacrifice, heroism) create double binds for women, who are neither respected nor valued – and may even be criticized – if they display these same characteristics (see, e.g., Price Waterhouse v. Hopkins 1989). In addition to the double bind problem, those attributes may also carry limits and expectations for men that strongly affect their identities and lives. This is connected to the difficulty for some men in achieving those qualities, or the anguish caused by rejecting those qualities. In addition, the negative defining characteristic of masculinities – that men should not be like women or embrace behaviours associated with women – discourages men from developing female-associated qualities (caring, emotional responsiveness, and expression) (Dowd 2010). An example is the lack of socialization of men to provide childcare. The consequences of these boundaries on the self imposed by masculinities are evident in suicide and health care statistics, as well as in men's difficulties in personal relationships due to the lack of support for the development of men's relational skills (Dowd 2008, 2010).

The second contribution of masculinities scholarship is to expose men's harms, to render them visible. Masculinities scholarship has exposed men's victimization. Making women's voices, inequalities and harms visible has been a core project of feminist analysis (Dowd 2008). Antiessentialist feminist analysis has further opened that perspective to the impact of intersections with other powerful sites of subordination in order to challenge and understand the scope of gender harms holistically rather than hierarchically (see, e.g., Dowd and Jacobs 2003, Crenshaw 1989, Harris 1990, Matsuda 1992). Men have largely been invisible in identifying gender harms because of the general pattern of male power and privilege. Exposing men's harms is critical, however, to a more realistic understanding of how gender inequality and other inequalities are constructed. Seeing men as gendered is the focus of masculinities analysis. That analysis has exposed how gender harm is connected to men's very identity as men. In particular, masculinity requires constant proof of one's manhood; it is a status never achieved, but one constantly to be established and to be tested (Dowd 2010). Daily proof of masculinity involves significant man-on-man hierarchy, denial of anything associated with being female, and living up to a standard that has been called the 'Big Impossible' (Kindlon and Thomson 1999). The 'Big Impossible' is the ideal of masculinity and part of the ideal is that it must be constantly proved, so it is inherently unachievable or the achievement is transitory.

It is disproportionately men's bodies that are sacrificed in war, and men alone are required to register for military service (Military Selective Service Act of 1967, 50 U.S.C. app. § 453[a] [2006]). Masculinities are the basis for violence against men that is broad, deeply embedded in culture, and frequently taken for granted as hardwired, as 'boys being boys', and 'men being men' (Dowd 2008). For example, the objects of the criminal justice system are boys and men, just as the punishments are meant to control boys and men at their most dangerous. We are not surprised to find boys and men in jails and prison, and this leads us to gender the system in ways that reflect our deepest fears about men, and which reinforce the power of all men because of men's implicit dangerousness. When linked with race, this triggers a disproportionate minority concentration linked to biases in policing and the judicial system (Dowd 2010, Feld 1999, Nunn 2002).

Another area where harms have been ignored is with respect to child abuse (Dowd 2010). Boys disproportionately are the targets of physical abuse, and disproportionately their batterers are women. In addition, boys have been largely ignored as victims of sexual abuse, with the exception of recent scandals involving public or institutionalized abuse particularly at the hands of priests (Ryan Report 2009). Identifying and making visible these harms in no way takes away from the harms of girls and women. Rather, it is to understand that gender is used in various ways to justify harm and identify victims. Masculinity as defined draws and creates much physical and psychic harm, and yet it sustains itself. The exposure of men and boys' harms is also critical to reimagining masculinity in a positive, egalitarian way.

The third area in which masculinities analysis can be especially helpful is to remind us to see gender where it is obvious, and to notice the difference between how gender operates in homosocial or male-exclusive or male-dominant environments, as compared to how gender functions in mixed gender environments. Where women are absent or in a minority, feminists frequently focus on how to integrate them into the environment, while assuming that gender is not operating at all or is only operating affirmatively for boys and men (see, e.g., Gilligan 1982, MacKinnon 1987, Schultz 1998, Williams and Segal 2001). This is the underlying assumption of the antidiscrimination norm, which prohibits deviation or discrimination of one gender/sex in comparison to a norm of presumed equality for the other. Each time we ask, 'Where are the women?' we should also ask the other question, 'What are the assumptions, structures and culture to which the men are subject?' or more simply, 'What about the men?' An example of this is the juvenile justice system, which is so overwhelmingly male that it might almost be called the 'boys' justice system' (Dowd 2010). Because of the predominance of boys and young men, the structure and assumptions of masculinities pervade the system, in a way that not only fails to account for female offenders, but also constructs and limits boys according to the masculinity code. As the number of girls has increased in the juvenile justice system, it has been recognized that they are in a structure not built for them or with them in mind, and this has generated gender analysis of the system (American Bar Association and National Bar Association 2001). But this analysis has been limited to thinking about girls: no one has asked, 'What about the boys?', 'What are the gender assumptions of this structure, and does it foster positive masculinities?' So the challenge of a place where one gender is sole or dominant is to resist the invisibility of the dominant gender. We also might compare how this works in dominantly male and dominantly female settings, for the dominant group and the outsider group. Both masculinities and feminist analysis of education, for example, suggest the likelihood that female-exclusive or female-dominant environments operate differently from male-exclusive or male-dominant patterns (Levit 2005).

In mixed gender settings, like education and many workplaces, we frequently assume a simplistic pattern when in fact the reality is more complex. In addition, the dialogue pushes towards a zero-sum game, where only one side wins. Debates over education are a good example of this, claiming it is boys' 'turn' or that boys' issues represent a crisis generated by policies meant to empower girls (Weaver-Hightower 2003). By noticing, then, how masculinities function differently or need to be noticed differently depending upon gender patterns, the study of masculinities adds to our vision and understanding of bias and our conception of equality.

Masculinities analysis reinforces antiessentialism. Masculinities scholarship is consciously multiple, reinforcing that masculinities are social constructs and are therefore not universal, but also recognizing that a critical piece of masculinities is hierarchies among men (Dowd 2010, Collier 2010a). Examining subversive and subordinated masculinities reminds us that not all men are privileged. By exposing the ways and factors that trump the patriarchal dividend associated with masculinity, masculinities analysis refocuses gender issues particularly on class and race. In a manner different from, but complementary to, antiessentialist critiques and methodology in feminist theory, masculinities analysis exposes what trumps male power. This calls, I believe, for feminists to embrace race as a feminist issue. Critical race feminists have demonstrated that gender is not an isolated identity characteristic; that priorities and understanding shift dramatically among different groups of women; and that unspoken points of view must be surfaced in feminist analysis. Their critique has made it central to feminism to be consciously antiessentialist. What the study of masculinities adds to this is that pluralism has been central to the development of the field and, arguably, is more robust. In addition, this analysis exposes the loss of masculine privilege, power and domination when masculinity is practiced by men of different races and class from the dominant heterosexual middle-class white male. I would argue that this analysis should be the basis for feminists making race and class feminist issues. So, for example, an analysis of the juvenile justice system – what I have called the 'boys' justice system' – leads to the recognition of the disproportion of black boys and young men in the system. The gender analysis cannot be separated from the race analysis. It is, to use Cheryl Harris's term, racial patriarchy (Harris 1996). Another example is the education system, where race inequities are far more disparate than gender inequities. I would argue that masculinities analysis exposes when male privilege is trumped or undermined; when it does, it demonstrates the tenacity and primacy of race and class at the core of injustice and inequality.

Finally, *masculinities theory generates risks and challenges*. While feminist analysis has sometimes been turned on its head or used for precisely the opposite effects from those intended by its advocates (see, e.g., Collier and Sheldon 2006a, Fineman 1991, Cahn 1991), masculinities scholarship carries even more risk. The biggest risk is displacing the focus on girls and women, or blaming women for men's harms in a way that feeds into old stereotypes. As an example, scholars who have worked on issues related to fathers know the tightrope between changing masculinities norms and hijacking fatherhood analysis to browbeat mothers (Dowd 2001, Gavanas 2004a). Masculinities scholars need constantly to be challenged to remain focused on issues of power, or what Jeff Hearn calls the hegemony of men (as opposed to their masculinities) (Hearn 1996, 2004). The enormous pull of non-egalitarian masculinities also raises sobering difficulties that impede the ability to recast masculinities in positive, affirming ways. Yet the scholarship also exposes how those changes have occurred, and therefore illuminates the potential for change.

* * *

Ultimately masculinities analysis contributes to the goal of equality and justice. At the same time, the difficulty of that task should not be underestimated. Much of masculinities analysis supports a deeply negative, constricting definition of manhood. One of the critical challenges for a reoriented masculinity is to imagine an affirmative identity. It is also a challenge to give up power, and much of masculinities scholarship does not provide a clear answer to how that can be achieved. But the way to achieve equality is to include all analysis, however difficult or uncomfortable. And it must be equality for all.

Chapter 3
Feminisms and Masculinities: Questioning the Lure of Multiple Identities

Martha Albertson Fineman

Introduction

It has been suggested that feminist legal theorists might productively use the scholarship on masculinities that has been developed over the past decade. There are several ways in which masculinities scholarship might interact with feminist legal theories. Masculinities scholarship could be seen as distinct from and complementary to feminist theories – an independent and parallel companion theory, developed by men. In this regard, from a feminist's perspective masculinities scholarship might be thought of as ethnography, helpfully providing insights into the operations and assumption of a distinct masculine culture. This approach would seem to validate the notion that there are significant differences between men's and women's experiences and perspectives, and consideration of both is necessary to form a complete legal theory picture. Feminist legal theory and masculinities theory are, thus, seen as both contrasting and complementary in nature.

On the other hand, masculinities scholarship can be understood as providing the basis for a critique of feminist legal theory. This approach begins with an allegation that feminist legal theory generally and incorrectly treats men as a monolithic group when there is in fact a multiplicity of male identities. Masculinities scholarship in this framing could be categorized as male-focused companion to critiques of feminist legal theory as excluding and essentializing that have been made by critical race and queer legal theorists over the course of the past thirty years. It is this understanding of the significance of masculinities to feminist legal theory that prompted this chapter.

I begin with summarizing some of the recent work on masculinities and reflecting on the relevance of masculinities scholarship to feminist legal theorists. Specifically, I am concerned with the role of identity-based approaches in critical legal theory (feminist or otherwise), particularly how they often result in unnecessarily vigorous, overly broad, and ill-conceived accusations about exclusion and silencing that have otherwise similarly oriented individuals at odds with each other. This form of academic criticism may build individual careers, but it also negatively channels energy and resources away from a comprehensive critical legal project in which the demand for social justice is a universal one.

This objective of universality is important. When we deal with law and the relationship between legal institutions and the structuring of power and authority, as well as their allocation among the individual, the state, and societal institutions, we employ a system dependent on the process of classification, generalization, and universal applicability. My reservations about masculinities theories, and other identity-focused approaches to law, reflect my belief that the most important task for those interested in a social justice project at this particular time in legal history in the United States and other countries with similar attachment to neoliberal legalism is to construct a legal subject with which to replace the abstract liberal political or legal subject with its accompanying and unrealistic constructs of autonomy, self-sufficiency and independence. This new conception of the legal subject must be based on an appreciation of the human condition in order to effectively displace the rhetoric of personal responsibility, small government, and condemnation of state intervention.

Since the reigning liberal political or legal subject is a universal construct, so must be its alternative. This is not an argument that identities are never important to the critical legal project or that discrimination on the basis of categories such as race, gender or sexual orientation is no longer a problem in the United States. Stronger remedies for discrimination are needed. But my project extends beyond current protected categories under equal protection and asks whether the fragmented multiplicity of modified legal subjects that remain after deconstruction of the categories of 'woman' and 'man' can aid in addressing within the confines of our imperfect system problems, such as poverty and lack of social mobility, that transcend those fragmented identities.[1]

Masculinities Claims

Basically, the argument of identity-focused scholars critical of feminist legal theory has been that the theory reflects a 'white women's heteronormative' perspective that both obscures the complexity and nuances of different experiences and excludes the voices, if not the actual women, who are not white, middle class and heterosexual (see, e.g. Spelman 1988, Harris 1990). Such exclusion necessitates the development of a separate feminist (or 'womanist') legal approach that adopts as a central element the experiences, narratives and stories of the excluded group – those with intersecting identities.[2] Concepts such as intersectionality bundle

1 Indeed, even the broad categories of woman and man obscure or distort structural problems by suggesting that it is the gender of the individual and not the social role, function or status occupied that is the problem. Introducing the idea of the 'Vulnerable Subject' to replace the liberal (autonomous) subject represents the attempt to replace the reigning universal legal subject with another, more appropriate universal subject.

2 The general nature of the charges often extends beyond the totalizing tendency of theory constructed by and for 'white middle-class heterosexual women' to offer theoretical

identity characteristics, locating the subject of such legal theory at the intersection of a multiplicity of categories (Crenshaw 1989, Harris 1990, Hutchinson 2001).

The general category of 'woman' is thus fragmented by its modification by other significant personal identity characteristics, often in a binary manner, so we now have white women and black women, heterosexual women and lesbians, or, perhaps more complexly, the black woman who is also a lesbian. The idea that differences among women mean that there cannot be a shared core of women's experience is foundational to the critical stance of perspective critiques. So too is the idea that the voices and perspectives of those who are different from some perceived dominant group (white, heterosexual middle-classed women) have been excluded. This different and excluded perspective critique has been labelled 'outsider' scholarship to reflect both of these premises (Coombs 1992). It is not always clear whether it is the law or the dominant feminist theorist being criticized for such exclusion, but the remedy is seen as the development of a distinct intersectional legal category.

Masculinities theory extends this critique of feminist legal theory's exclusionary bias by fragmenting the category of 'men'. Masculinities scholarship concedes that there are differences between men and women that might be theoretically relevant, as well as recognizing that men have been present in (not excluded from) feminist legal theory. The exclusion and silencing at issue here is the result of men, rather than women, being essentialized (Dowd 2010). The allegation is that men in feminist theory have been cast primarily as oppressors or subordinators of women.

In particular, the charge is that feminist legal theorists have not approached men as the objects of gender analysis (Dowd 2010, 23). It is argued that, if we were to do so, we would see that significant differences exist among men, just as we perceive among women (25–28). Further, recognizing differences among men would disrupt the narrative of gender subordination or domination, since feminist legal scholars would be compelled to concede that individual women may be in privileged positions compared to marginalized men (4–5). One goal in making multiple masculinities visible is that feminist legal theorizing would acknowledge and perhaps even address the barriers men encounter in interactions with each other and with women, as well as the prices men pay for the male or patriarchal privilege, which has so occupied feminist thought (45–61).

Some masculinities scholars argue that feminists must now take up the study of masculine identities, incorporating the insights thus revealed in order to correct an exclusionary feminist project as it is going forward (Collier 2010a, Levit 1996).

---

remedies for other cultural and social transgressors. *See, e.g.*, Capers 2007 (advocating 'reading black' to critically read opinions and narratives attentive to the race); Tehranian 2007 (contending people of middle-eastern descent need scholarship focused on them because of their unique position – having the same status as white people on paper but without recourse for legal action in the post-9/11 environment); Woan 2008 (arguing that women of Asian descent face 'white sexual imperialism', which has created a hyper-sexualized stereotype of Asian women).

Feminist legal scholars are admonished to explore men's experiences with women from the men's perspectives, rather than only considering women's experiences with men from women's perspectives (Collier 2010b, 9, 19). Additionally, we are told that men's relationships and interactions with other men affect the ways in which they express their masculinity, an interactive process that has significant implications for how they will contemporaneously interact with women.[3]

In a masculinities approach there seem to be two distinct ways in which men are differentiated from each other and then strewn along a hierarchical continuum of masculinities. First, it is asserted that a 'hegemonic'[4] masculinity is in operation, constructed in such a way that it is a status that few if any men are actually able to achieve (Connell and Messerschmidt 2005, Connell 1994). The idea is that every man is always in struggle to become or attain hegemonic masculinity, but the status is never arrived at in any stable form (Kimmel 1997b, Cooper 2009b). Hegemonic masculinity is a state or status that must constantly be defended (Dowd 2010, 28). Further, since heterosexuality is central in achieving hegemonic masculinity, individual men must be vigilant to act in ways that reinforce the fact that they are neither gay nor a woman (or woman-like). In this rendering, all men are subordinated, although it is to *an ideal*, rather than to some other defined group in society. Subordination in this form would seem to be in constant flux over an individual man's lifetime, as he could slide up or down the hierarchical scale that measures his masculinity against the hegemonic ideal.[5]

In addition to this generalized subordination, some subsets of men are seen to be in a position of relatively fixed or stable subordination due to the fact that hegemonic masculinity is also raced and classed (Kimmel 1997b, 33). The argument in this regard is that, when men have characteristics that are deemed inherently incompatible with the hegemonic masculinity, they can be further subordinated because of the way those characteristics intersect with their masculinity (Ehrenreich 2002). This line of argument, as well as the observations about the centrality of heterosexuality to hegemonic masculinity, reflects and

3 As part of that inquiry, we are to ask how race and class in particular intersect with and complicate the experience of masculinity for individual men (Dowd 2010, 28).

4 'Preponderant influence or authority over others; the social, cultural, ideological, or economic influence exerted by a dominant group', *Hegemony Definition*, Merriam-Webster.com, http://www.merriam-webster.com/dictionary/hegemony (last visited 28 January 2013). This definition implies that hegemonic masculinity is constructed and employed by actual people acting with awareness, intent – that it is a conscious and considered strategy of control that is only available to the most powerful, rather than the product of diffuse and undisciplined cultural and social forces. If it is a status seldom if ever achieved by individual men, however, one wonders just who constitutes the person or group that controls or dominates and just how that domination is accomplished if things are so fluid.

5 The hegemonic ideal could also evolve and change form over time. *See* Dowd 2008, 209 ('Seeing masculinity as a social construct rejects, and in fact critiques, the notion of a set or stable sex role that one acquires or masculinity as an inevitable phase of development from child to adult, from boy to man').

parallels some of the perspective-based criticisms of feminist legal theory. The larger category of 'men' is rejected as too essentializing and also as excluding individual characteristics that are as, if not more, relevant to the subordination analysis (Hearn 2004, Remy 1990). Individual men should not only be seen as men, but also seen as situated along axes of interacting hierarchies of race and class in particular, and perhaps also differences in ability, ethnicity, age or religion (Cooper 2006a). Therefore, it is as important to distinguish among men and look at the ways in which different men are both differently subordinated and differently privileged within dominant cultural, legal and socially imposed understandings of masculinity through those hierarchies.

Recognition that men are different from one another is not seen as suggesting that men as a group are in equivalent positions in regard to subordination when compared with women as a group. Most masculinities scholars concede that men as a group remain relatively privileged and that patriarchal privilege continues to matter in social, political and economic relations (Connell 2002a). What these scholars seek is that men not be treated as an undifferentiated monolithic group as women make claims about the ways in which gender operates in society in developing feminist legal theory. Since women's subordination is inevitably intertwined with men's – one cannot be understood without the other – the result of an excursion into multiple masculinities will be a clarification and reorientation of feminists' own explorations of inequality.

Some prominent feminist legal scholars have taken up the challenges offered by masculinities critiques. For example, Nancy Dowd uses insights from masculinities theory in examining the situation of boys in the contexts of education and the juvenile justice system and men in regard to fatherhood and sexual abuse (Dowd 2010, 73–100). Using this approach Dowd concludes in regard to education that, while it is expressly and formally 'gender-neutral', the structure, culture and norms in operation within the educational system are gendered and often work against the interests of both boys and girls, although differently (84). The juvenile justice system, by contrast, has been designed with boys in mind – or a version of boyhood that is criminalized. Thus it fails to meet the needs of girls who enter the system and, ironically, also fails the boys around whom it was designed. Dowd argues that, while fatherhood is an inherently male identified role, the specifically gendered nature of fatherhood has not been explored (105–111). As for sexual abuse, it typically calls to mind a male stranger and a female victim, while the reality is that men are also victims, women are also abusers, and quite often the abuser is a family member or person with a close relationship to the victim (125–134).

Dowd argues that a masculinities approach calls attention or 'exposes' male gendering and challenges us to think of boys and girls/men and women complexly and simultaneously, as in relation to each other rather than discreet and independent subjects (65–66). Considering masculinities also locates those relationships within specific societal institutions. As Dowd uses masculinities theory, it is not an end in itself but a way to try to understand complex social relationships and structures such as those found in the family or educational system (26–27). She concedes there is some danger that women might be excluded or marginalized in an analysis that also encompasses the position of men, who typically have more societal power and privilege than women, but she admonishes us to take not an 'either/or' but rather a 'both/and' perspective (67). Her ultimate focus on institutional arrangements and relationships she hopes will lessen the danger of excessively male-focused analyses, particularly when the expressed objective of including men's experiences is to show the true scope and nature of the harm under patriarchy – harm that is universal, shared by men and women, even if it is also differently experienced. Dowd's attempt to point out distortions and inadequacies in the functioning of institutions is admirable. However, her efforts also point out the limitations of an identity approach.

Using identities inevitably brings the inquiry back to a search for specific targeted discrimination based on those identities. Those so identified are splintered off from the universal legal subject (the liberal legal subject) and as a now differentiated part of the whole, measured against the universal ideal to see if there are differences in treatment, status or position that are impermissible. This comparative process is inevitable in a discrimination analysis, but if we want the inquiry to go to institutional and structural inequalities that are not (or are no longer) based on intentional impermissible discrimination, making multiple identities central to the analysis will be difficult to do in practice and may actually further obscure problems not captured by or transcending those identities. Dowd concedes that it is difficult to both hold multiplicities in mind (and not privilege one over others) and make the analysis relevant to the objective of suggesting institutional transformation through law. Interesting from my perspective is the fact that her book contains few concrete suggestions for engagement with law and law reform. This is not a criticism of the book, which does offer, even if in abstract terms, suggestions and admonitions directed to feminist legal scholars:

> Adding men should not mean displacing women, and it requires a willingness to consider the position of the dominant gender group while demanding that the dominant group acknowledge and commit to the achievement of liberation and justice for women while raising men's and boys' issues. (85)

And in regard to sexual abuse:

> [T]he focus on child sexual abuse has unintentionally meant that other forms of abuse have been given less attention. The negative consequences of that focus are disproportionate for boys. In addition, this focus has avoided the reality that women constitute the majority of offenders. The dynamic of that pattern of maltreatment and abuse is a critical part of understanding motherhood that must be addressed. (138)

My concern with such insights is not that either is inappropriate, but that each seems more directed at giving guidance for the reform of feminist legal scholarship than focused on how legal institutions and practice might be approached and reformed.

I am also concerned with the way that a focus on identities can narrow or constrict the critical imagination. In focusing on the gendered categories of 'mother' and 'father', for example, we may fail to see and critically explore the institution of the family and its role in the larger society. Looking at the examples Dowd uses, I would ask different questions. For example, why isn't the fact that we routinely incarcerate children, regardless of their gender, the issue, not the fact that incarcerated boys and girls are differently disadvantaged in a system that treats everyone inhumanly?[6] Isn't the more pressing question in regard to education the lack of resources for public schools, the overcrowding, and other problems that have resulted from significant ideological shifts in the United States around privatization? The whole idea of public education is under attack, not because it is failing boys and girls differently, but because, increasingly, politicians and powerful interests assert that the government should not be in the business of providing it.[7]

In regard to parenting, isn't the dilemma not that fatherhood has been differently gendered, but that both genders have been shaped by the fact that dependency is perceived politically as primarily the responsibility of the private family, and this necessitates some role division as between wage earner and caretaker (Fineman 2005)? Historically, this role division was gendered, but the disadvantages are attached to the role or status of caretaker, not the sex of the person performing the care. What is needed is not more gender equality in law, but a more responsive state and accommodating workplace policies (Fineman 2005). Similarly, understanding the extent and nature of child abuse in all its forms would not only look at and compare abusive fathers' with abusive mothers' behaviour, but also critique the condoning effects of religious and cultural premises that parents 'own' their children and have not only a right but a duty to discipline them.[8] The legal manifestation of

---

6 *See* Hechinger 2011, 494 ('The politics of criminal law [in the United States] have generally resulted in a one-way ratchet toward harsher policies and punishments'). *But see* de Jonge 2004 (explaining some of the measures taken towards a more humane juvenile detention system in Netherlands).

7 *See e.g.*, Hing 2012; Colleluori and Powell 2012.

8 *See* Woodhouse 2008, 138 (explaining how notions of 'parental authority' have worked as an impediment to fostering the rights of children in the United States). A great amount of deference is given to the parents in upbringing their children in United States law because of the presumption that they act in the child's best interests. *See, e.g.*, *Meyer v. Nebraska* 1923 (holding that parents have a right to direct the upbringing of their children, including control over the child's education); *Pierce v. Society of Sisters* 1925 (reiterating that the 'liberty of parents and guardians' includes the right 'to direct the upbringing and education of children under their control'); *Prince v. Massachusetts* 1944 ('[i]t is cardinal with us that the custody, care and nurture of the child reside first in the parents'); *Stanley v. Illinois* 1972 (recognizing the privacy right of parents to make decisions concerning the care, custody and control of their children).

this state abandonment of its responsibility to children is found in the extensive parental rights doctrines that shape policy in regard to education as well.

If the use of even the broad categories of male and female and the critical tool of gender construction can obscure structural issues, it seems wrong to suggest that further deconstruction of those categories will help in the reformation of complex social relations and structures. Critical legal scholarship should be generative as well as critical.[9]

Legal Theory and Societal Transformation

The masculinities critique, as well as other critiques of feminist legal theory, raises a question with which I have grappled my entire academic career: should feminist legal theorists give up on the possibility that law can be used to advance a positive social justice and equality project because the legal categories we are compelled to use are inevitably imperfect? This question suggests an even broader issue as to how the law in general and critical legal theory in particular should respond to socially produced economic, political and structural differences among and between individuals and groups in society. The problems inherent in using the general categories of women and men to explore one aspect of difference – that of gender – and its implications for institutional relationships are multiplied in the contexts of intersectional or multidimensional identifies. Perhaps feminist legal theorists should confine themselves to criticism as outsiders, to the deconstruction of legal categories and the ferreting out of situations not addressed or interests seemingly ignored, and abandon the idea of constructive legal reform.

Of course, a great deal would have been lost if feminist legal theorists had abandoned reform aspirations in the past. Feminist legal theory brought into existence innovations in legal thought and generated substantive changes in the way gender is addressed in law. Using the now vilified category of 'women', feminists in law used gender equality as the concept with which to suggest reforms of significant sites of inequality, such as the workplace, family, and public sphere. Reforms in those areas benefited many women across their differences (and some men in spite of their gender difference) (Bartlett 1974, Finley 1986, Kay 1985, Williams 1982).

In fact, when legal feminists entered the field the categories of women and men were defined as different and contrasted with each other in laws that structured many of society's institutions. One could even say that historically the law actually recognized two distinct legal subjects: one male and one female. The object of legal feminism was to challenge those different ideological and institutional constructions, which tended to disadvantage and exclude women as a legally

9 I am not referring to the generation of yet more law review articles here, but to the creation of progressive social legal policy that can actually make a difference in the ways in which the system operates.

defined group (Fineman 2005). Feminist legal theorists imagined utopian gender-neutral and egalitarian visions for society (some might label them dystopian) and brought concepts reflecting gendered institutional arrangements such as 'care-work' (which was to be valued equally with paid work) and 'marital property' (which recognized different, but equally important, forms of contribution to the accumulation of wealth and property) into mainstream legal and political discourse and made them the basis for reform. They also created legal harms from what had been invisible gendered experiences for many women, 'discovering' things like domestic violence and marital rape, and toppled the common law concept of husbands as disciplinarian heads of households. The idea of using law to get at such inequalities is hard to abandon, at least for feminist scholars of that generation.

There should be significant questions about how far fragmenting the legal subject along multiple axes of identity characteristics can get us in using law to develop a reconstructive social justice project.[10] In fact, it could be argued that the turn to multiplicities of identities has actually worked to derail a social justice project that began in the 1960s using broad categories of race and gender. Have fragmented identities contributed to shattering old alliances and impeded the formation of broad and effective new coalitions? Differences can be used to divide groups who might otherwise come together in the interest of working towards greater social justice.

Equally harmful to a broadly conceived and inclusive social justice project is the way in which identity categories have become proxies through which we articulate and understand social inequalities such as poverty and other forms of social disadvantage. Attribution of socially produced disadvantage to the mistreatment of only some groups detracts from the development of a more comprehensive systemic analysis of the political and economic organization of the United States at the beginning of the twenty-first century and the ways in which subordination and disadvantage are generated and distributed across identities. Equally problematic for the likely success of the approach is the way in which identities-focused analysis tends to concentrate attention on identifying 'victims' and is also generally premised on the assumption that there are, or have been in the recent past, individual or institutional villains. Such assumptions are often difficult to prove and many people, including judges and jurors, go to great lengths to find reasons other than discrimination for behaviour by focusing on plaintiffs' conduct or attitudes rather than defendants'.[11]

---

10 The approaches to the legal subject by categorizations of feminism might not be particularly useful. *See* Chamallas 2003, 15–22 (discussing the three stages of feminist legal theory: the equality stage, the difference stage, and the diversity stage).

11 *See generally* Eyer 2011, summarizing psychological literature on the fundamental background belief of meritocracy that makes a charge of discrimination extremely difficult for Americans to believe, even when the evidence is very strong and not contested.

Law as Discipline

Like feminist theory generally, masculinities theory was not initially developed by legal theorists but evolved first in other disciplines, particularly those of sociology and psychology.[12] The initial disciplinary origins of masculinities theory are important because there are significant differences between a legal approach and that of psychology or sociology. The subject and object of analysis are different, as are the focus and methodology, which leads the disciplines to ask different questions and be concerned with different norms and goals. Certainly the construction of a cultural, social or social-science subject involves different disciplinary considerations. The categories can be and often are mandated to be more nuanced, focused on distinguishing characteristics and used to create descriptive and explanatory categories than those in legal scholarship and theory. This does not mean that those disciplines are irrelevant to law or that theorists from other areas cannot use law within their disciplines. Rather, it is merely a reminder that the legal subject is an artefact that is constructed by and through law in part to hide the variedness of the various and varying realities of persons of flesh and blood and confine them within the roles that they are assigned in and through law (Fineman 2008). The actual legal subject at issue need not even be a real person; it can be a corporation or association.

Also significant is the fact that the relationship between social science disciplines and institutions of state power is different from that within law. Of course theorists from other areas can play a role in court proceedings as expert witnesses and their scholarship is used by legal theorists and in legal contexts. But legal scholarship directly and differently engages with state institutions that can and do exercise considerable power and influence over people's lives. Lawyers as judges, legislators, or even professors generate, explicate, manipulate and critique norms, rules and systems that punish and reward certain behaviours. The disciplining nature and force of law on an individual or institution is different – more immediate, focused, and more likely to have a direct impact on structuring people's lives than sociological or historical research. The legal subject formed by law has concrete and coercive implications for real persons and institutions. Further, there are unique characteristics associated with law and its uses that affect the legal system's ability to incorporate generalized insights about differences, be they sex- or race based or found in hierarchies of masculinities.

The tools available to legal scholars are limited in some important ways by the nature of legal institutions, the nature of law itself, and the constraining norms and values of legal scholarship. For one thing, law relies on broad categories that are rather entrenched within the law as it has developed over centuries as a coercive tool of the state. Law making relies on classification – the generation of broad generalizations about individuals, groups, or classes of things and people.

12 *See* Dowd 2010, 28–44 (outlining major sociological and psychological scholars in masculinities).

This classification process occurs initially at the legislative level, which generates systems of rules and norms that are intended to have universal application within categories. Generalizations and aggregation are inevitable in this process. Once the categories are drawn, the foundational principle of equality before the law demands the same treatment be applied to those who fit within the same classification. In other words, the legal or political subject is a universal subject. Individuals may be sexed, raced and classed, but the whole point of equal protection of the law is to erase difference in treatment.

On the other hand, adjudication is the means whereby individual circumstances are fitted into existing classification, the process whereby individual and specific facts are assigned legal meaning or consequences on a case-by-case basis.[13] Adjudication is not an ad hoc process and the same mandate of equal treatment applies. Courts make decisions using analogies and distinctions within the context of rules such as those governing 'precedent' and 'stare decisis', ideally tying like things together in a web of consistent, coherent and predictable doctrine using classifications.

Legal classifications are of necessity broad and take legal subjects outside of personal history, universalizing that which might appear as inherently different to scholars in some other disciplines. In order to 'speak' to law, legal theory, even of the feminist variety, must to some extent assimilate concrete and material differences into the dominant meta-narratives of law and, as a result, will have only a limited ability to theorize around particulars. Law is too general and reflective of the status quo, too rule- and precedent bound to easily and quickly absorb and reflect nonconforming experiences. Rather, operating in society as a dominant structural paradigm and discourse, law co-opts the experiences of diverse groups, while also homogenizing and standardizing those experiences as they are specifically subjected to law. Co-optation is achieved through classification and tinkering reforms, while standardization operates upon individuals caught in legal constructs, such as the adversarial process, rules of evidence, and the structured elements of causes of action and claims for relief, which make it impossible to tell stories outside of legal narratives.

---

13 Classification and principles governing the organization of objects into groups according to their similarities and differences or their relation to a set of criteria are evident in every body of knowledge. According to strict logic, organizing a domain of objects into classes must leave no two classes with any object in common; also, all of the classes together must contain all of the objects of the domain. This theory, however, disregards the frequency in practice of borderline cases – *i.e.*, objects that can with equal correctness be accepted or rejected as members of two otherwise exclusive classes (intersection). This is often seen in biology, where the theory of evolution implies that some animal populations will have characteristics of two distinct species. In practice, the principles used to classify a domain of objects depend upon the nature of the objects themselves. In law the articulation of perceived similarities and differences is particularly important because of the antidiscrimination mandate in equal protection jurisprudence. The classification of process in this situation requires a standard object against which all others are compared, the male norm identified in feminist legal theory.

Many years ago, in thinking about the imperfections of existing gendered classifications in law, I referred to motherhood as a 'colonized category' – a category occupied exclusively by women, but given legal meaning and content in institutions that were predominantly populated by men (Fineman 1995). I now realize that most, perhaps all, legal categories are colonized to some extent. This is as true with 'men' (or the masculine) as it is with 'women'. Colonization is inherent in the classification process and classification is essential to the operation of the legal system. The fact that broad, over- and under-inclusive classifications are inevitable does not mean that the resulting categories, imperfect as they are, cannot be employed to effect positive change (Fineman 1991, 51). Nor does it mean that the interpretation and content of legal categories are not worth fighting over.

Certainly, one way out from under the criticism and accusation of essentialism coming from masculinities scholars in regard to the category of men, and from others in regard to the understanding of 'women', is for feminist legal theorists to give up on the possibility of positive uses of law, perhaps pursue cultural and political engagement outside of formal institutions, even outside of academic disciplines altogether. This is the direction some former legal feminists are taking. Janet Halley in particular has argued that feminists should turn away not only from law but also from feminism (Halley 2006). Borrowing from Foucault's model of diffuse power, she asserts that any attempt to productively engage law will simply extend the reach of regulation, administration and discipline (119–132). In this analysis the law cannot be redeemed, and trying to transform or reform law poses risks of co-option and marginalization. Provocatively she couples this move away from law with a call to 'take a break' from feminism. This is justified because of the way that legal feminism has produced a legal subjectivity for women as associated with experiences of oppression and/or victimization, which are assumed to hold true for all falling within the legal category of women (346).

Halley's concerns are related to points also made by masculinities theorists. She is right to insist that issues about the construction of victimhood and conferral or denial of agency, as well as the problems associated with governance feminism's tendency to regulate sexuality, should be critically explored. The law can and does generate norms, rules and rationalizations outside of and above lived daily experience as a result of the co-opting/standardizing nature of legal institutions. But there is a paradox for the critical legal theorist, or at least those who are adherents to a law and society tradition when encountering the call to turn away from law: *law is everywhere*. One cannot turn away from law.

Law is not only found in statutes, cases, courts and legislatures, but spills over into and permeates the daily life of individuals, entities, institutions and relationships. In other words, critical legal scholarship must reconcile a paradox: inevitably legal classifications homogenize distinct individual experiences into some overarching whole, but law in society, and through the institutions it creates, profoundly shapes both individual and institutional experiences. We cannot stand outside of law any more than we can stand outside of culture. This realization for a feminist legal scholar means that we must engage with law, although it does not tell us what form that engagement should take.

Because we appreciate the co-opting potential and exclusionary tendencies of law, we might not want to undertake test-case litigation or draft ordinances or lobby for specific reforms. But I do think that critical legal scholars must use their unique understanding of law and legal institutions to bring forward a sophisticated critique of the role of law in the construction and organization of society and its institutions, particularly when those institutions perpetuate inequality. Further, we have a responsibility to suggest concrete reforms or changes when we can be reasonably confident that they will improve conditions for some, even if not for everyone, and this is particularly true when some in society are disadvantaged or harmed by or through law.

Feminist legal scholars recognize that legal categories or classifications have real-world consequences in people's lives, which is why there are political struggles over their meanings and applications. The struggles over meaning reflect both a legal and a political process – one that takes place within a pragmatic system recognizing that lines must be drawn and decisions made regardless of the incomplete or emerging nature of the underlying facts and theories. And, of course, those in power craft the categories and definitions and in ways that benefit themselves and their interests. Power permeates law and legal institutions. The limitations of the process can and do create problems, lead to distortions, injustices, subordination and discrimination.

Law and Society

My model for productive engagement with law is the Law and Society Movement.[14] Long before there was an anti-essentialist critique of feminist theory – long before there was anything labelled 'feminist legal theory', in fact – scholars such as Karl Llewellyn (1930), Willard Hurst (1977, 1950) and Stewart Macaulay (2005, also Macauley, Friedman and Mertz 2007) recognized that classification, while inevitably part of the legal process, was nonetheless susceptible to both over- and under-inclusiveness. They identified additional problems with the implementation of law, and the 'gap' between law on the books and law in action has been explored in countless articles and books.[15] They and other law and society scholars exposed the ways that 'unintended consequences', which were often also unforeseen, were all too frequently the lasting product of well-intentioned law reform efforts (Sarat et al. 1998).

14 The movement grew out of the legal relist tradition. *See* Garth and Sterling 1998 (outlining the history of the movement); Macaulay 2005 (discussing the legal realist roots and influence on the Law and Society Movement).

15 *See* Pound 1910, 15 (originating the distinction between law in books and law in action). *See also* Ehrlich 1936; Kessler 1995, 771; Nelken 1984; Page 1977.

The work of legal feminists following this tradition in the 1970s and 1980s was very attentive to the position of non-middle-class and non-white women. Their work documented the negative repercussions that feminist-inspired law reforms, asserted to benefit women generally, actually had on the subset of poor women's lives (Gordon 1990, Becker 1987). I, myself, did this type of analysis in regard to gender-neutral family law reforms and welfare reform proposals addressing the 'dilemma' of single motherhood using empirical data (Fineman 1991). My work urged would-be reformers to try to lessen the possibility of unintended consequences by self-consciously 'grounding' analyses of existing and proposed laws in women's experiences broadly. I adopted an approach developing 'middle-range theory', as advocated by Robert K. Merton (1967: 7–8). Middle-range feminist legal theory can be distinguished from the approach of feminist legal theorists like Catherine MacKinnon, who is more inclined to engage in the construction of grand theoretical overarching concepts and claims about the category of 'women'. MacKinnon's work has been criticized as 'totalizing' insofar as it transforms 'experience into objective truth', and middle-range theory sought to escape that sort of condemnation (Smart 1989).

In fact, MacKinnon has become the target of choice for those who want to employ the essentialist critique in regard to feminist legal theory (Cornell 1991, Franke 2009, Rhode 1989, Bartlett 1990, Harris 1990). Law and society feminist scholars' work is typically not under discussion, perhaps because its focus on poverty, imbalance of power, and so on, would disrupt the mantra of 'white middle-class heterosexual' feminism that is the main entry point for so much of perspective- or identity-based scholarship. Middle-range theorists try to understand and engage with the complexity of lives as they are lived and ground their theoretical insights in those lives. Feminist legal theorists have done this without giving up on the category of woman itself. The recent reinvigoration of a law and society approach apparent in the 'New Legal Realism' movement provides examples of such work (Miles and Sunstein 2008, Nourse and Shaffer 2009). But even using middle-range theory, if you resort to law, you must eventually draw lines and make generalizations that may gloss over differences. So I am left with my dilemma about how to productively use law to accomplish progressive reforms, and also with a nagging concern.

Using law and legal institutions (including legal theory) can be risky, may produce unforeseen and unintended consequences, and may overlook some differences among people in the interests of furthering reforms to benefit the larger group. But the tendency of some schools of critical legal theory over the past decade or so to primarily focus on identities also may have had unintended and unwanted consequences. In particular, identity-based analyses can obscure the ways in which subordination is shared across identities. Masculinities scholarship makes this point explicit when considering different groups of men, but it does so by differentiating men into more- or less-privileged cohorts and distinguishing all of them from women.

The continued focus on identities risks distorting and limiting analyses and reform proposals. The most salient danger is that continuing to primarily think about inequalities within an identities context risks leaving unexamined and unchallenged wider structural disadvantages that would not be considered discrimination under our equal-protection jurisprudence. One can begin with identities and build outwards to institutional structures. But, all too often, analysis that begins with identities also ends up there. Even approaches focused on intersectionality (or multidimensionality) will tend to direct critical attention to discrimination by and against individuals or, at best, individual institutions, and not to the failure, distortions or corruption of societal structures more systemically.

Identity-focused critiques, because they ultimately rely on identity as the basis for the disadvantaged (or advantaged) status or treatment, are anchored in antidiscrimination logic and individualized assessments of behaviour. Recent theories of unconscious or implicit bias,[16] while more institutionally focused, nonetheless are tied to identities and histories of intentional discrimination based on certain identity categories. While discrimination, intentional or unconscious, remains a problem, and certainly should be addressed in law, discrimination does not capture the universe of legal inequalities.

Defining the Universal Legal Subject

If the legal subject must be abstract, based on general principles or theories rather than on specific instances, as I have argued it has been historically, then it seems to me that the task for a critical legal scholar is to argue for a conception of the legal subject that is flexible, powerful, and able to incorporate a panoply of circumstances and positions. This is an argument that we must move beyond the impoverished legal subject of Locke and liberal thought, with its characteristics of autonomy and independence. Perspective scholars try to do this through intersectionality and multiplicities of identities, but I suggest we move in exactly the opposite direction: away from the fragmentation of the legal subject to the creation of a vigorous universal conception that will bring under consideration not the differences among individuals, but the relationship among and complementary shared responsibilities of the individual, the state, and societal institutions in regard to responding to the realities of the human condition.

16 *See* Kang 2005; Parks and Rachlinski 2008 ('Recent research from social psychologists indicates that unconscious race and gender biases are widespread and influence judgment. Because existing anti-discrimination law is designed to combat overt, or explicit, biases, it does not address unconscious biases well').

The Vulnerable Subject

In my recent work, I have used the idea of a universal 'vulnerable subject' to replace the one-dimensionally deformed liberal subject that is used to render natural and inevitable relationships of dependency, need, and vulnerability pathological and deviant (Fineman 2010a). The concept arose from asking two fundamental questions: (1) What should be the political and legal implications of the fact that we are embodied beings – which means we are born, live and die within a fragile materiality that renders all of us constantly susceptible to destructive external forces and internal disintegration? (2) If bodily needs and the messy dependency they carry cannot be ignored in life, how can they be absent in our theories about society, economics, politics and law? Unlike the liberal legal subject, the vulnerable legal subject is built around the idea of 'life-course', reflecting the range of developmental and social stages through which individuals are likely to pass in the course of a normal life span (Fineman 2008, 10–12).

The liberal legal subject at best captures only one stage – the likely least vulnerable of the human condition. By contrast, the vulnerable legal subject recognizes that, during their lives, individuals will encounter a myriad of possible opportunities, frustrations, challenges and experiences necessitating a wide range of differing and interacting abilities. We shall be dependent, weak, in need, as well as empowered and strong at different developmental stages in our lives. Throughout our lives we may be subject to external and internal negative, potentially devastating, events over which we have little control – disease, pandemics, environmental and climate deterioration, terrorism and crime, crumbling infrastructure, failing institutions, recession, corruption, decay and decline. We are situated beings who live with the ever-present possibility of changing needs and circumstances in our individual and collective lives. We are also accumulative beings and have different qualities and quantities of resources with which to meet these needs of circumstances, both over the course of our lifetime and as measured at the time of crisis or opportunity.

Vulnerability and Difference

One issue for a perspective- or identity-focused scholar at this point might be the question of just where and how individual identity categories fit into a vulnerability analysis. The theory argues, paradoxically, that, while human vulnerability is conceived as universal and constant on an abstract theoretical level that a construction of the legal and political subject requires, on the individual or experiential level it is realized in particular, varied and unique ways. This approach allows us to see two different roles for law and policy in regard to human vulnerability.

Two forms of individual difference are relevant: the first form is the physical/mental/intellectual and other variations are differences in human embodiment. These differences are not socially neutral, and historical reaction to some human variations, particularly race and gender, has led to the creation of hierarchies, discrimination, and even violence. Individuals who have certain characteristics have been subordinated and excluded from the benefits of society, often because their differences are thought to indicate they are dangerous, or interpreted as inadequacy, inferiority or weakness. These differences are often the basis for segregation of individuals into a 'vulnerable population' category, which both obscures the reality of universal vulnerability and stigmatizes the designated population (Fineman 2008, 8–10). The appropriate legal response to such instances is an improved and strengthened antidiscrimination system, perhaps complemented by affirmative action and social welfare processes to make up for past discrimination and reduce the probabilities that discrimination will reoccur in future.

The second forms of relevant difference are the differences in social location that are produced as the result of institutional practices and operations (15–20). While it is the case that such differences are manifested on the individual level, attention to the functioning of institutions is the specific focus in this part of the analysis. We are all differently situated within webs of economic and institutional relationships that structure our options and create opportunities. All individuals are dependent on institutions, be it the family or market and state institutions, because institutions provide the primary access and pathways to gain the resources necessary to address our vulnerability (7–8). Interestingly, this institutional and structural approach also allows for much more recognition of individual differences than does an identity-based analysis, which groups individuals according to their characteristics even if nuanced and multiplied. However, the focus is not on those distinguishing characteristics but on the institutions that produce them.

This focus on institutions is to my mind one of the most significant aspects of the vulnerability analysis. Societal institutions are theorized as having grown up around vulnerability (Fineman 2008, 12–13). They are seen as interlocking and overlapping, creating layered possibilities of opportunities and support but also containing gaps and potential pitfalls. These institutions collectively form systems that play an important role in lessening, ameliorating and compensating for vulnerability (Turner 2006, 255–284). Together and independently they provide us with resources in the form of advantages or coping mechanisms that cushion us when we are facing misfortune, disaster and violence. Cumulatively, these assets provide individuals with resilience in the face of our shared vulnerability.[17] There are at least five different types of resources or assets that societal organizations and institutions can provide: physical, human, social,[18] ecological or environmental, and existential (12–15).[19]

---

17 Urie Bronfenbrenner's ecological child development model, for example, examines systems and assets that influence the child. *See* Woodhouse 2009, 822 (citing Bronfenbrenner 1979, 6–7).

18 Among the social resources are group affiliation and identification based on the first form of embodied differences or distinctions.

19 'Physical resources are the physical goods or material things that determine our present quality of life, such as housing, food, entertainment, and means of transportation.

There is a link between these various types of resources and state responsibility. Many of the institutions providing resources that give us resilience can only be brought into legal existence through state mechanisms.[20] Entities such as corporations, schools, workplaces, families or churches are legitimated and given a status that confers on them benefits and protections by law.[21] Their very content and meaning is defined through state processes. The dissolution of many of these entities is also accomplished only through state processes. To the extent that these legally constituted institutions distribute significant social goods, they should be monitored by the state. State involvement in the creation and maintenance of these institutions requires that the state be vigilant in ensuring that the distribution of such assets is accomplished with attention to public values, including equality or justice, or objectives beyond private or profit motivation. Instead, what we find in the United States is that, within these various asset-conferring systems, individuals are often positioned differently from one another. Specifically, some are privileged by the structure and operation of these institutions, while others

---

Physical resources also can provide us with the means for accumulating additional resources when they take the form of savings and investments. … Human resources affect material well-being. They are those goods that contribute to the development of a human being, allowing participation in the market and making possible the accumulation of material resources that help bolster individuals' resilience in the face of vulnerability. These resources are often referred to in terms of "human capital," primarily developed through systems that provide education, training, knowledge, and experience. … Social assets or resources are provided by less tangible, not so easily quantifiable relationships. These include social networks from which we gain support and strength. The family is a major institution providing social resources. … [So too are] other associations, such as political parties or labor or trade unions. … In recent decades, a sense of community organized around identity characteristics, such as race, ethnicity, and gender, has constituted powerful networks of affiliation and belonging. Ecological resources can be conferred through our position in relation to the physical or natural environments in which we find ourselves. We live in an environment and are dependent on things like clean air and water. We experience the environment in immediate and cosmic senses. … A variety of external factors and physical actions can alter the environments in which we live and have profound influence over our needs and wellbeing. Existential resources are provided by systems of belief or aesthetics, such as religion, culture, or art, and perhaps even politics. These systems can help us to understand our place within the world and allow us to see meaning and beauty in our existence. These resources may help ensure individuals when faced with hardships or opportunities, providing the requisite resilience to survive and flourish' (Fineman 2010a, 270).

20 *See*, *e.g.*, 26 U.S.C. § 501(c)(3) (2006) (granting churches and other religious organizations tax-exempt status). Robert Dahl, Yale professor, observed that, without the protection of a dense network of laws enforced by public governments, the largest American corporation could not exist for a day. *See* Alperovitz and Daly 1982, 138 (quoting Dahl 1982, 183–185). Dahl also noted that the view of economic institutions as private is an ill fit for their social and public nature. *Id.* at 139.

21 Legal documents such as charters, documents of incorporation, licences or permits come to mind.

are relatively disadvantaged and left to cope with their shared vulnerability on an individual level. The responsibility to overcome existing systemic inequalities is seen as an individual, not a state, responsibility.

Conclusion: A Beyond-identities Vision

Legal reforms are by definition institutionally focused and the trick is how to effect a turn away, not from law (or feminism), but from identities to institutional structures. When the urge for change begins with identities, all too often that is where the energy for reform ends up being absorbed. Even an approach focused on intersectionality (or multidimensionality) will tend to direct critical attention to discrimination by and against individuals, not to the real or potential failures, distortion or corruption of societal structures that affect everyone in society. If we focus on institutions, the significant intersections might very well be those we see when systems, such as the educational, financial, political, familial and employment systems, work in unison to produce privilege and structure disadvantage.

Gender and/or race have been the entries into progressives thinking more complexly about equality for many decades, but the 'best' contemporary feminist legal theory (in my opinion) has moved beyond gender and other identity markers and engages with institutional and structural relationships (including ideological structures). An antidiscrimination model will not help us understand the institutional mechanisms through which economic resources are generated and distributed, as well as the allocation of power within society. Critical theory must engage with theories of regulation and institutionalization and define how we can access the multiplicity of power relationships we call 'the state'. We should be rethinking contract, corporation, family and education law – not from the perspective of identities, but from the perspective of privilege and disadvantage and with a firm grounding in a theory of state responsibility for the vulnerable legal subjects who actually populate society.

PART II
Deconstructing Masculinities in Location

Chapter 4
Martyred Women and Humiliated Men

Roja Fazaeli

Introduction

In January 2008 the well-known Iranian feminist journal *Zanan* (women) was closed down by the order of the Media Supervision Committee of Iran's Ministry of Culture and Islamic Guidance. The closure was prompted by *Zanan*'s publication of a report a year earlier titled *Koshte Mishavand ta Bokoshand* (They Die in Order to Kill), which focused on the Iranian martyrdom movement (*jonbesh-e esteshhadi*) (Zarabadi 2007).[1] The movement under the directorship of the World Islamic Organization Headquarters for Remembering the Martyrs (*Setad-e Pasdasht Shohaday-e Nehzat-e Jahaniy-e Islam*)[2] has been recruiting both men and women for potential suicide missions since its inception in 2003 (Zarabadi 2007, Ayandey-e Roshan 2006).

More than a year after the closure of *Zanan*, the Iranian opposition movement, which coalesced in the wake of the contested 2009 Iranian presidential elections, hailed Neda Agha Sultan as its symbolic martyr, a symbolism that until now was reserved mostly for men (Zarabadi 2007, Nissimov, Mansharof, Savyon 2009). Not only did Neda become a martyr, but also a symbol of the oppositions' unity. The fatalism of Neda's martyrdom differs to that desired by women martyrdom

1 *Zanan*'s licence was revoked after 16 years since the publication began its work. According to news articles as cited in a report by Amnesty International, *Zanan* was accused of having 'endangered the spiritual, mental and intellectual health of its readers, gave the impression of insecurity in society, and drew a dark image of the situation of women in Islamic society by publishing certain articles' (Amnesty International 2008: 3). Some reports indicate the links between *Zanan*'s closure and Zarabadi's (2007) report on female martyrdom seekers (e.g. Nissimov, Mansharof, Savyon 2009: 4). However, given that the closure came more than a year after the publication of the article, it could not have been the sole catalyst.

2 The World Islamic Organization Headquarters for Remembering the Martyrs (*Setad-e Pasdasht Shohaday-e Nehzat-e Jahaniy-e Islam*, hereafter *Setad-e Sasdasht*) announced their establishment by a press release on December 2003 in protest to the proposal by the Iranian foreign minister (Kamal Kharrazi, b. 1944) to change the name of a street in Tehran, which was named after Khaled Eslamboli (d. 1982), a member of Egyptian Islamic Jihad who assassinated Anwar al-Sadat on 6 October 1981. See the declaration of *Setad-e Pasdasht* to the Iranian Parliament and the Iranian Ministry of Foreign Affairs in protest to the name change, Mehrnews 2004.

seekers (*zanan-e shahadat talab*), who were the focus of the article in the 2007 issue of *Zanan*. In a broad context and from the outset one could say that these women are willing signatories to martyrdom operations, whereas Neda did not choose to be killed or martyred.[3] Both Neda's martyrdom and that desired by the female martyrdom seekers,[4] are politically charged and should be examined in their particular contexts. Nonetheless, Neda and these women all shared the experience of having lived and living in a patriarchal nation. They lived through eight years of war[5] in a country where martyrdom is revered historically as a male domain.[6] One could raise the question whether Neda's celebrated status as a female martyr and the growing numbers of women volunteers for martyrdom operations

3 Neda was shot dead on 20 June 2009. According to some news sources the director of *Bonyad Shahid va Omor Ithargaran* (Foundation of Martyrs and Veterans Affair) of Iran, Masoud Zaribafan, stated that if the relevant security forces were to prove that Neda was killed by the conspiracy of the enemies (of the regime) then Neda would be declared a martyr (formally) (Khabar Online 2009).

4 Note the word in Persian that translates to martyrdom seeker is *esteshhadi*, whereas the word meaning suicide bomber is *entehari*. Although the meanings of both words are clearly distinct, often the word *esteshhadi* is used instead of *entehari* by recruiters and those who sign up to such operations. In Arabic the word *shahid* translates to both witness and martyr, and is thought to have its roots in the Syriac Bible, the *Pshitta*. In the Qur'an the word *shahadat* is used to indicate the 'bearing of witness' rather than 'dying in the path of God'. Farhad Khosrokhavar (2002: 11) suggests that the word *shahid* only came to mean 'martyr' after the conquest of Palestine by the Muslims in the seventh century B.C. Martyrdom in a general sense as declared by both Fouad Ibrahim (2009: 111) and Manochehr Dorraj (1997: 490) is a conscious or an intentional act of sacrificing one's life by embracing death for one's faith or political cause. *Entehari* (suicide bomber) like martyrdom seeker sacrifices her or his life for a cause but with a knowledge that her or his life will end by killing others (usually who they consider as enemy). Both context and politics are important factors in differentiating between the two terms. In an article from an online publication (*hozoor*) published by Hawza.net (online portal of Islamic sciences linked to the seminaries in Qom), the two terms *entehari* and *esteshhadi* are juxtaposed very broadly. According to the article, 'the authorities of the Zionist regime, the US and some media have labeled these operations [referring to suicide attacks] as "suicide attacks (*entehari*) and terrorism." This term has a negative connotation and pre-condemns such actions. In contrast, the Palestinians, some Arabic sources and the majority of the Iranian political and media circles refer to such operations as "martyrdom seeking (*esteshhadi*)." From this point of view, such martyrdom seeking actions are regarded positively which are carried out by Palestinians in self-defense' (Pourhossein 2003).

5 The Iran and Iraq war (1980–1988) (e.g. Rajaee 2003, Karsh 2002).

6 One of the most celebrated martyrs of the Iran–Iraq war was the 13-year old Hossein Fahmideh, who died by strapping grenades to his body and throwing himself under an Iraqi tank. Fahmideh was made into a national hero. Ayatollah Khomeini referred to him as the country's leader: 'Our leader is that 13 year old child whose little heart is bigger than hundreds of written words or speeches, who threw himself under an enemy tank and drank the juice of martyrdom' (e.g. Saeid 2005).

point to a feminization of martyrdom in Iranian society. Also, could one say that this feminization extends to elsewhere in the Middle East given the surge in the number of female suicide bombers in the past ten years? Noteworthy is the increase in the number of female suicide bombers in Iraq and also the 'black widows' in Chechnya. According to *The New York Times* there were 'some 60 suicide bombings attempted or carried out by women' in Iraq in one year (2007–2008) (Rubin 2009, T. Williams 2009).

This rise in the number of suicide attacks in the Middle East coincides with and is perhaps not unrelated to the so-called 'war on terror' and occupation. In an interview with Mehrnews, Mohammad Ali Samadi, the head of communication of *Setad-e Pasdasht*, links the inception of the organization and the readiness of martyrdom seekers for deployment to 'the presence of foreign occupiers in strategic positions in Islamic lands' (Mehrnews 2004). He describes this presence as an aggression to the honour of Muslims. Mohammad Hafez (2007) in a study of suicide bombers in Iraq identifies three mobilizing narratives used by Jihadists to recruit and mobilize martyrdom seekers. Although the present context of Iran differs to that of Iraq, nonetheless the narratives used by recruiters seem to show striking similarities. The three commonalities are: the use of language of honour leading to humiliation of the Muslim man, the inability of the regional governments allied to superpowers to defend their nation's honour (land, holy shrines or Muslim women), and the need for the ultimate sacrifice and heroism of martyrdom. *Setad-e Pasdasht* held a membership drive in May 2004 in Tehran for volunteer martyrdom seekers who proclaimed their readiness to be deployed to defend the Shi'a holy cities of Najaf and Karbala. The head of the organization Rajaifar publicly declared that these recruitment drives were symbolic gestures and a warning to the US and the UK (Hamshahri 2004). Although the transgression against Iraq's holy Shi'a cities is used in this imagery as a show of offensives towards Shi'a Muslims, the narratives and imagery of suffering of Palestinians is often used by recruiters in Iran and elsewhere to exacerbate and personalize the sense of threat and humiliation faced by Palestinians as one that should be shared and ultimately defended by Muslims globally (Hafez 2007: 100–101).

Although the rise of female suicide bombers in the Middle East and particularly in Iraq[7] is noteworthy, this chapter will only concentrate on the contexts of Palestine and Iran given the significance of the Palestinian martyrs and suicide bombers as role models for Iranian martyrdom recruits by their recruiters.

7 Studies of suicide attacks in Iraq show that the number of such attacks 'has surpassed the number of suicide operations by all previous insurgent groups combined, including those by Hezbollah in Lebanon, the Tamil Tigers in Sri Lanka, and Hamas in Israel' (Hafez 2007: 3).

Women Martyrs and Suicide Bombers:[8] Changing Notions of Masculinities or Feminization of Martyrdom?

The first recorded female suicide mission in the Middle East was that of 16-year-old Sana'a Mehaidli, a member of the Syrian Socialist Nationalist Party (SSNP), 'who detonated her car bomb on 9 April 1985, in Lebanon, killing two Israeli soldiers and injuring two others' (National Counterterrorism Center 2007: 2). It was not, however, until after the death of Wafa Idris the first Palestinian suicide bomber in January 2002, that subsequent waves of suicide bombings by women were carried out. Dareen Abu Ayshe,[9] Ayat al-Akhras,[10] Andaleeb Taqatqah,[11] Hiba Daraghmeh,[12] Hanadi Jaradat[13] and Reem al-Riyashi,[14] amongst a number of other women, also undertook suicide missions (e.g. Hasso 2005, Victor 2004). It is the stories of these Palestinian women suicide bombers that are used as propaganda to recruit female martyrdom seekers in Iran (e.g. Samadi 2005).

Given the suddenness in the rise of women as suicide bombers[15] in the Middle East since 2002, the question arises as to what has changed in the last decade that attracts or forces women to seek martyrdom, a realm that was not only nearly exclusive to men but also in some ways defined their masculinities. In her paper 'Mullahs, Martyrs, and Men', Shahin Gerami describes martyrdom as one type of hypermasculinity created by the Islamic republic of Iran. The Islamic republic's depiction of a martyr, according to Gerami, 'is a young, unmarried (virgin, innocent)

8 The first Muslim martyr who died for the faith was a woman, Summaya bint Khayyat. Summaya's martyrdom has never been as celebrated as has the martyrdom of men (Khosrokhavar 2002: 11).

9 Twenty-one-year-old woman who lived in the Nablus village of Beit Wazan with her family. Dareen was a student at An-Najah University. Like Wafa Idris, Dareen carried out the suicide bombing under the banner of al-Aqsa Martyrs' Brigades.

10 Ayat was 18 years old at the time of her mission. As a high-school senior she lived with her family in the Deheisheh refugee camp in Bethlehem. Ayat was also a member of al-Aqsa.

11 Andaleeb Taqataqah, 20 years old from Bethlehem, was also a member of al-Aqsa and carried out a suicide mission on 12 April 2002 at Mahane Yehuda Market bus stop in Jerusalem, killing six and injuring 104 people.

12 Nineteen-year-old Hiba Daraghmeh, a member of Islamic Jihad and Al-Aqsa, blew herself up at the entrance of a shopping mall in Afula, killing three and injuring 70 others on 19 May 2003.

13 Hanadi Jaradat, a 29-year-old lawyer from Jenin, carried out her suicide attack at a restaurant in Haifa on 10 March 2003, killing 21 and injuring 60 people. Hanadi was affiliated to Islamic Jihad.

14 Reem al-Riyashi is the first woman to carry out a suicide mission in the name of Hamas. Reem was at the time of the attack 22 years old and mother of two young children. She died on 14 January 2004.

15 Please note that the terms suicide bomber and martyrdom seeker are used contextually rather than interchangeably in this chapter.

man, fearless and strong … Sometimes he is depicted in the foreground, leading a group of women and older male martyrs, or he is depicted in the foreground of fully veiled women and young girls, protecting them and the country's honor' (Gerami 2003: 267). The rise in the number of female martyrdom seekers challenges the status quo of women as the protected as they become the protectors.

Can one identify female suicide bombers or martyrdom seekers as agents capable of acting in their own capacity? How do these women relate to their own notions of self and their relationship to the society, and what is the role of politics and religion within such self-definitions? How much choice do these women exert in seeking martyrdom as compared to their male counterparts in 'this supposedly "male territory"' (Whaley Eager 2008: 4)? Also of importance is the question, what has prompted militant Islamists movement such as *Setad-e Pasdasht* and Hamas to recruit an increasing number of women to carry out suicide operations? Does this point to change of policy of these movements or to a change in women's perceived public status? Or is this simply a propagandist game in humiliating and shaming men who have failed to protect their 'honours'?

There is no doubt that women martyrdom seekers defy the mainstream traditional interpretation of women's roles in the public sphere (Pitcher 1998: 16) in their participation in operations, which would previously have been regarded as male domains. Women have been taking part in active combat throughout history; however, women's participation in any violent resistance is deemed difficult to reconcile with their roles as mothers, daughters, sisters or wives. As Paige Whaley Eager notes,

> women's roles as warriors and mothers have been difficult to reconcile. While the 'image of the women holding a rifle and baby was found in liberation movements throughout the third world' (Goldestine 2001: 81), many women were expected to retreat to the private sphere of the home once the conflict was over or national liberation was achieved. (Whaley Eager 2008: 3)

According to some it is this exact perceived character of a woman as motherly, and hence less violent, that leads to their recruitment by militant Islamic groups. According to Yoram Schweitzer, the use of women as suicide bombers stems from the militant groups' realization that the women's 'seemingly innocent outward appearance and the universal perception of their non-violent character' (2003: 2), makes it easier for women to circumvent security as they are generally regarded as less suspicious.

One could also juxtapose women martyrdom seekers with their young male counterparts. Linda Pitcher in her anthropological study refers to the Palestinian youth martyrdom seekers as 'young people trapped in circumstances beyond their control' (1998: 9). Pitcher's view of martyrdom in this study is that of escapism from 'the confines of a military occupation' (1998: 9). Palestinian children both male and female grow up in the midst of fear and vulnerability, which forms their individual and collective identities. The emotions of those living under occupation range from vulnerability and despair to anger and resentment. It is against the backdrop of these emotions and at times physical violations[16] that the body becomes 'the locus of displacement' (Pitcher 1998: 13). Pitcher's study of the Palestinian youth, although mainly concerned with the male gender, can also be applied to women. Women's experiences of occupation and authority would be similar to an extent to their male counterparts but would differ through society's differentiation of gender roles, entailing different levels of vulnerabilities and discriminations. Pitcher further states, 'Beatings, bullet wounds, harassment, and interrogation violate the intimacy of the body, yet are representative of a larger, collective, and systematic displacement: the displacement of Palestinian refugees evicted from their homes now inside Israel, the displacement of an entire population denied the authenticity of a homeland' (1998: 14). Violation of the intimacy of the body is demasculinizing for the male subject, whereas for women it may imply a question of honour.

The self-perceptions of martyrdom seekers are also formed against the backdrop of the 'authority' of the occupier (Pitcher 1998: 10). The concept of authority itself is of paramount importance in ascertaining these martyrdom seekers' agency. Not only are they affected by repression under the direct and indirect 'authority of occupier', but the authority of charismatic religio-political leaders is also equally effective.

It is imperative to look into the individual agencies of these women through their own taped testaments before their deaths. The testimonies provide us a glimpse of the context in which these women act. One can then attempt to find out whether their actions can be called their own and how and if their actions create change at the physical, interpersonal and social levels. The taped testaments chosen for the purposes of this chapter are excerpts from the dubbed Persian documentary *Dokhtaran-e Zeytoon* (Daughters of Olive), which the Iranian martyrdom recruiters screen in their recruitments forums (*Dokhtaran Zeytoon*, Anisi 2005).

The documentary begins with the testimony of 21-year-old Dareen Abu Ayshe before her death. Dareen, a student at An-Najah University in Nablus, became the second Palestinian female suicide bomber after detonating her bomb 'at the Israeli Maccabim roadblock in West Ramallah (West Bank)' (Alvanou 2007: 20). Dareen's testimony is important in her awareness of her role as a *female* suicide bomber, as she declares:

> Because the role of the Muslim Palestinian woman is no less important than the role of our fighting brothers, I have decided to be the second female martyr to continue the path that was forged by the female martyr Wafa al-Idris. I give my humble self in the path of God to avenge the limbs of our martyred brothers and in revenge for the sanctity of our religion and mosques, and in revenge for the sanctity of the Al-Aqsa mosque …

---

16 Physical violence that Pitcher refers to here is that endured by Palestinian youth inflicted by the Israeli army during protests (being targeted by plastic bullets, being beaten or even shot).

> Let Sharon the coward know that every Palestinian woman will give birth to an army of martyrs, and her role will not only be confined to weeping over a son, brother or husband, instead she will become a martyr herself. (Muhammed Hafez 2006: 89–90)

Miriam Cooke, using an explanation of the sociologist Islah Jad,[17] states that 'these women are not imitating men; they are demanding a "fatal equality" that will allow them to protect men through a "spectacular self-sacrifice"' (Cooke 2008: 96). She adds,

> The right to bear arms on Islam's behalf has long been a bone of contention between women and religious authorities: Where does the armed woman fit into the Muslim imaginary? Since the unmarked religious warrior is presumed to be male, these *istishhadiyat* unveil and challenge the exclusion of women from this identity-conforming, citizenship-conferring arena. (2008: 96)

The last sentence of Dareen's testimony not only attempts a redefinition of the women's role but also demasculinizes Sharon's role as 'the authority', against a backdrop of not only male martyrs born of women but also women martyrs.

The second part of the documentary represents the life and the last testimony of Ayat al-Akhras, the 18-year-old who detonated her bomb on 29 March 2002 in Jerusalem, killing two and injuring 28 others. Ayat became the third Palestinian female suicide bomber (Alvanou 2007: 19). The documentary highlights Ayat's wish to become a journalist and her numerous failed attempts in doing so. The documentary also tries to persuade the viewer of Ayat's self-expression through the act of martyrdom, as her mother states 'each human being would talk about their views, some by voting, some by the pen and some with Jihad.' Ayat like Dareen attempts a demasculinization of 'authority', but this time of the Arab rulers: 'to the Arab rulers I say enough sleeping, betrayal, and failure to fulfill Palestine's duty', as Ayat declares. This narrative of demasculinization and humiliation is not unique to the testimonies of female suicide bombers but is according to Hafez (2007: 99) a theme used 'at the heart of the mobilizing narrative of insurgents.'

The third part of the documentary is about Hanadi Jaradat, the 29-year-old lawyer from Jenin, who bombed the Maxim restaurant in Haifa, killing 19 people and injuring many others (Alvanou 2007: 21). Hanadi's testimony (*Dokhtaran Zeytoon*) is different from the other two in its deliberations of overly violent images:

> with the strength of God and his resolve I decided to be the sixth martyr who will make her body splinter and explode to kill the Zionists and destroy each settler. At last it's not only us who must pay the price and harvest the tears and pain of their crimes. In order not to keep our mothers paying the price of Zionist

17 Islah Jad is a lecturer in Women's Studies at Birzeit University.

> criminality, in order not for our mothers not to cry and wail at the loss of their children and sons, we must make their mothers cry, so mother, don't cry for my martyrdom. I decided after reliance on God to make the death that they surround us with, surround them also, and to make their mothers cry tears and blood, my call for God to make us eternal in the heaven and make them eternal in hell.

The tone of Hanadi's testimony is more vengeful than the other two, and her personal circumstances prior to her mission may provide a partial explanation for this. Hanadi's younger brother Fadi and her cousin Salah were killed a few months earlier during an Israeli raid on Jenin; Hanadi was distraught by her brother's death. Hanadi's friend Sana recalls Hanadi's reclusion:

> Hanadi did not leave the house much after her brother's death, she only spoke about religion, she read all of the Qur'an twice in the space of two months. Here with all that happens you become progressively more religious. You see death in front of your eyes at every moment. You may not be very religious either but when you are faced with death and you know that every second you could die then the issue is different. (*Dokhtaran Zeytoon*)

This progressive 'religiosity' has gained popularity amongst the younger generation of Palestinians. One way in which women valorize their cause is by donning the veil. Other causalities underlying violence such as suicide bombings are deemed to stem from socio-economic factors. Poverty, lack of education and unemployment could be viewed as both oppressive and depressive for the individual and for the society. Also, family relations and mental health may be seen as contributing factors.

Other studies, such as those conducted by Massimo Introvigne and Claude Berrebi, highlight that 'a large majority of suicide bombers have a better than average level of schooling and income' (Introvigne 2009: 44). According to Introvigne, contrary to some beliefs and demonstrated in the study of Alan Krueger and Jitka Maleková (2003) there is very little direct connection between education, poverty and suicide bombings or other terrorist activities. One could also apply this to the cases of female suicide bombers, while keeping in mind that motives could be individual, ideological or structural (Whaley Eager 2008: 1). The majority of female suicide bombers in Palestine were educated women from middle-class families. As Kai Adler writes, 'Far more than just a religious symbol, the veil has come to signalize a woman's identity, and her commitment to the "Palestinian Cause"' (2006). This form of religiosity is present in all of the women's testimonies as presented in the documentary.

The fourth celebrated martyr in the documentary (*Dokhtaran Zeytoon*), Reem al-Riyashi, 22-year-old mother of two, was the first woman suicide bomber to be associated with Hamas who was a mother. Reem is referred to in the documentary as 'the martyrdom-loving mother'. Reem's final speech is both violent and full of religious rhetoric:

> I swear to God that even if my bones are broken and my body parts are cut into pieces they cannot take away my faith from me … this is how I feel … I hope that the shredded limbs of my body will be shrapnel, tearing Zionists to pieces. Knocking on heaven's door with the skulls of Zionists.

Hanadi's understanding of her body as an agent politicizes the female body. Pitcher writes that such politicization of the body is 'an expression of cultural resistance' (1998: 14).

All three testimonies share the message of corporate revenge, and this fact begs the question of whether their personal agency is restricted in the face of their involvement with a political organization. That is to say, the element of choice may be curtailed if they are acting as a member of a collective.

However, regardless of the meaning one attempts to extract from these testimonies, they are used in this documentary to entice other women to do the same. Therefore, all three women are depicted as heroic. What Pitcher writes regarding the martyrdom of youth in Palestine can also be applied to these women, she states: 'The story of a martyr is a tale of heroism and sacrifice. He is a figure who in death achieves that which is unattainable in life – a union between freedom and control, between the past and the future, between the individual and the collective' (1998: 19).

Palestinian female suicide bombers have changed the status quo image of the male martyr by sacrificing their own body and blood. This sacrifice, according to Frances Hasso, challenges 'the sexual and feminized forms usually associated with menstruation, childbirth, heteronormativity, maternal sacrifice, and the violated or raped woman' (2005: 24). The male domination of martyrdom operations in Palestine changed on 14 January 2002 when 28-year-old Wafa Idris, a volunteer medic with the Red Cross, became the first Palestinian female suicide bomber (BBC 2002). Laleh Khalili writes that, only days after Wafa's death, her mural commissioned by the Martyrs' Affairs Bureau appeared in Haifa. According to Khalili, 'By highlighting a woman's self-sacrifice – considered to be the duty of men – it pointed to the extremity of Palestinian despair [that] had driven women to self-sacrifice; but it also, paradoxically, highlighted the gender egalitarianism achieved in performing a suicide operation' (2007: 119). Khalili notes that Wafa's mural was replaced by 'other commemorative images' (2007: 120) as more young women followed Wafa's path of suicide operations. She adds, 'The ephemeral commemoration, nevertheless, had its intended effect of valorizing heroism, now embodied in a woman's much debated violent act, intended for the local camp audience' (2007: 120). Hasso (2005: 24) writes,

> In addition to defying their own placement within this normative gender–sexual grid with various levels of explicitness, the women militants communicated a dramatic objection to Israeli military occupation of Palestinian land and repression of the Palestinian population. They also challenged Israeli gendered assumptions that it is Palestinian male and not female bodies that militarily

> threatened their racialized social order. Moreover, they concurrently called men to arms in defense of community, and participated in that defense themselves, destabilizing the construct of men as defenders of community and women as the protected.

According to Hasso, not only have these women suicide bombers changed the role of women as militant political actors but they have also changed some notions of Arab and Middle-Eastern masculinities. The narrative of desperation and humiliation of the Palestinian men is also captured by Hasso in her mapping of the responses of Arab political and religious leaders to these acts of violence by women. In these responses she notes that 'women gain some of the attributes of Arab masculinity conventionally deemed positive – bravery, courage, and willingness to sacrifice their lives to maintain honour and dignity – and men gain the attributes of femininity conventionally deemed negative – economic and political dependence, weakness, empty talk, and the inability to defend their honour and dignity' (Hasso 2005: 36) Saddam Hussein's response to Wafa's death is particularly interesting, as he stated, 'What is this injustice suffered by the Arabs in general and the Palestinians in particular that could prompt women to carry out fadayeen operations? Moreover, this operation will impact on men, all men, the Arab homeland. The fact that women have turned themselves into rifles will evoke men's sense of shame before their own women, before God, and before themselves' (Saddam Hussein in Republic of Iraq Television 2002, cited in Hasso 2005: 37).

Under the Shadow of *Dokhtaran Zeytoon* (Daughters of Olive) and the Army of Roses

Palestinian female suicide bombers are the iconic heroes of the Iranian women who subscribe to suicide missions. In 2005 the World Islamic Organization Headquarters for Remembering the Martyrs held a forum titled *Dokhtaran-e Zeytoon* (Daughters of Olive) in Tehran in an attempt to recruit Iranian female martyrdom seekers (BBC Persian 2005). It was declared in the gathering that 'the Iranian women and girl martyrdom seekers who are present in this union are ready to walk in the footstep of the martyred and *mujahid* Palestinian women martyrdom seekers and will create dreadful nightmares against the Zionists' (BBC Persian 2005). During the forum the abovementioned documentary *Dokhtaran-e Zeytoon* was screened.

Forooz Rajaifar, secretary-general of the World Islamic Organization Headquarters for Remembering the Martyrs (*dabir kol-e Setad-e Pasdasht Shohaday-e Nehzat-e Jahaniy-e Islam*),[18] in an interview with *Zanan* indicates

18 Rajaifar, according to an interview published on the website of the World Islamic Organization Headquarters for Remembering the Martyrs, she holds an engineering degree and a master's degree in political science and is currently studying for her Ph.D. at Tehran

that the number of women martyrdom seekers in Iran is about a third of the total martyrdom seekers, 20 thousand of the total 55 thousand. The recruits include seminary students (*tolab*), college students and graduates, teachers, and a small number of housewives (Sarmaye 2006).[19] According to Rajaifar, the Organization began enrolling martyrdom seekers after the US invasion of Iraq. She asserts, 'After the US invasion of Najaf and Karbala, and their mistreatment of the holy Shi'a sites, we decided to recruit and enroll volunteers for martyrdom missions to show the discontent of the Iranian people and against those who threaten material and spiritual sources of the Islamic world' (BBC Persian 2005).

These volunteers are grouped into different martyrdom units depending on their age, education, and physical and mental abilities. It is remarkable that gender does not play a role in the grouping of these volunteers in a society where gender segregation envelops the public sphere. Accordingly women are given the same training as the men. According to the Organization, the training is mainly cultural and political, in order to familiarize the volunteers with the issues pertaining to the world of Islam. The volunteers are also given psychological training, where the martyrdom seekers are coached to be spiritually and psychologically ready for their martyrdom missions (Zarabadi 2007). In a separate interview, Rajaifar speaks of the philosophy behind the martyrdom missions. She states:

> [The] martyrdom mission in my opinion is a type of defense but a level of defense which takes place with the minimal resources. You are faced with an enemy who is armed head to toe. The enemy has a full army and different kinds of weapons from nuclear to chemical and biological. You have nothing but your body as defense in front of this enemy … *Shari'a* and *urf* come to play here, in particular when *Shari'a* has made it the duty of both men and women to defend [land/faith] if an Islamic country is occupied by the enemy. To give one's life in this manner does not even require the permission of a *Shari'a* judge, meaning that one should know and feel when one reaches the point where she/he is under attack and needs to defend herself/himself. (Zarabadi 2007)

Rajaifar also asserts that there are three main targets for the volunteers to choose from. The first is the occupiers of the holy land, the second is Salman Rushdie, author of *The Satanic Verses*, and the third comprises other occupiers and those who threaten the material and spiritual fibre of the Islamic world. However, she adds that the goal of their organization is not only to train martyrdom seekers to carry out missions in Palestine or against Salman Rushdie: the fundamental motive of their training is to enable core *Hezbullah* resistance groups to be formed all around the world and in conflict areas. She asserts, 'this is Imam Khomeini's command that there should be such cores all over the world' (Zarabadi 2007).

University, Faculty of Politics. She also proudly asserts her involvement in the US Embassy hostage crisis in Iran in 1979.

19 It is also noteworthy that, according to Rajaifar, most recruits register as a family.

Martyrdom in Islam: A Changing Gender Paradigm?

The increase in the number of female suicide bombers and female martyrdom seekers brings forth a need for the re-examination of the notion of martyrdom in Islamic societies. This re-examination must keep in mind that the tradition of martyrdom is not unique to Islam. For example, in the history of monotheistic religions both Judaism and Christianity have understood 'martyrdom in the path of God as a noble act' (Dorraj 1997: 490).

In Shi'a Islam, no other martyrdom event has contributed more to martyrology than the martyrdom of the Shi'a Imam Hussein in Karbala on *Ashura* (10 October 680).[20] The martyrdom of Hussein is seen not only symbolic as a model for all martyrdom seekers: it has become 'a defining symbol for Shii Muslims of the profound injustice of the world' (Esposito 2003: 33). Dorraj consequently declares that 'martyrdom in the struggle against social injustice and oppression is said to be the noblest of all causes. A Muslim's sincerity and devotion to the faith are measured by his/her readiness to sacrifice his/her life' (Dorraj 1997: 494).[21]

The role of women in martyrdom in Shi'a Islam is intrinsically linked to the events of Karbala. The women of Karbala, in particular Zaynab,[22] are on the one hand regarded as those who needed protection and on the other hand revered as strong women who coped with the loss of their men. In his sermon on 5 June 1989, Khomeini, in what is known to be his last will and testament, refers to Zaynab as a symbol of the sacrificial woman who gives everything in the way of God:

---

20 The story of Karbala begins with Hussein's attempt to move from Medina where he was residing to Kufa in Iraq on learning that the Shi'a in Kufa were planning a revolt against the Umayyad regime. Yazid's army defeated the revolting Shi'as in Kufa and subsequently killed Hussein and his family (apart from his youngest son and his sister Zaynab) in Karbala in 680.

21 Also note that Manochehr Dorraj (1997: 491) claims that the culture and religions of pre-Islamic Iran have also influenced the late Shi'ite martyrology. According to Dorraj, one of the major iconic influences was Mani, who preached rituals such as fasting, living ascetic lives and practising self-castration. Furthermore Dorraj makes a link between the prevalence of tragedy in Iranian culture and the culture of martyrdom. This tragedy is reflected in the Persian literature, such as Ferdowsi's *Shahnameh* (The Book of Kings). Ali Shariati and Ayatollah Motahari, the ideologues of the Islamic republic, transformed the narrative of the death of Hussein by applying his heroic and symbolic role to the ordinary male populace; in other words, Hussein, who previously was a saintly figure, became humanized. During the Iran–Iraq war this popularization of Hussein's martyrdom was used to urge the young Iranian males (as young as 11) to go to the front in their thousands in the hope of either becoming a martyr (with the keys around their necks representing the keys to heaven) or reaching Karbala. As Manouchehr Dorraj notes, 'thousands of Iranian youth voluntarily walked through Iraqi mine fields to clear a path for Iranian tanks and artillery divisions' (1997: 489). The image of Saddam Hussein as Yazid was often used during the Iran–Iraq war to mobilize the Iranian masses.

22 Grand-daughter of Muhammad and daughter of Ali ibn Abu Talib and Fatima bint Muhammad.

> We have repeatedly seen great Zaynab-like women cry out that they have lost their children and sacrificed everything they have in the way of God the Exalted and beloved Islam, and are proud to have done so. They realize that what they have achieved instead is higher even that the gardens of paradise, let alone the unimportant chattels of this world. (Khomeini 1982: 127)

The story of Karbala as one of the major historical accounts of martyrdom in Islam is one dominated by the male martyrs, with Hussein often being called *Sayyed al-Shohada* (Lord of the Martyrs). Women have more often been regarded as the proud mothers of martyrs, self-sacrificing, becoming the emblematic symbols of a nation at war (Khalili 2007: 127). As Mateo Mohammad Farzaneh states, 'Women were accordingly encouraged to send their sons along the path of martyrdom just as Zeynab, Hussein's sister had done' (Farzaneh 2007: 91). This notion of the sacrificial mother also reverberates in the Palestinian narratives, as Laleh Khalili (2007: 127) writes: 'An important iconic figure in commemorations of martyrs is the martyr's mother, an older Palestinian woman who encouraged her son to fight at any cost, and who rejoices rather than mourns his death.' This image of the sacrificial mother was also used during the Iran–Iraq war, a mother who sacrifices his son for her homeland and her faith. The well-known slogan of the eight-year war was *behesht zir-e paye madarn ast* (paradise is underneath the feet of the mothers).

In an interview, Mrs Fahmideh, the mother of Hossein Fahmideh – a 13-year-old child soldier who became known as a heroic martyr and whose life and sacrifice Iranian school children studied in government-issued textbooks[23] – speaks of her pride in having offered her son to the path of God. She states, 'I am proud of being the mother of a martyr and of a child such as Hossein who I offered as a present in the path of God, Islam and my faith and I hope God will accept this small gesture from me' (Sheikhani 2008). The mothers of martyrs fill a very specific gendered role, similar to the role Zaynab filled in Karbala. However, with the rise in female martyrdom volunteers, one can point to the shift from mothers, sisters and wives of martyrs to martyrs themselves.

In his book on suicide bombers, Khosrokhavar writes of the previous exclusion of women from suicide bombings both in Iran and by Al-Qaeda. He links this exclusion to the traditional notion of the family and the traditionalists' perceived complementarity of genders (Khosrokhavar 2002). However, the rise in the number of female suicide bombers and martyrdom seekers appears to be linked to a change in the traditionalist notions of women's agency to defend their faith and their land from the so-called 'aggressors'. For example, Hamas spiritual leader Sheikh Ahmad Yassin's reaction to Wafa Idris's death was in the first instance allied to traditional notions of gender:

---

23 At the age of 13, Hossein joined the war as a volunteer to fight against the Iraqi insurgence. He died by throwing himself under a tank while holding grenades.

> The Palestinian woman has an important role in society and in supporting the fighters … In our Palestinian society, there is a flow of women towards Jihad and martyrdom, exactly like the young men. But the woman has uniqueness. Islam sets some restrictions for her, and if she goes out to wage Jihad and fight, she must be accompanied by a male chaperon. (MEMRI 2002)

However, Sheikh Yassin was quick to change his position as he declared only a few days later that a woman who goes out to wage Jihad is to be accompanied by a *mahram* (a male immediate member of the family) only 'if she is to be gone for a day and a night. If her absence is shorter, she does not need a chaperon' (MEMRI 2002).

The World Islamic Organization Headquarters for Remembering the Martyrs insists that the women volunteers do not need the permission of their husbands or fathers in order to sign up for martyrdom operations. In Forooz Rajaifar's words,

> It has been stated in all *fatawi* that defense [religion or homeland] is a religious duty of both Muslim men and women and there is no need for women to acquire the permission of their husbands or fathers, there is even no need for the permission of the *Vali-e Faqih*. There are many married women who have signed up as volunteers and if a problem arises during their classifications into units which would require their husbands' permissions we leave it up to them if they wish to acquire such permission. We do not interfere with such matters. Families who express their willingness to carry out martyrdom operations usually regard this as a religious duty. We have [entire] families that have proudly signed up [for martyrdom operations] – from the seven-year-old child to the 70-year-old grandmother, wishing to walk the path [of the martyrs] as a family. (Zarabadi 2007, Nissimov, Mansharof, Savyon 2009)

Rajaifar's indication that women martyrdom seekers do not need the permission of their husbands or fathers to participate in suicide missions presents a picture of equality between men and women in their duty and ability to defend their faith and their country. However, one should not forget that these women live in societies where they do not possess rights comparable to those of their male counterparts. For example, *shahadat* (bearing of witness) of a woman is worth half of that of a man in a court of law in most Muslim majority countries.[24]

---

24 Article 74 of the Iranian Islamic Penal Code declares, 'Adultery, whether punishable by flogging or stoning, may be proven by the testimony of four just men or that of three just men and two just women.' Likewise, articles 75 and 76 set the testimony of a woman at half that of a man's. Article 75 states, 'If adultery is punishable only by flogging it can be proven by the testimony of two just men and four just women.' And article 76 declares, 'The testimony of women alone or in conjunction with the testimony of only one just man shall not prove adultery but it shall constitute false accusation which is a punishable act.'

Conclusion

Gender roles are being reinvented in societies that have experienced years of war, violence and occupation. In neo-colonial Middle-Eastern societies the conventional expressions of manhood are threatened both by the occupying forces and by the global ideals of modernity. This in turn entails women's increased presence in what were previously defined as male spaces. The notion of martyrdom, which traditionally has been male territory, seems to be changing in ways that challenge not only the Middle-Eastern views of femininity but also the perceived masculinities. One can neither homogenize the Middle East as a static culture, nor pretend that there is only one type of femininity or masculinity that defines the region. Yet even this short discussion on female martyrdom and suicide operations points to a contested and confused notion of gender in the Middle East that needs clarification. A place where men and women are equal in martyrdom but not in witness may be a place of increased female agency, but at what cost to social justice and human rights?

Chapter 5

Colonial Optics: Dancehall and Legal Imperatives against the 'Unnatural'

Camille A. Nelson

In an era of monumental technological advancements, the permeable nature of national borders is evident. Not only is worldwide travel easier, but information is also more accessible around the globe. This chapter focuses upon a particular type of 'information', the transnational dissemination of what might be characterized as a type of cultural art and ethos, Jamaican dancehall music (hereinafter 'dancehall'). Dancehall is a genre of reggae music that evolved from the earlier roots rock variety most commonly typified by the music of Bob Marley, Peter Tosh, and other international reggae stars of the '70s and '80s.[1] Given the proliferation and transmission of this type of music not only in Jamaica, but also around the world, it is little wonder that increasing attention is being paid to the messages in the art, and also to its underlying ethos. For the purposes of this chapter, I am interested in the transnational dispute that has revolved around the way in which Jamaican masculinity is lyrically constructed in some dancehall music.

As the Jamaican equivalent to American hip-hop music, dancehall is susceptible to some of the same critiques, specifically excessive violence, misogyny and hyper-masculinity. Dancehall, however, has been most critiqued, not on the basis of these concerns, but on account of the explicit homophobia[2] evident in some lyrics.[3] Indeed, Jamaica has been cast as 'the most homophobic place on earth',[4] partly on the basis of some dancehall music that has been dubbed 'murder

---

1 *See* L. Bradley. 2001. *Reggae: The Story of Jamaican Music*. Grove Press; S. Barrow and P. Dalton. 2004. *The Rough Guide to Reggae: The Definitive Guide to Jamaican Music from Ska through Roots to Bashment*. Jonathan Buckley Edition. Rough Guides Ltd.

2 Human Rights Watch. 2004b. *Hated to Death: Homophobia, Violence and Jamaica's HIV/AIDS Epidemic* [hereinafter, Human Rights Watch]. Available at: http://www.hrw.org/en/node/11894/section/14 [accessed: 8 January 2013] (listing significant social and legal challenges faced by LGBT individuals and finding fault in a homophobic culture and national leadership).

3 T. Padget. 2006. *The Most Homophobic Place on Earth?* Time [online]. Available at: http://www.time.com/time/world/article/0,8599,1182991,00.html [accessed: 8 January 2013] (basing that statement on an interview with Rebecca Schleifer, author of Human Rights Watch, who in speaking about homophobia in Jamaica states, 'Jamaica is the worst any of us has ever seen').

4 *Id.*

music'.[5] I take issue with this qualitative descriptor of Jamaica due to the curious relative and self-interested omissions inherent in such nomenclature. Through an examination of controversial dancehall music, this chapter will analyse an ongoing transnational masculinity contest.

The optic through which I explore this contest is the persistent manifestation of colonialism. Dancehall, as a culturally informed and productive site, constructs a post-colonial hyper-hetero-masculinity that is contested in the North-west. Unpacking this terminology focuses attention not just upon a cultural studies interrogation of neo-colonialism and a reparative approach thereto, but also upon an intersectional concern for masculine gender construction, religion, race, and sexual orientation. It is my concern that some dancehall music artists, in an attempt to empower subordinated masculinities, exaggerate traditional notions of masculinity partly through violent hetero-masculinist identity construction. In turn, this manifestation of masculinity is exported via the lucrative and far-reaching musical economy, of which Jamaica plays a role out of all proportion to its size and population. At the global level, the significance of this manifestation of masculinity is compounded, given that musical exports from Jamaica significantly inform the substance of what many people know of the small island nation and its people.

The goals of this chapter are twofold. First, it seeks to complicate the supposed internal Jamaican embrace of homophobic norms by revealing the connections to colonial legal impositions that were used to further the interests of empire. Second, it challenges the allegations that Jamaica is 'the most homophobic place on earth'[6] as righteous cultural imperialism that demonizes Jamaica based upon a de-contextualized a-historical reading of Jamaica and its music. Importantly, the chapter criticizes some of the recent boycotts of Jamaica as ultimately self-serving and not genuinely motivated by interest in the advancement of local Jamaican equality rights.

Thus, I do not wish to displace the agency of Jamaicans who participate in discriminatory behaviours or worldviews. I do, however, wish to challenge our understanding of such cultural homophobia as indigenous, abstract, and decidedly post-colonial. It is my opinion that we can read neither dancehall, nor any music of the subaltern, uncoupled from its colonial past. Moreover, we cannot read legal texts, the 'buggery' laws in this case, as untethered from colonial norms or edict. This chapter serves as an interdisciplinary intervention into third-world feminism, queer theory, cultural studies and the law, in order to make the connections between music and jurisprudence more transparent. In order to analyse any Jamaican

---

5 A. Topping. 2007b. *Victory for Gay Rights Campaign as Reggae Star Agrees to Ditch Homophobic Lyrics*, The Guardian [online]. Available at: http://www.guardian.co.uk/uk/2007/jul/23/musicnews.gayrights [accessed: 8 January 2013] (referring to Peter Tatchell's 'Stop Murder Music' campaign, which ultimately forced a 'settlement' with some dancehall artists in July 2007). The details of this settlement will be elaborated upon in this chapter: see notes 28–34 and accompanying text.

6 Padgett, *supra* note 3; Human Rights Watch, *supra* note 2.

embrace of homophobia, as demonstrated in dancehall, one must simultaneously interrogate the music and the legal enforcement of the colonial agenda with respect to this small island nation. They are both, the music and the law, constituted by and responsive to colonial ideals.

The Power of Music: The Jamaican Heartbeat

> In Jamaica it is virtually cliché to observe that musical performers are the most influential voices among the general population.[7]

As with other forms of art, music can be incredibly influential. Just as rap music was referred to as 'the Black CNN',[8] dancehall is the main cultural conduit in Jamaica. Music transmits meaning and messages across the frontiers of race, class, gender and nationality. This is particularly the case given that certain forms of music are increasingly accessible not only through traditional radio broadcasts, but also through the internet and other twenty-first-century technological advancements such as satellite and internet radio. Thus, in an increasingly small world, music can easily infiltrate beyond national boundaries.

Unlike what is typically cast as 'high art', music is simultaneously readily accessible, malleable to existing social norms, and hard to contain. One need not attend a special venue to listen to music; rather, music can reach us, even second hand. In this way, music has a potency seldom found in other art forms. The scope of music gives it temporal socio-political currency. It can be an agenda setter and an agenda follower. As Professor Cooper has written, '[m]usic is not mere entertainment but ideological weaponry'.[9] This is particularly the case in Jamaica.

Music can be centred as the heartbeat of Jamaica. Despite having a relatively small population, Jamaica produces a disparately large quantity of music.[10] With worldwide sales and distribution garnering billions of dollars annually, the Jamaican music industry is an important part of the national economy.[11]

---

7 A. Ross. 1998. *Real Love: In Pursuit of Cultural Justice*. NYU Press (at 38).

8 Sacramento State News. 2004. *Chuck D to Present his 'State of the Union'* [online]. Available at: http://www.csus.edu/news/012004chuckD.stm [accessed: 8 January 2013] (calling rap 'the black CNN', Chuck D gave notice to the world that the genre was more than entertainment: it was a voice for the under-represented and a force for social change).

9 C. Cooper. 2004. *Sound Clash: Jamaican Dancehall Culture at Large*. First Edition. Palgrave Macmillan (at 75).

10 Central Intelligence Agency. 2009. *The World Factbook 2009, Central America and the Caribbean: Jamaica* [online]. Available at: https://www.cia.gov/library/publications/the-world-factbook/geos/jm.html# [accessed: 8 January 2013] (estimating a population of 2,825,928 as of July 2009).

11 Worldwide sales of reggae recordings have been valued at about $1.2 billion USD annually; an estimated 25 per cent of that, or $300 million USD, flowed to Jamaican musicians and producers, and live performances in Jamaica netted an additional estimated

Moreover, the Jamaican music industry 'provides access to jobs, the opportunity to achieve relatively great success, and a means to sell one's labor and produce on the foreign market',[12] thereby making it a transnational economic sector. The prolific nature of the Jamaican music industry has meant that this important export is not only consumed by the Jamaican 'transnational society',[13] who comprise the Jamaican Diaspora, but that dancehall has a far greater reach. Given technological advancements, dancehall, even more so than its predecessor genres of reggae, has transnational implications in an increasingly small world.

This globalization of music has made possible a confrontation over Jamaican dancehall. Focus has been placed upon the controversial lyrics at the heart of some dancehall music. Thus it is not just the transnational nature of the music, but the message contained therein that has led to an international confrontation. The site of this cross-border conflict is complex as it implicates culture, language, gender, class, race, sexuality and, of course, nationality. Inherently intersectional, the questions posed also beg interdisciplinary and contextual thinking in order to generate appropriate solutions. It is my sense that, in light of this identity complexity, the international response to homophobic dancehall lyrics has not been a thoughtful one. Rather, the international reaction has revealed an ironic disconnect between Western respect for individual rights discourse and a quasi-colonial approach to developing nations resistant to following such discourse. Thus the matter begs the paradoxical question of whether a transnational discourse of individual rights may properly be imposed, rather than freely adopted.

Musical Confrontation on the Global Stage

For many people Bob Marley was, and still remains, the international standard against which the music of Jamaica, and indeed the Caribbean, is measured. Despite the fact that many of Bob Marley's lyrical messages were profound and revolutionary, he was, as the 'world's first "Third World Superstar"',[14] incredibly

---

$50 million USD. *See* R. Henry. 2006. *Jamaican Music is a Multi-billion Business, but Tax Avoidance High*. Jamaican Observer [online]. Available at: https://www.jamaicaobserver.com/news/97063_Jamaican-music-is-a-multi-billion-business--but-tax-avoidance-high [accessed: 8 January 2013]; N. Stolzoff. 2000. *Wake the Town and Tell the People: Dancehall Culture in Jamaica*. Duke University Press.

12 Stolzoff, *supra* note 11, at 8.

13 *See* O. Patterson. 2001. *The Roots of Conflict in Jamaica*, New York Times, 23 July, at A17 (referring to Jamaica as a 'transnational society' as 'between a quarter and a third of all Jamaicans live abroad, most in the United States').

14 National Geographic. *Reggae: National Geographic World Music* [online]. Available at: http://worldmusic.nationalgeographic.com/view/page.basic/genre/content.genre/reggae_775 [accessed: 8 January 2013] ('Jamaican reggae phenomenon Bob Marley was truly the world's first "Third World Superstar": a pop icon for the whole world').

charismatic and comprehensible.[15] As a musical ambassador, Bob Marley's persona had international caché. This reach was due both to his exotic Jamaican authenticity as well as to his simultaneous mainstream intelligibility. Unlike many contemporary dancehall artists Bob Marley can be praised, or condemned, for his malleable international identity construction. As noted reggae scholar Lloyd Bradley comments,

> Bob's subject matter may have been roots reggae but his application was mainstream rock. Just as he'd learned how to behave like a rock star off stage too, playing the part to the hilt – the combination of exotic and earthy, the locks, the licks and Rastafari, the women, the weed, the almost otherworldliness … *Bob Marley could conform to every stereotype of a black man abroad, but at the same time rewrite the book on what that same black man could be.* And he fully understood just how vital this was to his crowd's appreciation of his music: people wanted to buy into the whole Bob Marley experience, which he skillfully delivered as a package without ever losing sight of who he was.[16]

Thus, while the music itself is crucial, the reality is that the packaging of Jamaican masculinity is a central issue in the marketability, saleability and success of Jamaican musicians. The 'Marley experience' centred on a particular framing of Jamaican masculinity that was consistent with North-western ideals, or at least North-western fantasies. Authentically Jamaican or otherwise, the Jamaican masculinity performed by Marley was an appealing, earthy 'live and let live', yet simultaneously revolutionary posture that remains enticing to many in the North-west.

Thus, while Bob Marley was sophisticated in his self-construction as a sexual, yet spiritual, reggae icon, it would seem that many contemporary dancehall artists are not inclined towards mainstreaming their music for an international market if it means mitigating the violent hyper-masculine and hetero-normative messages contained therein. Theirs is an exclusive masculinity crafted out of raw gender performance, simultaneously hypersexual and hetero-normative. Nonetheless, they cannot escape being compared to Marley.

For instance, Peter Tatchell, leader of the United Kingdom-based gay rights organization OutRage!, drew this comparison by claiming that contemporary dancehall artists had betrayed the authentic reggae script in deviating from Marley's message of 'One Love'.[17] In an interview following OutRage!'s successful protests

---

15 Bradley, *supra* note 1, at 486 (stating, 'Over and above his sheer raw talent and extraordinary charisma, the difference between Bob's mainstream success and almost every other reggae act was down to his presentation of both himself and his music as being so user-friendly').

16 *Id.* at 487 (emphasis added).

17 *See* lyrics of Bob Marley's famous song of unity, 'One Love', Bob Marley & The Wailers, *One Love/People Get Ready*, *on* Legend (Island Records, 1984). Available at: http://www.metrolyrics.com/one-love-lyrics-bob-marley.html [accessed: 8 January 2013].

to have the English Music of Black Origin (MOBO) nominations revoked from dancehall artists Capleton, Elephant Man, and T.O.K., Tatchell stated:[18]

> Some singers in a bid for publicity to boost their sales have resorted to sensationalist bigotry … They grab the headlines but lesbian and gay people have to live with the violent consequences of these murderous lyrics. *Whatever Bob Marley's personal views about homosexuality were, he never went down the road of inciting homophobic murder.*[19]

Marley has thus become the man and the message. This singular insistence on reggae's musical message is striking, especially given the loaded legal language of incitement.[20] Admittedly part of a larger context of political activism,[21] Tatchell's rhetoric is in stark contrast to popular notions of Jamaica as a place of sun and sand. Of course, many people have fantasies of Jamaica as a tropical utopia. This may actually form part of the musical confrontation – specifically, the lyrics at issue in some dancehall seem radically out of step with foreign fantasies of Jamaica as

---

18 B. Didcock. 2005. *How Jamaican Stars Turned from One Love to Homophobia and Violence*. Sunday Herald [online]. Available at: http://sunday-herald.vlex.co.uk/vid/jamaican-turned-homophobia-violence-66078124 [accessed: 8 January 2013].

19 *Id.* (emphasis added).

20 The United Kingdom boasts legislation addressing freedom of speech and incitement of violence in both the Human Rights Act of 1988 and the Public Order Act of 1986. The Public Order Act of 1986 was recently amended to include language that prohibits incitement of violence on the grounds of sexual orientation. United Kingdom Human Rights Act, 1998, 42, sched. 1, pt. I, arts. 10, 12, 14. Available at: http://www.legislation.gov.uk/ukpga/1998/42/schedule/1/part/I [accessed: 8 January 2013]; *see also*, Criminal Law Policy Unit Ministry of Justice, *Offences of Stirring Up Hatred on the Grounds of Sexual Orientation*, 2010 (Circular 2010/05). Available at: http://webarchive.nationalarchives.gov.uk/20100505212528/http://www.justice.gov.uk/publications/docs/circular-05-2010-sexual-orientation-stirring-up-hatred.pdf [accessed: 8 January 2013].

21 Mr Tatchell has critiqued legislation aimed at the creation 'of an offence of rallying hatred against gays and lesbians' as impotent in tackling 'anti-queer prejudice' and as possibly infringing free speech. Notably, Tatchell critiques such legislation given the traditional failure of the police, prosecutors and government to enforce existing legislation aimed at protecting sexual minorities. He states: 'For nearly two decades, despite repeated appeals from the gay community, the government, police and prosecution service have allowed record stores and radio stations to promote "murder music" songs inciting the killing of queers. Jamaican artists such as Buju Banton, Beenie Man and Bounty Killa have released CDs that openly encourage and glorify the shooting, burning, hanging and drowning of gay and lesbian people.' P. Tatchell. 2007a. *Hate Speech v. Free Speech*, The Guardian. Available at: http://commentisfree.guardian.co.uk/peter_tatchell/2007/10/hate_speech_v_free_speech.html [accessed: 8 January 2013]; *see also* T. Branigan and A. Travis. 2007. *Straw Moves to Ban Incitement against Gays*. The Guardian [online]. Available at: http://www.guardian.co.uk/uk/2007/oct/09/gayrights.immigrationpolicy [accessed: 8 January 2013].

an 'irie' place of rum and fun.[22] Undoubtedly more nuanced understandings of the on-the-ground reality in Jamaica exist in the minds of many outside of Jamaica, but the ostensible self-interest in reacting so strongly to Jamaican instances of homophobia possibly reveals a longing for paradise not similarly imbedded in Western cultural imaginings with respect to other locations also known for their homophobia, i.e. Iran or Uganda.[23] Thus, the imagination of Jamaica as a place for foreign frolic is starkly at odds with the construction of Jamaica as the violent, homophobic and impoverished nation depicted in some dancehall. Indeed, it is my sense that the North-western unease with this Jamaican alter-ego undergirds the focus of Western advocates upon Jamaica, as opposed to other less tropically inviting places. Thus, the contested construction of the transnational space that is Jamaica frames these issues – is it an inviting paradise awaiting foreign vacationers, or is it a sometimes reactionary, developing nation struggling with societal violence, some of which is evident in dancehall? In reality, it is both.

The Music and the Boycotts

Despite this duality, over the course of a fifteen-year campaign against homophobic lyrics in dancehall music, gay rights activists in North America and the United Kingdom were able to bring considerable attention to controversial lyrics found in some dancehall music.[24] Together with the organizational efforts of Gay and Lesbian Alliance Against Defamation ('GLAAD') and Gay Men of African Descent

---

22 Indeed, the Jamaican tourist industry is certainly complicit in this construction of Jamaica as a place for foreign frolic. The marketing of several hotels plays on a wild party theme and helps to create a pervasive sense of Jamaica as a scandalous party place. For examples, *see* websites for Hedonism Resorts including the Men of Hedonism 2011 calendar and connecting to the link to Hedonism and the link to the Facebook page featuring a Playboy radio interview: http://hedonismresorts.com/, VisitJamaica.com, http://www.visitjamaica.com/, and Sandals resorts, http://www.sandals.com/general/included.cfm [accessed: 15 January 2011].

23 *See* D. Ottoson. 2010. *State-sponsored Homophobia: A World Survey of Laws Prohibiting Same Sex Activity between Consenting Adults*. International Lesbian, Gay, Bisexual, Trans and Intersex Association [online]. Available at: http://ilga.org/historic/Statehomophobia/State_sponsored_homophobia_ILGA_07.pdf [accessed: 8 January 2013].

24 Topping, *supra* note 5 ('Peter Tatchell, of the gay rights group Outrage! [*sic*] which has coordinated the campaign, said the move was a big breakthrough in a battle that has raged between gay rights activists and a number of dancehall artists for 15 years'). OutRage! and Peter Tatchell have also done anti-homophobia work in other countries such as Iran, Malawi, Uganda, Russia and Zimbabwe, and have occasionally partnered with groups like Black Gay Men's Advisory Group, GMAD (Gay Men of African Descent, an organization based out of Brooklyn, New York, and indicating that they represent 'the largest constituency of Black gay men on the East Coast' of the United States, *see* http://www.gmad.org/, accessed 28 May 2013) and GLAAD (Gay and Lesbian Alliance Against Defamation, an organization based out of Los Angeles, California and New York, *see* http://www.glaad.org/, accessed 28 May 2013).

('GMAD'), OutRage! convinced concert promoters, sponsors and venues to remove their financial support of dancehall artists or to cancel their concerts or sponsorship deals.[25] Tatchell commented, 'Our No 1 priority is to stop murder music.'[26]

According to cultural theorist Dr. Andrew Ross, these boycott campaigns proved immensely successful. The campaigns achieved notable success in the prevention of Jamaican dancehall artists from securing visibility on television and led to the cancellations of several concerts in both North America and the United Kingdom.[27] Perhaps the greatest, if rather short-lived, success of these early boycotts was achieved when several high-profile Jamaican dancehall artists agreed to sign an agreement that has come to be known as the 'Reggae Compassionate Act' ('RCA').[28]

This Act is actually a pledge by four of dancehall's leading performers, Beenie Man, Sizzla, Capleton and Buju Banton, to refrain from promoting hatred against gays and lesbians.[29] While worded generally to promote tolerance against all marginalized groups,[30] the Stop Murder Music campaign was admittedly focused exclusively upon homophobic lyrics, to the exclusion of all other identitarian concerns, such as misogyny. Indeed, the exclusive focus of the campaign was upon errant homophobic dancehall artists who gay rights activists felt had to be brought into line.[31] There now seems to be some dispute as to the durability of this agreement, with some of the reggae artists renouncing it,[32] and others having never agreed to sign on.[33] Ultimately, however, the foundations of the RCA were imperial and were thus shaky from the start.

---

25 *Id.*; *see also* National Public Radio. 2004. *Dancehall Reggae Artists under Fire for Anti-gay Lyrics*. Available at: http://www.npr.org/templates/story/story.php?%20storyId=3837073 [accessed: 8 January 2013] (referencing the interception of Jamaican dancehall artist Beenie Man at London's Heathrow airport and the cancellation of his London show by organizers reluctant to deal with protesting gay rights activists).

26 Topping, *supra*, note 5.

27 Ross, *supra* note 7.

28 Petertatchell.net. 2007b. Reggae Stars Renounce Homophobia. Available at: http://www.petertatchell.net/pop_music/reggaecompassiondeal.htm [accessed: 8 January 2013].

29 *Id.*

30 *Id.* (The act states: '[T]here's no space in the music community for hatred and prejudice, including no place for racism, violence, sexism or homophobia.')

31 *See* Topping, *supra* note 5 (addressing the goal of the Stop Murder Music campaign in targeting Buju Banton, it was noted that he had 'signed the "reggae compassionate act" set up by the gay rights campaign group Stop Murder Music, after a three-year campaign to bring him into line').

32 P. Tatchell. 2007b. *Reggae Tips: Top Jamaican Singers have Signed a Deal to Renounce Homophobic Hatred and Halt 'Murder Music' – But Do They Really Mean It?* The Guardian [online]. Available at: http://www.guardian.co.uk/commentisfree/2007/aug/02/reggaetips [accessed: 8 January 2013].

33 *See* R. Swash. 2007. *Beenie Man, Sizzla and Capleton Renounce Homophobia: Three Prominent Dancehall Artists Known for their Anti-gay Lyrics have Signed the*

If, as the RCA states, its premise was that '[r]eggae artists and their music have fought against injustices, inequalities, poverty, and violence even while enduring some of those same circumstances themselves',[34] the campaign might more properly have taken on a more informed grassroots focus. The existence of even more recent boycott campaigns makes this point well.

In the spring of 2009, determined Western gay rights activists launched yet another boycott of Jamaica on the basis of cultural homophobia. American gay rights activists spearheaded the 'Boycott Jamaica' campaign in an attempt to use economic pressure to propel movement on gay rights issues in Jamaica.[35] Kicking off the boycott with a rum and beer dump outside of the famous Stonewall Inn, the website for Boycott Jamaica stated, 'The sewer in front of the Stonewall Inn is set to flow with Red Stripe beer and Myers's Rum tonight when gay rights advocates hold a "rum dump" as part of their "Boycott Jamaica" campaign against the island nation that gave the world rastas, reggae, and dance hall lyrics that encourage the burning and killing of "Mister Fagoty"'.[36] The organizers of this event claimed to be acting in concert with their Jamaican gay and lesbian brothers and sisters, stating that they 'see the boycott of products and tourism to the island as a sign of solidarity with their Jamaican brothers and sisters'.[37] However, the boycott seems to have been unilaterally Western in origins and goals.

In response to the boycott and the publicity surrounding its kickoff, J-FLAG, the Jamaican Forum for Lesbians, All-sexuals and Gays, issued a pointed response

Reggae Compassionate Act. The Guardian [online]. Available at: http://www.guardian.co.uk/music/2007/jun/14/news.rosieswash [accessed: 8 January 2013] ('several other high-profile Jamaican artists have been singled out for not complying. "The other five murder-music artists, Elephant Man, TOK [*sic*], Bounty Killa, Vybz Kartel and Buju Banton, have not signed the Reggae Compassionate Act. The campaign against them continues," said Tatchell. He added: "These artists have openly encouraged the murder of lesbians and gay men, which is a criminal offence in every country … [They] are the moral equivalent of neo-Nazis and the Ku Klux Klan"').

34 *See* Petertatchell.net. 2007a. *Buju Banton Says Boom Bye Bye To Homophobia* [online]. Available at: http://www.petertatchell.net/pop_music/bujubantonbyebyehomophobia.htm [accessed: 8 January 2013]; Risingstarstv.net. 2010. *Here's a Copy of The Reggae Compassionate Act Allegedly Signed by Dee-Jay Vybz Kartel aka Adidja Palmer* [online]. Available at: http://www.risingstarstv.net/profiles/blogs/heres-a-copy-of-the-reggae [accessed: 8 January 2013]; Soulrebels.org. [n.d.] *The Reggae Compassionate Act* [online]. Available at: http://www.soulrebels.org/dancehall/w_compassionate_001.htm [accessed: 8 January 2013].

35 *See* Mitchell, *infra* note 45.

36 E. Brady. 2009. *Gays to Boycott Jamaica Tonight*. Village Voice [online]. Available at: http://blogs.villagevoice.com/runninscared/2009/04/gays_to_boycott.php [accessed: 8 January 2013].

37 *Id.*

against the proposed dump and boycotts, which was not heeded.[38] Given the sheer brilliance of the letter, it deserves to be quoted at length:

> Dear Friends and Supporters:
>
> We thank our international allies for their continued interest in the state of LGBT affairs in Jamaica. Your support over the years has strengthened our voice and made it possible for us to make progress where we hardly thought it possible.[39]

However, after these initial pleasantries J-FLAG goes on to chastise the North-western advocates for an ill-timed, misguided and uninformed boycott campaign. The organization makes the point about cultural sovereignty abundantly clear. They continue,

> In the global arena in which we operate today, events in one place can and do have repercussions in another. Concomitantly, information about occurrences in different places across the globe is easily accessible everywhere. We believe that any overseas entity or organization seeking to agitate for change in a context with which it has only passing familiarity should first do its homework to ensure that it does not do harm to its credibility and ultimately to the cause of the local community whose interest it seeks to defend.[40]

Not only could the boycotts have done more harm than good to gays and lesbians on the ground,[41] they were carried out despite the prior requests of Jamaican grassroots organizers who had asked the North-western organizers to refrain from their planned campaign. Such disregard is troubling and smacks of the same type of colonial ignorance against which many dancehall artists rebel. Ironically the purportedly well-intentioned North-western advocates left the actual people in the

38 International Gay and Lesbian Human Rights Commission. 2009. *Jamaica: Don't Boycott Us!* [online]. Available at: http://www.iglhrc.org/cgi-bin/iowa/article/takeaction/partners/888.html [accessed: 8 January 2013].

39 *Id.*

40 *Id.*

41 Indicating their general view of boycotts, J-FLAG has commented on previously scheduled boycotts by stating that proposals had led to additional homophobic violence. '"We've had about four cases [of attacks attributed to the boycott] which have come to us," says Jason MacFarlane. "Our perspective is still the same. A boycott is not helpful, especially since the prime minister has made a statement that he won't be [denouncing homophobic violence or repealing laws criminalizing homosexuality]."' K. Rau. 2008. *Jamaica Boycott Called Off.* Xtra! [online]. Available at: http://www.xtra.ca/public/viewstory.aspx?STORY_ID=4808&PUB_TEMPLATE_ID=9 [accessed: 8 January 2013].

trenches, as it were, with more work to do and in a far more precarious position post boycott:[42]

> Jamaica's deeply ingrained antipathy towards homosexuality and homosexuals is a social phenomenon that will not be undone by boycott campaigns or government dictate. It requires the painstaking effort of confronting the society and talking to social actors who can bring change in the way society sees LGBT people. We have been doing this through a small but growing group of increasingly aware opinion leaders who are concerned about the damage homophobia does to our society. We need those ears to continue being open to us and we need the relative safety that some of us have been given to speak to them.[43]

My concern for dialogue, as opposed to dictates, is most evident in the last paragraph of the J-FLAG response to the recent boycotts. It highlights the arrogance of some advocates in their attempt to impose a rights discourse in the absence of either dialogue or discussion. Who better to work with than Jamaican gay rights advocates in order to address Jamaican homophobia? Yet in an officious display of a masculinity contest run amok, a boycott was launched that may well have set the cause of gay rights in Jamaica back some years:

> It is important that our international allies understand the nature of our struggle and engage us in a respectful way about it. Unless they are willing and able to lead the struggle in the trenches as we have done, it is important that they be guided by us. To do otherwise would be to act in a manner that destroys the space for dialogue that we have managed to create over the past decade and to set back our struggle. It is for this reason that we urge those in the international arena who seek to act in our name and on our behalf to do so not only with the

42 A. James-Johnson. 2007. *Fort Lauderdale Church Faces Furor for Starting Gay Congregation in Jamaica*. South Florida Sun-Sentinel, 29 May (detailing the ongoing controversy surrounding gay rights and Christianity in Jamaica and noting that attempts to improve relations between Jamaicans in South Florida and the gay and lesbian community have been met by hostility. In commenting upon a radio broadcast attempt by an American minister to address homophobia through inclusive Christianity, the article noted, 'Jamaican callers chastised him for promoting homosexuality in their country. One caller said [he] would get a bullet through his head if he set foot on the island.' Additionally, the radio host who asked the minister to appear on the call-in radio show said, 'anti-gay sentiments are common in Jamaica and some who grew up there don't want to see more gays and lesbians in their homeland. I don't like seeing two men hugging and kissing. It's sending the wrong message, and our children are going to be spoiled in the long run'); *see also* J. Monteagudo. 2010. *The Odysssey of Rev. Grant Lynn Ford*. SouthFloridaGayNews.com [online]. Available at: http://www.southfloridagaynews.com/sfgn-columnists/columnists/jesses-journal/1578-the-odyssey-of-rev-grant-lynn-ford.html [accessed: 8 January 2013].

43 International Gay and Lesbian Human Rights Commission, *supra* note 38.

> utmost care and responsibility but also with due consideration for our efforts and concerns as members of the local activist community.[44]

Little more can be said about the imperial manner in which Western gay activists behaved. Not only did their unilateral campaign not work in concert with on-the-ground activists most directly involved in the struggle for human rights for sexual minorities in Jamaica, but it alienated local activists and perhaps rendered them more vulnerable. Such bald transnational moves that presume to know best should be avoided, especially when the stakes are so high and when progress is being made, albeit slowly.[45] We in the North-west do not necessarily know best. Cooperation and consultation are the most appropriate way of proceeding, especially when the lives of others are put at risk. This is particularly important when Western dictates are made in the absence of true grassroots engagement at the local level – it is easy to issue edicts from afar instead of working in concert in the trenches.

The Western impatience with the pace of change is part of the quasi-colonial assumption of a universal performance of human rights norms. As Delroy Constantine-Simms, another voice from the Jamaican Diaspora[46] and editor of *The Greatest Taboo: Homosexuality in Black Communities* has noted, homosexuality, like atheism, is near the top of the list of taboos for many black people.[47] As such, socio-cultural transformation on so powerful an issue demands collegial cooperation between nations that cannot be achieved through top–down means such as boycotts. Indeed, truly breathing life into a broad sexuality rights paradigm necessitates a respect for the ways in which the quest for those same rights plays out beyond our borders. In this case, leading also involves learning. However the dynamic demonstrated by Western advocates, with respect to the

---

44 *Id.*

45 S. Mitchell. 2009. *Gays in US 'Boycott Jamaica'*. Jamaica Gleaner [online]. Available at: http://www.jamaica-gleaner.com/gleaner/20090401/news/news2.html [accessed: 8 January 2013]; *see* comments of J-FLAG leaders and Red Stripe spokesperson in the Jamaica Gleaner ('J-flag deplores boycott: However, Jason McFarlane, programmes manager at the Jamaica Forum for Lesbians, All-sexuals, and Gays (J-FLAG), said it deplored the boycott, particularly because Red Stripe had withdrawn support from entertainers – particularly of the dancehall genre – who promoted violence against gays. "We had spoken to them not to go ahead with the boycott when they first contacted us last week, but they went ahead despite our response," McFarlane told The Gleaner. Meanwhile, Maxine Whittingham-Osborne, head of corporate relations at Red Stripe, said the company was surprised by the gay advocates' apparent random targeting. "Over the years, by our actions and our policies, we have demonstrated that we do not advocate any bias or prejudice against any individual or group(s)," she said yesterday').

46 S. Fullwood. 2001. *The Greatest Taboo: An Interview with Delroy Constantine-Simms*. Africana.com [online]. Available at: http://www.hartford-hwp.com/archives/45a/758.html [accessed: 8 January 2013].

47 *Id.*; *see also* D. Constantine-Simms, ed. 2000. *The Greatest Taboo: Homosexuality in Black Communities*. Alyson Publications.

most recent boycotts against Jamaica, reveals a quasi-colonial entrenchment and Western self-interest.

Why Jamaica? Advocating Self-interest

My suspicion is that the impatience with change in the area of sexual identity politics in Jamaica has as much to do with Western interests and preoccupations as it does with a genuine empathy for the plight of Jamaican sexual minorities. The nature of the boycott campaign was overbroad in its reach through time and place. By this I mean to highlight the fact that the boycott, whose underlying concern for sexual equality I agree with, was misguided and antagonistic to the very principles of equality on which it was purportedly founded. If a genuine concern for Jamaican sexual minorities was the motivating factor, surely listening to and acting in concert with these same people would have been a priority. In addition to being careful not to increase physical risks to sexual minorities in Jamaica, North-western advocates would do well to consider the impact of their actions upon the local community at the level of cultural discourse.

Specifically the RCA and subsequent boycotts were misguided as they served to concretize Jamaican opposition to same-sex equality. Admittedly, homophobia existed in Jamaica before the RCA and the boycotts, but many Jamaicans see both as punishing external attacks on Jamaicans' right to make a livelihood and to have opinions and perspectives in keeping with free and independent people. For instance, the venerable Jamaican newspaper, *The Gleaner*, referred to the contestation as 'gay attacks on local artistes'.[48] Of course, central to this assertion is a gendered defensiveness that seeks to protect local understandings of Jamaican manhood, but it is also founded upon assertions of free speech, agency and autonomy.

Allegations of cultural homophobia with corollary demands for change from the West prove incendiary to many Jamaicans. As a result, many Jamaicans consequentially rally around a national independence agenda,[49] even if they were not initially engaged with the issue of sexual orientation as cultural homophobia. In this way the international scorn levied at Jamaica, by way of boycotts, has ingratiated neither the Jamaican population nor their political leaders to issues of sexual equality. Instead, the North-west campaign against 'murder music' and the strategy of boycotts against a supposedly sexually intolerant Jamaican society have had the exact opposite effect, pitting North-western demands for sex-equality

48 K. Henry and T. Evans. 2007. *No Compassion for Dancehall*. Jamaica Gleaner [online]. Available at: http://www.jamaica-gleaner.com/gleaner/20071007/ent/ent2.html [accessed: 8 January 2013].

49 See L.R. Helfer. 2002. *Overlegalizing Human Rights: International Relations Theory and the Commonwealth Caribbean Backlash against Human Rights Regimes*. 102 Columbia Law Review, 1832.

against Jamaican assertions of autonomy, agency and independence.[50] In short, the activism outlined above has backfired and has, unfortunately, negatively affected the gay rights movement in Jamaica.

Right or wrong, in Jamaica the boycotts are largely seen as external attacks on Jamaican independence.[51] As Dr. Cooper has posited, 'given the historical context of a dislocating politics of euro-american imperialism in the region, "hard-core" Jamaican cultural nationalists are likely to resist any re-examination of indigenous values that is perceived as imposed on them by their imperial neighbour [*sic*] in the North.'[52] What remains to be addressed, however, is this notion of "indigenous values".

One of the central aims of this chapter is to interrogate and respond to this normative homophobia as an indigeneity claim and to re-source it as closely tied to the colonial project. It is a curious matter that post-independence Jamaican culture remains tethered to constructions of sexuality that are deeply informed by the colonial agenda of our former masters. Homophobic dancehall music is an unfortunate manifestation of this oppressive past. To paraphrase Edward Said, in mapping the affiliations of this musical art form we can perceive its involvement in expanding empires.[53] The social poets of the island, its musicians, have attempted to construct a post-modern masculinity. However, in doing so some of them have ironically clung to hyper-masculine displays of hetero-normativity that made our former colonial masters wealthy.

Building Nation, One Heterosexual Man at a Time

Inevitably, for many in the North-west, the explicit, homophobic lyrics of some dancehall artists[54] create a lasting unfavourable impression of Jamaica and Jamaicans. Like some of the other controversial homophobic dancehall lyrics, they are violent and crude. Unlike their American counterparts in gangsta rap, or homophobic or misogynistic hip-hop,[55] Jamaican dancehall has attracted

50 Topping, *supra* note 5 (for instance, Vincent Nap, a UK-based reggae artist, acknowledged that there was indeed a problem of homophobia in dancehall music, but took issue with the boycotts. He remarked, 'If they keep attacking us, we will fight back. If they try to stop our music we are going to have to defend ourselves').

51 Henry and Evans, *supra* note 48 (see remarks of Clyde McKenzie of Shocking Vibes Limited, *id.*: 'I think sometimes the artistes are being penalised for things they say here (in Jamaica) because people (worldwide) can hear your utterances in Jamaica and they judge you and form protests against you based on what is said').

52 Cooper, *supra* note 9, at 25–6.

53 E. Said. 1993. *Culture and Imperialism*. Alfred A. Knopf, Inc.

54 *See e.g.*, Human Rights Watch, *supra* note 2, at 75–9 (providing explicit homophobic lyrics to various dancehall tracks).

55 *See e.g.*, lyrics of Eminem, 50 Cent and Nelly. Note the video of Nelly's 'Tip Drill' featuring hyper-hetero-masculinity as demonstrated through excessively sexualized black

international scorn and motivated concerted political action.[56] However, there is much else for which dancehall could be criticized and condemned by concerned North-western activists. The music can also be vicious towards women and girls and can be downright vulgar.[57]

Despite this, there has been no international organizing around these important issues of violence. Dancehall has not been condemned internationally as misogynistic or abusive beyond its explicit homophobia, despite the well-known connection between misogyny and homophobia.[58] Rather, the attention of the international community has been focused squarely upon dancehall's adamant stance on masculinity as hetero-normative. Thus, one must wonder about the goals behind the isolated boycott and international approbation directed solely to only one problematic aspect of dancehall. One must further query why there have not

---

womanhood. Available at: http://www.youtube.com/watch?v=235TXjL9nd0&feature=fvsr [accessed: 19 December 2010].

56 *See* Ross, *supra* note 7. Dr Ross points out the disparate approach taken by international activists towards dancehall versus hip-hop when he states, 'Many commentators who had explained away rappers' lyrical flights about killing cops as an escapist or therapeutic fantasy of the oppressed regarded the[se] song's targeting of gays as an oppressor's fantasy and thus as an abhorrent incitement to real violence. Even when such songs were perceived as a desperate attempt on the part of the down pressed black male to retain power, any kind of power, over his immediate environment, the condemnation of batty boy-bashing was as sharply pronounced as the censure of misogyny, its structural counterpart in hip hop.'

57 C. Cooper. 1995. *Noises in the Blood: Orality, Gender and the 'Vulgar' Body of Jamaican Pop Culture*. First US Edition. Duke University Press, at 142 ('Eschewing respectability, the DJs operate subversively at the low end of the scale of accepted social propriety. Their privileged subjects are DJing itself, and sexuality. Heterosexuality most often requires a precise listing of body parts, almost exclusively female, and an elaboration of their mechanical function … and sexual skill are often indistinguishable'); *see also* Stolzoff, *supra* note 11, at 106 ('[W]omen were now more a focus of attention than ever before, but they were still being treated as sexual objects rather than sexual agents. While a few songs from this period did deal with a male DJ's love and respect for women, feminist critics are right to point out that many more songs are actually filled with misogyny and sexual violence aimed at women. Women's body parts become objects of lurid fantasies of male desire for sexual dominance, as evidenced in countless songs such as Shabba Ranks's "Love Punaany" (i.e., "Love Vagina")'). *See e.g.*, Vybz Kartel, *No Dutty Panty* [No Dirty Panties], *on* The Reggae Masters: Vol. 2 (D & E) (Don Corleon Records, 2009). Available at: http://www.elyrics.net/read/v/vybz-kartel-lyrics/no-dutty-panty-lyrics.html [accessed: 8 January 2013]. Similarly, the lyrics to a song by Don Youth and Spagga reference the term 'naany', which Stolzoff clarified: '[n]aany is a shortened form of punaany, a Jamaican term for vagina that is roughly the equivalent of "pussy" in American vernacular' and '[p]um-pum is a synonym for punaany.' Stolzoff calls this a 'typical example of slackness … romaticiz[ing] rough sex', Stolzoff, *supra* note 11, at 214, 271.

58 *See also* A. Harris. 2000. *Gender, Violence, Race, and Criminal Justice*. 52 Stanford Law Review 777, 793.

been similar international boycotts against other countries with official policies antagonistic to the rights of sexual minorities.

We must therefore consider that what is at stake is the construction of Jamaican masculinity on the world stage. A masculine persona that is not 'in line' with contemporary North-western norms around sexuality attracts heightened scrutiny. The importance of this misalignment clearly pits the subaltern voice against the power of the metropole. So when Gayatri Spivak asks, 'Can the subaltern speak?',[59] the response would seem to be, 'Only when it is consistent with metropolitan values.' Nonetheless, the emergent voices represented in dancehall declare a masculine subject that is contingent upon and derivative of the power of the former colonial lords. Indeed, as will be explored in the next part of this chapter, the homophobic incitement found in some dancehall is related to Jamaica's positioning within the British Empire. While attempting some semblance of civil disobedience to 'contest their inclusion in an international formation that denies them freedom and equality',[60] some dancehall artists have not unshackled themselves from ways of thinking that echo colonial edicts. In this way, the masculine construction of the Jamaican nation is at stake and its evolution is directly responsive, in a restitutionary way, to the Jamaican colonial experiences.

The Crafting of a Restitutionary Hyper-hetero-masculinity

There can be no doubt that the United Kingdom, the last official colonizers of Jamaica, reaped tremendous economic benefits, wealth, assets, labour and geo-political prominence, from its colonial holdings. This metropolitan enrichment wrought a corollary impoverishment of Jamaica and its people – the experience of slavery was certainly debilitating and has had serious long-term ramifications, as has the larger experience of colonization.

In the absence of a legal remedy for slavery or colonization, many people who feel exploited by these legacies and their entrapment thereby seek extra-judicial remedies. This search is manifest in Jamaican music.[61] To a large extent dancehall governs cultural production in Jamaica. As Stolzoff has described it, dancehall is the 'most potent form of popular culture in Jamaica.'[62] Dancehall thus has incredible salience for the manner in which Jamaicans attempt to assert

59 G. Spivak. 1988. Can the Subaltern Speak?, in *Marxism and the Interpretation of Culture*, edited by C. Nelson and L. Grossberg. University of Illinois Press.

60 R. Fletcher. 2005. *Reproducing Irishness: Race, Gender, and Abortion Law*. 17 Canadian Journal of Women and the Law 2, at 368 (stating, 'Sometimes the imagined community of the nation performs a justificatory role in enabling civil resistance to colonial domination. People are drawn together as a nation in order to contest their inclusion in an international formation that denies them freedom and equality').

61 *See e.g.* the lyrics of music by Bob Marley, Third World, Culture, Luciano, Sizzla, and Buju Banton.

62 Stolzoff, *supra* note 11, at 1.

independence and sovereignty on the world stage. Dancehall is not simply a noun, but it is also a verb as it defines the manoeuvre by which 'black lower class youth articulate and project a distinct identity in local, national and global contexts.'[63] Thus, it is possible to conceptualize dancehall as a post-colonial restitutionary move whereby marginalized voices seek recompense, both monetary and in terms of respect, in the international music economy. The nexus between the national and the international becomes evident when one considers that the essential questions at stake are of self-definition and self-identity. As Ross has noted, this question is particularly relevant for Jamaica, a nation facing colonizing forces in a post-colonial world.[64] Not to be let off the hook, post-independence governments are part of this conspiracy, 'adopting strategies that have locked these nations into a world economic and political system, the effect of which is re-colonization.'[65]

Definitions of citizenship and nationality, as identity constructs, become the currency through which the formerly disenfranchised assert a voice in a post-colonial world. Dancehall artists proclaim a quintessential Jamaican voice and posit an 'authentic' Jamaican identity in gendered and sexualized terms. Like all identities, 'Jamaican-ness' becomes defined in exclusive and oppositional terms – to be Jamaican, according to these artists, is to not be gay, lesbian, white or weak; rather, it is to be straight, of African descent, and strong. In this regard, cultural theorist M. Jacqui Alexander has noted that 'citizenship … continues to be premised within heterosexuality and principally within hetero-masculinity.'[66] But, as will be explored in the next section, insofar as some dancehall artists seek to make an international restitutionary move, their manner of seeking such remedy is paradoxical as the hyper-masculine demands of dancehall founded upon hetero-masculinity replicate and reconstitute in modern form the essential oppression of colonization.

Expanding from this point, I want to push one definition of hyper-masculinity in a transnational direction. Noted legal scholar Angela Harris defines hyper-masculinity as 'a masculinity in which the strictures against femininity and homosexuality are especially intense and in which physical strength and aggressiveness are paramount.'[67] Once taken beyond the individual frame, this notion of hyper-masculinity can be viewed through the lens of post-colonial nation building. As Ruth Fletcher has commented, it is important to 'understand nationalism as a historical process that works through gendered and racialized practices in order to achieve its aim of unifying people in the name of the nation

---

63 *Id.*

64 Ross, *supra* note 7, at 38–9.

65 M.J. Alexander. 1994. *Not Just (Any)Body Can Be a Citizen: The Politics of Law, Sexuality and Postcoloniality in Trinidad and Tobago and the Bahamas*. 48 Feminist Review 5, 15.

66 *Id.* at 7.

67 Harris, *supra* note 58, at 793.

and claiming authority over their resources.'[68] Pushing Fletcher's premise, gender, race *and* sexuality serve the ends of nationalism through inclusions *and* exclusions.

Masculinity, as a gendered identity, becomes an important conduit through which the nation is constructed. In the post-colonial transnational context, the contentious relationship between metropole and subaltern takes on a defiant tone as the colonized paradoxically seek to exert power in ways that mattered to the former governors – masculinity thus comes to the fore, but ironically on the reified terms of the former colonizer. Social theorist Carl Stychin notes, '[n]ations have been historically constituted in gendered and sexualized terms'.[69] I would add that nations have also been constructed in racialized ways and are internationally classed and ordered.[70]

For instance, these intersecting identity constructs – nation, gender, race, and sexuality – are simultaneously doing work in dancehall artist Sizzla's X-rated song *Nah Apologize*.[71] Sizzla, a dancehall artist who otherwise also has many spiritual

68 Fletcher, *supra* note 60, at 367.

69 C.F. Stychin. 1998. *A Nation by Rights: National Cultures, Sexual Identity Politics and the Discourse of Rights*. Temple University Press (at 7).

70 Stolzoff, *supra* note 11, at 8. Stolzoff states, '[D]ancehall is not only important to poor blacks but central to the society as a whole, because Jamaicans of all races and classes define themselves in relation to it. For the lighter-skinned middle and upper classes, glossed as uptown people, opposition to dancehall has galvanized their sense of cultural superiority—hence, their right to govern—because they think it demonstrates black lower-class cultural inferiority and lack of morality. However, for the black lower classes, glossed as downtown, dancehall provides a medium through which the masses are able to ideologically challenge the hegemony of the ruling classes and state apparatuses. Dancehall is thus a marker of a charged cultural border between people of different races and class levels.' *Id.* at 6.

71 Sizzla, *Nah Apologize*. Available at: http://www.metrolyrics.com/nah-apologize-lyrics-sizzla.html [accessed: 8 January 2013]. See also EGALE Stop Murder Music Canada. Available at: http://archive.egale.ca/smm/docs/background.pdf [accessed: 16 April 2013]. Loosely translated: 'The girls, they are sexy and their pussies are fat / Yes all the girls the boys are looking at / Some boys bow down [alternatively meaning perform cunnilingus or render themselves subservient], doing what! / Nothing in this world could ever make me do that / I don't care if they ban me / Because if you burn faggots that's not wrong with me / Yo, I wasn't born in England, I'm a real African / I am a real real real Rastaman, boom!' Chorus: 'Rastamen don't apologize to any faggots / Because if you disrespect black people then I am going to shoot you boy / Give me all the girls because they're the source of joy / Into the lake of fire is where I will dash you boy / Rrrrrrr!!! We do not apologize to any faggots / If you disrespect King Selassie then I will shoot you boy / Into the lake of fire is where I will dash you ahoy! / Give me all the girls because they're the source of joy. They act like they're smart … / Shoot them in their heads as they are too nasty / The girls have the pussy and the stiff breasts and the cute faces / Yet these boys walk past it / Damn it's the lyrical praise that it what makes them fret / In the biblical days we used to stone them to death / Whoa! It's the sexy girls who I have sex with/ I say burn faggots don't vex damn!'

songs, or what might be dubbed 'conscious reggae',[72] excoriates gay men in *Nah Apologize*. In thumbing his nose to the possibility of being banned ('I don't care if dem ban mi'), Sizzla, like fellow dancehall artist Elephant Man,[73] asserts that gay men should be burned ('Cause me seh fi bun battyman yuh caan wrong mi') or stoned ('inna de Biblical days we used to stone dem to death'). While focusing upon women's bodies, Sizzla chastises gay men for their lack of appreciation for women as sex objects ('Di gal dem have di pussy and di stiff titty and di cute face / And di bwoy walk pass it'). In refusing to apologize to gay men for his homophobia, Sizzla further situates himself as authentically black ('Rastaman don't apologize to no battybwoy / Yuh diss black people then mi gun a shot yuh bwoy'), thereby casting homosexuality as white and un-Jamaican. Implicit in such words is an indigeneity claim that is made more explicitly elsewhere in his lyrics. To dancehall artists like Sizzla it is simply abnormal and alien to be gay. Thus, 'the relationship between the national and the global … is multidimensional.'[74]

Dancehall thus becomes a cultural regulator of identity boundaries along the lines of race, sexuality and gender. Certainly in Jamaica, 'these are the boundaries around which power coheres.'[75] Stychin notes that notions of 'normalcy' for newly independent nations play out through a post-colonial fixing of gender relations. Specifically, 'anything that could be construed as undermining that fixity was construed as the nation's other.'[76] Thus identity constructs 'are contingent upon an oppositional framework' that is exclusive of antagonistic identities.[77] In this way, Sizzla's lyrics are telling as he situates homosexuality itself as foreign, specifically English, and fixes himself and other Rastas as African, and thus heterosexual. ('Yo mi nuh born ova England a real African this; Real real real Rastaman this, BOOM.') Thus dichotomously defined, homosexuality is oppositional both to Jamaican nationality and Jamaican masculinity.

Perhaps even more directly, popular dancehall artist Beenie Man sings in one song, 'I'm dreaming of a new Jamaica, come to execute all the gays'.[78] In

72 C. Salewicz and A. Boot. 2001. *Reggae Explosion: The Story of Jamaican Music*. Harry N. Abrams, Inc.

73 *Log On* by Elephant Man indicates that 'log on' is '[a] dance with foot motion as if squashing a cockroach – the lyrics boast about crushing gay men.' *See also* Human Rights Watch, *supra* note 2, at 75–8. To hear this song and for a demonstration of this dance *see* YouTube for 'how fi dance reggae'. Available at: http://www.youtube.com/watch?v=sz8WydzXePI [accessed: 12 August 2009].

74 *See* Stychin, *supra* note 69, at 6.

75 Alexander, *supra* note 65, at 1.

76 *See* Stychin, supra note 69, at 9.

77 C.A. Nelson. 2008. *Lyrical Assault: Dancehall Versus the Cultural Imperialism of the North-west*. 17 Southern California Interdisciplinary Law Journal 231, 247.

78 G. Younge. 2006. *Troubled Island: In Jamaica, where Politicians are Openly Homophobic and Song Lyrics Incite Violence against Gay People, Coming Out Can Be Fatal*. The Guardian [online]. Available at: http://www.guardian.co.uk/world/2006/apr/27/gayrights.comment [accessed: 8 January 2013].

doing so he flatly exposes his heterosexual construction of post-colonial Jamaican nationhood. In Jamaica, we are told, heterosexuality is celebrated musically and otherwise. Indeed, pre-eminent scholar Dr. Cooper, Professor of Literary and Cultural Studies at the University of the West Indies, asserts that dancehall has been misunderstood, as we are missing the 'power of metaphor':[79]

> It is the music of young, working-class black people and I think that makes it an easy target. Homophobia is one part of dancehall but you shouldn't reduce it to its homophobic lyrics. *It's a heterosexual music. It celebrates heterosexuality by denouncing homosexuality.*[80]

Unfortunately, this musical denunciation has produced a contestation of international import – it represents a clash of masculinity constructs in the global arena. It brings to the fore the Jamaican 'nationalist project'[81] and the international response of condemnation. Nonetheless, the site is unquestionably the construction of masculinity in relation to other identity constructs. Specifically, the construction of masculinity is situated within a field of competing identity concerns. What we are witnessing in Jamaica, therefore, is the national prioritizing of gender *qua* masculinity over race, sexuality and class. As Philip Dayle, the Jamaica legal officer at the International Commission of Jurors, has commented, '[i]n Jamaica nationalism trumps sexual orientation and race trumps sexual orientation. So when faced with nationalism and race together, issues of sexual orientation don't stand a chance.'[82]

This is a remarkable prioritizing of identity. It orders and prefers certain statuses above others. As such, the notion of simultaneity[83] seems anathema to this post-colonial national project. Such either/or exclusive identity constructs defy what we know of intersectionality.[84] Seemingly, there can exist no hyphenated gay-Jamaican citizen – that intersection is erased as existing only outside of the

79 *Id.*

80 *Id.* (emphasis added).

81 *Id.*

82 *Id.*

83 M. Kline. 1989. *Race, Racism and Feminist Legal Theory*. 12 Harvard Women's Law Journal, 115.

84 K. Crenshaw. 1989. *Demarginalizing the Intersection of Race and Sex: A Black Feminist Critique of Antidiscrimination Doctrine, Feminist Theory, and Antiracist Politics*. University of Chicago Legal Forum 139, 140 (1989); D. Hutchinson. 1997. *Out Yet Unseen: A Racial Critique of Gay and Lesbian Legal Theory and Political Discourse*. 19 Connecticut Law Review, 561; F. Valdes. 1995. *Sex and Race in Queer Legal Culture: Ruminations on Identities and Inter-connectivities*. 5 Southern California Review of Law and Women's Studies, 25 (arguing that subordinated sexual minorities ought to strive for interconnectivity between and among their communities); M. Matsuda. 1992. *When the First Quail Calls: Multiple Consciousness as Jurisprudential Method*. 14 Women's Rights Law Reporter, 297; K. Crenshaw. 1991. *Mapping the Margins: Intersectionality, Identity Politics, and Violence against Women of Color*. 43 Stanford Law Review 6, 1241.

national geo-political space that is Jamaica. Politicians have also seen fit to weigh in and have firmly labelled the discussion of homophobia in Jamaica as foreign meddling about domestic issues. As the information minister Senator Burchell Whiteman stated, '[w]e are certainly not about to respond to any organisation external to this country that may want to dictate to us how and when to deal with the laws of our land.'[85] Former prime minister P.J. Patterson went further in personalizing the debate by taking offence at the possible relaxing of anti-gay laws by his government. He stated on a live radio programme, '[m]y credentials as a life-long heterosexual person are impeccable'.[86] Capping off this political debate, the immediate past prime minister Bruce Golding, while being interviewed on Hard Talk, a BBC television programme, conceded that gays and lesbians would form no part of his Cabinet.[87]

This dialogue reveals the truism that '"homosexual" difference is indispensable to the creation of the putative heterosexual norm.'[88] The power of Jamaican dancehall music is that it engages nationally and internationally in identity construction and maintenance. But these dynamics do not operate in isolation. Indeed, 'the social relations of dancehall productions are to a great extent structured by the same social variables found in Jamaica's national economy: massive exploitation, racism, sexism, homophobia, and violence.'[89] While I surmise in the next section that dancehall replicates imposed colonial legal norms of homophobia, dancehall certainly entrenches these sentiments. Like no other social force in Jamaica, dancehall is a cultural regulator of identity with more reach than the church, the education system, and the government.[90]

The Power of the Law: Cultural Assimilation on Pain of Punishment

The power of the law is stark in the domain of sexuality. In Jamaica, the sodomy laws were colonial impositions enacted and enforced to further British interests. Paradoxically, these laws have been maintained despite their nefarious origins. Betraying their latent homophobia, the relevant section of the *Offences Against the Person Act* is entitled '*Unnatural Offences*'.[91] This nomenclature blatantly situates

85 Younge, *supra* note 78.

86 G. Davis. 2001. *Homophobia Remains High.* Jamaica Gleaner [online]. Available at: http://www.jamaica-gleaner.com/pages/gay/homophobia.html [accessed: 8 January 2013].

87 BBC News. 2008. *In a HARDtalk interview shown on 20th May 2008, Stephen Sackur talks to Jamaica's Prime Minister Bruce Golding* [online]. Available at: http://news.bbc.co.uk/2/hi/programmes/hardtalk/7410382.stm [accessed: 8 January 2013].

88 Alexander, *supra* note 65, at 6.

89 Stolzoff, *supra* note 11, at 8.

90 Stolzoff, *supra* note 11.

91 *See* Government of Jamaica Ministry of Justice. 2005a. *Offences Against the Person Act*, § 76, L.N. 111/2005 [online]. Available at: http://www.moj.gov.jm/laws/statutes/Offences%20Against%20the%20Person%20Act.pdf [accessed: 8 January 2013].

heterosexuality as the norm by maligning homosexuality as unnatural. Section 76 reads,

> Whoever shall be convicted of the abominable crime of buggery, committed either with mankind or with animal, shall be liable to be imprisoned and kept to hard labor for a term not exceeding ten years.[92]

The law conflates anal sex (between men) with sex with animals and punishes both sodomy and bestiality as serious criminal offences; in doing so, the language and spirit of the law treats sex between men as abnormal, unnatural and freakish. In finding the requisite 'carnal knowledge' upon 'proof of penetration only', as opposed to the 'emission of seed',[93] the act reveals an interesting concern for gender performance.

It would seem that there is national concern for being perceived as effeminate – in not wanting to appear non-manly, the nation is constructed as non-feminine, the concern being the vulnerability implicit in penetration.[94] Specifically, the law seems structured to prevent and punish male, not female, penetration. This implicitly references the 'threat of the effeminized non-Western state.'[95] Of course, non-consensual sex acts whether with adults or children are an entirely appropriate subject matter for the law, but there is something else driving these laws. The concern is as equally steeped in gender as it is in protectionism.

I think that masculinity, its construction and operation, is the central driving force behind much of this legislation. Section 79 of the Jamaican *Offenses Against the Person Act* is explicit in its masculine concern.[96] There is no room for ambiguity as, unlike the other sections addressing 'unnatural offences', it fixes the subject as 'any male person'. This section, '*Outrages on Decency*', reads:

> *Any male person* who, in public or private, commits, or is a party to the commission of, or procures or attempts to procure the commission by any male person of, any act of gross indecency with another male person, shall be guilty of a misdemeanor, and being convicted thereof shall be liable at the discretion of the court to be imprisoned for a term not exceeding two years, with or without hard labour.[97]

---

92 *Id.*

93 *Id.*

94 Harris, *supra* note 58 (noting the role of symbolism in articulating a national masculinity that is 'properly heterosexual'); *see also* Stychin, *supra* note 69, at 12.

95 *See* Stychin, *supra* note 69, at 12.

96 *See* Government of Jamaica Ministry of Justice. 2005b. *Offences Against the Person Act*, § 79, L.N. 111/2005 [online]. Available at: http://www.moj.gov.jm/laws/statutes/Offences%20Against%20the%20Person%20Act.pdf [accessed: 8 January 2013].

97 *Id.* (emphasis added).

In their entirety, these Jamaican laws seek to criminalize non-procreative sex.[98] There is a long colonial history of incentivizing profitable sexuality to ensure wealth creation.[99] Indeed, in holding Texas anti-sodomy laws unconstitutional the majority of the United States Supreme Court stated, 'early American sodomy laws were not directed at homosexuals as such but instead sought to prohibit non-procreative sexual activity more generally.'[100]

In seeking to legitimize themselves post independence, Jamaicans struck a legislative bargain with their former colonizers. Jamaica paradoxically replicated the colonial edict in an attempt to gain global respect. As Alexander notes, 'the effects of political and economic international processes provoke a legitimization crisis for the state which moves to restore its legitimacy by recouping heterosexuality through legislation.'[101] This bespeaks an independence paradox, as the very methodology of post-colonial legitimization is colonial in its origins and object. Specifically, *post*-independence Jamaica re-enacted the same oppressive legislation that had been imposed upon it *pre* independence, and now refuses to release it.[102] Adding to this dynamic, development programmes (sponsored by the IMF, World Bank, USAID) coupled with globalization, 'help to reconfigure definitions of masculinity and femininity and simultaneously undermine the ideological bases upon which the state organizes, separates and draws from the "public" and "private" domains.'[103]

A review of the pre-independence provisions reveals that very little has changed over the course of hundreds of years. While the contemporary criminalization of the 'abominable act of buggery' as an unnatural act remains static, the potential penalty has been lessened insofar as the mandatory minimum of a three-year sentence is removed from the provisions. Section 66 of the 1938 Act read,

---

98 Alexander, *supra* note 65, at 5.

99 *See* C. Nelson. 2007. American Husbandry: Legal Norms Impacting the Production of (Re)productivity. 19 Yale Journal of Law and Feminism, 1 (discussing breeding practices during slavery).

100 Lawrence v. Texas, 539 U.S. 558, 559 (2003) (noting that '[b]eginning in colonial times there were prohibitions of sodomy derived from the English criminal laws passed in the first instance by the Reformation Parliament of 1533').

101 Alexander, *supra* note 65, at 7.

102 *See* Offences Against the Person Act, § 76 and §77, L.N. 123/2011, available at http://www.moj.gov.jm/sites/default/files/laws/Offences%20Against%20the%20Person%20Act.pdf ; *see* comments by immediate past Prime Minister Bruce Golding and his refusal to abolish buggery laws, '[w]e are not going to yield to the pressure, whether that pressure comes from individual organisations, individuals, whether that pressure comes from foreign governments or groups of countries, to liberalise the laws as it relates to buggery', D. Luton. 2009. *Buggery Laws Firm – PM Says Life or 15 Years for Same-sex Offence Breaches*, Jamaica Gleaner [online]. Available at: http://www.jamaica-gleaner.com/gleaner/20090304/lead/lead1.html [accessed: 8 January 2013).

103 Alexander, *supra* note 65, at 16, 18.

Unnatural Offences

> Whoever shall be convicted of the abominable crime of buggery, committed either with mankind or with any animal, shall be liable, at the discretion of the Court, to be kept in penal servitude for a term not exceeding ten years, and not less than three years, or to be imprisoned and kept to hard labour for a term not exceeding two years.[104]

The contemporary, post-independence, sodomy legislation is thus virtually identical to the pre-independence, i.e. colonial legislation of 1938.[105] 'By maintaining the logic and essence of these provisions, the post-colonial Jamaican legislators chose to re-inscribe the very same colonial sexual imperatives – that is, sex for procreation is prized and profitable for the building of the nation state.'[106] The problematic colonial prerogative is even more remarkable when one traces the legislative roots further into our past. Note the striking similarity to the buggery provision from the time of King Henry VIII:

An Acte for the Punysshement of the vice of Buggerie

> Forasmuch as there is not yet sufficient and condigne punishment appointed and limited by the due course of the laws of the Realm for the detestable and abominable vice of buggery committed with mankind or beast, It may therefore please the King's Highness with the assent of his Lords spiritual and temporal and the Commons the present parliament assembled that it may be enacted by authority of the same, that the same offence be from henceforth adjudged felony, and such order and form of process therein to be used against the offenders as in cases of felony at the common law.[107]

In the face of such a legislative history, it is ironic that many in contemporary Jamaican society situate their conception of homosexuality as foreign, as opposed to the laws addressing 'buggery' as foreign. Preference for this notion of 'colonial contamination',[108] where 'homosexuality is attributed to the white colonizer', seems at odds with the reality of foreign imposed legal dictates.[109] This theory 'situates homosexuality as a foreign concept and the societal exclusion of homosexuals

104 *The Laws of Jamaica*, 1938. Vol. 5, Unnatural Offenses, § 66.

105 *See* Central Intelligence Agency, *supra* note 10 (Jamaica gained independence on 6 August 1962).

106 Nelson, *supra*, note 77, at 259.

107 An Acte for the Punysshement for the vice of Buggerie, 1533–4, 25 Hen. 8, c. 6 (Eng.); *see* L.J. Moran. 1996. *The Homosexual(ity) of Law*. Routledge.

108 Stychin, *supra* note 69, at 11.

109 *Id.*

as organic[ally Jamaican].'[110] The legislation, however, reveals the fallacy in this position. The foreign imposition is the legal framework, not the sexuality. The colonial contamination is legal. The paradox is that the colonial laws have been adopted as indigenous, while many Jamaican sexual minorities are cast as national outsiders. What has to be routed out are the sodomy laws themselves. Through a colonial optic one can see that these laws are the colonial impositions that have come to be thought of as organic, indigenous, and authentically Jamaican.

As I have stated elsewhere, '[w]hile [other] remnants of colonization are deplored and routed out as localized examples of imperial domination and exploitation of the "sufferers,"[111] the laws criminalizing homosexuality are paradoxically upheld and applauded as "righteous examples of respectability."'[112] Alexander sees this paradox as an attempt to gain status on another's terms, 'as if colonial masters were still looking on, as if to convey legitimate claims to being civilized.'[113] What appears to be in order, therefore, is a dismantling of the underlying colonial prerogatives that percolate throughout the *Offences Against the Person Act*. In short, an essential first step would be some national political recognition of the colonial resonance, if not mimicry, found in the sodomy laws.

As the keepers and amenders of national legislation, the government must take leadership on this. As powerful as dancehall artists are, they cannot be expected to undertake legislative review. Instead, the government is best situated to open the matter up for discussion by recognizing the colonial paradox of national legislation. Dancehall artists will be key participants in any such national discourse. These artists have attempted to assert independent post-colonial voices as cultural leaders. Their recognition of the colonial duplicity of supposedly post-colonial laws, and the consequent cultural contamination, should assist in the formation of discursive strategies furthering sexual equality. If cultural leaders, including dancehall artists, are willing to cast their colonial informed homophobia aside, the rest of the society might follow, thereby allowing for the achievement of an important hallmark – the repeal of the sodomy laws as one part of a process towards wiping the colonial slate clean.

---

110 Nelson, *supra* note 99, at 260.

111 The reference to sufferers is a reference to the poor masses in Jamaica. They form the majority of Jamaicans and they occupy the lowest rung on the socio-economic ladder. For a musical reference to the plight of the sufferers, listen to Bob Marley's Babylon System *on* Songs of Freedom (Island Records 1992). Lyrics available at: http://www.metrolyrics.com/babylon-system-lyrics-bob-marley.html [accessed: 8 January 2013].

112 Nelson, *supra* note 77, at 260–61.

113 *See* Alexander, *supra* note 65, at 14.

Chapter 6
Towards Multidimensional Masculinities Theory: Policing Henry Louis Gates

Frank Rudy Cooper[1]

On Thursday 16 July 2009, white male police officer James Crowley was called to the home of prominent black male Harvard scholar Henry Louis Gates, Jr. on a report of a potential break-in (J. Crowley 2009). Crowley immediately asked Gates to exit his home and to prove his residency and identity (J. Crowley 2009). Gates took offence and loudly called Crowley a racist (J. Crowley 2009). The conflict escalated as more police officers arrived and onlookers gathered (J. Crowley 2009). When Gates exited his home to complain about Crowley to another officer, and despite knowing both that no break-in had occurred and Gates's identity, Crowley arrested Gates for disorderly conduct (J. Crowley 2009). The Cambridge Police Department promptly released Gates without charges, but the arrest became a national controversy (Jan 2009). Gates claimed he had been racially profiled and demanded an apology, while Crowley defended his actions (J. Crowley 2009). President Barack Obama, also a black male, first fanned the flames of the controversy by saying the police acted 'stupidly', then put out the fire by hosting a 'beer summit' between the parties at the White House (J. Williams 2009, Milbank 2009). The Gates controversy dominated news across the United States, and indeed, the world, for two weeks. It may thus serve as a case study in how identity operates in the context of law enforcement.

Some commentators suggested Crowley's arrest of Gates was solely a product of race (Doherty 2009). They argued this was an instance of racial profiling (Harcourt 2009). A smaller group of commentators thought class had produced the arrest because of 'town/gown' tensions (Hughes 2009). A few commentators blamed the arrest on the machismo of both parties (Vennochi 2009). In other words, the fact that Crowley and Gates are both men created a greater likelihood that the parties would not back down from their positions. All of those commentators are right, and all of them are wrong. It was the *interaction* between race, class and gender that caused the arrest.[2]

---

1 Special thanks to Ann Brown, Suffolk 2009, for assistance above and beyond the call of duty. I also thank my research assistant Lia Marino and research librarians Rick Buckingham and Diane D'Angelo. I may be reached at fcooper@suffolk.edu

2 Treating the Crowley arrest of Gates and subsequent controversy as largely a product of masculinities or race or class alone in various places is done strictly for heuristic purposes (Carbado and Gulati 2003).

This chapter analyses the Crowley arrest of Gates through the lens of masculinities studies in order to demonstrate the necessity for a broader conception of masculinities, one that acknowledges the ways they are cross-cut by race, class, and other identities. The Hegemonic Masculinities approach to masculinities studies is the dominant strand in law (Cohen 2009, Cooper 2009b, Dowd 2010, Harris 2000, McGinley 2008). It analyses the impact of masculinities by describing how men were influenced by and/or sought to deviate from the hegemonic, or dominant, ideal of masculinity (Cooper 2009b). This chapter departs slightly from the Hegemonic Masculinities approach to masculinities studies and instead proposes a Multidimensional Masculinities approach. Multidimensionality theory is a concept from critical race theory of law. It says that masculinities (1) are always intertwined with all other categories of identity and also (2) create different effects in different contexts (Cooper 2010). Merging a Hegemonic Masculinities approach and multidimensionality theory creates a Multidimensional Masculinities approach.

In addition to advocating for a Multidimensional Masculinities approach, this chapter makes the more specific argument that Crowley's arrest of Gates was a result of a 'masculinity contest' between the parties, albeit one heavily influenced by race and class. First, it summarizes how multidimensionality theory can help address the criticisms levelled against the Hegemonic Masculinities approach and create a theoretical framework for a Multidimensional Masculinities approach. Second, it develops a model of the hegemonic form of police officer masculinity to explain why officers are especially prone to respond to challenges to their masculinity by initiating masculinity contests. Third, it demonstrates that Crowley's arrest of Gates was a masculinity contest while emphasizing the ways that race and class influenced the event. It concludes by drawing further insights about the interactions between different forms of identity.

Theoretical Framework: From Hegemonic Masculinities to Multidimensional Masculinities

The Hegemonic Masculinities approach to masculinities studies has been by far the most prevalent in masculinities studies of law (Cohen 2009, Cooper 2009b, Dowd 2010, Harris 2000, McGinley 2008). The 'hegemonic masculinity' is the definition of manhood that is dominant in a given cultural context (Connell and Messerschmidt 2005). The hegemonic man is an ideal of manhood that tries to set the norm by which all men will tacitly agree to be judged (Dowd, Levit and McGinley 2012). Leading masculinities theorist Michael Kimmel thus says that men are engaged in 'homosocial' competition (Kimmel 2005b). That is Eve Kosofsky Sedgwick's term for competition between men (Sedgwick 1985). As Kimmel says, what seems to be men showing off for women is really men showing off for men. Men collect evidence of success – money, power, women, and so on – to show other men they are manly (Kimmel 2005b). According to Kimmel, 'We test ourselves, perform heroic acts, take enormous risks, all because we want other men to grant us our manhood' (Kimmel 2005b: 33). If that is so, masculine self-esteem will require the affirmation of other men.

This need for the affirmation of other men makes masculinity fundamentally anxious. Men tend to grant affirmation of masculinity when they see behaviours that they already associate with masculinity. Manhood is thus a never-ending test of whether your behaviours measure up to the ideal form of manhood (Kimmel 2005b). But the rules of the hegemonic form of US masculinity – (1) denigrate contrast figures, such as women, (2) accrue tokens of success, (3) hold one's emotions in check, and (4) be aggressive – are unrealizable (Kimmel 2005b). It is difficult, if not impossible, for any man to embody these characteristics of the ideal man at every given moment and over the course of his lifetime. We are always subject to being 'unmasked' as less than manly (Kimmel 2005b). The need to prove our masculinity is thus a constant source of anxiety.

The role of the denigration of contrast figures deserves further elaboration. The idea is that men have often identified other groups of men from whom they distinguish themselves. For the historically dominant straight white Christian male, gay men, racial minorities, Jews and women have served as contrast figures. The denigration of those figures has allowed dominant men to bolster their masculine esteem. In policing, there is a long history of special scrutiny of blacks and gay men (Maclin 1998, Messerschmidt 1993, Sklansky 2008). As will be discussed, that history is related to the bolstering of the officer's masculine esteem. For now, it suffices to say that homosocial competition and anxiety are structured into masculinity and lead to the denigration of contrast figures.

The idea that there is a hegemonic man or that we should refer to hegemonic masculinity has come under criticism. For instance, Christine Beasley argues we should limit the term to its political meaning – that images of masculinity are propounded as 'a political mechanism producing solidarity between different masculinities in a hierarchical order' (Beasley 2008a: 93). That idea takes us back to the roots of the concept as imagined by Marxist theorist Antonio Gramsci. Gramsci meant hegemony to connote that 'a social group will try to describe the world in a way that accounts for, but coordinates, the interests of other groups such that they will consent to a structuring of society that promotes the dominant group's interests' (Cooper 2002: 859). Meanwhile, Jeff Hearn calls for a move from hegemonic masculinities to 'the hegemony of men' – the idea that masculinity has allowed men to exercise power over women, as well as subordinated men (Hearn 2004). The Beasley and Hearn critiques seem to allow for the possibility that there are both attempts to establish a generally hegemonic masculinity in the US and also attempts to establish alternatives to that masculinity, either in general or in specific cultural contexts (Cooper 2012). As critical race feminist Angela Harris says, 'though one way of doing masculinity may be "hegemonic" … within a friendship network or a social institution, there may be many other ways of being a man that conflict, compete, or form a relationship of interdependence with the hegemonic form' (Harris 2000: 783). This chapter thus uses the term Hegemonic Masculinities, but in more of the political sense that Beasley advocates and while conscious of the risk of forgetting men's collective power over women that Hearn warns of.

With those thoughts in mind, this chapter seeks to modify Hegemonic Masculinities theory using multidimensionality theory. Critical race theorist Athena Mutua has conducted the most comprehensive investigation of multidimensionality theory (Mutua 2012). Using the work of critical race theorists Darren Hutchinson, Francisco Valdes and Nancy Ehrenreich, among others, she synthesizes five aspects of multidimensionality (Hutchinson 2000, Valdes 1998, Ehrenreich 2002). First, multidimensionality describes individuals as having many dimensions, from appearance traits – biological sex, skin colour, hair texture, and so on – to performance traits – gender, dress, religious expression, and so on – to role – nurse versus police officer, and so on (Cooper 2012, Mutua 2012). Second, it recognizes that groups are also multidimensional, being composed of not just 'blacks', but black men and black women, queer blacks and straight blacks, black cops and black museum curators, and so on (Mutua 2012). Third, it concentrates on the materially relevant characteristics, which are so because they have been hierarchized (Mutua 2012). For example, we can speak of the 'scaling of bodies', which ranks people as more or less valuable based on hierarchies of white over non-white, male over female, abled over disabled, and so on (Cooper 2006a; Young 1990). Fourth, it recognizes that these overlapping hierarchies of identities create a matrix of privilege and oppression (Mutua 2012). This principle might be thought of as having two implications. On the one hand, each characteristic is co-constituted by other characteristics, such that gender and sex orientation are imbricated within each other, class dynamics are shot through with race, and so on. For instance, masculinity has often been defined through relational difference from both femininity and gayness, meaning that gay men are feminized, which is a narrative that is both an effect and a reproducer of the intertwining of gender and sex orientation in our culture (Valdes 1995a). On the other hand, the interaction of privilege and oppression may produce counter-intuitive results. So, black men may be more vulnerable to racial profiling on the street than black women, even though black men are privileged by gender and black women are oppressed by both race and gender (Mutua 2012). Finally, though, cultural context often affects an individual's treatment as much as their location in the matrix of privileges and oppressions (Cooper 2012, Mutua 2012). Thus, even though black men are more profiled on the street, black women may actually be more prone to harassment by customs officials (Sharma 2003).

Multidimensionality theory's insights can be boiled down in a way that has implications for the critique of the Hegemonic Masculinities approach. Note that the first three multidimensionality insights are largely background for the last two. Recognizing that both individuals and groups are multidimensional and that we should focus on how characteristics are made materially relevant by being hierarchized sets the stage for acknowledging that identities are both co-constituted and affected by context. The focus on how identities are hierarchized seems to address Beasley's criticism that the Hegemonic Masculinities approach needs to emphasize its political content. To say that all identities are subject to hierarchization makes it more reasonable to assert that there is a competition to establish a hegemonic man. Meanwhile, multidimensionality theory's focus on context helps explain why there can be dominant norms of masculinity in general and still alternative norms that govern under certain circumstances (Cooper 2012). As to Hearn's criticism of the Hegemonic Masculinities approach, it does not seem inconsistent to say that we will pay attention to men's collective power over women, but also note the homosocial competition between men. Some contexts will require an excavation of the effects of men's collective power, while others will require revealing homosocial competition. The Crowley arrest of Gates, having been argued to be merely a matter of race or class, seems to require explication of the way it was also a competition between men.

Hegemonic Masculinities Theory of Police Masculinity

A core aspect of the hegemonic pattern of police officer identity, as distinguished from the hegemonic pattern of US masculinity in general, is the officer's sense that he must enact a command presence. One has command presence when one takes charge of a situation (Newman 2006, Chemerinsky 2001). The officer projects confidence and decisiveness (Newman 2006). Command presence is also associated with the physical control of suspects. It is justified by the need to control dangerous suspects (Newman 2006, Chemerinsky 2001). When it is misused, it can amount to police brutality (Newman 2006). As has been demonstrated elsewhere, seeing the enactment of command presence as the core of the job is a characteristic of policing throughout the country (Cooper 2009b, Newman 2006).

A corollary of the fact that policemen's senses of self are tied up with their ability to enact command presence is an unwritten rule that civilians must show deference to the badge. That attitude has its roots in what sociologists Dov Cohen and Joe Vandello call the culture of honour (Cohen and Vandello 1998). In a culture of honour, one must protect one's social stature or suffer being taken advantage of. For instance, herdsmen often cannot keep an eye on every member of their roving flock. To discourage poaching, they must have a reputation for punishing anyone who messes with them (Cohen and Vandello 1998). Accordingly, protecting one's honour becomes paramount and insults are treated as grave threats to one's identity and livelihood (Cohen and Vandello 1998). Police officers seem to fear that, if they let an instance of disrespect pass, they will be subject to constant challenges (Harris 2000). Because officers feel they might need to impose command presence on a situation at any moment, they often feel they must constantly enforce a rule of deference to the badge. Police officers are often on the lookout for any sign of disrespect of their authority, which they will then punish (Cooper 2009b).

The rule of deference to the badge should be linked to masculinity. That is so because police officers associate their police authority with their masculine authority. As early as 1970, sociologist James F. Scott concluded that 'to make depreciatory remarks about the police role is to cast aspersion upon the policemen's conceptions of themselves as men' (Scott 1970: 12). As late as 1999, criminologist Susan Ehrlich Martin determined that, '[s]ince a key element of policing – gaining and maintaining control of situations – remains associated with manhood, male officers do gender along with doing dominance' (Martin 1999: 117). Both of these scholars suggest that police officers conflate their masculine authority and their police authority. So, what seems to be the product of their role – the rule of deference to the badge – is also a product of gender identity. This is made obvious by the fact that jobs are often gendered: nurses are stereotypically female and police officers are paradigmatically male. Thus, it should not surprise us that police officers sometimes use their role to boost their individual masculine esteem.

Criminologist and masculinities scholar James Messerschmidt argues that police officers assigned to street duty seek to reinforce their masculine self-esteem through their occupational behaviours. According to Messerschmidt, police officers are divided into street-cop and office-cop cultures (Messerschmidt 1993). 'Street-cop masculinity,' he contends, 'reflects, in part, street-cop desire to deny a subordinate position within hierarchical department power relations among men' (Messerschmidt 1993: 179). The hegemonic pattern of US masculinity emphasizes the dominance, control and independence characterizing office-cop positions (Messerschmidt 1993). Street-cops are thus in 'penalty status' because of class. Penalty status is the condition of already having something about your identity that makes your masculinity suspect (Cooper 2010). If the idealized masculinity is heterosexual, white and upper middle class (and, arguably, Christian), men who do not fit one of those categories start off knowing that their quest to measure up to the ideal is hampered. Street cops can respond to their penalty status (and thereby reinforce their masculine self-esteem) by denigrating contrast figures, such as gay men, racial minority men and lower-class men (Messerschmidt 1993). According to Messerschmidt, 'the police construct a white, heterosexual form of hegemonic masculinity through the authorized practice of controlling "deviant" behavior of "inferior" men' (Messerschmidt 1993: 184).

Having seen that men generally suffer from masculine anxiety and that police officers often express such anxiety through the rule of deference to the badge, we should consider the possible results of this situation. It will thus be helpful to define and apply the theory of masculinity contests. This theory emerges from, but distinguishes itself from, Messerschmidt's theory of the 'masculinity challenge'. One's masculinity is challenged when one is threatened in a way that denigrates one's masculinity or when expectations of masculine behaviour are unachievable (Messerschmidt 2000). One's manhood is obviously threatened when one is challenged to a fight (Cooper 2009b). The challenge is in being put in the position of either backing down and seeming less manly or fighting and risking harm. One also has his masculinity challenged when the manly way of acting is hard to achieve. A prime example is when men are expected to act unemotional in the face of tragedy. The challenge is to either let your grief show and be perceived as unmanly or be stoic and risk harming yourself emotionally. When men find their masculinities challenged, they will often seek ways to boost their masculine self-esteem (Messerschmidt 2000). One way to do so is to initiate a masculinity contest.

A masculinity challenge ripens into a masculinity contest when each of two or more people are subject to a masculinity challenge and only one person or one side will be able to boost their internal or attributed masculine esteem (Cooper 2009b). A masculinity contest is thus inter-relational: it arises from the conflictual relations between two or more people. It is also a zero–sum game: for someone to win, someone must lose. When someone issues a challenge to a fight, he creates a masculinity contest. He has challenged the masculinity of the other, as noted above. He is also under a masculinity challenge, though. If the other fights, the initiator will now have his masculinity judged based on his performance. While there are nuances to what constitutes 'winning' a fight that affect one's internal and attributed masculine esteem, masculinity is clearly at stake in a masculinity contest.

There are some differences between a masculinity challenge and a masculinity contest that bear mentioning. First, a masculinity challenge is something experienced by an individual. A masculinity contest requires multiple people. Second, while a masculinity challenge is internally felt, a masculinity contest is intersubjective, and thus a shared experience. Third, a masculinity challenge can be resolved without harming another. In contrast, a masculinity contest is a zero–sum game that must be resolved at one party's expense. It is possible, of course, for both parties to simultaneously back down, but then it would cease to be a masculinity contest altogether.

Why might a police officer initiate a masculinity contest in response to a masculinity challenge? Here, it is important to note that the literature on the interactions between class and masculinities introduces the concept of 'compensatory subordination' to describe men's reactions to being of low status in an environment (Pyke 1996). That is, working-class men sometimes compensate themselves for their low status along one axis of identity by subordinating others who are below them along other axes (Ehrenreich 2002). So, the guys on the oil rig may harass the co-worker they consider gay and working-class men may be more likely to beat their partners (Ehrenreich 2002). As applied to Crowley, Messerschmidt's work suggests that his street-cop status would be expected to simultaneously emphasize his penalty status *vis-à-vis* class and provide him with a resource for compensatory subordination: the repression of deviant men. Gates's blackness would be expected to trigger this response in Crowley in the form of heightened suspiciousness and a lower tolerance for uncooperative behaviour (Harcourt 2009).

Crowley's Arrest of Gates as a Masculinity Contest

Having laid out the theory of masculinity contests, it is now time to apply that theory to Crowley's arrest of Gates. Consideration of the elements of the arrest makes it clear that masculinity was at stake for both parties. That is not to say that race and class did not play a role in the arrest. As becomes apparent in detailing the masculinity norms at play, those aspects of identity also influenced the arrest.

Crowley Challenged Gates's Masculinity

Analysing masculinity in the context of Crowley's arrest of Gates requires consideration of the ways the parties had their masculine esteem challenged and the resources they used for boosting that esteem. Crowley challenged Gates's masculinity in two primary ways. First, Crowley assumed Gates's illegality. Both Crowley's report and Gates's account suggest that Crowley's first words to Gates insinuated that he had broken into the house. Crowley immediately asked Gates to leave his house (J. Crowley 2009). This seems to have been an attempt to exercise command presence by controlling the situation. The relevant law required Crowley to obtain a warrant or Gates's consent to enter the house, so Crowley would have had more control if Gates had left his house at that time (*Vale v. Louisiana* 1970). As is suggested by Gates's lawyer's statement following the arrest, Gates seems to have interpreted the request to leave his home as an assertion that something illegal was going on (Ogletree 2009). To see why Gates might have reacted in this way, imagine an alternative means for Crowley to have initiated the encounter: he might have allowed Gates to stay in the comfort of his home and, after introducing himself and explaining his presence, requested to join him therein.

Second, and related to Crowley's initial assumption of illegality, was his disbelief of Gates's credentials. Almost immediately after asking Gates to exit his home, Crowley asked him to identify himself. When Gates said he lived in the home and was a professor at Harvard, Crowley required him to prove it with identification (J. Crowley 2009). Again, Gates's lawyer's statement suggests that Gates took offence at Crowley's seeming disbelief that Gates was the resident and a Harvard professor (Ogletree 2009).

The fact that Crowley assumed Gates's illegality and disbelieved his identity was particularly likely to offend Gates in light of the historic tensions between the police and black men. Masculine anxiety may have been heightened for Gates because he was in penalty status because of race. As many masculinities theorists have noted, the idealized masculinity is white (Kimmel 2005b). As a consequence, racial minority men have historically been defined as either un-masculine or all too masculine (Kimmel 2005b, Cooper 2006a). The definition of blacks as all too masculine is a source of the traditional police characterization of blacks as warranting greater suspicion and constituting a greater danger to officers (Thompson 1999). Gates probably perceived that he had to live down that reputation when confronted by Crowley. Gates's immediate accusation of racism is itself a tip-off that Gates also felt his masculinity was at stake. Racism has long been perceived by black men to be a means of emasculating them (Carbado 2000). Hence, the 1960s civil rights placards declaring 'I am a Man' (Carbado 1999).[3] As black feminists have demonstrated, 1960s black civil rights leaders often viewed the dismantling of racism as a means of restoring black men to their

3 The cover of this anthology of black men's writings depicts black men wearing 'I am a Man' signs at a civil rights protest (Carbado 1999).

rightful place as truly masculine heads of households (Williams 1998). At least at a subconscious level, then, Gates may have felt that Crowley's purported racism was an attack on his manhood.[4]

Finally, Gates's class privilege may have made him feel especially affronted by Crowley's behaviour. Given his many achievements (i.e., his class status), Gates would be particularly irritated by the need to overcome stereotypes about his blackness. Gates's eventual assertion of being a bigger man than Crowley (by saying Crowley did not know who he was messing with) was a way of reasserting his manliness in the face of a perceived racial emasculation (Cooper 2006a: 859).

Gates Challenged Crowley's Masculinity

Just as Crowley's behaviour challenged Gates's masculinity, Gates's actions presented Crowley with a masculinity challenge because they violated the rule of deference to the badge. Here again, the concept of penalty status bears mention. Crowley's masculine anxiety may have been exacerbated during the Gates arrest because he was in penalty status because of his class. For Crowley, this meant that his class status was a bit of an albatross. As a street cop, Crowley would commonly be described as working class. That might not matter in most interactions, but it certainly does when an officer is confronting a member of the cultural elite, such as a Harvard professor. As Gates demonstrated by getting the charges dropped and garnering international media coverage, these people have much greater power than everyday folk to make the officer pay for a bad decision. Crowley's consciousness of Gates's superior class status was primed by Gates's claim that Crowley did not know who he was messing with. That statement by Gates is just one of the ways in which he violated the rule of deference to police officers and thereby challenged Crowley's masculinity.

Gates seems to have violated the rule of deference, and thereby presented Crowley with a masculinity challenge, in four basic ways. First, by refusing Crowley's requests that he exit his home. Second, by demanding Crowley's name and badge number. Third, by calling Crowley racist. Fourth, by suggesting that he was a more important man than Crowley. The first challenge was created by the fact that, upon viewing Gates, Crowley requested that he exit his home (J. Crowley 2009). Gates replied, 'no I will not' (J. Crowley 2009). When Crowley explained that he wanted to speak with Gates because he was investigating a potential break-in, Gates said, 'why, because I'm a black man in America?' (J. Crowley 2009). Those initial refusals to cooperate with Crowley seem crucial to understanding Crowley's subsequent actions.

There are several signs that Crowley took offence at Gates's refusal to leave his home. The first is that Crowley took this event so far. He arrested Gates even after

---

4 To relegate Gates's masculine anxiety to the subconscious level would not be to denigrate it as superfluous, for our behaviours are often motivated by subconscious feelings (Lawrence 1987).

determining Gates's identity and that no break-in took place (J. Crowley 2009). This suggests that Crowley was personally offended by Gates's refusal to leave his home. A second sign that Crowley was offended by Gates's refusal to leave his home is the fact that Crowley made multiple attempts to get Gates to leave his home (J. Crowley 2009). Crowley really wanted Gates to leave his house. At some point, that desire was connected to an intent to arrest Gates. Hence, as soon as Gates walked out onto the porch, Crowley began the process of arresting him (J. Crowley 2009). Another sign that Crowley was offended by Gates's refusal is the lengths he went to in order to explain why he asked Gates to leave his home. Crowley writes in his police report that the 'acoustics' in Gates's kitchen made it hard for him to hear (J. Crowley 2009). On its face, this seems to be a stretch. Nowhere has it subsequently been suggested that Gates's kitchen was in fact so cavernous as to have unusual 'acoustics'. While getting Gates out of the house eventually facilitated a disorderly conduct charge by bringing Gates into the public, the initial desire to get him out of the house is based only on the flimsy 'acoustics' rationale. That suggests that one real reason for wanting Gates out of the house was solely because Crowley had requested it and Gates had refused. The need to spuriously justify the request is a sign that the fact of the request itself was the important thing, not the reason for the request. Gates was violating the rule of deference to the badge, which Crowley may have experienced as a disrespect of his masculine standing. Finally, the challenge to Crowley's masculinity was probably heightened by the fact that Gates's refusal to leave his house took place in front of Crowley's police officer peers. Crowley thus faced a loss of masculine esteem in front of other men. Further, since police officers are especially concerned with exhibiting command presence and punishing disrespect, Crowley may have felt his peers would disapprove of his backing down. In view of the scholarship on police officer masculinity, the strength with which Crowley clung to his request suggests he did so because his masculine self-esteem had been pricked (Cooper 2009b, Harris 2000, Messerschmidt 1993).

Second, Gates also violated the rule of deference to the badge by repeatedly demanding Crowley's name and badge number. This response to Crowley's request that Gates exit his house constituted a defiance. Officers are quite sensitive to the suggestion that they may be rebuked for the way they exercise discretion. That sensitivity seems manifest in the 'blue wall of silence' (Chin and Wells 1998) as to officer misbehaviour and police union resistance to civilian review boards (Armacost 2004). For present purposes, we can expect an officer in Crowley's position to have been sensitive to the suggestion that Gates would not only refuse his request, but seek to punish him for it. Gates's perception was, 'when I demanded – which I did – his name and badge number, I think he just got really angry' (Gates 2009). Crowley thus seems to have perceived Gates as violating the unwritten rule of deference to the badge by requesting his badge number and to have punished Gates's disrespect with the arrest.

A third reason that Crowley might have perceived Gates as violating the rule of deference to the badge is that Gates called him a racist. Doing so violated the rule of deference. To see how this is so, one needs only note that calling someone racist has become a grave incivility. Because the challenge has become downright rude, it violates the rule of deference.

The final way that Gates challenged Crowley's masculinity was by suggesting he was a bigger man than Crowley. He did that by saying Crowley did not know who he was messing with and had not heard the end of this (J. Crowley 2009). Gates's relative importance was implicit in the prestigious and expensive location of his home. Ware Street is close to Harvard Square and located in one of Cambridge's 'better' neighbourhoods. The eventual revelation of Gates's status as a professor at Harvard also made his relative stature implicit (J. Crowley 2009). In contrast to professors, who are considered upper middle class, at least (Fussell 1983), policemen are generally considered working class despite their above-average incomes because the job is identified with the working class (Fine et al. 1997). Growing up going to the public schools in Cambridge, Crowley would have been considered a 'townie' by the many university-affiliated students and staff. There is certainly a 'Town/Gown' split in Cambridge. Further, the area Crowley grew up in is considered largely working class compared to the upper-class neighbourhoods of Harvard Square, Porter Square or West Cambridge.[5]

The prestige of Gates's status as a Harvard professor is obvious. Crowley's consciousness of Gates's class status (even if only at a subconscious level) was potentially primed by Gates telling Crowley he did not know who he was messing with (J. Crowley 2009). That statement implied that Gates was a big shot and Crowley a small fry. Of necessity, the statement implied that Crowley was a lesser man than Gates. We might expect the general resentment of black males that is sometimes held by working-class whites (Fine et al. 1997, Kimmel 2005b), as primed by Gates's class-based insult, to make Crowley more likely to arrest Gates. Gates was violating the rule of deference to the badge (Cooper 2009b), which helped transform this event into a masculinity contest.

The Masculinity Contest between Crowley and Gates

As a result of Gates's challenges to Crowley's masculinity, and Crowley's simultaneous challenges to Gates's masculinity, the parties were in a masculinity contest at the time of the arrest in at least three ways. First, there was the 'will he or won't he' as to Gates leaving the house. As was noted, Crowley's police authority, and thus his masculinity, was challenged by Gates's refusal of his request (Scott 1970, Martin 1999). Simultaneously, Gates's masculinity was challenged by Crowley's insistence on the departure. Would Gates stand his ground or back down? The interaction thus produced a contest wherein masculinity was at stake.

A second sign that this was a masculinity contest was Crowley's claim that Gates said derogatory things about his mother (J. Crowley 2009). If we take this

5 No disrespect to working-class neighbourhoods; the author grew up in, and is currently a resident of, a mixed-income neighbourhood in Cambridge.

as true, it is the classic challenge to a fight. After all, a real man stands up for his mother. If Gates did say something about Crowley's mother, he thereby initiated a masculinity contest with Crowley. Certainly an arrest would be an adequate response. We might not accept the claim of a 'your mama', though. Gates denies it (Warner 2009). It also seems particularly unlikely that a black man would say this to a cop, since black men are generally raised to believe that police officers are prone to beating black men (Carbado 2002). Nonetheless, the claim of such a statement still seems indicative of a masculinity contest. If Crowley believed Gates said this, he would certainly have felt his masculinity was challenged. If Crowley knew Gates made no such statement, he might have believed he needed to concoct an insult in order to justify the arrest. Such a false claim would ratchet up the masculinity contest that seems inherent in making an arrest in the midst of Gates's refusal to cooperate. Both parties had suffered insults that they were likely to take as challenges to their manhood. The claim that Gates said 'your mama' would thus stand as a move in the game of opposing claims of bad behaviour.

A third way in which the Gates arrest became a masculinity contest was in Gates's later request for, and Crowley's refusal to give, an apology (Sweet et al. 2009). Crowley had accused Gates of bad behaviour with his arrest for disorderly conduct. Gates had counter-claimed bad behaviour by calling Crowley a racist. The request for an apology was a continuation of the masculinity contest. Now Crowley was the one about whom we asked, 'Will he or won't he?' Would he stand his ground or back down? Of course, he stood his ground, and this masculinity contest became a national event (Sweet et al. 2009).

Conclusion

This chapter conducts a masculinities studies analysis in that it focuses on the ways that societal assumptions about gender are formed and individuals respond to those assumptions when performing their gender (Cooper 2009a). But this chapter began by contending that Crowley's arrest of Gates is best understood as the product of the *interaction* between race, class and gender. That is what a Multidimensional Masculinities approach is about: attending to the ways that masculinities interact with other forms of identities to produce certain behaviours in particular cultural contexts. Consequently, this concluding part of the chapter will emphasize the ways race and class have been crucial to understanding Crowley's arrest of Gates.

The conclusion that the arrest resulted from the confluence of identities makes sense given that the very assumptions of the hegemonic form of US masculinity include race and class dimensions. As McGinley (2004) points out, the various forms of masculinities are created through the process of relational difference. Men constitute themselves as groups by distinguishing themselves from other men along lines of race, class, age, sex orientation, religion, region, and so on. This process of distinction is why we must refer to masculinities in the plural (Smith 1996). There is no one masculine experience, only clusters of related experiences of manhood.

Men are advantaged and disadvantaged in a variety of ways based on their precise combinations of identities. Our subject positions – where we fit in terms of privileged and subordinated identities in the three-dimensional matrix of identities (Mutua 2012) – affect both how we are treated and how we experience ourselves.

We saw the difference that the differentiation of masculinities makes in this case study. As a high-status black male, Gates had certain expectations and certain sensitivities. He thought he had earned his way out of racial profiling. As critical race theorist Devon Carbado (2002) has shown, a significant impetus for the critique of racial profiling is the sense that a Good Black Man (Cooper 2006a) should not be subject to suspicion. As a Harvard professor, and among the most famous of them at that, Gates was likely used to being treated with deference. Simultaneously, as a black man, and a chronicler of racism, Gates may have been particularly vulnerable to feeling challenged by the suggestion that he might be a criminal. Simultaneously, Crowley's white working-class status could be expected to make him especially vulnerable to being challenged by perceived arrogance from a black man (Fine et al. 1997). As a Cambridge-raised 'townie'[6] rather than someone who came to Cambridge to attend one of its many post-secondary schools, he would be all too familiar with the air of entitlement sometimes exhibited by those affiliated with Harvard. Crowley's sensitivity to feeling challenged by Gates would have been magnified by Gates's calling him racist. At best he would be hurt by the unfair stereotype of a white cop. At worst, he would have felt vulnerable to the charge and seen an arrest as a way to counter-accuse Gates of bad behaviour. On top of that, Crowley's status as a cop, with its implied need to be in charge of situations, provided another way for his manhood to be challenged. In sum, then, Gates and Crowley were very differently positioned vis-à-vis their manhood while sharing the general masculine preoccupation with perceived disrespect. That combination was explosive in this case.

So we end this chapter having confirmed the hypothesis that we began with: the purely race-based, class-based and gender-based explanations of Crowley's arrest of Gates are all insufficient. While it is hard to imagine that a famous white Harvard professor, say, Alan Dershowitz, would have been arrested after the officer identified him and determined there had been no crime (Goodnough 2009), it is also hard to imagine that a famous black female Harvard professor, say, Lani Guinier, would have been arrested (Vennochi 2009). In order to fully understand the arrest, it is necessary to see it as a multidimensional product of Crowley and Gates's races, Gates's claim of racism, Crowley's sensitivity to that charge, the relative class positions of the parties, and the fact that these were men. A Multidimensional Masculinities approach is the one that can best consider the interactions between those factors.

6 No offence meant; the author is also a Cambridge 'townie'.

PART III
Confronting Law

Chapter 7
HIV/AIDS and Male Circumcision: Discourses of Race and Masculinity

Marie Fox and Michael Thomson

Introduction

At an early stage of the HIV/AIDS pandemic, male circumcision was mooted as a possible biomedical response to the public health crisis it generated (Fink 1989, Moses et al. 1994, Cardwell and Cardwell 1996). Indeed, some advocates promoted the procedure as a 'natural condom' (Fink 1989). Over time the purported relationship between circumcision status and HIV status has been an increasing focus for scientific enquiry. A key aim of this chapter is to contextualize and problematize the increasingly influential public health discourses that posit circumcision as a key prevention technology in the 'war' on HIV/AIDS in sub-Saharan Africa (Waldby 1996). We suggest that these discourses need to be read against a historical backdrop of attempts to use medicine to manage the bodies of African and African-American men. We are influenced in this project by scholars who have traced the ways in which the bodies of black men, women and children have been (mis)used in medical research (Duh 1991, Washington 2008), and also, more generally, how they have been subjected to oppressive medical regulation rooted in negative stereotypes of black sexuality. Often this results in the application of different standards of consent to bodily interventions (Roberts 1997). In our contribution to this volume we seek to explore the implications of these public health policies for managing the sexuality of the men and boys who are most directly affected by pro-circumcision policies, but we also examine the significant implications of these policies for women's health, an issue that is often neglected when public health policies target the male body.

In order to historicize and problematize contemporary accounts and practices, we begin by outlining the initial Anglo-American medical colonization in the second half of the nineteenth century of a procedure that had previously been contained within tenets of religious observance. By providing this context, we seek to complicate a commonplace understanding of the relationship between male genital cutting and race, which regards the procedure as an aspect of religious or cultural practice. To better understand the contemporary policy developments at the centre of this chapter, we highlight two aspects of the pro-circumcision discourse of that era. First, we explore the role that circumcision was seen to play in controlling male sexuality. Secondly, we address the place of race, and specifically of racialized masculinities, in medical recourse to circumcision in earlier decades. Thus, we examine medical discourses of the 1880s–90s that advocated circumcision of African-Americans on grounds of hygiene, disease prevention, and curbing excessive sexuality. We then turn to contemporary discourses that promote circumcision in sub-Saharan Africa as a public health response to HIV/AIDS (Fox and Thomson 2012). We suggest that this contemporary advocacy carries echoes of those earlier debates.

Our contribution to these debates moves across centuries and between continents. These shifts in focus are anchored by recognition of a cultural drive for circumcision in the United States in earlier decades and in contemporary US and Western funding of programmes in Africa, and by the fact that across these different contexts it is the black male body that is the focus of public health interventions. A further justification for aligning these discourses across different eras and different jurisdictions is that this serves to demonstrate the ways in which research findings from sub-Saharan Africa are currently filtering back to influence domestic policy formulation in the United States. Thus, US-sponsored research in Africa is now being used to legitimate a renewed focus on circumcision in North America. This process is not, of course, new. Colonial medicine from the nineteenth century onwards made use of biological sciences to advance colonial activities, as well as to promote science at home through the colonial experience (Metzl and Kirkland 2010). Analysing these discourses we find an enduring focus on the black male body – and specifically its construction as promiscuous and a source of infectious disease – and an exchange and circulation of circumcision rhetoric and practice.

In its preoccupation with the black male body, we also seek to highlight how the mobilization of circumcision as a public health measure in various African jurisdictions leads to a marginalization of the health needs of women. We conclude by suggesting that greater critical attention needs to be devoted to public health policies that have attracted less ethico-legal scrutiny than other areas of medical practice. As Deborah Lupton has argued,

> The tendency has been to accept the prevailing orthodoxies of public health and health promotion, focusing upon statistical measures, cost-effectiveness and the evaluation of measurable effects, but devoting comparatively little attention to the critical analysis of the political implications of such endeavours. (Lupton 1995: 1)

Yet, as Lupton has shown, the discourses and practices of public health are highly political and socially contextual (Lupton 1995: 2). While accounts of the emergence and development of public health often plot a progression driven by advances in medical science, analysis of the birth and growth of the public health movement reveals a series of stages characterized by regressions and political struggles:

> The histories have shown that while it is standard to describe the 'old' public health and the 'new' public health as related but very different traditions, much

> of the discourses and practices of the 'old' health movement can be currently seen in the 'new' public health. (Lupton 1995: 17)

Building on this analysis, we argue that a responsible approach to health promotion must be attentive to the resurfacing of 'old' social and political anxieties and the recoding of these in new as well as familiar ways. Our key argument is that a genealogy of the medical promotion of circumcision must inform current policy development and practice.

Historicizing Contemporary Debates

This section explores the emergence of circumcision as a medical procedure. Specifically we focus on medical discourses prevalent in the 1880s–90s in the US that advocated the circumcision of African-Americans. We begin, however, by outlining a more general account of the ways in which medical knowledge has been mobilized to legitimate the subordination of African-Americans. The classic example of racially abusive medical research is, of course, the Tuskegee, Alabama syphilis experiment, although this is far from an isolated incident (see, for example, Corea 1985, McClain 1988, Golner 1993, Sharp 2006). At Tuskegee, over a 40-year period from 1932, 399 subjects, all African-American males, were denied standard medical treatment for the disease. As Allan Brandt has argued, this 'essentially racist' study was shaped by the notion 'that blacks, promiscuous and lustful, would not seek or continue treatment' (Brandt 1978: 23, see also Reverby 2000), while Sander Gilman has observed that it was also premised on the belief that 'American blacks had a greater immunity to syphilis because of the "African" origins of the disease' (Gilman 1988: 100). Anne Marie Hickey offers a concise account of the vision of black masculinity that underpinned the Tuskegee experiments:

> Whereas white masculinity was (and is) constructed as a powerful and impenetrable force, the protector as well as the dominator, black masculinity is seen as an exaggeration of normal masculinity, a masculinity that is sexually animalistic, deviant, and in need of regulation. (Hickey 2006: 168)

We suggest that similar understandings continue to influence current public health discourses, which echo earlier debates about syphilis in constructing HIV/AIDS as of African origin. In both cases, as Gilman notes, 'Blacks were deemed to be at risk because of their perceived sexual difference – their "hypersexuality" [was] … associated with images of sexually transmitted disease' (Gilman 1988: 102). And, as the history of medical practice illustrates, the medical profession met the regulatory imperative to 'deal with' black male sexuality. As Hickey continues,

> By the nineteenth century, the system of domination of black men's bodies exhibited by medical officials and scientists had its premise in sexual and racial

> stereotypes. Medical science began to go to great lengths to affirm that black men and white men differed in terms of sexual morals and behaviours, and the primary way in which black men and white men were dichotomized was through the medicalization of black male sexuality. (Hickey 2006: 171)

In such medical constructions the depiction of black male sexuality and sexual anatomy as animalistic was a primary means of differentiating black men from white, prompting Arthur Saint-Aubin to contend that, by the late nineteenth century, physicians and scientists viewed black men as 'closer to the lower animals … when it came to sexual appetite, lack of morality, and to a certain degree sexual anatomy' (Saint-Aubin 2002: 264). Indeed, such views persisted into the twentieth century in other medical contexts. Thus, in her analysis of early xenotransplantation experiments conducted in the southern United States in the 1960s, Lesley Sharp suggests that the use of black male subjects as recipients of animal organ transplants may have been as much a product of medical perceptions of their substitutability with primates, as it was to do with their availability as research subjects (Sharp 2011). Perhaps significantly, by the 1990s the preferred organ recipients in such experiments were HIV patients – a similarly stigmatized and marginalized group, many of whom were black men. Importantly, as Dorothy Roberts observes, such abuses and assumptions have meant that 'many Blacks harbor a well-founded distrust of technological interference with their bodies … at the hands of white physicians' (Roberts 1997: 260). These shameful aspects of US medical history resurface when new studies of research into sexual transmitted infections come to light, often revealing a racial or colonial context. For instance, in September 2010 the US government apologized to the Guatemalan government following the revelation that between 1946 and 1948 American public health doctors infected nearly 700 Guatemalan prison inmates, mental patients and soldiers with sexually transmitted diseases in order to study the effectiveness of penicillin (McNeil 2010). The National Institutes of Health paid for infected prostitutes to have sex with prisoners. When this method of transmission was not effective, some prisoners had the bacteria poured into wounds on their penises, arms and faces, while in other cases it was injected into the spine. Dr John C. Cutler, who led the experiment, later had an important role in the Tuskegee study, an experiment he continued to defend after the abuses were exposed.

An Emerging Practice

As we have noted, male genital cutting was originally embraced by the Anglo-American medical professions in the second half of the 1800s. We have detailed the history of medicalized male genital cutting elsewhere (Fox and Thomson 2005), and a number of fuller accounts exist (Gollaher 1994, Darby 2005). Here we simply trace how male sexuality and race were articulated in these early medical discourses. Thus, we map the transformation in the second half of the nineteenth century of religious genital cutting into medicalized circumcision and its refiguring as a secularized medico-religious practice (Dozor 1990). This period saw the adoption, by a predominantly white middle-class profession, of what had in these jurisdictions hitherto been an almost exclusively Jewish practice. We are acutely conscious of the need to avoid simplified attempts at an overarching motivation for, or account of, male genital cutting. Yet it is important to acknowledge a historical tendency to look for rationalizations – including from within biomedicine – that allow us to justify genital cutting across geographical, cultural and religious boundaries (Hellsten 2004). Indeed, circumcision has long existed as a procedure in search of a biomedical justification or rationale (Fox and Thomson 2005), which historically has prompted extravagant medical claims lacking scientific justification (Gollaher 1994, Darby 2005). We see this perennial turn to circumcision as an important backdrop against which more recent assertions regarding the procedure should be viewed. In this context it is worth noting that advocacy of circumcision as a public health response to HIV transmission existed well in advance of any credible data (Szabo and Short 2000).

Medicalized male genital cutting developed during an infamous period of experimentation in genital surgery on both sexes (Barker-Benfield 1975), when a belief emerged that both male and female genital cutting cured masturbation, which was thought to cause degeneracy and insanity. Circumcision allowed the Victorians to manage cultural anxieties regarding masturbation (Miller 2001, Hodges 2005) and, arguably, it was curing masturbation that was understood as the most important health benefit of circumcision (Miller 2002, Darby 2003). This 'war' on masturbation was connected to the more general desire to curb or tame masculine sexuality. Indeed, the efficacy of circumcision was so widely accepted that it was enthusiastically advocated as a prophylactic for all manner of ills, exemplified by J.M. McGee's promotion of the practice in the 1880s:

> I would favour circumcision … independent of existing disease, as a sanitary precaution [because] … (1.) The exposure of the glans to friction etc., hardens it, and renders it less liable to abrasion in sexual intercourse, and consequently venereal ulcer. (2.) It is acknowledged to be useful as a preventative of masturbation. (3.) It certainly renders the accident of phymosis and paraphymosis impossible. (4.) It prevents the retention of sebaceous secretion and consequent balanitis. (5.) It probably promotes continence by diminishing the pruriency of the sexual appetite. (McGee 1882: 103–5)

By 1910 circumcision had become the most common surgery in the United States and it remains so to this day (Miller 2002, Bell 2005). Almost identical arguments appeared in British publications. For instance, in 1900 E. Harding Freeland called for universal circumcision in response to syphilis. In his paper, he noted a countervailing argument based on damage to the penis:

> [I]t has been urged as an argument against the universal adoption of circumcision that the removal of the protective covering of the glans tends to dull the sensibility

> of that exquisitely sensitive structure and thereby diminishes sexual appetite and the pleasurable effects of coitus. Granted that this is true, my answer is that, whatever may have been the case in days gone by, sensuality in our time needs neither whip nor spur, but would be all the better for a little more judicious use of curb and bearing-rein. (Freeland 1900: 1869)

The central importance of managing male sexuality is also evident later in the twentieth century when, in the *British Medical Journal*, R.W. Cockshut argued that one benefit of removing the foreskin was the diminishment of the libido:

> I suggest that all male children should be circumcised …. Civilization … requires chastity, and the glans of the circumcised rapidly assumes a leathery texture less sensitive than skin. Thus the adolescent has his attention drawn to his penis much less often …. (Cockshut 1935: 764)

Such accounts highlight key themes that recur within the pro-circumcision discourses that have dominated the medical literature for 150 years. This confluence of Victorian (and later) preoccupations goes some way to explaining the rapid up-take of circumcision in the early years of the last century and how and why it has endured.

A Racialized History

Turning to the specific history of campaigns to circumcise African-American men, pro-circumcision advocacy in the late nineteenth century was underpinned by depictions of black masculinity as bestial and uncontrollable. In this context the medical profession inflated general concerns about male sexuality when their attention turned to black masculinity. The (familiar) focus for these medical discourses was the connected tropes of hygiene, venereal disease and male sexuality. In line with Hickey's assertions above, a general desire to curb male sexuality was heightened by constructing black masculinity as an extreme or more animalistic version of 'normal' white masculinity (Weinberg and Williams 1988). While circumcision was promoted as part of a general preoccupation with hygiene, such concerns were regarded as especially pressing for black men. Thus, an editorial in *Daniel's Texas Medical Journal* in 1889 supported J.M. Vandavel's call for compulsory circumcision of black male infants. The journal reprinted a talk given by Dr Vandavel to the Coloured Physicians' Association where he had advocated such compulsion: 'the coloured people, being ignorant of the laws of hygiene, should be enlightened, while taken under a kind of sanitary protectorate' (Editorial 1889). Vandavel's main argument was couched in terms of preventing venereal disease, which was linked in the popular imagination with hygiene and race. In arguing for compulsory circumcision, principally to prevent syphilis, he noted that this would be especially advantageous for 'the coloured people of the South land, where virtue is so slovenly and so loosely worn by our women, morality so little valued, and the marriage relationship so easily adulterated, or sullied' (Vandavel 1889: 10). This rhetoric casts circumcision as the medical solution to ignorance, bad hygiene and low morals in the black population. It is premised on an understanding of the black man as 'a sexual predator, a threat to White southern womanhood and White male sexual hegemony' (Nagel 2000: 12).

As Hickey has argued, this preoccupation with black male sexuality after Emancipation marks a shift from the focus on black women's sexuality during slavery (Hickey 2006: 169). The medical and popular demonization of male sexuality as a threat to white womanhood had underpinned racist laws designed to maintain white hegemony (Bardaglio 1999). As Hazel Carby explains,

> White men used their ownership of the body of the white female as a terrain on which to lynch the black male … [A] patriarchal system that had lost its total ownership over black male bodies used its control over women to attempt to completely circumscribe the actions of black males. (Carby 1986: 308–9)

Characterizing black male sexuality as excessive and primitive in this way legitimated scientific attempts to manage it. In seeking to explore 'the causes that drive [black males] to seek the females of the white race', circumcision campaigner Peter Charles Remondino turned predictably to circumcision:

> From our observations and experience in such cases, we feel fully warranted in suggesting the wholesale circumcision of the Negro race as an efficient remedy in preventing the predisposition to discriminate raping so inherent in that race. (Remondino 1894: 3)

The *Maryland Medical Journal* remarked of his proposal, 'whilst male Jews are noted for their strong sexual proclivities, such a character as a Jewish rapist is never heard of' (1894: 345). As Remondino continues, echoing his earlier and equally polemical *History of Circumcision* (1891), this was not true for African-Americans – a difference he attributed to the foreskin:

> It would certainly be more humane for a State legislature to pass an act legalizing and enforcing circumcision as a preventive measure, just as it would enforce either vaccination or quarantine regulations, than to enact laws to castrate or eunuchize the accused after his infraction of the laws. The many burnings, hangings, shootings and stonings that have of late taken place should suggest the search for the physical cause of this law-breaking and of some preventive measures; the radical means adopted by mobs certainly cure the burned, hung, shot or stoned to death, but they seem in no wise to act as preventative in others. Circumcision, as a preventive measure, certainly stands at the head of all possible suggested measures. (Remondino 1894: 4)

While he was undoubtedly an evangelical supporter of circumcision as a cure for most of Victorian society's ills, Remondino's work exemplifies a trend in medical discourse throughout the eighteenth and nineteenth centuries to justify, rationalize and legitimate racist beliefs through the racialized body, and to invoke science to support 'natural' differences between the races, between 'civilized' and 'primitive' (Saint-Aubin 2002: 248).

His attention to the foreskin, and his assertion that circumcision could avert lynchings, resonates with Robyn Wiegman's description in 'The Anatomy of Lynching' of nineteenth-century understandings of black sexuality as tied to the 'bestial excess of an over phallicized primitivity' (Wiegman 1993: 458). These racist constructs, and the interplay of race, sexuality and disease that has characterized circumcision discourses, persisted well into the twentieth century, as the following quotation from 1949 illustrates:

> Through the ages, Jews have universally been circumcised on the eighth day after birth. This procedure has given them protection against venereal disease even when they have been exposed. Though they may be promiscuous in their own race, Jews certainly are less promiscuous than Negroes .... The sex education of most Negroes is meager. In Negroes there is little circumcision, little knowledge or fear of venereal disease and promiscuity in almost a hornet's nest of infection. Thus the venereal rate in Negroes has remained high. (Hand 1949: 345–6)

Context

By attempting to historicize contemporary debates and policy developments, we are not suggesting that contemporary advocates of circumcising African men are racist. Nor do we impugn the motives of those seeking a solution to this health crisis. The imperative for action in this region is clear. The majority of the world's population infected with HIV live in sub-Saharan Africa. Sixty-eight per cent of adults and nearly ninety per cent of children infected with HIV globally are located in this region (Esacove 2010). Nevertheless, the historical context is particularly relevant since public discourse on the pandemic displays a strong racial overtone, with AIDS 'no longer represented as a gay plague but an African one' (Montgomery 2007: 267). Uncovering earlier medical debates about circumcision that are located within wider discourses of sex, infection and race demonstrates the need for extreme care in formulating health policy – which is reinforced when similar constructions of black sexuality emerge in some contemporary African AIDS discourse. As Esacove observes,

> As is the case with the epidemics in the West, African AIDS is attributed to bad moral character and unbridled desire. The difference is that sexual identity (i.e. male homosexuality) was understood to drive the early epidemics in the United States and Western Europe, while African AIDS is understood to be driven by an inherent, animalistic and ritualistic 'traditional' African sexuality. (Esacove 2010: 85)

In a similar vein, Tamsin Wilton argues that the white imaginary has constructed the epidemiological trend in the West

> as the global norm and declared that the (putatively *abnormal*) high rate of heterosexual transmission in the so-called Third World – specifically sub-Saharan Africa – was due to pre-existing abnormalities, failures or pathologies among the (black) indigenous populations. (Wilton 1997: 5)

We agree with Simon Watney's suggestion that these responses to HIV/AIDS deploy a 'discourse of "promiscuity" which drifts out and across the Mediterranean to incorporate the entire African subcontinent and beyond, recharging "the Orient" with a deadly cargo of exoticism that reminds "us" that negritude has always been for whites a sign of sexual excess and death' (Watney 1988: 74). Thus, in the history of Western responses to the spread of the virus in Africa it has been – and continues to be – suggested that black African men covertly engage in homosexual sex or abnormally violent heterosex, are uncontrollably promiscuous, have multiple sexual partners including prostitutes, and so on (Esacove 2010).

In summary, we have offered a history of the emergence of medical male genital cutting in the second half of the nineteenth century that reveals the central concerns with hygiene, sexually transmitted disease, and controlling male sexuality. Specifically, we have drawn attention to the racist constructions of black masculinity as bestial and excessive that underpinned public health campaigns to circumcise African-American men. We have also highlighted the ongoing relevance of this history when we noted the persistence of racist constructions of black masculine sexuality in some contemporary public health discourse and the continued social contingency of our understandings of disease and health. In the following sections we outline the emergence of circumcision in response to the contemporary HIV/AIDS crisis in sub-Saharan Africa. We stress the limitations of the evidence gathered to date and how this threatens the role of circumcision as an effective health intervention, particularly since women's health is not directly protected by the procedure. Thus, although we have been concerned with constructions of male sexuality that underpin the advocacy of circumcision, we are conscious that such a preoccupation with public health interventions on men renders women who are affected by these policies invisible. Further, contemporary public health policies, like earlier circumcision discourses, construct specific subjectivities and recode familiar anxieties. They fit within a public health model whereby a focus on already marginalized groups allows privileged groups to negotiate or manage anxieties, much as past circumcision policies have done. Identifying marginalized groups who are labelled 'unhealthy' or 'risky' allows privileged groups to articulate and project anxieties regarding chaos, excess, disease and death (Lupton 1995: 75). Given the impact of these policies on women, the remainder of this chapter underscores the need for feminist scholars to engage with the social construction of masculinity and the male body within health and other discourses.

Circumcision and HIV/AIDS

As we have sought to demonstrate, the complex history of medically justified male genital cutting is tied, in part, to concerns about male sexuality, hygiene and race (Gollaher 1994, Darby 2005). Given the repeated turn to circumcision as a 'solution' or partial solution to sexually transmitted disease, notwithstanding the lack of conclusive scientific data as to its efficacy in preventing such infection (Bonner 2001), it is perhaps unsurprising that it figured prominently at an early stage in the HIV/AIDS crisis. To some commentators it was clear that there was a drive on the international stage to link circumcision status and HIV status, and that this had the effect of silencing many questions and marginalizing sceptics (Dowsett and Couch 2007).

A randomized controlled trial in Orange Farm, South Africa in 2005 was the first to establish a connection between circumcision status and the rate of HIV transmission in a clinical setting (Auvert et al. 2005). The results were subsequently duplicated in Uganda (Gray et al. 2007) and Kenya (Bailey et al. 2007). These trials, in countries where the virus is endemic and where penile–vaginal intercourse is the predominant mode of virus transmission, established that over a 24-month period circumcision reduced the risk for men of acquiring HIV by 51–61 per cent. In each trial, those men assigned to the group who were circumcised had a lower incidence of HIV infection in up to two years of follow-up study compared to men assigned to a control group who did not have the procedure. The Joint United Nations Programme on HIV/AIDS (UNAIDS) and the World Health Organization (WHO) subsequently hailed the results of the three African studies as 'an important landmark in the history of HIV prevention' and recommended that mass circumcision programmes be introduced throughout sub-Saharan Africa (WHO/UNAIDS 2007). In April 2009 a Cochrane Review reported on the effectiveness of male circumcision as a prevention strategy (*Cochrane Database of Systematic Reviews* 2009). It concluded that there was strong evidence that medical male circumcision reduces the acquisition of HIV by men engaging in heterosexual sex by a rate of between 38 and 66 per cent over a two-year period. The Review called for further research to assess the feasibility, desirability and cost-effectiveness of implementation within local contexts. We argue that the absence of an adequate evidence base raises concerns when countries across Southern Africa are currently promoting circumcision as an official part of their HIV campaigns (Arie 2010). While the internal validity of the randomized controlled clinical trials has been generally albeit not universally accepted, the external validity, that is the generalizability of the scientific results from the specific contexts of the trials, remains unproven (Green et al. 2010). Indeed, there has been a notable lack of research aimed at verifying this essential aspect (Green et al. 2010: 479).

In the next section we respond to the concerns raised in the Cochrane Review regarding implementing these policies in the light of evidential gaps pertaining to external validity. Specifically, we raise an issue that is glossed over in the scant ethico-legal debate on the circumcision trials and resultant policy, which is the desirability or otherwise of rolling out mass circumcision programmes that, whatever their protective potential for men, have potentially adverse consequences for women (see Fox and Thomson 2013). Being attentive to the male body imagined within circumcision discourse therefore leads us to question the impact of these policies across the populations affected – that is, the circumcised men and their sexual partners.

Male Circumcision, HIV, and Making Women Visible

Critical commentaries on the circumcision trials highlight the barriers to translating clinical trials into effective health policy, and the importance of distinguishing efficacy (health improvement under ideal circumstances, in expert hands) from effectiveness (impact on health, under real-world conditions, for entire populations) (Imrie et al. 2007, Fox and Thomson 2010). Yet public health programmes are being rolled out without the necessary additional research having occurred and with scant regard for meeting ethical criteria (Fox and Thomson 2012). Clearly this poses considerable health risks to the men and boys upon whom surgery is performed. However, it is also salient, in a volume on feminism and masculinities, to examine how pro-circumcision policies have implications for women's health too. In our view, these policies pose risks to both men and women given that they are incompletely supported by research and rely, in part, on particular and problematic understandings of masculinity.

In 1998 Peter Piot, then executive director of UNAIDS, characterized AIDS as a 'women's epidemic' (Piot 1998). Indeed, as a virus transmitted largely through sexual intercourse, HIV inevitably poses questions about the patterns and dynamics of gender relations (Bujra and MKake 2000). We suggest here that, given dynamics in heterosexual relations, there is a danger that the mass roll-out of circumcision may exacerbate the already disproportionate effects of the health crisis on women (Wilton 1997). It should be remembered that the majority of new HIV infections in high-prevalence areas are in women (Jewkes et al. 2010). Women between 15 and 24 are at the greatest risk of HIV acquisition, and in some areas – such as South Africa – the prevalence of infection for women in this age group is nearly four times that of young men (HIV Incidence, Behaviour and Communication Survey 2008). Finally, women represent about 60 per cent of all people living with the infection in sub-Saharan Africa (UNAIDS/WHO 2009). These statistics, coupled with how the caring burden created by the disease predominately falls to women, clearly position HIV as a feminist issue.

Equally, 'responses to AIDS are influenced by cultural background and historical experience' (Sikwibele et al. 2000: 60), and it certainly appears that the strategies of supranational bodies including UNAIDS, and private foundations such as the Gates Foundation, have failed to recognize this cultural specificity. International responses tend either to be premised on medical interventions (drugs, vaccines, and so forth) or to stress the importance of prevention. Both types of response raise ethical issues. In the former case, the impoverished conditions that have contributed towards HIV/AIDS becoming endemic in sub-Saharan Africa mean that many of the most costly treatments will not be accessible to African HIV/AIDS patients (Saito 2000). Ethical considerations and cost effectiveness therefore frequently point to prevention. Circumcision straddles both the biomedical and preventative approaches, since it is clearly a medicalized intervention that, as we have illustrated, has had a chequered history as a prophylactic. Increasingly it is positioned as a preventive strategy alongside condom use, partner reduction, and abstinence before marriage and fidelity within it – what Baylies has termed the 'predominant trio' of prevention strategies (Baylies 2010: 17). Yet such health promotion strategies will succeed only if they acknowledge the gendered power differentials within many relationships. Crucially, these prevention interventions all depend on men complying with a regime of being tested, circumcised, using condoms and so forth, and are underpinned by an individualistic model that requires individuals to make the 'right choice' (Esacove 2010: 94). As Baylies notes, such models are often inappropriate to the lives of women who lack power to influence the behaviour of their male partners and they also 'take insufficient notice of the broader context in which behaviour and particularly gendered behaviour occurs' (Baylies 2000: 17). Moreover, the centrality of such attempts to 'responsibilize' individuals, relieves those involved in policy development of any obligation to consider the broader structural issues that contribute significantly to this and other health crises in this region. Esacove, in her analysis of AIDS prevention policies in Malawi, criticizes the emphasis in public health strategy on modifying individual behaviour. She details how Malawian public health discourse relies on a highly moralistic narrative of good and bad sex, with HIV transmission attributed to 'backward and ignorant villagers, particularly sexually powerless women and sexually brutish men' (Esacove 2010: 95). Her analysis shows how this narrative repeatedly returns to individual responsibility, even when purportedly addressing structural and social drivers of the epidemic (Esacove 2010: 87). It 'focuses prevention efforts on the form of relationship in which individuals have sex rather than on sexual practices themselves or the structural and economic context in which people have sex' (Esacove 2010: 104). We argue that it is against this backdrop of highly moralistic and individualistic interventions that pro-circumcision policy needs to be evaluated. Within this matrix of social forces, we are particularly concerned with how women's lower cultural and economic status and their lack of power to influence sexual relations are key to the heterosexual spread of the epidemic (du Guerny and Sjoberg 1999). As Heise and Elias observe, 'in large measure, women's vulnerability to HIV infections derives from their lower status in society' (Heise and Elias 1995: 931). This socio-economic inequality intersects with biological factors to leave them acutely vulnerable, yet public health initiatives often fail to make connections between gender, disadvantage and health, notwithstanding how they compromise women's health (Rogers 2005).

In the context of circumcision, the impact on women's health has too often been downplayed or ignored. Following the three African trials, further research has sought to test the parameters and limitations of the clinical findings. A study by Miller et al., for instance, concluded that circumcision had no protective effects for men who have sex with men (Miller et al. 2008), and research by Wawer et al. found that circumcision fails to offer the same protection to women as it does to men (Wawer et al. 2009). Nevertheless, circumcision is advocated as offering long-term benefits to women as it is argued that it will lower the overall viral levels in a population. However, Marge Berer has questioned whether circumcision will ever afford women adequate protection:

> Whether male circumcision will ever become an effective means of preventing sexual transmission of HIV to women at a population level is highly uncertain because it will require a majority of men to be circumcised in any given population where HIV is prevalent before women can benefit as a group from the reduced HIV prevalence. (Berer 2007: 45)

Her point is important. Even if they succeed in reducing transmission to men, circumcision programmes will not reduce the infection of women for at least 10–20 years, and even this would require an ambitious 70 per cent take-up among the male population over a very short period (Berer 2007). Indeed, such policies could increase harm to women, as the protection offered by circumcision is misunderstood, the ability to negotiate condom use is compromised, and risk compensation behaviour increases. Risk compensation behaviour (specifically 'condom migration' – the move away from condom use) is particularly dangerous should it occur before the wound has properly healed. Infected men who have sex in this period are likely to increase the chances of their female sex partners acquiring HIV (WHO/UNAIDS 2007). The Wawer study showed that the 'HIV acquisition rate in partners of circumcised men who resumed sexual activity before wound healing was 27.8%, compared with 9.5% in partners of men who underwent circumcision but delayed sex until healing and 7.9% in the partners of uncircumcised men' (Wawer et al. 2009). Serious ethical questions are thus raised by trials that appear to increase the risk of HIV transmission to partners who were HIV free when they commenced (Berer 2008, Okwusoa et al. 2009). Thus, Berer observes that insufficient attention has been paid to the 'highly problematic' fact that male circumcision policies are 'the only HIV prevention intervention that do not protect both partners to some extent' (Berer 2008: 171). Given that women are already disadvantaged, we would argue that it is crucial that public health intervention attend to issues of gender equity.

In addition to the risks that these policies pose to women, a further problem with the circumcision 'solution' is its potential to deflect attention and resources from proven prevention strategies. Women are rarely the target of HIV research, or the focus for media interest in research developments. This arises from the preoccupation with men's bodies and masculine sexuality, and a privileging of technology. As Green et al. argue, we should be concerned by the 'tendency of both men and women to ascribe undue power to a technical fix for what must remain a matter of human control, as in the use of condoms and other safe sex practices' (Green et al. 2010: 481). Yet, some research initiatives that aim to protect women from the virus support the need for further work in this area. An interesting example is a study in Malawi that confronts the gender power imbalance identified as at the heart of women's experience of the disease. This research, by Baird et al., randomly assigned 3,796 young women aged 13–22 years to two groups, with half the women receiving cash payments of varying amounts. For some women, payment was dependent on school attendance, but this was not the case for others. After 18 months' follow-up, girls in the cash group who were in school at the start of the study had a 60 per cent lower HIV prevalence than those who received no payment. This held whether the payment was conditional or unconditional. It is hypothesized that the result was attributable to a reduction in transactional sex with older men. The effect increased with the amount of money paid, suggesting that extreme poverty was a key influence on these women's sexual choices (Baird et al. 2010). A further study of note is the CAPRISA 004 trial, where investigators found that a microbicide containing 1 per cent tenofovir reduced a woman's risk of infection by 39 per cent. The protective effect of the gel increased with consistency of use. Women who used the gel in more than 80 per cent of sex acts had a 54 per cent reduction in HIV infections (Centre for the AIDS Programme of Research in South Africa 2010). This is the first positive trial result after 20 years of microbicide research. Commenting on a number of trials on women, McCoy et al. note that such research illustrates that 'serious investment in upstream, economic prevention approaches that respond to the realities faced by adolescent girls and women is still needed' (McCoy et al. 2010).

Of course, addressing structural societal problems inevitably entails adopting a long-term perspective. Yet since the international community is willing to fund circumcision programmes where any potential benefit for women from a successful population level roll-out will only be felt after 10–20 years (if at all), it does not seem unreasonable to argue for the simultaneous resourcing of similarly long-term programmes that are designed to tackle structural problems that exacerbate the burden that HIV/AIDS imposes on women. In this regard Jewkes et al. have recently established that inequitable gender relationships and intimate partner violence increase the risk of HIV infection in young South African women and account for a substantial proportion of HIV infections:

> Qualitative research has shown that the links between HIV/AIDS, gender inequity, and gender-based violence lie in the patriarchal nature of society, and the ideals of masculinity that are based on control of women and that celebrate male strength and toughness. These ideals readily translate into risky sexual behaviours, predatory sexual practices, and other acts of violence against women. (Jewkes et al. 2010: 41)

This demonstrates how particular masculine ideals make it difficult for women to insist on the condom use that is a necessary complement to circumcision. As

UNAIDS and others have reiterated, since circumcision only provides a partial protective effect against the transmission of the virus, it must be understood as one part of a broader prevention strategy. Yet, as we have seen, this too often ignores the impractical and moralistic tone of such polices, particularly where women lack power to persuade male partners to reduce multiple and concurrent partners and commit to consistent condom use. Furthermore, misunderstanding the partial nature of the protection afforded by circumcision may make it even harder to negotiate condom use in such relationships. Such factors are still more difficult to address in a violent relationship: 'Violence prevents women from influencing the circumstances of sex, resulting in more frequent sex, and less condom use' (Jewkes et al. 2010: 42). Additionally, violence intersects with activities that increase risk to women: 'exposure to gender-based violence … is associated with high-risk sexual behaviour, including multiple and concurrent sexual partnerships, substance use, transactional sex and prostitution' (Jewkes et al. 2010: 42). The study by Jewkes et al. concluded that 13.9 per cent of HIV infections could be avoided if equity in heterosexual relationships was enhanced (Jewkes et al. 2010: 46). Engaging with questions of gender inequality and how masculinity is implicated in such relationships takes us back to our earlier discussion of the racist construction of African-American masculinity in medical responses to sexually transmitted diseases, notably syphilis. In order to engage critically with the role of masculine norms in the HIV/AIDS pandemic we must be wary of reifying stereotypes of excessive black masculinity, while recognizing that the place of ideals of masculinity and their impact on women's health has generally been absent from public health debates and initiatives. Furthermore, highlighting gender inequalities should not obscure the complexity of structural problems and the ways in which poverty and colonial histories permeated with racial and gender discrimination contribute to the HIV/AIDS crisis (Coovadia et al. 2009).

In considering public health initiatives, we therefore argue that the ways in which women are marginalized must be addressed. Specifically, any potential negative impacts on women need to be taken into account in formulating policy and allocating resources. As we have shown, a number of interventions to promote women's health have had positive outcomes, yet attract much less attention than circumcision. It will not, however, be enough simply to attempt to encompass women within public health policies or to shift the focus of such policies from men to women. Such strategies could prove equally problematic, especially if women continue to be represented as vectors for – or victims of – the disease. Baylies and Bujra criticize a continuing tendency in NGO discourse 'to focus on women rather than on gender relations and, in spite of apparently adopting a gender neutral discourse, to treat women as merely victims' (Baylies and Bujra 2000: 48). This, they argue, contributes to the construction of powerful ideological imagery that blames the victims, and (further) deflects attention away from basic causes (Baylies and Bujra 2000).

Conclusions

Presenting a draft of this work at Emory, Atlanta was a task with considerable resonance. It was timely in that the Centers for Disease Control and Prevention in Atlanta were reconsidering domestic circumcision policy in the light of the African HIV/AIDS research. It was also laden with many troubling histories, specifically the history of racial human rights abuses committed by medical practitioners and scientists, often in the southern states, and as recently as the 1970s. The effects of Tuskegee continue to inform African-American attitudes to medical practice and research (Hickey 2006). Tuskegee, the historic pro-circumcision narratives considered in this chapter, and the many other medical and scientific campaigns that yoked black male subjectivity to a hyper-sexualized, deviant and animalistic physiology suggest that it is incumbent on us to pause and assess critically the clamour for mass circumcision programmes in sub-Saharan Africa and elsewhere. As Dowsett and Couch note, such advocacy cannot be confined to the specific region or sub-regions:

> The collateral wash-over of the heretofore poorly managed international debate and loosely generalised discussion … is already having effect in other places. That effect is not related to the evidence – available only from sub-Saharan Africa – a very specific type of evidence from specific places. (Dowsett and Couch 2007: 35)

More generally in terms of concern for equality, the lack of specifics – the 'collateral wash-over' – generates broader questions about Western responses to public health crises in Africa. Responses to the three African trials – that is, the desire to generalize across the sub-Saharan region and further afield – collapse differences in a way that homogenizes the continent, ignoring ethnic and racial differences. Practically, there is a scientific failure to recognize 'the quite specific contribution of places, times, social networks, populations and cultures to all successful prevention programmes' (Dowsett and Couch 2007: 35).

The repeated return to circumcision in shifting public health contexts also suggests caution. Enthusiasm for circumcising African men (ironically after at least three decades where female 'circumcision' has been an international human rights issue) needs to be weighed against this history and earlier racist constructions of black masculinity within pro-circumcision campaigns. More generally, the history of public health interventions is littered with campaigns that under the pretence of health promotion have attempted to regulate sexuality and gender (Esacove 2010: 86). Global AIDS policy can be located firmly within this trend:

> [H]istorical account[s] of venereal disease control efforts in the early- and mid-twentieth-century United States provide[] an eerie preview of contemporary global AIDS prevention policy and the specific configuration of heteronormativity on which it is based. These early campaigns enforced the ideas that idleness

> leads to irresponsible sexual activity and that men's sexuality is driven by an uncontrolled nature, as well as the division of women into 'good' (those in need of protection) and 'bad' (those who act as disease vectors). (Esacove 2010: 86)

Finally, and as we have argued, circumcision programmes endanger women's health and risk diverting attention from other intervention strategies that may better serve women's health and women's interests. As Jewkes et al. have asserted, organizations driving HIV prevention agendas need to ensure that policies, programmes and interventions to build gender equity are developed and implemented (Jewkes et al. 2010: 47). To continue to write women out of public health debate and policy, as we argue these policies do, could be devastating in the current context.

Chapter 8
The Challenge of Pleasure: Let's Talk About Sex in Feminist and Masculinity Studies Theorizing

Chris Beasley

Introduction

When I was initially thinking about the paper[1] that gave rise to this chapter, I was driven by two things. On the one hand I have a sense that we all – and perhaps young people in particular – are constantly bombarded with images of sexual identity by a range of cultural forms. This bombardment amounts to a provision of sexual education by privatized commercial sources, with sexuality presented in terms of material consumption: 'Buy this, be sexy.' On the other hand, I have a sense of missed opportunity. What I mean is that critical, non-commercial voices regarding sexuality seem to me to be offering a decidedly limited alternative. I assert that we need to undertake a rethinking of sexuality and sexual health (of sexual citizenship) that attends to significant existing absences in critical non-commercial writings concerned with sexuality.

These critical voices – which include writings arising from Gender/Sexuality Studies, and from the Preventive Health field such as sex education policy materials – aim to offer alternative understandings of heterosexuality and masculine sexuality to those that are on offer in the popular media. Yet such critical approaches remain undeveloped, largely negative and/or focussed upon danger/risk rather than considering *heterosexuality* in terms that might encourage young men in particular to be inspired by the possibilities of egalitarian sexual practices and embrace the aim of ending sexual violence.

There appears to be a gap between the cacophony of popular commercial voices about (hetero)sexuality and the comparatively silent and largely negative critical voices in Gender/Sexuality Studies that might be expected to provide a counterpoint. As Michael Kimmel and Rebecca Plante note in *Sexualities* (2004: xv), there is a concerning conjunction of a proliferation of sexuality throughout

1 This chapter draws on a paper originally titled 'Problems and Possibilities for Masculinity Studies in Relation to Violence', presented at the Feminism, Law, and Masculinity Conference, The Feminism and Legal Theory Project, Emory University School of Law, Atlanta, Georgia, USA, 11–12 September 2009.

modern culture (or at least a proliferation of certain forms of it) with a simultaneous lack of serious substantive 'conversation' about it. The gap leaves heterosexual pleasure to privatized voices and effectively abandons a strategy for alternative visions and social change. While I certainly acknowledge that presently it seems almost impossible to get away from (hetero)sex, there is a lack of critical address. As in drugs policy (where the coolness of drugs in popular culture is poorly countered by drug policy that fails to attend to its pleasures) (Race 2008, Diprose 2008), so for (hetero)sexuality.

However, while I intend to question the primarily negative orientation of such critical approaches towards heterosexuality, this questioning is not undertaken in order to reinscribe heteronormativity or fixed sexuality/gender categories. In looking to reconsider heterosexuality and its pleasurable possibilities, I reject both the idea that sexual relations are a power-neutral, 'free' zone for individual pleasure-seeking construction and the revisionist account of heterosexuality as an option in a fluid smorgasbord. Rather, I wish to open up the possibility that, like gender (Gatens 1996: 178), heterosexuality is not monolithic (Flood 2008), that it encompasses constraints and possibilities. Heterosexuality is located as a form of 'being' organized by 'collective assemblages' (legal, medical, and so on) (Deleuze and Guattari [1980] 1987: 94), yet it is also a plane of unpredictable practices that exceed such containment. Moreover, I focus on heterosexuality because of its significance in terms of developing policies/strategies regarding sexual violence and because I see it as the most problematic arena in analyses of sexuality at this time.

My concern is to develop this overall analysis by outlining three interconnected arguments. Writings in (1) the Gender/Sexuality field and (2) in Preventive Health, share a particular approach to heterosexuality. The Gender/Sexuality field involves approaches that inform Preventive Health with regard to sexual health. Yet this field contains heterogeneous trajectories that have had the effect of leaving heterosexuality stuck in the mire of the old 'sex wars' debates, such that it remains almost exclusively aligned with the second-wave Modernist 'sex-as-danger' camp of the sex wars debates. Preventive Health agendas attending to sexuality – in particular, sex education in schools – draw upon Gender/Sexuality writings. However, despite certain elements of the 'pro-sex' approach, the crucial focus on prevention/pre-emption of danger and risk within Preventive Health (including sex education) also predisposes it to fall back upon the primarily negative sex-as-danger orientation with regard to heterosexuality. Writings in both the Gender/Sexuality field and in Preventive Health, in short, have a primarily negative sex-as-danger approach with regard to heterosexuality. What this means is that, (3) the two critical non-commercial voices that are the focus of this chapter are not able to attend to hetero-pleasure. This is perhaps particularly of interest when considering Masculinity Studies and its approaches to sexuality, in the light of the problem of sexual violence.

But why would lack of attention to hetero-pleasure matter? Existing research indicates that recognition of pleasure in sexual health education results in increased negotiation of sexual practices. As will be outlined in greater detail later in the chapter, it would seem that attending to hetero-pleasure generates greater gender equity. Philpott et al. (2006b), for example, note examples from several countries that indicate the variety of ways in which consideration of pleasure in sexual health education and campaigns encourages greater negotiation and choices in heterosex – including more active arbitration by women, the possibility of enhancing women's arousal and thus involvement in sexual activities, and increased acceptance and enjoyment regarding negotiated usage of both male and female condoms to reduce the risk of STIs (including HIV/AIDS) and unwanted pregnancy (see also Garcia and Goldman 2004). Hetero-pleasure, in other words, has ramifications for a range of strategies concerned with encouraging more equitable relations between men and women, such as anti-violence strategies. This means that *not* attending to hetero-pleasure in Gender/Sexuality – and specifically Masculinity – Studies, as well as in Preventive Health writings, begins to look like a problem.

Heterogeneous Trajectories in the Gender/Sexuality Field

The Gender/Sexuality field (which is a crucial source for alternative understandings of masculine sexuality and anti-violence agendas) contains disparate subfields – importantly, the three major subfields of Feminist, Sexuality and Masculinity Studies – with distinguishable trajectories. Tensions between these heterogeneous trajectories in the Gender/Sexuality field then impact upon analyses of heterosexuality.

I have suggested elsewhere that the three main subfields of Feminist, Sexuality and Masculinity Studies in the Gender/Sexuality field are not simply commensurable bits that fit together neatly like pieces of a jigsaw. The subfields contain differing knowledge cultures involving (amongst other things) different theoretical underpinnings and emphases (Beasley 2005). On this basis I argue that, since the 1960s/70s, the subfields have aligned in shifting ways, and that this is particularly evident in relation to sexuality. Initially Feminist and Masculinity Studies developed closely linked Modernist theoretical paradigms under the rubric of the term 'gender'. However, with the rise of Postmodern approaches Feminism and Sexuality Studies have moved closer to one another in terms of overarching theoretical frameworks. By contrast, Masculinity Studies increasingly appears as 'the odd man out' (Beasley 2009). This dissonance between the subfields became explicit in the 1980s so-called 'sex wars' and has continuing effects in relation to analyses of heterosexuality.

Feminist/Sexuality/Masculinity Studies and the Sex Wars

Feminist and Masculinity Studies literatures – that is, Gender Studies literatures – have been in an ongoing 'conversation' with Sexuality Studies writings. A crucial theme in this conversation may be summarized as the 'pleasure and danger' 'sex wars'. The sex wars amounted to a debate between on the one side *Modernist radical feminist* (Gender Studies) thinkers like Catherine Mackinnon, Andrea Dworkin, Susan Griffin and Mary Daly, amongst many others, talking about 'sex as danger' in the 1970s/80s, and on the other side the growing influence from the late 1980s/1990s of *Postmodern* thinkers associated with Sexuality Studies, talking usually from a Foucauldian and Queer Theory perspective about 'sex as pleasure': the 'pro-sex' position. In short, the sex-as-danger stance became aligned with Modernist feminist thinking and the pro-sex stance with Postmodern thought in feminist and sexuality thinking.

Modernist radical feminist writers like Catherine Mackinnon and Andrea Dworkin in the 1970s/80s drew attention to the ways in which sexuality was socially constructed along gendered lines to uphold men's social dominance. They noted the links between normative heterosexuality and displays of men's power over women such as rape, and were rather courageously critical of penis-centred conceptions of sexuality. They were consequently inclined to depict women as a group as vulnerable and men as a group as predatory. In this analysis, men and women were categorically divided. The emphasis was on gendered power and in this context men's sexual power over women.

The Modernist radical feminist approach was, in short, focussed on the 'danger' of heterosex, and the evils of prostitution, pornography and rape. In this account men were 'hegemonically abusive' (Heise 1997: 423). Though men had access to pleasure, it was oppressive sexual pleasure. Lesbians, by contrast, because they were women, engaged in gentle womanly sexual pleasure. Heterosexual women appeared predominately as passive victims who had no fun at all, or at least not with their sexual partners (Kanneh 1996: 173). Importantly, this sex-as-danger position remains the most common viewpoint in Masculinity Studies today since – along with feminist work on violence – it remains one of the last bastions of support for Modernist radical feminist agendas. At a simple level this point about Masculinity Studies can be observed by means of a schematic content search of arguably the premier journal in the field, *Men & Masculinities*. In the 13 issues of the journal at the time of writing – from July 1998 to October 2010 – there are 252 articles in which 'sexuality' is referenced and at least 55 per cent of these are concerned with sexual violence, while out of 112 articles broadly referencing 'pleasure', less than 12 per cent could be said to consider this (at least in terms of heterosex) in ways that do not focus on pleasure as domination.

However, this sex-as-danger stance increasingly came under fire from the 1980s onwards with the rise of the so-called 'pro-sex' or 'sex-positive' approach (Echols 1983, Echols 1984, Rubin 1994, Califia 1996, Sullivan 1997, Epstein and Renold 2005). The pro-sex stance set itself in opposition to radical feminism in particular and was strongly associated with the rise of Foucauldian Sexuality Studies and Queer Theory developed by theorists like Judith Butler, Gayle Rubin and Steven Seidman. These theorists were considerably less attached to gender categories and, relatedly, were disinclined to presume that gender relations effectively determine sexuality (Beasley 2009). Moreover, sex in this approach was precisely about embracing danger, power, and even consensual violence.

This shift in focus towards pleasure did not, however, produce a renewed understanding of heterosexuality, because the pro-sex position was primarily, even almost exclusively, about minority sexualities, frequently named as queer sexualities. In such pro-sex theorizing, queer minorities were discriminated against, but at least they now all had fun. Heterosexual men were still sexual and still nasty. And heterosexual women largely disappeared from sight, probably because of the sheer embarrassment in this pro-sex context of being so boring. They were still stubbornly having no fun at all (Beasley 2005: 122–3, Jackson 1999: 13–15).

The pro-sex stance was a new development but it basically attended to minority (queer) sexualities, and largely ignored heterosexuality, except as that which was mentioned in passing in order to be refused. Minority sexualities were deemed as the 'home' of queer (Ahmed 2006, Chancy 2008, Shugart and Waggoner 2008), or at least oppositional to the extent that they resist approaching heterosexual normalization (Richardson 2004). Heterosexuality, by contrast, was largely simply cast as 'compulsory' sexuality; its transgressive pleasurable possibilities remained invisible. Heterosexuality was for the most part merely the starting point against which the pro-sex approach constituted itself.

Although theorists like Valocchi (2005) have asserted that Queer thinking offers a challenge to the heterosexual/homosexual dichotomy, conceptions of transgression in Queer theorizing that make any reference to heterosexuality are typically restricted to slippages in heterosexual identities towards the non-heterosexual (see for instance, Jagose 1996: 3, Muňoz-Laboy 2004). A 'queered' (transgressive) heterosexuality is, with few exceptions, seen as an oxymoron (Beasley 2011, Beasley 2005: 112). In sum, while the pro-sex stance has become important in Gender/Sexuality Studies, this pro-sex viewpoint has almost never been applied to heterosexuality.

The upshot of theoretical tensions and shifts in the Gender/Sexuality field expressed in the sex-wars debates is that heterosexuality is simply rarely examined nowadays in Gender/Sexuality Studies writings. There are, for example, very few current (post-1998) books on heterosexuality (Jackson 1999, Holland et al. 1998, Johnson 2005, Scott and Jackson 2007, Hockey et al. 2007, Ingraham 2008). Heterosexuality is largely taken to be of little critical interest, as simply to be equated with heteronormativity, and remains mired in the old sex-wars divide. In that debate heterosexuality is cast by the sex-as-danger perspective as immured in gendered inequality with an emphasis on its nasty and normative features. More recently, the combined Feminist/Queer pro-sex perspective has become prevalent, but in this approach non-heterosexual queer becomes the site of subversive, transgressive, exciting and pleasurable sex, while heterosex continues to be locked into its earlier constitution as problematic. Insofar as heterosex is mentioned at all in such pro-sex theorizing, the emphasis only shifts somewhat from earlier conceptions of it as largely nasty and normative to the implication that it is boring and normative (see Halley 2008). These existing accounts of heterosex as either primarily nasty or boring, but in any case normatively exclusionary, do not provide much room for manoeuvre (Beasley, Brook and Holmes 2012).

In essence critical scholarly voices in the Gender/Sexuality field have almost frozen and remain largely undeveloped regarding *heterosexuality*. To the extent that it is discussed, these voices effectively confine heterosexuality to the abandoned backblocks of theoretical history by leaving it stuck in the predominately negative sex-as-danger camp. For example, it is almost impossible to find any account of heterosexual men's pleasure in Masculinity Studies that does not presume desire = damage. Only gay men's desire involves permissible pleasure. Similarly, if we look at International Studies writings attending to sexuality it would seem that predatory men and vulnerable women abound (Peterson and Runyan 1999, Bayliss and Smith 2001, Tickner 1992, Tickner 2001). More specifically, most of the limited debate on sexuality in a global context has been fashioned by themes of trafficking, slavery and rape in war, themes largely dominated by gendered representations of male victimizers and feminine victims (Sabo 2005, Re-public 2008, Women's Worlds Congress 2008).

Such themes are unquestionably crucially significant. As noted earlier, I do not intend to discount the weight of Feminist and Masculinity Studies critiques of heterosexuality. However, I do want to challenge heterosexuality's comparative absence in contemporary Gender/Sexuality thinking and challenge its continuing restrictive constitution as unremitting cruelty and pain in the service of oppressive normativity. Heterosexuality is a majority orientation but, relative to other sexualities, it is under-theorized as a potential source of pleasure, interest and transgression, and over-determined as a source of domination (Beasley, Brook and Holmes 2012).[2] Such a stance offers little in the way of strategic directions for positively engaging young men (or young women) in the development of an egalitarian heterosexuality. This failure regarding strategies relevant to young men is perhaps particularly ironic in the case of Masculinity Studies.[3]

It is here that the intriguing status of Masculinity Studies as 'the odd man out' in Gender/Sexuality thinking – as at a distance from the now more thoroughly pro-sex agendas of Feminist and Sexuality frameworks – comes home to roost, since Masculinity Studies' general advocacy of a sex-as-danger stance may well have concerning implications for its capacity to reconceptualize heterosexuality, hetero-masculinity and sexual violence strategies (Beasley 2009).

The problematic analysis of heterosexuality in Gender/Sexuality theorizing reoccurs in odd ways in the Preventive Health field and thus in sex education materials.

Preventive Health, Sexual Health

Preventive health has constituted itself as a field of thinking that moves beyond the narrowly instrumentalist medical model of health, which emphasizes disease

2 I am indebted to Heather Brook for this way of expressing the problem.

3 The comment is also relevant to feminist work on violence.

and illness. The way in which the more expansive Preventive Health theoretical framework is expressed in sexual health is evident in the definition of the World Health Organization (WHO), revised in 2002. This definition states,

> [s]exual health is a state of physical, emotional, mental and social well-being related to sexuality; it is not merely the absence of disease, dysfunction or infirmity. Sexual health requires a positive and respectful approach to sexuality and sexual relationships, as well as the possibility of having pleasurable and safe sexual experiences, free of coercion, discrimination and violence. For sexual health to be attained and maintained, the sexual rights of all persons must be respected, protected and fulfilled. (WHO 2002b)

In the Preventive Health framework, sexual health not only has physical and mental aspects (biomedical aspects), but is also defined within a social framework. Sexual health is further defined in an *affirmative* way, stressing *positive well-being* and not just stating *the absence of negative qualities*. In other words, there are important links here with the pleasure-oriented pro-sex position I outlined in the sex-wars debate previously. This association is evident in the WHO (2002a) definition of sexuality:

> [s]exuality is a central aspect of being human throughout life and encompasses sex, gender identities and roles, sexual orientation, eroticism, pleasure, intimacy and reproduction.

What, then, is the problem? Preventive Health appears to be attending to pleasure quite adequately. However, while Preventive Health sometimes has a rhetorically expansive pro-sex framing, it frequently fails to live up to its promise. It frequently falls back into more traditional models of health. This is because Preventive Health as a field – at least in relation to sexuality – draws upon a dual legacy: the influence of Gender/Sexuality field (evident in its attention to gender/sexuality justice) and a concern with health as management of risk. Broom (2008) and Diprose (2008), amongst others, have outlined and problematized the crucial focus on prevention of danger and risk within Preventive Health. This dual legacy induces a predisposition to fall back upon the primarily negative sex-as-danger orientation with regard to heterosexuality. In many, if not most, accounts of sexual health, the sex-as-danger feminist position I discussed earlier is reborn as populations and individuals being exposed to health 'risk' (on 'risk' see also Beasley and Bacchi 2007). More affirmative and expansive accounts of (hetero)sexuality, which enable consideration of hetero-pleasure, become sidelined. The question is, how does this regression to a primarily negative account happen?

Sexual Health becomes aligned with danger and 'risk' with regard to sexuality via *both* medicalized and social versions of risk management. In the first instance it lapses into an instrumental *medicalized* account of sexuality, reinforcing a focus on sexual 'problems' conceived in biomedical terms. For an example of this, consider the first World Congress for Sexual Health in April 2007. With a classic Preventive Health conference theme of 'Achieving Health, Pleasure and Respect', the main topics were as follows: Sexual Health, Basic Science on Sexual Function, Desire Disorders, Arousal Disorders, Orgasm Disorders, Sexual Pain Disorders, Sexually Transmitted Infections, Cultural Studies on Sexuality, Sexuality Education, Endocrine Disorders, Gender Dysphoria, Sexual Paraphilias, Sexual Violence, Issues in Reproductive Health, Sexuality in Special Populations, Studies in Human Sexuality, Sexual Orientation, Ethics. This rather grim and decidedly medical-looking list contains an awful lot of disorders, infections and dysfunctions (First World Congress for Health 2007). The list reveals the tendency in Preventive Health to discard its more expansive pro-sex claims in favour of returning to medical management.

Secondly, even when Preventive Health models of sexuality do not lapse into miserable medicalization, more socialized versions of 'risk' frequently still dominate. For example, in the fourth edition of *The Puberty Book* (Darvill and Powell 2007), a book recommended by a doyen of Preventive Health in the arena of sexuality, Family Planning Australia, in answer to the question 'Can sex be fun?' the answer is,

> [s]ex can be lots of fun … it depends on the circumstances. If both partners want to have sex together and are protected against unwanted pregnancy or catching an STI, it is more likely to be enjoyable. (Darvill and Powell 2007: 127)

A pro-sex agenda quickly becomes, 'avoid pregnancy and don't get STIs'. Tellingly the clitoris gets four lines in this book, while vaginas get over twenty. This is, I should add, one of the better Australian books for adolescents.

Non-consensual heterosexual sex and sexual violence is undoubtedly a worldwide concern. Obviously paying attention to sex as danger/risk *is* important. For example, the 2003 Australian Study of Health and Relationships (ASHR 2003) and the 2003 National Survey of Australian Secondary Students (Smith et al./NSASS 2003) both show a significant pattern of forced sexual activity (Combes and Hinton 2005). Yet sex education is not compulsory in Australian schools and there is no nationally consistent curriculum for teaching teenagers about relationships or sexual and reproductive health. This is not a problem in Australia alone. Furthermore, most sexual health education programmes throughout the world remain restrictively focussed upon biomedical and reproductive information. As the 2003 Australian Study of Health and Relationships – the largest and most comprehensive survey of sexuality undertaken in the country – has revealed, sex education in schools gained 'top marks' from young people in terms of learning about technical 'mechanics', but apparently gave little clue about the interactive including pleasurable aspects of the enterprise (Powell 2007, ARCSHS 2003). SHine SA (Sexual Health Information Networking and Education 2008), the leading sexual health agency in South Australia, also reports that 80 per cent of young people regard sex education in schools as useless or fairly useless. Similarly, a joint report to the British government on sexual health in 2005, fuelled by the 'risk' of teenage pregnancy rates, stated that sex education in schools provides basic factual biological information but beyond that was extremely limited and even confused (Campbell 2005). Sex education of even this meagre sort is, of course, under threat in the USA (Irvine 2000).

However, perhaps an even more important limitation of sex education programmes is the insistent use of fear and risk of disease to try to motivate people to practice 'safer' sex (Philpott et al. 2006a). In this setting it is no wonder that there is considerable evidence that 'the "official" discourse of sex education [does] not relate to teenage lives' (Chambers et al. 2004: 397–415). Specifically, the sex education curriculum almost entirely evades minority sexualities, but it also all too often neglects the complicated process of choices regarding sexual behaviour, and is *de-eroticized*. My point here is that a proudly pro-sex orientation in sexual health agendas can still involve a heavy dosage of regulatory imperatives and does not necessarily produce attention to pleasure, even to hetero-pleasure.

For example, the SHARE Project (a sexual health programme for upper-level high-school students in South Australia that ran between 2003 and 2005 under the auspices of SHine SA) strongly emphasized its holistic Preventive Health framing. Yet SHARE was explicitly shaped by concerns about risk and danger, and although the programme did stress being positive about sex, at the same time it could barely mention pleasure. This is not a criticism of SHARE, which faced vitriolic attack by Christian right-wing lobbyists precisely for its 'pro-sex' stance (Gibson 2007), but simply to point out that Preventive Health in sexuality – even in its more progressive manifestations – is rarely in practice about sexuality. It is rarely about doing sex, let alone about experiencing or giving pleasure, and much more about health as regulatory management of social risk.

Debra Lupton, along with many others who offer critical perspectives on Preventive Health, employs Foucault's work on the modern surveillance of bodies to discuss its risk/danger orientation (Lupton 1994: 20–40, Lupton 1995). Is this the answer? Should we simply turn away from the Modernist sex-as-danger approach and adopt a Postmodern Foucauldian pro-sex stance? While I see advantages in the latter perspective, I am not sure this analysis is sufficient either. The Foucauldian pro-sex camp does at least bring Queer sexualities into view. However, it is inclined to equate pleasure almost exclusively with Queer sexualities, while heterosexuality = heteronormative and heterosexual women simply disappear from view. The Foucauldian pro-sex stance may not be the answer. Indeed, as I have noted in relation to sex education programmes such as SHARE, a pro-sex framework, affirming sex is 'healthy', does not get us very far. It certainly does not necessarily involve recognition of pleasure.

Recognition of Pleasure in Sexual Health and Strategies for Sexual/Gender Equity

What if we refused the sex-wars binary of danger versus pleasure and took a different direction? What if a concern with risk – with making sex safe – and a concern with pleasurable sex were not mutually exclusive? In this context, existing research indicates that recognition of pleasure in sexual health has resulted in greater safety, in increased use of condoms by men, and greater involvement of women in negotiation of sexual practices (Philpott et al. 2006a, Ingham 2005, The Power of Pleasure 2010, Holland et al. 1992). There are now, for example, a number of studies in a variety of settings, including Cambodia, Thailand, Senegal, Mexico, the Dominican Republic and India, indicating both that failure to attend to sexual pleasure is a key factor in non-use of condoms and that increased acceptance of pleasure in sexual health programmes and campaigns is highly effective in producing safer, more enjoyable and more actively negotiated sexual practices (Philpott et al. 2006b, Philpott 2004, Cornwall and Jolly 2006, Scott-Sheldon and Johnson 2006; see also The Sambhavana Trust 2010, Easy on the Eye 2010, Masturbate-a-thon 2010, SHEPP 2010, Chi Chi LaRue 2010). One example of the effective employment of pleasure to support progressive innovations in gender/sexual relations may be found in campaigns promoting the female condom as an erotic accessory.

Recognition of pleasure paradoxically appears to produce more egalitarian rather than non-consensual sexual relations between men and women. This research information is not just relevant to prevention of disease. Recognition of hetero-pleasure can in other words inform a shift towards *positively* reconstructing men's identities. Positive, pleasure-and-safety-focussed approaches are capable of evoking what White terms 'alternative' or 'subjugated stories' concerning gender/sexual equity. They are a strategic resource in supporting and promoting forms of masculinity that can embrace egalitarian negotiation and that exclude violence against women (White 2000, White 2005, Jenkins 1990).

I have attempted here to indicate the limits of a primarily negative orientation that emphasizes danger and warnings. I have suggested that both Gender/Sexuality scholarly writings and Preventive Health sex education materials remain captured by precisely such a *narrow* agenda. Yet it is possible, even likely, that without attention to hetero-pleasure we shall not engage young heterosexual men. Moreover, without engaging young men, anti-violence discourses run the risk of continuing by default to leave young women with the task of being responsible for 'risk management' of sexuality and sexual violence (Carmody 2005). While pleasure is not the answer to everything, we must face growing evidence that promoting pleasure when discussing sex is likely to encourage forms of sexuality that are safer and more egalitarian. Talking about pleasure is *not* necessarily at odds with safety, but instead may well produce it.

Conclusion

I suggest we may need to move away from the standard binary thinking of the old 'sex wars'. Both Gender/Sexuality writings and Preventive Health in the form of the sexual health literature tend to be populated by vulnerable wombs and vaginas and troublesome penises. Perhaps we could instead learn from aspects of the HIV/AIDS work and refuse to accept the established binary of pleasure versus danger, such that 'safe sex' can also be hot sex. For Masculinity Studies this must mean a rethinking of understandings of (hetero)masculinity and sexual pleasure. As Moira Carmody (2005) puts it, we need an 'ethical erotics'.

Strategies to encourage egalitarian (hetero)sexuality, and to end sexual violence, must move beyond conceptions of heterosexuality simply as a problem and instead *generate* positive identification with forms of hetero-masculinity attuned to egalitarian sexual practices. Putting hetero-pleasure back into Masculinity Studies, and into sex education, is not just a question of getting out the aromatic oils and an exotic massage book, but is a deeply political question.

Chapter 9
Gender, Masculinities and Transition in Conflicted Societies[1]

Fionnuala Ní Aoláin, Naomi Cahn and Dina Haynes

Introduction

We are overwhelmed with information about countries undergoing transition from conflict to post-conflict status with the assistance of the international community. Importantly, such a transition is not always a move from war to peace – consider Afghanistan, the Congo, Iraq, or arguably Sudan – but instead, from conflict to less conflict. In this chapter we seek to explore the role that gender plays in the construction and implementation of the post-conflict transitional process. We focus on examining the gendered dimensions of societies emerging from extreme, systematic and institutional violence by multiple parties. Our question in regard to all of these countries, in all of these varying transition processes, is what we term 'the gender question'. Where are women to be seen, and how are they visible within the processes that define and shape the cessation of communal violence? How should peace processes approach the forms of masculinity that dominate in situations of endemic violence? How should peace processes address the emergence of 'hyper' masculinity in such contexts? What does the absence of gender signify, and how does such absence affect the substance of any particular agreement (whether local or international) to end violence? How does the failure to properly ask and answer 'the gender question' undermine the short-, medium- and long-term reconstruction of post-conflict societies?

In this chapter, we first explore how conflict affects men and women differently, and introduce the gender lens that we use throughout our analysis. We then examine issues related to the emergence of certain kinds of 'hyper' masculinity in situations

1 The ideas in this chapter were first presented at the Feminism, Law and Masculinity Workshop at the Emory Law School in November 2009. An earlier version was presented at New England Law | Boston as the Hirsch Lecture, which honours the memories of Anna Hirsch and Mary Jo Frug. We thank Martha Fineman for all of her support on this project, and the *New England Law Review* for allowing us to republish the Hirsch Lecture article in this collection (Naomi Cahn and Fionnuala Ní Aoláin, *Hirsch Lecture: Gender, Masculinities, and Transition in Conflicted Societies*, 44 New Eng. L. Rev. 1 [2009]). This chapter is derived from our book on gender and post-conflict reconstruction, titled *On the Frontlines: Gender, War and the Post-conflict Process* (2011, New York: Oxford University Press).

of conflict and in subsequent peace-building attempts. Next, we argue that a failure to account for and to be cognizant of these specific masculinities has a significant effect for women in particular, as well as the success of the conflict transition process. Finally, we show the critically significant impact of a gender lens by considering the effect of violent masculinities on Disarmament, Demobilization and Reintegration ('DDR') programmes.

Conflict and Gender: Women

Conflicts fundamentally affect the lives of men, women and children. Women face gender-specific issues during and after wars that men do not, including pervasive sexual violence, forced impregnation, reproductive violence, sexually transmitted diseases, and forced abortion. Women and their children experience internal displacement and dominate the refugee populations across conflicts. Women are also differentially affected because of their roles as primary caretakers of the household and family. In this regard, traditional gender dichotomies may be further entrenched and exacerbated during times of extreme violence.

Surprisingly, the transitions born of conflict may yield positive social, economic and political changes for women. For example, during some conflicts in which aspects of a functioning state and economy continue to exist, women can take on roles as workers and labourers outside of the home, opportunities that would never be available were the society not in conflict. Rosie the Riveter, the archetypal woman who was employed in the Second World War to help with the military effort and subsequently transformed the war experience into economic opportunity in the post-war period for women, exemplifies a well-known American illustration of this phenomenon.[2] In this way, conflict can open up intended and unintended spaces for empowering women, 'effecting structural and social transformations and producing new social, economic and political realities that redefine gender and caste hierarchies' (Manchanda 2001: 99).

Despite these potentially positive aspects, in most contexts the result of conflict for most women is a negative sum. Economies stall during and after conflict or operate in black and grey markets where women are the least often employed or employable because of their legally enforced second-class status. Across most post-conflict transitions, women are the first to be fired and the last to be hired with the large exception of the false (and temporary) economy built up around the presence of the international community, in which women are paid to fill the 'camp follower' positions as housekeepers, cooks and administrators, and, of course, for sex. Women and children also constitute the overwhelming number

2 Family law and feminist scholars have noted that the post-war opportunities came with a later backlash in the 1950s with a renewed conservatism about the role of women in society and a return to fixed roles in a way that reversed many of the earlier advancements (May 1999: 49–80, McEnaney 2000: 448).

of refugees, and of people displaced from their home communities. The very fact of war can contribute to undermining the limited social stability and security of women in many societies, which is the precursor to any exertion of economic or social autonomy.

We stress that women's roles should not be essentialized, even in the context of war. Women are frequently violent actors themselves in violent and conflicted societies, both in undertaking primary acts of violence and in lending substantial support to men who carry out such actions. Importantly, recognizing that women can be violent has practical consequences. For example, it provides the means to acknowledge that women who have also been combatants face an array of social and cultural challenges that simply never arise for men during and after war. Accepting and accommodating a more diverse range of roles for women both in war and post war facilitates a greater conceptual and practical understanding of the lived intersectionalities of most women's lives. Equally, a practice of gendering our analysis of violence thus 'cannot be conceptualized without understanding the process of knowledge production as such epistemic practices intersect with the specific prevailing cultural and political conditions' (Shalhoub-Kevorkian 2009: 65). In reality, however, these diverse and highly gendered patterns are rarely identified as coexisting simultaneously for women and not factored into peacemaking agreements and transitional structures.[3]

Conflict and Gender: Men

A fairly substantial amount of literature has been generated over the years regarding the forms of masculinity that emerge in times of armed conflict and war (Goldstein 2001, Yuval-Davis 1997). Theorists have identified an organic link between patriarchy, its contemporary outworkings, and various forms of masculinity as they arise within societies and institutions. A preponderance of literature across disciplines has deepened our understanding of how masculinities are constructed and differentiated (Chodorow 1994, Connell 1987). While war literature across many disciplines has made significant conceptual and practical use of the term 'masculinity', the concept has been less applied and less understood to be relevant in the post-conflict context. In accepting that masculinities study is a diverse and burgeoning field, we stress that it has significant insights to offer to the analysis we wish to advance here (Connell 1987, Kimmel 2005a).

Masculinity theorists and feminist analysis have not always worked in tandem, and it is only relatively recently that feminist scholars have sought to address what

3 In this context Shalhoub-Kevorkian uses the concept of 'frontliners', women who occupy parallel and sometimes conflicting roles in violent societies. They are both constrained by highly patriarchal systems and yet, as a result of the limitations placed on men, have access to and agency within the public sphere (Shalhoub-Kevorkian 2009: 4–5, 62–7, 96–7).

masculinity studies has to offer feminist theorizing (Dowd 2000). In this vein, we start by asking the 'man' question, interrogating where and how men are situated in relation to the creation, perpetration and institutionalization of violence. In what ways does hegemonic masculinity work, and how do masculinities operate to benefit even those men who are at the margins of masculinity norms and practice? Somewhat ironically, even within the hierarchies of masculinity, subordinated masculinities can benefit from the social construction of male privilege and value.

While an enormous amount of scholarship has been generated about the varying forms of masculinity and their effects, of particular interest to our analysis is the lens of 'hyper' masculinity. In our emphasis on hypermasculinity, we draw on Angela Harris's definition of 'a masculinity in which the strictures against femininity and homosexuality are especially intense and in which physical strength and aggressiveness are paramount' (Harris 2000: 793). We frame our analysis by affirming that other kinds of masculinities coexist with hypermasculinity, but notably in situations of conflict and endemic violence, hypermasculinity plays an enlarged and elevated role. Its social traction is intensified when violence is endemic, and other social strictures are slackened, and the unloosening of these patterns and hierarchies is particularly fraught in the post-conflict process.

One clear parallel for non-conflicted states is to analogize the emergence of hypermasculinity with the role of the military in multiple cultures and societies. The military is closely tied with manhood, and, indeed, militaristic actions are supported by an ideology of male toughness (Goldstein 2001: 5–6, Theidon 2007: 76). Self-evidently, men dominate most national and international militaries. By the time the conflict ends, men who have acted militarily and the (generally) male political elite are deeply enmeshed in this cultural vision of manhood. As former combatants in Colombia explained to anthropologist Kimberly Theidon, for example, joining a paramilitary group allowed the men 'to "feel like a big man in the streets of their barrios," to "go out with the prettiest young women," and to "dress well," privileges they insist would not have been possible if they weren't carrying a gun' (Theidon 2007: 76). We suggest that the prevalence of this kind of masculinity poses complex issues for undoing violence, for mainstreaming gender equality, and for remaking societies that have been fractured and deeply divided.

Post-conflict societies present a unique and under-analysed site of examination for masculinities. One of the main reasons for the lack of attention to masculinities in this domain is the presumption that the post-conflict context is equated to peace and that the absence of war makes moot any analysis of masculinity, which may be presumed 'tamed' by the end of violent contestation. This presumption fails to account for the ways in which women experience violence both in conflicted and in post-conflict societies. The result of this lack of attention to masculinities means a failure to account for the myriad of ways in which masculinities transform, adapt and reformulate in the post-conflict environment. Consequently, close attention to the forms and impact of masculinities in the post-conflict milieu is critical not only for women's experiences in the process, but also for the success of the transition itself.

Indeed, the post-conflict environment, like conflict, is also 'vividly about male power systems, struggles and identity formation' (Handrahan 2004: 433). There may be an enormous flux in the male post-conflict fraternity both on an individual and on a communal level. Moreover, international organizations and institutions, typically headed by male elites, are arriving to reconfigure the transitioning society. So, men who were in power are losing power, other men (domestic and international) are taking their place, and, as is often the case when a conflict stalemate arises, internationals (generally culturally and politically differentiated other males) are coming into a society to fill a vacuum.

One enduring question that emerges from the conflict and masculinities literature is, why do men engage in violence? Without over-digressing, we point out that violence, as an aspect of masculinity, is deeply linked to the assertion of social status and the value of self in particular contexts. Violence may literally 'make the man' in many societies, and not infrequently the site of the violence is the woman's body. In recognizing such deeply rooted links between the constructions of the masculine self, and the social acceptance of 'manhood', we acknowledge the difficulties that arise as we address the end of violence (as a formal legal matter). The end of violence is not a superficial engagement, but may require deep and difficult entanglement with the masculine construction of self in many societies. In post-conflict societies, such conundrums are compounded by the lack of other opportunities available to men to assert positive masculinities, and to have practical and symbolic roles within societies that struggle on the economic margins and are deeply politically dysfunctional.

This question of violence and its ending is central to the post-conflict experience because the cessation of public violence between (generally) male combatants is usually the litmus test by which the success of transition from war to peace is measured. We take issue with the presumption that the end of *public* violence and the measurement of security based on the safety of *male* combatants should constitute an adequate calculation of peace in any society. While analysis of the causality of violence is central to addressing transformation in the post-conflict environment holistically, issues of causality are extremely complex, dependent on variations in social and cultural contexts. The analysis is also made more complicated by a deeper recognition of the role that masculinities play in giving rise to violence, and the difficulties of transforming such practices on a fundamental level. Nonetheless, greater attention to causality is entirely relevant to addressing women's experience of violence as well as to implementing measures in post-conflict societies that meaningfully address the need for women's security.

The causes of violence and conflict in a range of societies are far too complex to explore here (Scherrer 2002). But a number of cluster causalities are useful to identify: first, economic and social insecurity; second, a lack of legal and political status particularly associated with group or ethnic identity; and third, the lack of opportunity for meaningful self-determination (whether external or internal) within the state. In multiple contexts, engaging in violence is a rational choice for men when few other opportunities may be provided to gain economic security (albeit that participation in violence provides a highly tenuous economic existence or longevity), social status and value within their communities, and security (again albeit tenuous and fragile) for their families and communities. As post-conflict literature has begun to explore, there is a strong overlap between all these causal categories and the emergence of certain forms of masculinity in conflicted societies. Without addressing the causalities outlined above within a framework that integrates masculinities, we may also fail to address the ongoing realities of how masculinities closely interconnect with post-conflict social, political and economic outcomes.

Beyond a more nuanced recognition of international masculinities, we also want to address a more complex set of role assumptions for men and women in post-conflict societies. This requires asking the fundamental question, what does it mean 'to be a man' in a violent society, when violence begets status and economic capacity? Even more relevant to our inquiry, what happens to such masculinities when societies transition from violence and move towards democratic or more liberal forms of political engagement? Which men lose and gain in such contexts? As both Brandon Hamber and Amy Maguire have explored in post-apartheid South Africa and transitionary Lebanon, women often bear the brunt of the flux in masculine roles (Hamber 2006: 22–4, 26, Maguire 2009: 226). The theoretical gains made by women in status and legal protection are much more complex in reality. One female participant in a study of women's experiences of post-conflict security in South Africa has noted,

> I think, in as much as the law of the country allows women to be empowered, that is going to have a spin-off effect on men's behaviour and men's attitudes towards women. In particular, those so-called empowered women. They'll always be the subject of abuse … everywhere you go … if you are perceived to be an empowered woman you are subject to a lot of abuse from society in general. (Maguire 2009: 226)

The link between formal (generally equality) gains made by women in many post-conflict legislative and constitutional enactments, conjoined with the political displacement of power for many men from the traditional routes provided during armed conflict, creates a complex social and legal terrain. It is upon this territory that women's gains and their intersection with masculinities in flux are played out. Formal gains for women may, in fact, be nullified or significantly constrained by the reality of social and community context, in which the accommodation of men's deeply entrenched social status may outweigh the enforcement of formal legal norms in practice (Rubio-Marin 2009: 63). Moreover, the social realities that women confront in highly patriarchal societies are propped up and perpetuated by masculinities in action – limiting in subtle and crosscutting ways the reach of law.

It is also vital to contextualize the reality of economic fragility faced in post-conflict zones around the world. Countries emerging from conflict are some of the poorest on the planet.[4] They have the highest number of refugee populations (who are predominantly female with child dependents) and internally displaced persons.[5] In this context, when one domain of status and economic subsistence is closed off (by the end of violent armed conflict), such societies struggle to replace the dysfunctional economy of war with a functional liberal economy of provision. The tools that for some men provided a means of survival in war are unreliable and may no longer be needed. Men and young boys who are under- or uneducated are at a considerable and material disadvantage in such settings. In this space of economic struggle, Gary Barker and Christine Ricardo illustrate the rise in the parallel economics of criminality and 'normal' violence, which allow certain forms of masculinity to endure and provide both status and material needs (Barker and Ricardo 2005: 31–2). They note the particular difficulties of confronting violent masculinities in social settings that have operated to seal off men spatially from women and children. This is further compounded in societies that have deeply stratified gender roles, leaving little room for the expression of positive masculinities in either the public or private sphere. The effects of such stratification are also intensified when one accounts for intergenerational transmission of violent norms, as well as in societies where age stratification is intense, creating intense competition for economic and sexual resources as well as opportunities.[6]

The Gender Lens

Having explored how conflict affects both men and women, we want to affirm the importance of a gender lens and investigate its impact. The independent value of a gendered assessment of post-conflict processes remains contested. In the legal and political space of ending or transmuting conflict, women still struggle to assert the magnitude of issues that affect them directly. They remain subordinated by dominant discourses that minimize or ignore the value of placing the needs and views of women at the centre of the conversation about ending violent communal behaviours, even though such placement is absolutely central to ending societal violence. It needs constant restatement that women are the group most historically

4 As of 2010, Somalia's Gross Domestic Product (GDP) per capita was $600; Rwanda's GDP per capita was $1500; Burundi's GDP per capita was $600; and Columbia's GDP per capita was $9800 (Central Intelligence Agency 2010).

5 As of January 2009, Rwanda had 55,062 refugees; Somalia had 1842 refugees and 1,277,200 internally displaced persons; Burundi had 21,093 refugees and 100,000 internally displaced persons; and Columbia had 170 refugees and 3,000,000 internally displaced persons (UNHCR 2009).

6 The limits on access to land in sub-Saharan Africa are pivotal for the transmission of social status, marriage opportunity, and independence for young men (Barker and Ricardo 2005: 12).

marginalized and excluded from the peacemaking and peace-building processes across all jurisdictions and conflicts (Bell 2000). Applying the gender lens is critical to ensuring the effectiveness of policies and practices involved in ending conflicts and ensuring that they do not recur. Without this attention, traditional gender dichotomies may be further entrenched and exacerbated during times of extreme violence and extended in the post-conflict phase.

While women are missing from key roles in peace negotiations and government, they often dominate in civil society movements that create 'safe' and neutral spaces in conflicted societies. In this latter role, women often provide the grassroots networking and social support structures that are relied upon by local and international elites to embed peace processes. But this raises the issue of whether those involved in the reconstruction process essentialize women by reducing and collapsing their varied roles into a single dimension that relegates them to 'soft' civil society roles, rather than tangible roles entrenched in the political infrastructure. We remain consistently wary of essentializing women as peacemakers and facilitators when we are deeply aware of the complex set of roles women as individuals and as members of broader communities play in enabling and encouraging violence. Such essentialization also underplays the extent to which women play an underappreciated role in supporting and enabling certain kinds of masculinities to thrive.

Using the gender lens helps us understand that gender must become central to conflict resolution, peacekeeping, reconstruction, and reconciliation efforts. Integrating gender into the post-conflict process is insufficient unless gender is incorporated into all aspects and levels of the newly developing or rehabilitating state. For gender to be absolutely involved it must be addressed in every issue and at every level. In this view, it is insufficient for formal legal norms alone to confront the inequalities, violence and discrimination that women may have experienced during conflict, or for women to have an impact solely through civil society. Rather, a broadly framed set of imperatives is required that includes legal reform to address harm and exclusion and also takes account of the broader psycho-social and customary practices identified earlier in our analysis of masculinity in action. For example, gender inclusion has often focused almost exclusively on holding war crimes perpetrators accountable for sexual violence. We cannot, however, evaluate the credibility and value of such accountability mechanisms without an eye to the broader transitional and gendered dynamic of the society in question (Cahn et al. 2011). Moreover, we cannot hope to dislodge practices of violence towards women (before, during and after conflict) unless we are prepared for a hard interface with the social embeddings of violence in the individual identities and social practices of men.

In its broader context, our approach challenges conventional notions concerning the role, and rule, of law in post-conflict situations. For those of us trained to think in terms of legal solutions; of justice via international, regional or local tribunals; of prosecutions and investigations; and of evidence and trials, these concepts must be tested in countries with a minimally functioning justice system, with no means of protecting victim witnesses, and with only minimal assurance that genocide and gender-based violence will not recur. In these countries, we must be particularly sensitive to what role the law can and should play in ending impunity and restoring confidence that the war wounds can be healed. An emphasis on the relationship between masculinities and violence in conflicted and post-conflict societies permits us to identify a much broader array of enabling phenomena resulting in women's experiences of systematic violence. In doing so, we become acutely aware that formal legal mechanisms provide only part of the solution.

Finding justice for victims and punishing perpetrators is critical, but there are important contextual issues on how best to proceed to ensure that accountability occurs as countries struggle to establish new governments. In our focus on legal approaches, we must remember the practical realities that confront victims of gender-based violence as they continue with their lives, often living in the same communities as the perpetrators, and thus craft remedies that account for these differing, potentially conflicting, realities that themselves may reflect divergent constituencies: a need for punishment; a need for rehabilitation for both victims and perpetrators; and a need for moving on politically in a divided society.

Sites of Masculinity Struggle in the Post-conflict Environment: Disarmament, Demobilization and Reintegration

To show how a gender lens might matter, we turn to the process of Disarmament, Demobilization and Reintegration ('DDR'). DDR efforts are integral parts of peacemaking and development processes in multiple conflict situations. An extensive general literature has emerged on the subject of DDR (UNDPKO 2000, Berdal 1996: 73–6, Clark 1996, Hagman and Nielsen 2002, Kingma 2001, Knight and Özerdem 2004), as well as more particular case-study analyses, looking at particular countries and how they have reintegrated and demobilized (or not) former combatants (Brown and Hauswedell 2002: 22, Koth 2005: 5, Alden 2002, Schafer 1998: 208). DDR comes with strong instrumental and policy goals. At its essence it may function as the most important preliminary step in ending or limiting violent conflict. It can act instrumentally to facilitate control over armed forces (both state and non-state). Less obviously, DDR can create extraordinary vulnerabilities in societies where guns are 'both a threat *and* a source of security' (Theidon 2009: 19). Thus, addressing the full spectrum of gendered issues for men and women is a complex and highly variable task. The demobilization, demobilization and reintegration (with equal emphasis on all three elements) of former combatants clearly overlap with the production, control and maintenance of masculinities in conflicted and post-conflict societies.

DDR programmes do not follow one template, but they are typically discussed during the peace process and established after the peace accord has been signed, as one of the first components of implementation (UNDPKO 2000, Berdal 1996: 9, 73–6, Clark 1996, Hagman and Nielsen 2002: 1, Kingma 2001, Koth 2005: 25–6,

Knight and Özerdem 2004). Recall that women are significantly absent or excluded from the peacemaking process. Moreover, even where women are present at peace negotiations, the specific negotiation sites in which demobilization and security are agreed tend to be exclusively male and lack gender parity in representation, going hand in hand with the reality of women's lack of high-level status in the military and/or at the commander level of non-state paramilitary forces (Ní Aoláin 2009: 1080–82). Examples of the integration of demobilization with the formal peace deal include the Good Friday Peace Agreement in Northern Ireland, various versions of the Colombian peace process, and the demobilization of former combatants in Mozambique. It is generally agreed that DDR programmes should only be undertaken with certain conditions present, such as a peace accord that establishes the framework for DDR; a general sense of confidence in the peace process itself; minimal and meaningful levels of security; ownership of DDR by all relevant stakeholders; and basic guarantees of information and transparency (Aplon 2008, Ball and van de Goor 2006). Given the fractured nature, form and implementation of peace agreements, however, this rarely happens.

Traditional or 'classical' DDR programmes, which assume ideal – and rare – conditions, conceive of DDR as a set of technical interventions to assure, for example, effective containment of armed groups, collection and destruction of weapons, division of former combatants into those who will remain in or join the country's armed forces and those to be demobilized, and then the effective reinsertion, reintegration and rehabilitation of those demobilized into their communities of origin (Laplante and Theidon 2006: 57–8). The obvious point, of course, is that there is a variance of emphasis across most DDR implementations, but a general pattern is that demobilization gains considerable and quick traction while the reintegration and rehabilitation portion draws much less reflection, funding and applied enforcement from the state and the international community. DDR requires some minimal levels of security as a baseline for establishing the institutional structure for disarmament and for making former combatants feel safe in relinquishing their weapons. It also requires that all parties, including the former combatants and new government as well as international actors, commit to its implementation with consensus as to the basic outline of the process (Ball and van de Goor 2006: 5–6).

The most intensive operations occur post stabilization, during the transition and recovery period (UNDDRC 2006: 5–7). The actual implementation often starts with combatants voluntarily entering reception centres turning in weapons to begin the demobilization process (McKay and Mazurana 2004: 98). Such programmes are typically administered by a multilateral organization and/or the United Nations, and the World Bank and the United Nations are significant financial contributors (UNODA, Escola de Cultura de Pau 2009). These programmes, world wide, cost more than $1.5 billion per year, and they generally occur in some of the poorest countries (UNDDRC 2009). Because DDR processes depend on broader developments towards a peaceful environment, they are subject to frequent disruptions, and they seldom proceed in a linear fashion (Ball and van de Goor 2006: 11).

The existence of DDR raises complex questions in post-conflict or regime-change societies from a gender perspective. For example, disarmament has a high crossover with political decisions and compromises involving amnesty for human rights and humanitarian law violations, including amnesty for crimes involving sexual violence or violence against women.[7] In contexts where women are the least likely to be present at the negotiation, deals are struck that include amnesty for crimes involving sexual violation, mutilation, reproductive harms, the transmission of sexually transmitted diseases and HIV/AIDS, and forced impregnation (Transitional Justice Institute 2008). The amnesty is often the precursor to the DDR programme, and given that gendered harms may not be viewed as necessarily threatening the growing international consensus that certain crimes against humanity cannot be subject to amnesty (Mallinder 2008), the gendered fault line may simply not be noticed or assessed as a fundamental bias to such processes. This challenging nexus between gender and disarmament is important to highlight. Political compromises, including amnesty for serious human rights violations that have occurred during a conflict, mostly made by elite men, often fail to engage with the particular vulnerabilities created for women by partial or excluded accountability.

Gender perspectives are important to DDR for numerous reasons. First, armed conflict affects women and men differently, and that difference is seldom taken into account in designing and implementing DDR programmes. The obvious point is that women are often hugely affected in their day-to-day lives by the way in which a DDR programme is implemented. The range of effects includes the frontline exclusions that fail to accommodate women in compensation schemes and the internal effects that may include the return of violent men to their communities with little, if any, recognition of the potential harms that they may visit on their home environments, and little, if any, support to victims when subsequent harms occur. Second, under many existing programmes, women and men have unequal access to resources following conflict. Particularly in light of the gender bias and inequalities that underpin many societies, DDR may focus only on male combatants. What this means in practice is that the economic benefits that flow from DDR will rarely flow to women (even when they have been combatants in the traditional sense), and distortions of post-conflict economy can be linked to DDR payments. Third, achieving peace requires the inclusion of all members of society, male and female, and it is a long-term process. Peace remains elusive after civil wars in most post-conflict situations. Though DDR may be conceived as the means to deliver conflict endings in the short term, we caution that inadequate or poorly managed DDR programmes may in fact create further cycles of instability in a post-conflict

7 For example, Section 8 of the Belfast, or 'Good Friday', Agreement in Northern Ireland deals with security, referring to the 'normalisation' of security arrangements and practices. This is to include the reduction of armed forces, the removal of security installations and emergency powers, and other measures appropriate to and compatible with a normal peaceful society (Northern Ireland Office 1998).

society, leading inexorably to the perpetration of further communal violence. Finally, adding a gender analysis requires focusing specifically on men and issues of masculinity (U.N. Department for Disarmament Affairs and the Office of the Special Adviser on Gender Issues and the Advancement of Women 2001, Theidon 2009, Hamber 2007). By this we mean that close attention must be paid to the psycho-social dimensions that create and elevate the emergence of certain kinds of masculinity in society and rewards those men who exhibit these characteristics. Attention to this dimension requires valuing gender equality as a core dimension of the DDR process and preparing to posit the success of these programmes on the extent to which they actually operate to bring about a lessening of overall violence in a society (in both private and public spheres) as well as in handing over arms. We acknowledge, of course, that for DDR interventions to succeed, they must be designed in the context of each country's special circumstances, and consistently deploy gender as a centralizing mechanism.

Accordingly, using a gender perspective leads to a series of additional issues concerning the structure of DDR programmes. First, what constitutes disarmament sufficient to satisfy a ceasefire requirement in the political/military sense may not in fact entail the removal of all such weapons from the public and, more importantly, the private sphere.[8] An obvious linking issue is how to measure the success or failure of demobilization from a gender perspective (Cahn et al. 2011). This benchmarking for success through a gender-sensitive lens is markedly absent through many of the programmes that are heralded as success stories by the international community. Second, demobilization generally fails to address the deep imprinting of violent masculinities in former combatants and the effects of a militaristic culture on the civilians that surround him in the transitional and post-conflict context.[9] The underlying psycho-social dimensions that, in a conflicted society, have supported the resort to violence and the elevation of particular forms of masculinity that accompany it, are not in any sense undermined or addressed by a formal demobilization process. Thus, a key issue to be addressed concerning violence is what is meant by the term 'ending violence'. In the parlance of ending public violence or internal conflict, this conversation revolves around decommissioning weapons and getting armed paramilitaries/insurgents to swap violent confrontation for peaceful debate about contested issues. However, this kind of discussion rarely engages with the fundamental requirement of changing

8 Specifically, according to the UNDP, there are some 550 million small arms circulating in the world today (United Nations 2002). Only 41 per cent of these weapons are in the hands of the regular armed forces (European Union Press Release 2006). Many women express 'deep disappointment in the disarmament process'. For example, security threats have impeded women's ability to travel, study and work in post-Taliban Afghanistan (Human Rights Watch 2004a: 2, 4).

9 Notably, addressing masculinities requires paying attention to the ways in which women often actively participate in facilitating and supporting men's militarized masculinity (Theidon 2009: 29, Goldstein 2001: 306).

deep-seated social attitudes towards the use of violence (Amnesty International 2005).[10] Self-evidently, where discharged-but-not-disarmed combatants return to their homes and families with their weapons, the sites of violence may simply move from the public to the private sphere (Ní Aoláin 2009).

Attention to Masculinities

As societies transition from violence and move towards democratic or more liberal forms of political engagement, close attention must be paid to masculinities as part of the project of ending violence. Failure to account for and to be cognizant of these specific masculinities has significant effects for women, but more generally for the success of the conflict transition processes. DDR programmes struggle with 'what to do with the "morass of malignant male muscle" ... Men unable to positively manifest masculine roles may return to violent and destructive means of expressing their identities' (UNIFEM 2004). Factoring this psycho-social reality into the design and implementation of DDR programmes is a means to avert inevitable structural barriers to the success of a key element of conflict-ending processes.

Masculinities appear in several different ways throughout the DDR and other processes. First, socialization into male roles as both traditional head of household and then – as a result of the conflict – into the assumption of violent roles may be difficult to undo. The complexity and difficulty of this task should not be underestimated by policy makers, and it underscores that processes and policies sensitively attuned to the dynamics of embedded socialization will reap both immediate and intergenerational benefits.

The magnitude of this socialization lies with the complexity of managing the forms of violence that emerge in many transitional societies, a context that is acutely illustrated in the relationship between disarmament and intimate violence. As a starting point, underlying endemic sexual and domestic violence is never calculated into an overall accounting for the experience of violence during conflict. There is a strong and maintained presumption that sexual violence in war is a thing apart, an experience capable of being parsed out from the 'regular and normal' violence that accompanies women's lives in many societies. As feminist international law scholars have long noted, sexual and gender-based violence rarely conforms to the timelines of peace treaties and ceasefires but endures past them. The kinds of violence and sexual acts perpetrated upon women in conflicted societies endure as a form of entrenched 'othering' in such societies, and pervade

10 The study contains a sustained and detailed cross-jurisdictional study of the 'ordinary' impact of gun violence against women, and notes that, 'although available data supports the widespread assumption that most direct casualties of gun violence are men, particularly young men, women suffer disproportionately from firearms violence, given that they are almost never the buyers, owners or users of such weapons' (Amnesty International 2005: 6 [footnote omitted]).

the way in which women subsequently experience inequality, discrimination and exclusion. Many observers and commentators on post-conflict societies have asserted that there is a marked rise in the violence that women experience post conflict (Meintjes 2001: 4–18). Statistics in a number of post-conflict societies that measure such acts suggest, at least, a marked increase in reported violence (Sideris 2001: 153–7). There is, however, still a need for additional empirical evidence to document such an overarching trend, but at the very least, there is room to acknowledge the continued pervasiveness of violence for women when peace is theoretically won. This ongoing violence undoes a pervading premise that women and men experience the post-conflict gains in the same way.

Re-socializing Men

One of the central quandaries for the DDR process is how to undo the masculinities learned during wartime. Where discharged combatants return to their homes and families, the sites of violence may simply move from the public to the private sphere. From the gendered critique of accountability mechanisms, what we learn is that truth processes may examine the prior violence in the public sphere, but will not engage in any way with the continual violence that is facilitated in the private sphere by non-rehabilitated former combatants. The disconnect between the operation and scope of the transitional justice mechanism and the intimate and everyday realities of living with a former combatant for women could hardly be more starkly contrasted.

This disconnect has been graphically identified in such transitional societies as South Africa. For example, the perceived escalation of domestic violence rates post apartheid have raised deep concerns about the relationship between pre-existing apartheid violence and its spill-over to a transitional society. There is some evidence that post-conflict societies do (at least) statistically experience greater proportions of domestic and intimate violence (McWilliams et al. 1995). Thus, increased reporting at the end of conflict may not mean absolute empirical increases in violence per se; rather, it may simply mean that reporting is possible where it was not previously, and in fact, the forms of violence may be more muted. Nonetheless, while it remains open to further empirical investigation to assess the fullness of the relationship between violence during conflict and increased violence post conflict, what remains clear is that there is a continuum of violence for women and that the end of conflict is not the end of gendered violence. The normality of ongoing violence for women is itself broadly sustained through political transformations.

The reassertion of violence in the private sphere during the transitional phase may constitute a form of compensation for male combatants, for their loss of public status and hegemony (Pillay 2001: 36–45). This is graphically shown by the psychological phenomena of the returning warrior who has, through conflict, normalized the use of violence and views the home as another site in which to exercise power and control through physical force (Ní Aoláin and Turner 2007: 252).

DDR programmes can help to separate manhood from its violent and military meaning by providing positive, non-violent role models and means for achieving status. Kimberly Theidon observes that many of the former combatants in Colombia told her they were 'tired' of combat; she suggests that 'the DDR program [could] make more explicit what these men gain in the transition from combatant to civilian' (Theidon 2009: 32). In the Congo, for example, the DDR programme is collecting information on how programmes that involve men can dissolve gender stereotypes (MDRP 2007, MDRP 2009). Offering vocational education and creating employment opportunities in both the public and private sectors can serve to channel aggressive energy into more productive uses (Peacebuild 2008: 15). It is also evident that integrating men more positively into their family and parenting responsibilities offers some means to redress the complex roles that men must manage in the post-conflict context. Here, relatively simple moves, such as ensuring that families and children are integrated into the DDR process, can operate as positive transitionary measures to support both men and women and open up spaces for social transformation. Another important and related move is to extend and broaden the categories of combatants for the purposes of DDR programmes, ensuring that women who have provided support roles to military or paramilitary forces (as well as women who have been involved in direct hostilities) are included and fully integrated into structured DDR programmes (Alison 2009). This would assist both in ensuring that women combatants are not doubly marginalized by their involvement in military and paramilitary organizations, and that the opportunity is provided to affirm the status of women combatants (who frequently languish and suffer the post-conflict stigma of non-conforming gender roles as society returns to 'normal') and to include women fully in the benefits that flow materially and otherwise from demobilization.

Re-socializing men requires integrating the information known about the effects of hyper- and other forms of heightened masculinities into the planning and delivery of what are generally internationally constructed and supported DDR programmes. It means moving the emphasis away from merely handing over guns to neutral arbitrators and instead integrating psychological and reflective counselling into the demobilization of combatants. It requires a commitment to gender integration for DDR programmes, literally bringing the wives, partners and children of combatants where possible into the demobilization space, and utilizing the social connectedness of men to their families and children to affirm individual and group capacity for a different and positive masculinity. It mandates modelling for such men – bringing into the demobilization space men who have the capacity to act as accepted role models and who offer a different life perspective, functioning in a post-conflict yet perhaps still violent society. Ultimately, and far more difficult, it requires providing other economic and social opportunities for men to express masculinities in ways that are not socially and politically destructive. As a result, there is a significant overlap between the reconstruction of violent masculinities in post-conflict societies with the provision of meaningful economic opportunities for men (and women).

Attention to Male Victimization

It is also important to acknowledge that men and boys may also have been victimized throughout the conflict, possibly by abduction, possibly by sexual violence, as well as by the violent ritualization that frequently accompanies male initiation into predominantly male military fraternities. As is generally noted in the context of sexual violence experienced by women, under-reporting is rife in this regard, and we do not have a deep understanding of the form, dynamics and scale of sexual violence that men experience in times of conflict. There is some nascent literature that suggests a link between sexual violence of men by men and deeply rooted practices of feminization (UNOCHA 2008). In this telling, sexual violence experienced by men is a direct playing out of wider social (and violent) practices that are generally directed towards women. For many men who experience rape, the result is to undermine their own masculinity in fundamental ways and put in doubt their sexual identity. Sexual violence experienced by men is, we know, significantly under-reported, although empirical proof other than anecdotal evidence is difficult to establish. The statistics of the Peruvian Truth and Reconciliation Commission ('TRC') suggest that men may under-report (even as the statistics illustrate that women are the most prevalent victims of sexual violence). Of the 538 cases of sexual violence reported to the TRC, 527 correspond to women and only 11 were attributed to male victims (Duggan et al. 2008: 202).

Equally evident in this context are the unique vulnerabilities of young men and male children who have been conscripted into militias, insurgent groups, or paramilitary forces. As the initial indictments from the International Criminal Court illustrate in relation to the harms visited upon child soldiers, acts of sexual violation were intentional and systematic, clearly intended to break bonds between children and their families/communities of origin and force relationships of dependency and shame into the paramilitary organizations (Prosecutor v. Thomas Lubanga Dyilo 2006). All of these multiple contexts of male victimization (made more complex by the victims' parallel roles as perpetrators) require melding into the conceptualization and delivery of DDR programmes. In particular, DDR programmes need to develop special counselling and training programmes addressing the harms experienced directly and more broadly, forcing difficult conversations about men's roles post conflict (United Nations 2006, Bastick 2008: 18).

Male victims may feel caught between the hypermasculinization of war and their own feelings of vulnerability and stigma (Gettleman 2009). Recognizing that gender-based issues are not merely instrumental goals for the benefit of women can help in developing programmes to aid this population. These programmes might include specially trained counsellors, targeted educational opportunities for boy soldiers, and specific healthcare measures. Like others undergoing the DDR process, they too will benefit from forms of economic empowerment that may help them to resolve their feelings of victimization.

Conclusion

There is a need for a fuller recognition that gender cannot be fully addressed in the post-conflict environment by addressing women's rights in legal documents. Gender must be addressed in multiple ways, including through close attention to masculinities as part of the high-priority (and funded) measures to end violence. Programmes specifically focused on disarming and reintegrating former combatants need to account for masculinities in their mandates and programme deliveries.

Notwithstanding the cultural, legal and social variations between countries facing post-conflict challenges, navigation around the centrality of and response to gender remains universal. In undertaking this analysis, we are convinced that addressing gender and the differing needs of men and women is not only good policy and practice on its own merits, but that it meets the first principle of conflicted and post-conflict societies – namely, ensuring that violence ends for all, is not reignited, and is sustainable far into the future.

Chapter 10
Migrating and Mutating Masculinities in Institutional Law Reforms

Jamie R. Abrams[1]

As the newest class of trainees in the Navy's elite SEAL unit convenes on the quad, Navy Master Chief Jack Urgayle in the movie *G.I. Jane*[2] invokes the D.H. Lawrence poem 'Self-pity' (1986: 189) as he prepares these soldiers for the hardships they will endure:

> I never saw a wild thing
> sorry for itself.
> A small bird will drop frozen dead from a bough
> without ever having felt sorry for itself.

The movie depicts the fictional struggle to formally integrate women in the Navy SEAL unit. The word 'self-pity', is defined by Merriam-Webster's dictionary as 'a self-indulgent dwelling on one's own sorrows or misfortunes.'[3] Notably, Master Chief Urgayle continues his memorable welcome address, '[t]he ebb and flow of the Atlantic tides, the drift of the continents, the very position of the sun along its ecliptic. These are just a few of the things I control in my world! Is that clear?' The Master Chief's remarks reveal vividly his view of the incompatibility of military service and vulnerability. Tellingly, the female candidate endures a brutal assault by the Master Chief, shaves her head, and ceases menstruation as

---

1 An earlier version of this chapter was published in volume 16 of the *William & Mary Journal of Women and the Law* 703 (Spring 2010). The author extends her deepest appreciation to participants in the Feminism and Legal Theory Project's Conference on Feminism, Law, and Masculinity at Emory University School of Law, the LatCrit Works-in-Progress forum, and the Hofstra University School of Law junior scholars workshop for their feedback and commentary. Thanks also to the American University Washington College of Law, where Ms Abrams was previously an Instructor, for providing generous research grant funds to support this project. Thanks for the substantive guidance and input provided by Beth Burkstrand-Reid, Daniela Kraiem, Jason Pletcher and Rachel Rebouche, and the invaluable research and editing assistance provided by Lisa Coleman, Maggie Donahue, Mary Huff, Kate Lukeman, Erica McKnight and Naree Nelson.

2 This 1997 film starred Demi Moore as Lt. Jordan O'Neil, a fictional female trainee selected to integrate the US Navy's elite unit. Directed by Ridley Scott.

3 At http://www.merriam-webster.com/dictionary/self-pity [accessed: 31 May 2013].

she proves her SEALs compatibility, suggesting that her femininity itself risked connoting vulnerability in the all-male military unit. This scene reveals the defeatist paradox of women's military integration whereby hegemonic masculine constructs demand that women occupy perpetual vulnerable, outsider status, yet vulnerability is castigated.

The symbolic use of D.H. Lawrence in *G.I. Jane* reveals vividly the central thesis of this chapter: just as law reforms transform institutions so too do they transform masculinities and, inversely, prevailing masculinities within institutions can thwart, transform – even mutate – law reform objectives. Feminist legal advocacy has generally compartmentalized law reforms by institution, generating separate and distinct responses to military integration, domestic violence, etc. Masculinities scholarship and feminist scholarship also have a complex, interconnected history, in tension in some regards and catalysing in other, yet the scholarly intersections are predominately theoretical.

This chapter suggests symbiotic value to feminist law reforms incorporating a masculinities analysis to the efficacy and implications of institutional law reforms on the praxis side. This chapter explores its thesis using domestic violence and military integration law reforms in the United States specifically. These law reforms both challenged institutions (the military and the family) that were (are) constructed and framed heavily around male control, power, and exertions of strength and violence, receiving deference from the state historically. These law reforms necessarily transformed masculinities in intended and unintended ways and realigned the relationship of the state to masculinities. They also overlapped at critical times historically and are active ongoing law reform efforts, suggesting a unique ability to see the praxis implications of masculinities intersecting with feminist law reforms.

Masculinity imperatives distinctly plague and impede law reform successes in both the military and the family. Today women in the United States military have recently achieved formal equality, yet they face ongoing integration barriers. Even where women are serving in the military, it remains a paradigmatically masculine institution. Domestic violence also remains a pervasive problem for men and women alike as millions of men and women report domestic violence each year, and data suggest that only a fraction of crimes are reported (K. Kelly 2003: 1). Masculine imperatives in the family and military do not just harm women. Men are also plagued by the complexities of male violence in their complicated and often stigmatized role as victims of domestic violence and in the stigma surrounding male military personnel's mental health needs after armed conflict, among others.

Although feminist law reforms sought most directly to engage *the state*, these reforms inherently impacted institutional and normative masculinities. This chapter begins by exploring its central thesis in the context of domestic violence reforms. Domestic violence law reforms not only successfully changed the relationship of the family to the state, but also transformed masculinities within the family and the relationship of the state to masculinities. This chapter explores how layering domestic violence law reforms on the paradigmatically masculine law enforcement agencies and the conservative crime control agenda complicated and transformed law reforms. It positioned law enforcement agencies as the surrogate protectors of women and family, positioning men as both the perpetrators and the protectors – reinforcing masculinity norms, not necessarily gender equality. The inherent line drawing in the criminal law reform agenda also entrenched masculinized violence, reinforcing artificially binary characterizations of women as vulnerable to male victimization and men as potential perpetrators impenetrable to violence.

The chapter then examines the ways in which transformed masculinities within the family and vis-à-vis the state migrated to alter military masculinities. Re-entrenched masculinized violence in domestic violence law reforms complicated military integration efforts where reforms had to necessarily navigate the dominant and pervasive 'masculine-warrior paradigm' (Mazur 1999). This chapter ultimately suggests that making historically invisible masculinities visible within law reforms stands to achieve more sustained and pervasive law reform successes and to address the underlying gendered dynamics of vulnerability and violence.

Masculinities Examined

Masculinities, comprising the study of how men relate to each other and the social dynamics that construct male identities, were largely unexamined in scholarship until the 1970s. The study of masculinity *in the law* has emerged even more recently yet. The realities of unexamined masculinities are particularly striking given the sweeping role that masculinities have had in shaping institutions, histories, politics and human relations. Michael Kimmel notably claimed in his pioneering work, *Manhood in America* (2006: 1), that '[m]en have no history', and he began the monumental task of documenting the history of manhood and male relations in the United States. Unravelling the complexities of masculinities has proven to be no easy feat for even the rapidly expanding cast of masculinities scholars. As Kimmel explains, in *Misframing Men* (2010: 1), 'the spotlight itself seems to obscure as much as it illuminates.'

Masculinities are particularly difficult to identify and examine because of their relational and institutional constructs. Todd Reeser (2010: 20) explains the symbiotic relationship of masculinities and institutions: '[M]asculinity can be thought of both as created by institutions and as creating them, and the process of the construction of masculinity as a constant back-and-forth movement between masculinity and institutions.' Masculinity is fluid (Reeser 2010: 38). As scholars define, articulate, examine and chronicle masculinities, the lens only expands as it becomes clear that masculinities cannot be understood without institutional, historical and relational understandings, and institutions, history and relations cannot be understood without understanding the underlying masculinities that shape them.

Hegemonic masculinity describes a form of dominant masculinity anchored in an exclusionary paradigm, systematically excluding women and gays (Kimmel 2006: 62), and expressing and reaffirming strength and physicality (Cohen 2009:

144). Hegemonic masculinity theory defines masculinity as synonymous with power (Kimmel 1997b). It explains how the definition of manhood in American culture reinforces the power that some men maintain and wield over women and other men (Kimmel 1997b: 61). Expressions of hegemonic masculinity inherently position women in a perpetual outsider status within institutions and social groups, and are thereby keenly relevant to feminist theory and praxis. Hegemonic masculinity is a relational concept, 'constructed around people, institutions, and cultures' (Dowd 2008: 214). Men are socialized, from the time they are young boys, to suppress emotion and live in a 'narrowly defined world of developing masculinity in which everything [they] do[] or think[] is judged on the basis of the strength or weakness it represents: you are either strong and worthwhile, or weak and worthless' (Dowd 2008: 219).

Though hegemonic masculinity exerts pressure on men to conform to its ideals, it need not correspond closely to the actual personalities of the majority of men (Connell 2005a). Indeed, while men as a group may be dominant and powerful, many men as individuals do not feel powerful (Dowd 2008: 213). For these men, a critical underpinning of this feeling of powerlessness is their perceived inability to achieve this dominant picture of masculinity, despite the constant pressure to do so (Dowd 2008: 213). From their sense of powerlessness, men can develop a desire for control (Dowd 2008: 213).

Wielding physical strength is essential to dominant masculinity. Many scholars see male violence as 'extensions of "normal" masculinity' (Dowd 2008: 220). It is simply a way of 'doing gender'. Violence is a resource that men can use when other resources are not available to accomplish masculinity (Harris 2000). As Angela Harris (2000: 781) explains, '[V]iolent acts are also, sometimes, the result of the character of masculinity itself as a cultural ideal. In these cases, men use violence or the threat of violence as an affirmative way of proving individual or collective masculinity, or in desperation when they perceive their masculine self-identity to be under attack.' Failure to wield violence or express strength can position men in outsider status too.

Hegemonic masculine imperatives distinctly pervade and define the military. The military has been described as a microcosm of hegemonic masculinity in action (Cohen 2009: 144). Historian John Keegan (1993) explains, 'If warfare is as old as history and as universal as mankind, we must now enter the supremely important limitation that it is an entirely masculine activity' (Morgan 2008: 46–7, Clatterbaugh 1990: 41). The military is largely designed around masculine traits (Ralston 1998) and entrenched in a 'masculine-warrior' paradigm that actively excludes those who threaten this warrior image (Dunivin 1997), most notably women and gays historically. The archetypal military man resembles hegemonic masculinity ideals in many respects (Harris 2000: 781). He is white, heterosexual and male, and he must demonstrate and continually affirm his strength (Ralston 1998: 672).

Masculine values pervade military culture and define the essence of the job – to fight and to win wars (Dunivin 1997: 2). The military is a 'proving ground for masculinity', frequently seen as 'a rite of passage, transforming boys into men' (Carreiras 2006: 41, Clatterbaugh 1990: 41). Male within this definition means more than just biological sex – it requires the right amount of masculinity (Ralston 1998: 672).

Much of military custom and culture is structured around a hegemonic masculine imperative that subordinates women and gays (Vojdik 2005b: 343). The historic exclusion of women from certain combat positions reinforced that 'true soldiers' were men (Ralston 1998: 676). Women were excluded from the ground combat positions that were considered to be the most 'macho' until 2013 (Ralston 1998: 677, Dunn 2009). The ground combat exclusion positioned women as second-class citizens, judged by their biological womanhood that inherently did not conform to the universal male warrior image (Dunivin 1997: 18).

The military centrally reveres and refines violence, positioning soldiers 'by doctrine' as 'managers of violence' (DeYoung 2001). Strength and aggression are requirements of the job (Dunivin 1997: 2). Combat positions are highly respected and regarded (Dunivin 1997). Combat instruction is taught through a well-delineated and uncompromising chain of command (Toth 2005: 335–9).

Dominant hetero-masculine norms historically defined the family too, positioning men as the defender or king of his castle. Male family roles historically had clear limits, leaving men to find 'masculine-affirming' work to achieve fulfilment (Clatterbaugh 1990: 17), and relegating parenting as secondary to financial providing (Dowd 2008: 239).

Given the institutional and relational frame of masculinities and the dominance of masculine imperatives in the military and the family, domestic violence and military integration reforms offer an effective lens to examine the masculinities implications of feminist law reforms.

Domestic Violence Reforms Make the 'Invisible Visible', Yield Sweeping State Responses, and Migrate to Military Integration; Yet Masculinities Remain Invisible within Law Reform Agendas

Domestic violence reforms successfully moved male violence against women from a private harm to a public issue and achieved expansive success on the state and federal level. These law reforms changed institutions, yet they also show how feminist institutional law reforms can be transformed, if not mutated, by unexamined pervading institutional masculinities.

The family unit was historically largely impervious to state interference with male violence (Felter 1997, Schechter 1982). The criminal justice system effectively codified and emboldened men's dominant role over the family, and thus over women and women's bodies (Gruber 2007). Law enforcement traditionally failed to enforce crimes against women in the home by 'looking the other way' (Alleman and Muraskin 1993). The system treated domestic violence as a purely private matter – outside of legal enforcement. This framework privatized and endorsed unrestrained male governance of the family. In so doing, it reinforced masculine conceptions deeply rooted in traditional conservative views presuming men to be the defender and king of his castle (Suk 2009). The law thus implicitly endorsed male violence against women as an extension of 'normal' masculinity and familial governance.

Because of the state's implicit endorsement of women's subordination to male familial power, feminists positioned domestic violence reforms prominently on the equality agenda (Halley 2006). The 'battered women's movement' in the United States evolved out of the anti-rape and women's liberation movements; it was fuelled by women supporting and empowering a community of women (Schechter 1982: 29–43). The movement responded to unfettered male familial power by making the 'invisible visible', naming and framing violence against women and constructing legal responses to it.

The domestic violence movement implicitly challenged prevailing dominant masculinities. The first United States domestic violence shelter began as a 'consciousness raising group' intended to provide a 'utopian community' for battered women (Schechter 1982: 33). Many early activists were themselves survivors of domestic abuse (Schechter 1982: 56). These activists, inspired by their personal experiences, worked at the local level to establish safe spaces for battered women in their communities (Schechter 1982: 53–79). Shelters did not treat victims as clients receiving professional services; rather, they were active participants in the work of the movement and shelter maintenance (Schmidt 1995: 58). The shelter movement avoided hierarchies and distinctions between residents and staffers, creating inclusive, egalitarian spaces built around consensus and collective action (Schechter 1982: 76–9). This movement therein rejected male hierarchical constructs and power as it challenged hyper-masculine violence.

While domestic violence law reforms grew out of the grassroots feminist movement, they intersected prominently with the historically overlapping criminal reform movements (Gruber 2007: 748–9) and involved strategic alliances with social and religious conservatives (Halley 2006). President Reagan's politics of the 1980s positioned crime as a major social ail, demanded a return to law and order, and sought stricter criminal enforcement and punishments (Marion 1994). Domestic violence on the federal agenda intersected with the crime control agenda and transformed the movement. By 1984, the United States Attorney General's Task Force on Family Violence recommended that family violence should be recognized and responded to as a criminal activity and it encouraged law enforcement to establish arrest as the preferred response (Arnold 2004). National politics thus met the local domestic violence movement squarely in the criminal justice system, which in turn positioned the dominant and hegemonic masculinities of law enforcement to transform underlying feminist law reform objectives.

The resulting criminal laws positioned domestic violence as a general 'law and order' issue (Daniels et al. 1997: 79). States nationwide enacted criminal laws that formalized victim protections and prosecuted domestic violence. New policies ensured that police responded to 'domestic incident' calls, rather than trivializing or ignoring them as non-criminal calls (Sack 2004: 1663, Sparks 1997: 40). States reformed their criminal laws to expand police power to arrest suspects in cases of domestic assault (Sparks 1997: 45, Schechter 1982: 159). Historically, domestic violence victims had to sign formal complaints positioning the victim as the accuser initiating criminal charges (Sack 2004: 1667–8). 'No-drop' reforms empowered the state to prosecute domestic violence offenders absent witness testimony or a formal victim complaint (Sack 2004: 1672–4). Prosecutors instead relied on the arresting officer's documentation, empowering state intervention (Sack 2004: 1672–4). Mandatory arrest policies legislated a polar shift from a 'do-nothing' response or a 'cooling-off period' to an affirmative requirement that police officers arrest a domestic violence suspect when the victim shows signs of injury, a weapon is involved, or the officer has probable cause to believe that the accuser has violated a restraining order (Sack 2004: 1662–4, Sparks 1997: 42–5, Schechter 1982: 157–61). Other states did not affirmatively require arrest, but nonetheless imposed an affirmative reporting obligation on officers to complete a domestic violence incident report and document why an arrest was not made.

These sweeping criminal reforms occurred at the federal level too. Advocates successfully mobilized in the early 1990s to pass the Violence Against Women Act ('VAWA'), creating a civil rights remedy for gender-motivated violent crimes (Violence Against Women Act of 1994). Congress heard extensive legislative testimony recounting personal experiences of domestic abuse. Congress recognized the insidious effects of domestic violence as a gender-motivated crime and passed VAWA as a piece of consolidated crime legislation. VAWA reinforced state reforms by prohibiting interstate domestic violence. It allowed victims to testify at pretrial detention hearings to vet issues of safety, provided a means of victim restitution for losses resulting from violence, and mandated enforcement of valid protection orders across state lines. VAWA also created a new federal cause of action for victims of violent crimes motivated by gender under a civil rights theory of liability, although the Supreme Court subsequently invalidated that provision.[4]

With domestic violence on the federal agenda, it intersected in transformative ways with the overlapping military integration movement. Activists had long sought legal and institutional military reforms to include and integrate women, gays and lesbians. Notably, it was the exposure of wide-scale violence against service women that led to some of the largest law reform military integration successes in the early to mid-1990s. The 1991 Tailhook sexual abuse scandal[5]

4 The Supreme Court in 2000 invalidated VAWA's civil rights remedy in *United States v. Morrison*. The Court held that the civil rights remedies exceeded congressional authority under the commerce clause and Section 5 of the Fourteenth Amendment because violent crimes motivated by gender did not comprise economic activity in and among the states.

5 At the Navy's 35th Annual Tailhook Symposium in September 1991, at least ninety victims experienced indecent assault in a high-profile scandal that captured congressional and media attention (Office of the Inspector General 2003).

revealed widespread systematic sexual assaults of service women. The direct military responses tightened prohibitions on violence against service women committed by fellow soldiers, increased penalties, and improved reporting mechanisms, following civilian law reform responses to gendered violence.

Yet the indirect Tailhook aftermath was about women in combat as much as sexual abuse. In 1991, with VAWA on the federal legislative agenda and the Tailhook scandal in the spotlight, Congress considered women's formal combat military exclusion. Outrage surrounding Tailhook combined with the unprecedented involvement of women in the Persian Gulf War of 1990 and 1991 led to increased combat opportunities for women in the Navy and Air Force. Reforms expanded women's access to over 90 per cent of active-duty jobs across all branches (Segal 1998). Substantially more combat positions were opened to women (Donnelly 2007), particularly in the Navy and Air Force; military academies integrated women (*United States v. Virginia* 1996); and the military enacted policies to address sexual violence and harassment of military servicewomen (Rimer 1996). Tailhook was thus a catalyst in 'shifting from an exclusionary masculine-warrior paradigm to a more inclusionary, egalitarian paradigm of warrior' (Dunivin 1997: 25), made possible through the contemporaneous success of the domestic violence movement.

While the military expanded career service opportunities for women dramatically, the legal codification of hegemonic masculine imperatives remained evident in the formal legal exclusion of women from certain direct ground combat roles (Cloutier 2008, Murnane 2007), an exclusion that prevailed until 2013. Women still comprise less than 15 per cent of military personnel, making the military a clearly male-dominated organization (Gruber and Morgan 2005, Women in Military Service for America Memorial Foundation, Inc. 2011).

Feminist law reforms yielded sweeping successes that transformed relations between the state and the family and expanded military opportunities for women. These sweeping law reforms necessarily impacted masculinities too.

Law Reforms both Transformed and are Transformed by Masculinities

Masculinized Violence

Domestic violence and military integration law reforms simultaneously challenged masculine norms, reinforced them, and redefined them. So too did masculinities mutate law reform objectives. If male violence is an 'extension … of "normal" masculinity', the exclusion of certain forms of male violence from legal codes transformed the state's relationship to both the family and to masculinities. Criminalization of domestic violence succeeded in removing the implicit immunity afforded to men in violent male family governance and penalized it, positioning the state to explicitly respond to hyper-masculine expressions of violence.

Yet the criminal law reforms necessarily had to simplify complex aspects of domestic violence from its theoretical feminist underpinnings (Hanna 1998). Law reforms inherently present a 'double-edged sword' in the legislative line drawing that needs to occur (Römkens 2001: 267). The lines that are drawn carry the risk of 'misrecognition', entrenching underlying masculinities imperatives.

As Gruber examines, the shared goals of state conservative politics and the battered women's movement did not align perfectly. The crime control alliance offered certain tangible benefits such as criminal deterrence of violent behaviour and the symbolic value of prominently placing violence against women on the national agenda (Gruber 2007: 759–60). Central to the feminist response to domestic violence was the positioning of domestic violence as a form of male aggression and a mechanism of state-sanctioned subordination of women (L. Kelly 2003: 844–8). The statistic often cited historically is that approximately 95 per cent of domestic abuse is committed by men against women, but implicit in this statistic is the reality that approximately 5 per cent of these acts are committed by women and victimize male or lesbian partners (K. Kelly 2003: 35).

Catapulting domestic violence to the national criminal agenda as a women's issue paradoxically risked normalizing male violence generally even as it criminalized aspects of it. Pathologizing women's violence and normalizing male violence in turn risked reinforcing aspects of hegemonic masculinity. Criminal domestic violence reform agendas ran into this complexity squarely as binary characterizations in the mainstream public sentiment polarized victims as helpless and defendants as monsters (Hanna 1998). Inherent in the masculinization of the aggressor are assumptions about male behaviour, assumptions that all men are prone to and capable of violence, reinforcing underlying dominant masculinities. As Stemple (2009) articulates, 'Assumptions that real men are sexual aggressors and never victims promote harmful perceptions about the "one" way to be a man. They can justify violent behavior as an archetypal manifestation of maleness, promoting a sense of inevitability about its continuation' (634).

Indeed, study findings suggest that respondents react more strongly to men as perpetrators and deem them more deserving of punishment, whereas they experience more sympathy for female abusers. Respondents rated the exact same conduct as more serious when the perpetrator–victim gender dynamic was male–female than when it was female–male, female–female or male–male, believing that the police should intervene in male–female abuse and that the other situations should be left alone (Schmesser 2007: 178). One interpretation of these findings is that people perceive men as more capable of inflicting injury and women more vulnerable to injuries (Schmesser 2007). These findings underscore the entrenchment of 'gender-role stereotypes of women as weak and vulnerable and men as dominant and threatening' (Schmesser 2007: 175–6). Conceptions of 'men as a monolithic perpetrator class' can perpetuate 'regressive norms about masculinity rather than challenging the harmful status quo' (Stemple 2009: 605).

Another interpretation of these findings is that they reinforce the distinct compatibility of law enforcement personnel policing male behaviour to protect women as a vulnerable class, and a disconnect between policing female violence or protecting male victimization. Indeed, male victims face legal and social bias within the criminalized domestic violence enforcement framework. Research suggests that 'police are two times more likely to arrest male perpetrators of domestic violence than female perpetrators' (Schmesser 2007: 174). Frequently, when police officers learn that the victim of a domestic crime is male, they will not take the male victim's charges against the female perpetrator seriously (Schmesser 2007: 174). Male victims often face a higher burden when requesting a restraining order against the female perpetrator, and prosecutors are much less likely to bring charges against a female perpetrator than a male perpetrator of domestic abuse (U.S. Department of Justice, Bureau of Justice Statistics 2000). Male victims may also face other barriers when they seek restraining orders against women, such as more hesitation, slower processing, higher standards, and an increased likelihood of receiving a mutual restraining order. The 2000 National Violence Against Women Survey reported that domestic violence committed against male victims was less likely to be prosecuted than domestic violence committed against a woman (U.S. Department of Justice, Bureau of Justice Statistics 2000). Convicted female perpetrators of domestic abuse are much more likely to be sentenced to a term of probation, and much less likely to be sent to prison than men (Schmesser 2007: 199).

These findings may suggest entrenched gender stereotypes about men and women, but they may also suggest the extent to which masculinities have interplayed with law reforms. They may suggest that law enforcement personnel are more aptly policing masculinities in male–female domestic violence than violence as an act. Male victims may complicate the heroic masculinity frame of criminalizing male–female violence.

Pathologizing a 'women's syndrome' through the Battered Women's Syndrome ('BWS') also suggests that there is something pathologically different about female violence. BWS emerged as a psychological explanation of women in abusive relationships who kill their abuser (Burke 2002: 220). It involves two common symptoms of domestic abuse survivors: the 'cycle theory of violence' and 'learned helplessness' (Burke 2002: 222). BWS suggests that abused women develop a heightened ability to cope and survive in an abusive environment at the expense of the development of 'escape skills', and perpetually perceive their environment as hostile and dangerous, even when the male perpetrator is exhibiting non-confrontational behaviour (Burke 2002: 224). It fulfilled a need to educate jurors and mental health professionals about the common attributes shared by survivors of domestic violence (Burke 2002: 221). BWS emerged as a pattern of symptoms to describe the effects of abuse on its victims and how it might lead to acts of violence against abusers in self-protection (Buel 2003: 296–7). It plays a critical role in providing women a legal defence when they use violence as a means to protect themselves from ongoing abuse.

BWS distances – indeed, pathologizes – female violence from male violence. Creating an evidentiary legal argument rooted in 'the myth of a helpless, hysterical, unstable woman' further masculinizes violence (Daniels et al. 1997: 64). Buel asserts that 'BWS has been used to buttress insulting, unrealistic, female stereotypes such as docility, instability, weakness, and inability to protect oneself' (2003: 297).

It allows for a consistent preservation of women as victims as the 'helpless … powerless, pure-of-heart battered woman' (Gruber 2007: 792–3). It reinforces a societal message that 'women are not supposed to use physical violence in self-protection; it is not our prerogative, our role, our right' (Daniels et al. 1997: 60).

Indeed, certain statements of military stakeholders weighing in on women's military integration have revealed problematic entanglements in reconciling women's physical vulnerability to male violence with women's military qualifications, a defeatist paradox. Opponents to integration have invoked women's vulnerability in problematic ways that essentialize women as victims and distort vulnerability to violence in myopic ways as somehow incompatible with women's military service. Perhaps this tension is best revealed by the Master Chief's invocation of the D.H. Lawrence poem 'Self-pity', which expresses vulnerability as patently incompatible with military service.

L. Miller (2001: 129) summarizes the complexities for military women in the views of certain stakeholders, explaining that '[t]he simultaneous agenda … to portray military women as victims to male power and to argue their potentially equivalent strength to men in battle, works against itself in the minds of many soldiers.' Mazur (1990: 50) likewise highlights the tensions for women in military service in transporting the victim methodology that emerged from domestic violence reforms to the military integration agenda:

> Identification from the standpoint of victims seems to require enemies, wrongdoers, victimizers. Those identified as victims ('we') stand in stark contrast to others ('they'), whose claim to superior knowledge becomes not only false but suspect in some deeper sense: conspiratorial, evil-minded, criminal. You (everyone) must be either with us or against us. Men are actors – not innocent actors, but evil, corrupt, irredeemable. They conspire to protect male advantage and to perpetuate the subordination of women.

As Mazur's quote poignantly reveals, there is risk in positioning women as categorically vulnerable to victimization that it may undermine the perceived status and responsibility of military women as a class. Indeed, military personnel have used women's vulnerability to male violence in harmful ways. Consider one particularly chiding articulation of this view: 'if women whine about guys having a little fun, how will they handle combat and enemy abuse as a POW?' (Fenner 2001: 19) Other opponents to women's integration have expressed that they find it irreconcilable to position women as 'helpless victims of sexual harassment' by male service members, while contemplating women as 'fearless warriors' in direct ground combat (L. Miller 2001: 103, 129). This paradoxically perpetuates the outsider status of women and immunizes hyper-masculine expressions of violence.

Even less malevolent or explicit articulations of this view reveal problematic tensions for military women in the perceived irreconcilability of warriors and victims. As Mazur (1990: 50) explains, 'Oversimplifying women as vulnerable to victimization and men as potential aggressors may undermine the long-term success of military women by casting women as sexual targets and men as sexual hunters, without fully embracing the existence of successful women service members.' This characterization may communicate that military women are '"pejoratively, debilitatingly different"' from their male peers (Mazur 1990: 66, quoting Abrams 1993: 228).

Masculinized violence harms military men too. The tragic Fort Hood shootings and the mental health debate that it exposed revealed complex and symbiotic layers of insider/outsider masculinities in the military rooted in expressions of hegemonic masculinity. The pervasive mental health issues of service personnel returning from combat that have received national attention following the Fort Hood shootings reveal that men are vulnerable in the deployment of violence, yet masculinity norms and the hegemonic masculinity paradigm of the military dictate the suppression of this narrative. This discourse revealed that some men – heterosexual men otherwise positioned to wield the full advantages of male power and control – are outsiders within military culture and that there are harmful consequences to a sound, efficient fighting force that derive from even the outsider status of men that hegemonic masculinity supports and reinforces.

The aftermath of the Fort Hood shootings quickly shifted national attention to the mental health issues facing the United States military. The nation's military is strained at unprecedented levels, having fought simultaneous and protracted engagements in both Iraq and Afghanistan (Schwartz 2009). Soldiers are serving multiple tours of duty, placing unique strains on soldiers and their families (Jamail 2009). The impact on service personnel has been real. The Army has reported a record increase in the number of suicides every year since 2006 and increased soldier-on-soldier violence (Jamail 2009). One board-certified psychiatrist treating Marines warned that these mental health issues will lead to more violence, suicides, domestic abuse and dysfunction (Jamail 2009). Some experts have predicted that the shootings may have a transformative impact on the military's mental health framework. General Cone suggested that Fort Hood may establish itself as a 'baseline for our real mental health needs' after the tragic shootings (Kingsbury 2009). One expert recently described the mental health care at Fort Hood as a 'current crisis' and called for extensive redeployment of providers and the elimination of stigma (States News Service 2009).

Service personnel face well-documented access barriers to obtaining mental health services that are further layered on top of deep-rooted, yet rarely discussed, masculine norms that stigmatize the provision of mental health services. Certain barriers are institutional. Critical shortages exist in the availability of mental health providers (Schwartz 2009). Military policies also jeopardize the confidentiality of military counsellors, presenting considerable risk to service personnel (Schwartz 2009). These institutional barriers position military chaplains and other civilian service providers to treat the military's mental health needs. Other barriers to mental health services are grounded deeply in expressions of hegemonic masculinity. There is a resounding stigma associated with military personnel obtaining mental health services. As one soldier who served in Iraq and now helps others seek mental health explained, 'It's humiliating, first of all, for a male. We're men; we're alpha. To admit we're broken is a big, big ego thing' (Schwartz 2009).

Feminist law reforms thus intersected squarely with prevailing institutional masculinities. These law reforms altered prevailing masculinities as the prevailing masculinities transformed, even mutated, the law reform objectives.

The Masculinized State

The state can act to reinforce masculine norms and 'maintain[] and strengthen[] the gender order' (Tosh: 2004: 41). Indeed, many domestic violence laws position the state to reinforce traditional family structures. Some state mandatory arrest laws, for example, directly excluded unmarried couples or same-sex couples (Roberts and Kurst-Swange 2002: 111–12). This suggested an underlying state value in responding to intimate violence only when the integrity of hetero-normative family values was jeopardized. This feeds into the imperatives of hegemonic masculinity and positions the state to reinforce them.

Efficacy studies have concluded that mandatory arrest policies are a more effective deterrent when the abuser is married and employed, but they actually increase the likelihood of future violence when the abuser is unemployed or unmarried (Roberts and Kurst-Swanger 2002: 112). Some further efficacy analysis suggests that mandatory arrest policies actually deter domestic violence victims from reporting the abuse in the first place, suggesting that the mandatory arrest policy actually 'mirror[s] the battering relationship itself, reinforcing the patriarchal dynamic in which women have little power' (Roberts and Kurst-Swanger 2002: 112).

The state is thus driven to reform family violence to 'clean up its public face and to restore its legitimacy as a safe institution for women'; in doing so, the state ensures that 'these sacred institutions of patriarchy are preserved intact and patriarchal gendered relations are reaffirmed, reproduced, and represented as in the best interests of women and children' (Radford and Stanko 1996: 78). It suggests that male violent behaviour is immutable absent state intervention (Suk 2006: 21). Aspects of the criminal domestic violence approach empower the state to act as the surrogate protector of women, a role 'smacking of paternalism' (Gruber 2007: 748).

Examining the domestic violence reforms' interplay with masculinities suggests that the state is driven more likely by family preservation protectionist instincts than by ending violence or achieving equality. Criminal responses to domestic violence work best when heterosexual men deviate from their masculine imperatives to protect women and women are perceived as vulnerable victims in need of protection. This paradigm positions the state to re-entrench dominant or hegemonic masculinities within the law. It marginalizes the men who function outside of these dominant structures, frames women as inherently vulnerable and in need of state protection, and leaves unexamined the use of violence as a response to perceived masculinity 'failures' directly, as a way of 'doing gender'.

The state acting as a surrogate to protect women and traditional families likewise feeds the underlying protectionist stereotypes that simultaneously impede women's meaningful military integration. The state's role of intervening in the family to police masculinity norms risks legitimizing the state role in other contexts too. These protectionist roles complicate military service in opponents' view because they argue that men are inherently inclined to protect women from enemy harm (Katzenstein 1999: 48, 50), risking that they become 'overprotective' of their female comrades and may jeopardize the success of a mission (Morgan 2008: 52). Democratic Representative George Hochbrueckner articulated this perspective (Saul 1991: 4): '"Most men don't want to put women in jeopardy. We're willing to put ourselves in jeopardy more readily than we are with women. It's a visceral reaction."' Late former Marine Corps commandant and retired general Robert H. Barrow agreed (*The Victoria Advocate* 1991: C1), characterizing women killing in combat as '"uncivilized"' and stating matter-of-factly that '"women can't do it."' He said (*The Victoria Advocate* 1991: C1): '"Women give life, sustain life, nurture life, they can't take it … If you want to make a combat unit ineffective, assign women to it."'

Examining the state as a masculine actor reinforcing masculine imperatives yields important takeaways to examining law reforms. To the extent that the state is limiting the 'power, prestige, [and] privilege' of men, the state acquires that power over the family and thus over women itself (Clatterbaugh 1990: 37). This dynamic risks mutating law reform objectives if it remains invisible.

Making Visible the Invisible: Vulnerable Masculinity and Aggressive Femininity

This chapter has examined how masculinities intersect with law reforms. Law reform strategies and critiques have historically generated within institutions, rather than across them. Masculinities and feminist scholarships have intersected predominantly at the theoretical level. Given the relational and fluid construct of masculinities, this chapter has suggested symbiotic value to examining the masculinities implications of law reforms across institutions. This analysis, conducted narrowly by examining the domestic violence and military integration reforms, has uncovered complex intersections between masculinities and the state, masculinized violence within law reform agendas, and the ways in which hegemonic masculinity reinforced in the law harms both men and women.

Returning to the grassroots law reform that so aptly positioned the domestic violence movement for its law reform successes offers a useful frame for responding to the analysis in this chapter. Successful domestic violence reforms were informed by effectively ascertaining and using the direct and lived experiences of women as advocacy tools (Pleck 1987: 183–4, 199). Just as victimization narratives achieved lasting change in the domestic violence movement, so too might narratives that make visible the vulnerable masculinity and the aggressive femininity advance the broader feminist law reform agenda. Such an approach would be useful in re-conceptualizing masculinized violence. Such narratives might transform prevailing mythical warrior images to represent more accurate and informed legal and societal understandings of service in today's military, revealing innumerable military roles that are not defensive or protective and extend far beyond strength, aggression and violence (Dunivin 1997: 19). More inclusive narratives might alter exclusionary stereotypes of men as warriors and define roles in inclusive ways that transcend race, sex, and sexual orientation (Dunivin 1997: 25).

PART IV
Education

Chapter 11
Thinking through the 'Boy Crisis': From Multiple Masculinities to Intersectionality

Juliet A. Williams

Contemporary gender scholars regard it as axiomatic that masculinity, both as an ideal and as a set of embodied practices, is multiple. As legal scholar Nancy Dowd observes, 'a key piece of masculinity theory is that masculinity is not unitary; hence the name of the field is masculinities, plural' (2010, 27). In disclosing the false universalism of a generation of sociological, anthropological and psychological studies of the male sex role, masculinity studies has encouraged gender scholars to move beyond traditional ways of conceiving patriarchal power and to address the heterogeneity and uneven distribution of male privilege.

In the effort to deepen and complicate prevailing accounts of gendered power, masculinities studies scholars have dedicated significant critical energies to the theoretical elaboration and the empirical exploration of 'hegemonic masculinity'.[1] In the field-defining work *Masculinities*, R.W. Connell characterizes 'hegemonic masculinity' as 'the configuration of gender practice which embodies the currently accepted answer to the problem of the legitimacy of patriarchy, which guarantees (or is taken to guarantee) the dominant position of men and the subordination of women' (2005a, 77). While the term 'hegemonic masculinity' often is used loosely to designate dominant ideals or norms of masculinity, in its original formulation, the Gramscian notion of 'hegemony' was invoked specifically to underscore the plurality of hierarchized masculinities and the complicity of all men, even those who enjoy a lesser share of the 'patriarchal dividend', in maintaining regimes of masculine privilege.[2]

In seeking to transcend one-dimensional accounts of masculinity, however, the imperative to recognize multiple masculinities has produced dilemmas of its

1 Christine Beasley offers an especially trenchant critique of the slippery use of the term 'hegemonic masculinity' in masculinities scholarship. Beasley contends that the term commonly has been used simply to indicate dominant ideals of masculinity or socially dominant men. Instead, Beasley emphasizes the neglected mandate, implied by the term 'hegemonic' itself, to address the specific way dominant ideals of masculinity operate 'as a political mechanism producing solidarity between different masculinities in a hierarchical order' (2008a, 93).

2 Connell defines the 'patriarchal dividend' as 'the advantage men in general gain from the overall subordination of women' (2005a, 79).

own. Among the most widely pondered has been the question of how to engage diversity without depoliticizing difference. If the classificatory project comes to displace critical analysis, masculinities studies may do more to reproduce stereotypes than to illuminate diverse experiences. As sociologist C.J. Pascoe warns, efforts to elaborate the range of masculine types may be 'intended to highlight patterns of practice in which structure meets with identity and action, but they have the effect of slotting men into masculinity categories: a hegemonic man, a complicit man, a resistant man' (2007, 8). To resist this tendency, Pascoe exhorts masculinities studies scholars to 'always pay attention to power relations when we think in pluralities and diversities; otherwise we are simply left with a list of differences' (8). When masculinity is regarded not as a social fact, but rather as an effect of beliefs, practices and institutions that regulate gendered identities, we gain insight into the social and political processes though which social hierarchies are produced and maintained. And in questioning the presumption that masculinity is the natural expression of embodied maleness, we are led to consider the very different ways masculinity is performed, and disciplined.

In directing attention to the role that power plays in constituting gendered identities, masculinities studies engages a question at the forefront of recent debates over the future of intersectional analysis more generally. Mirroring the critique levied against masculinities studies, some worry that, as intersectional analysis has gained acceptance as a research methodology, it has lost its commitment – explicitly embraced by early innovators of the approach – to challenge social and economic inequalities based on hierarchies of race, gender, sexuality and class. Legal scholar Joanne Conaghan acknowledges that intersectionality 'can generate a rich stock of data, for example, about how categories of women are differently situated in relation to education, the family, the labour market, and the political system', but she finds that contemporary intersectional scholarship 'is less able to capture the processes through which these disparities are produced or the relations of subordination of which they are expressive' (2009, 41).

In what follows, I take up the charge to attend more rigorously to the politics of intersectionality. Specifically, this chapter offers a critical reassessment of prevailing, but largely unexamined, assumptions about the political dynamics associated with complex identity. The next section traces intersectionality theory to the influential writings of Kimberlé Crenshaw, whose analysis of intersectional politics centres upon the erasure and exclusion of marginalized subjects in political discourse and public policy. Arguing for an enlarged understanding of the political dynamics that produce and maintain social inequalities, I then turn to a discussion of the recent discourse of a 'boy crisis' in the United States to illustrate the way the acknowledgement of multiple masculinities has been leveraged through tactics of selective representation and hyper-visibility. In this way, I suggest that the unfolding discourse of a 'boy crisis' in the United States holds valuable lessons for masculinity studies scholars, while also pointing to the important contribution masculinities studies can make to developing more richly nuanced understandings of the operation of intersectional politics more broadly.

Beyond Intersectionality?

The term Intersectionality designates a critical perspective that rejects single-axis approaches to identity. As a methodology, intersectionality aims to address 'the relationships among multiple dimensions and modalities of social relations and subject formation' (McCall 2005, 1771). In the turn to address 'multiple masculinities', the field of masculinities studies has come to centre intersectional analysis – although the term 'intersectionality' itself has ignited significant controversy within the field. In a recent survey of two decades of intersectional scholarship, Leslie McCall remarks that 'feminists are perhaps alone in the academy in the extent which they have embraced intersectionality' (2005, 1771). As I discuss below, precisely because intersectionality has been so closely associated with the study of multiply marginalized women, some have questioned its appropriateness as a method for understanding the condition of men who may bear gender privilege and yet be socially subordinated. Indeed, masculinities studies have proven an especially lively site for critiquing intersectionality.

Citing the early association between intersectionality theory and work that specifically focuses on the experiences of black women, prominent voices in the field of masculinities studies advocate for use of the term 'multidimensionality' in the place of 'intersectionality' (see e.g. Cooper and McGinley 2012). In *Progressive Black Masculinities* (2006a), legal scholar Athena Mutua contends that intersectionality theory has not proven adequate to address phenomena like racial profiling or mass incarceration – practices that disproportionately disadvantage 'blackmen' that cannot be accounted for by conventional explanations of the operation of racism or sexism alone. Mutua finds that intersectionality has been 'often interpreted to suggest that black men were subordinated by race but privileged by gender', an understanding that quite evidently fails to explain the proliferation of racial profiling as a policing tactic (19). The shift to 'multidimensionality theory' – a theory that 'grew out of intersectionality', according to Mutua – enables a 'focus' on 'the various and multiple social structures that oppress and constrain the agency of individuals and groups in uniquely distinctive ways' (20). Mutua's rendering of multidimensionality emphasizes the need to balance a recognition that 'no group or community effort can represent every person in his or her individuality' with the fact that some modes of identification nonetheless have become 'materially relevant' within 'systems of domination including class, race, and sexuality' (21).

Legal scholar Darren Hutchinson similarly acknowledges that his 'multidimensional' approach 'arose, primarily, out of an impressive body of feminist and critical race literature' (1999, 10). Hutchinson characterizes multidimensionality theory 'as both a substantive and conceptual extension and redirection of the literature' on the '"intersectionality" of oppression' (11). According to Hutchinson, however, intersectionality theory is 'limited, almost exclusively, to understanding and exploring the operation of just two sources of oppression—patriarchy and racism—in the lives of women of color' (11). That is, Hutchison contends that intersectionality theory has had an unduly narrow analytic reach, failing to address the range of experiences of subordinated subjects. In his view, the 'limited relevance of intersectionality' is prescribed by the pervasive assumption that 'social identity categories of systems of oppression only "intersect" in the lives of persons burdened by multiple sources of disempowerment, such as women of color' (12).

The emergence of parallel but separate theoretical vocabularies to address complex identity in masculinities studies and feminist legal theory could be construed as an instance of the tendency of these two fields to 'occupy separate academic silos', as legal scholar Nancy Levit puts it (2010, 2). There does not appear to be much distinguishing intersectionality from multidimensionality at the conceptual level; rather, the disagreement turns on the question of how to address what some take to be the unduly narrow deployment of intersectional analysis in the past. Of course, the problem of narrow application becomes a self-fulfilling prophecy if the term intersectionality is abandoned instead of extended when other identity conjunctures become the subject of critical attention. Perhaps the most compelling case to be made for separate terms is to insure that intersectionality's historical focus on the long-neglected nexus of racism and sexism is sustained. Nonetheless, there are serious costs to endorsing an artificially cabined purview for intersectional analysis. On the one hand, we deny the broad range of work currently being done under its auspices. At the same time, we risk reinforcing the suggestion that intersectionality theory, with its roots in the 'life narratives' of black women, somehow lacks the explanatory power to develop into a broader analytic for legal and social scientific inquiry.[3] For these reasons, I retain the term intersectionality here, even while suggesting areas for development of the theory itself.

Reconsidering the Politics of Difference

Intersectionality analysis commonly is traced to the galvanizing work of Kimberlé Crenshaw, whose canonical law review articles, 'Demarginalizing the Intersection of Sex and Race' and 'Mapping the Margins', played a pivotal role in stimulating academic inquiry into complex identity. In these well-known pieces, Crenshaw offered an incisive analysis of the way the voices, experiences and interests of black women have been marginalized, silenced and erased by legal, social and political logics premised on one-dimensional approaches to identity.[4] In 'Demarginalizing',

3 Laura Kang sharply observes that, in McCall's account, '[t]he theoretical work of "feminists of color" are epistemologically demoted as "personal narratives" bounded by and merely expressive of a "partial perspective"' (manuscript on file with author, 10).

4 While Crenshaw is rightly credited with popularizing the term 'intersectionality', key aspects of her conceptual framework are rooted in earlier work by women of colour feminists and critical race theorists among others. Nonetheless, it is unfair to dismiss Crenshaw, as Jennifer Nash recently has done, with the suggestion that Crenshaw merely 'recycles black feminism without demonstrating what new tools it brings to black feminism to help it fashion a more complex theory of identity' (2008, 9). This assessment overlooks

Crenshaw argued that 'the single-axis framework *erases* Black women in the conceptualization, identification and remediation of race and sex discrimination' (emphasis added, 1989, 140). Crenshaw uses terms like 'erase', 'silence' and 'obscure' throughout the article to describe the way single-axis frameworks position those 'who are multiply-burdened' (1989, 140). She offers several examples of legal decisions in which courts have refused to acknowledge black women as a distinct class, and goes on to explore the way black women have been silenced, even by feminist and antiracist commentators. For example, reflecting on the controversy in the black community surrounding the film *The Color Purple*, Crenshaw explains how concerns that the film would reinforce 'negative stereotypes of Black men ... *seemed to compel the subordination of certain aspects of the Black female experience* in order to ensure the security of the larger Black community' (emphasis added, 1989, 163). Crenshaw identifies a similar dynamic at play in progressive critiques of the Moynihan Report and attendant diagnoses of 'the deterioration of the Black Family'. While commentators have developed compelling analyses of the white cultural norms undergirding the Moynihan Report, Crenshaw notes that critics often have failed to examine their own patriarchal assumptions (1991, 1254–5).

In 'Mapping the Margins', Crenshaw further develops her account of the silencing and erasure of black women. Focusing on efforts to address violence against women of colour, Crenshaw shows that the needs, interests and experiences of 'the most marginal' women are often the least likely to be taken into account. Indeed, Crenshaw demonstrates that even well-meaning domestic violence programmes have at times 'reproduced the subordination and marginalization of women of color', for example, by limiting access to shelters and support groups to English-speaking women (1991, 1262). As in her earlier article, emphasis is placed on the way 'women of color can be *erased* by the strategic *silences* of antiracism and feminism' (emphasis added, 1991, 1253).

Returning to those path-breaking articles today, it is striking that virtually all of the examples of intersectionality Crenshaw provides centre dynamics of silencing and erasure. Whether she is discussing antidiscrimination law or popular culture, the emphasis in these pieces is placed on the way that 'the political interests of women of color are *obscured* and sometimes jeopardized by political strategies that ignore or suppress intersectional issues' (emphasis added, 1991, 1252). There is one notable exception, however, appearing near the end of 'Mapping the Margins'. Crenshaw examines the controversy that arose in 1990 when members of the popular hip-hop group 2 Live Crew were arrested and charged with obscenity. Insisting that 2 Live Crew is a deeply 'misogynist' act, Crenshaw nonetheless makes the case for an intersectional analysis to 'consider whether an exclusive focus on issues of gender risks overlooking aspects of the prosecution of 2 Live Crew that raise serious questions of racism' (1991, 1285). Taking on an essay George Will published in *Newsweek* magazine shortly after the obscenity charges were filed,

---

the elaborate and nuanced account Crenshaw provides of the operation of intersectional logic in the fields of law, politics, community organizing, and popular culture.

Crenshaw contends that Will's profession of outrage on behalf of black women degraded by 2 Live Crew's lyrics is not merely superficial, but opportunistic. Noting that Will's commentary on the 2 Live Crew controversy quickly segues to a discussion of the Central Park jogger case, Crenshaw justifiably concludes that Will's attention to the degradation of black women by hip hop artists is merely a rhetorical device meant to temporarily 'dramatize' what he takes to be the real problem – the threat of sexualized violence that black men supposedly pose to white women. Reflecting on the 2 Live Crew controversy, Crenshaw underscores the fact that, '[a]lthough Black women's interests were quite obviously irrelevant in the 2 Live Crew obscenity judgment, *their images figured prominently* in the public case supporting the prosecution' (emphasis added, 1991, 1253).

Crenshaw's discussion of the 2 Live Crew obscenity prosecution is noteworthy precisely because it is so unlike all of the other examples of intersectional politics she presents. While her writings are peppered with the terms 'erase', 'silence' and 'exclude', in the 2 Live Crew case we have something different: an example in which black women 'figured prominently', if also highly problematically. In this instance, we glimpse the way in which complex identity may be exploited through a representational strategy that operates on a logic of hyper-visibility, not invisibility.

Twenty years after Crenshaw's path-breaking law review articles first were published, the dominant emphasis in intersectional analysis continues to be placed on the silences and erasures that produce social marginalization and thereby perpetuate inequality.[5] In contrast, much less attention has been brought to social and political dynamics that operate through selective acts of recognition to achieve these same ends. The familiar idea of intersectional politics as working primarily through mechanisms of silencing and erasure has led to a neglect of the way multiply marginalized groups are implicated in political dynamics that operate not through negation, but via strategies of visibility and representation.[6] The shift in analytic

5 McCall observes that '[m]any feminists who are trained in social science methods and who are interested in intersectionality use the case study method to identify a new or invisible group – at the intersection of multiple categories – and proceed to uncover the differences and complexities of experience embodied in that location' (2005: 1782). For example, Strolovich (2007) explores the representation of the multiply marginalized. Strolovich's impressive empirical study of leading social justice organizations in the United States finds that, even among organizations formed to represent marginalized groups, disproportionate resources are directed to issues affecting advantaged subgroups within the larger group.

6 I do not mean to suggest that the politics of visibility has been entirely overlooked. For example, in her innovative study of gender politics in the United States Congress, Mary Hawkesworth offers an especially insightful account of the marginalization of women of colour who serve in that body. 'Through tactics such as silencing, stereotyping, enforced invisibility, exclusion, marginalization, challenges to epistemic authority, refusals to hear, legislative topic extinctions, and *pendejo* games, congresswomen of color are constituted as "other"' (2003, 546). Hawkesworth notes several ways in which women of colour are 'silenced', but she also addresses tactics like 'tokenism', 'stereotyping' and 'patronizing' that operate through flawed gestures of representation rather than simple erasure.

focus I am gesturing at here has a certain resonance with Foucault's famous rejoinder to the 'repressive hypothesis'. To enduring effect, Foucault recast modernity, long characterized in terms of sexual repression, as an era marked by 'the multiplication of discourses concerning sex in the field of exercise of power itself: an institutional incitement to speak about it, and to do so more and more; a determination on the part of the agencies of power to hear it spoken about, and to cause it to speak through explicit articulation and endlessly accumulated detail' (1978, 18). Foucault's argument against the 'repressive hypothesis' might be useful in thinking about the prominence accorded to 'silence' and 'erasure' in accounts of intersectional politics, inviting us to consider the evidence – hiding in plain sight – of the appropriation of discourses of diversity and difference by policy advocates and state actors.

The 'Boy Crisis'

While intersectionality typically has been understood as a way of conceptualizing *identity*, I am suggesting that the term also has come to imply a distinctive way of thinking about *politics*. Through an examination of the shifting terms of the 'boy crisis' discourse in the United States, the following discussion aims to shed light on neglected dimensions of the politics of complex identity. What follows, then, is not a typical intersectional narrative. Such a narrative undoubtedly would address the way that the construction of the 'boy crisis' has led to the denial of intragroup differences and thus inattention to the distinct challenges poor boys and boys of colour face in the educational system. At the same time, an intersectional analysis might highlight the marginalization of concerns about girls, as the presumptively subordinated class, in recent education reform debates. The following discussion does not deny the significance or impact of these occlusions, but focuses nonetheless on a different aspect of intersectional politics: what we might think of as the dynamics of appropriation and strategic representation. As I explain below, the story of the unfolding of a 'boy crisis' discourse in the United States over the past two decades is not one in which the distinctive needs, interests and priorities of economically disadvantaged boys and boys of colour simply get silenced or erased in the name of addressing the universalized plight of 'boys' (although this does happen); instead, it is a story in which the images and voices of boys of colour are rallied as the very emblem of the crisis, lending the movement for policy interventions, such as 'boy-friendly' public school initiatives, legitimacy. Indeed, rather than seeing boys of colour marginalized in the United States 'boy crisis' discourse, we often find boys of colour foregrounded – a move that may in fact help to shore up claims of redress on behalf of racially and otherwise privileged boys. In this way, attention to poor boys and boys of colour has played an essential role in making 'boy crisis' rhetoric appear both credible and politically palatable.[7]

7 This dynamic has been closely analysed in the British case of the 'boy turn' and the emergence of a 'poor boys' discourse (see e.g. Epstein et al. 1998).

In seeking to elaborate neglected aspects of the politics of intersectionality, the account that follows is particularly indebted to Cathy Cohen's nuanced analysis of the dynamics of fragmentation and stratification presented in her groundbreaking study of AIDS and black politics. In the opening chapter of *Boundaries of Blackness*, Cohen observes that '[i]ncreasingly … black Americans and other marginal group members are faced with public issues, constructed or framed in ways that highlight not their relevance to the entire group but their limited or bounded impact on a fragment of the community' (1999, 13). These 'cross-cutting issues' challenge the premise of the shared group identity upon which political mobilization and resistance traditionally has been organized. Cohen emphasizes the way the fragmentation engendered by cross-cutting issues leads to a 'reduction in the probability and effectiveness of political mobilization by blacks as a group' (16). In what follows, I want to consider the flip side of this coin: the way cross-cutting issues enable a politics of strategic realignments that, while threatening some identity formations, may empower others. In particular, I draw attention to the way the movement for single-sex public education has exploited the 'boy crisis' as a cross-cutting issue that is inclusive of boys of colour but which nonetheless privileges narratives of 'essentialized masculinity' while displacing discourses that centre critique of racial and economic disadvantage.[8]

The so-called 'boy turn' has evoked significant interest and heated controversy among masculinities studies scholars, particularly as it has played out in education reform debates in Great Britain and Australia. Much of the scholarly commentary on the 'boy turn' has been critical, concluding that the crisis mentality has been promoted by those more interested in pushing an agenda of 'recuperative masculinity' than challenging dominant constructions of masculinity itself. Capturing the general tenor of work on this subject, one observer concludes that concern with boys' purported underachievement has led to the promotion of '"solutions" which, rather than questioning hegemonic versions of (white, heterosexual, able-bodied) masculinity, work to recuperate and reinstate them' (Epstein et al. 1998, 7).[9]

In the United States, the discourse of a 'boy crisis' has been traced to the late 1990s (Weaver-Hightower 2008, 182), a time when polemical works like Christina Hoff Sommers' *The War Against Boys* (1998) denounced the persecution

8 Legal scholar David Cohen (2009) demonstrates how recent advocacy for all-boys public education promotes an essentialist myth of masculinity.

9 Epstein's critique echoes Crenshaw's claim that domestic violence against women of colour too often has been framed as 'just another manifestation of racism' (1991, 1257). In Crenshaw's view, '[w]hen violence is understood as an acting-out of being denied male power in other spheres, it seems counterproductive to embrace constructs that implicitly link the solution to domestic violence to the acquisition of greater male power. The more promising political imperative is to challenge the legitimacy of such power expectations by exposing their dysfunction and debilitating effect on families and communities of color' (1991, 1258).

of boys at the hands of a feminism gone awry. In fact, another 'boy crisis', this one framed around the plight of 'young Black males', already had risen to national prominence by the early 1990s.[10] At that time, public attention was drawn to the situation facing 'at-risk' boys, particularly young black males living in the nation's economically depressed urban centres. The situation was presented as dire: black boys were referred to in media reports and scholarly articles as an 'endangered species' on the brink of extinction in the face of alarmingly high rates of poverty, violence and incarceration for black men, and distressingly low levels of academic achievement among young black boys (see e.g. Wright 1991–92, 14).[11]

Sommers' book, and others of its ilk, found resonance not so much with the 'Black male crisis', but rather with a very different cause, that taken up by those fixated on the purported decline and fall of the American male. As Michael Kimmel chronicles in *Manhood in America*, masculinity itself was widely construed to be in crisis as the United States entered the last decade of the twentieth century, caught between traditional ideals of 'cowboy masculinity' on the one hand, and a shifting social and economic landscape on the other in which women not only demanded respect at home but commanded ever-increasing salaries and influence in the workplace (2006, 197). Responding to depictions of the modern American man as an emasculated pawn of 'frenzied "feminazis" and a culture of entitlements, affirmative action, and special interests', a reactionary movement of 'angry white males' was born (197). Rhetorically, the new 'men's rights' movement appropriated the discourse of the historically marginalized, declaring the average white male the real victim of a culture of redress run amok (198). As the entitlements of white male privilege became less certain, men's movement activists insisted that women had 'already achieved equality' and it was men who now were subject to discrimination as the only class not treated to special rights and entitlements (198).

While rhetorically aligned with aspects of the 'angry male discourse', the movement to address the 'Black male crisis' in the early 1990s constituted a pointed challenge to the presumptive designation of the white male as a member of the aggrieved class – let alone its epitome. This challenge is evident in the fact that education reforms advocated for at the time to address the 'Black male crisis' advanced proposals for sex-segregated classrooms in the context of initiatives, such as the creation of Afrocentric academies, which explicitly identified persistent racial and economic inequalities as a primary cause of failure of inner-city boys of colour to thrive.

Notably, while single-sex education was being promoted as an intervention for at-risk boys in the early 1990s, the idea of sex segregation also was gaining

10 In 1996, educational sociologist Pedro Noguera noted that '[i]n recent years, terms such as "crisis", "at-risk," "marginal," and "endangered" have been used with increasing regularity to describe the plight and condition of young Black males' (219).

11 The term 'endangered species' circulated in tandem with a racist and dehumanizing rhetoric rooted in anxieties about a generation of young black men running 'wild' in an 'urban jungle'.

popularity as an intervention to address the challenges facing at-risk girls. In 1992, the American Association of University Women issued its report *How Schools Shortchange Girls*. Without denying the seriousness of 'the particular education problems of poor black and Hispanic boys', the AAUW report is sharply critical of the glaring 'absence of attention to girls in the current education debate' (3). Citing evidence that older girls lag behind boys not only in math and science achievement but also in measures of self-esteem, the Report offered a qualified endorsement of single-sex education (126). Soon thereafter, the movement gained an important ally in philanthropist Ann Rubenstein Tisch, who launched the Young Women's Leadership School of East Harlem in 1996. The success of the Harlem Girls' School helped create critical momentum in support of single-sex public education, and in 2001, a provision was added to the No Child Left Behind Act making federal funding available to public schools wishing to experiment with sex segregation.

In foregrounding the plight of poor kids and kids of colour, advocates for single-sex public education in the 1990s devised what proved to be a highly effective rejoinder to feminist and antiracist legal organizations like NOW Legal Defense, NAACP and the ACLU, which sought to equate sex segregation in public schools with a return to state-sanctioned discrimination. However, in the wake of the 2001 victory, proponents of single-sex public education – particularly those advocating on behalf of boys – increasingly began to supplement the strategy of framing single-sex education as an intervention targeting the nation's most disadvantaged kids with a new justificatory rhetoric for single-sex education – one that centres a biologistic discourse of 'natural', 'hard-wired', 'genetic' and 'biological' sex differences. Today, single-sex education is being widely promoted to educators, policymakers and parents on the grounds that 'boys and girls learn differently' due not simply to gendered socialization but rather to underlying biological factors affecting hormone levels, neurological function, and even hearing and sight. As a result of two decades of advocacy, there are now over 100 single-sex public schools in the US serving students in grades K–12 (up from just three in 1990), and over 500 additional schools offering single-sex classes within co-ed institutions. The impact of the movement for single-sex public education has reverberated far outside the classroom as well, precipitating in 2006 the first major change to the Department of Education's Title IX regulations in nearly 30 years – a change characterized by feminist legal organizations and other civil rights groups as a blatant attempt to slacken existing protections against discrimination in public schools.

The shift in public justifications proffered for single-sex education over the past two decades reflects changes in the 'boy crisis' discourse itself, which increasingly is framed to implicate boys as a class, rather than centring upon economically impoverished boys of colour. Boys of colour are not simply erased or marginalized in this discourse; rather, their plight is selectively deployed in ways that promote an image of diversity while simultaneously denying the challenges facing girls of colour and silencing efforts to critique racial and economic inequalities.

Consider, for example, this statement from journalist Peg Tyre's 2008 New York Times bestseller *The Trouble with Boys: A Surprising Report Card on our Sons, their Problems at School, and What Parents and Educators Must Do*:

> Almost every ill that befalls schoolchildren in America—from learning disabilities, to dropout rates, to rickets—disproportionately affects poor black and Hispanic children. And the boy problem is no exception. We should not downplay the heavy burden that poverty and racism place on poor kids and kids of color. That said, it's useful to hold this bit of data in your mind … boys in every racial subgroup do worse than girls in school *even though they come from identical environments*. (Emphasis in the original, 44–5)

To be clear, it is *not* the case that boys in every racial subgroup do worse than girls in school – boys in every racial subgroup only do worse in school than girls *in the same subgroup*. White boys, for example, do *better* than girls from every *other* racial subgroup than their own.[12] But Tyre's construction of the boy crisis denies the salience of race as an explanatory category, and in this way harkens back to a dynamic Crenshaw identified in describing the way domestic violence activists in the 1980s rebuffed efforts to publicize violence against women of colour, contending it was critical to the movement to portray domestic violence as 'everyone's problem' rather than 'just' an inner-city problem.[13] Tyre appears to be operating on the same suspect logic – making the case that the 'boy crisis' is not reducible to a crisis afflicting 'only' poor boys or boys of colour by privileging the standpoint of the most advantaged boys.

In this way, the contemporary 'boy crisis' discourse might seem to be a familiar instance of intersectional political dynamics – a case in which multiply subordinated subjects get erased by a single-axis framework. But as the passage quoted above illustrates, while the 'boy crisis' discourse insists that all boys – regardless of class or race – have been disadvantaged vis-à-vis their female counterparts in recent years, poor boys and boys of colour nonetheless may 'figure prominently' (to return again to Crenshaw's phrase) in the representation of the crisis, as is the case with Tyre's forthright acknowledgement that boys of colour are suffering 'disproportionately'. Rather than shifting attention to the most disadvantaged boys, Tyre's rhetorical recognition of their plight seems intended to justify alarmist rhetoric about white boys – even as disadvantaged boys remain front and centre in the rhetorical construction of the crisis. The language of marginalization does not capture the positioning of disadvantaged boys in a new

12 My argument here should not be taken to foreclose discussion of the ways schools might not be serving even the most advantaged boys.

13 Efforts to frame the boy crisis as 'everyone's' problem have been common throughout the past decade. For example, a 2003 *60 Minutes* report entitled 'The Gender Gap: Boys Lagging' made this point explicitly, opening with this line: '[I]f you think it's just boys from inner cities, think again. It's happening in all segments of society, in all 50 states.'

'boy crisis' discourse that foregrounds their images as the very emblem of the crisis facing 'all' boys (that is, white, middle-class boys). In this way, assertions of the acuteness of the education crisis in communities of colour have served to legitimate segregationist interventions being extended to all students, regardless of race or class background. Indeed, even those who have popularized a biologistic rhetoric of sex differences – differences proclaimed to exist regardless of race, class and even sexuality – have sought to shift the public debate over single-sex public education to centre on narratives of racial and economic disadvantage. Ironically, the result is that economically disadvantaged kids of colour have come to serve as the public face of a movement that, increasingly, subordinates attention to racial and economic disadvantage in favour of biologistic explanations in accounting for educational outcomes.

And so it is, for example, that in 2004, when the Department of Education announced its intent to amend its Title IX regulations, disadvantaged children were brought to the rhetorical centre. On the eve of the unveiling of the proposed new regulations, meant to encourage greater 'experimentation' with single-sex approaches, Sen. Kay Bailey Hutchinson declared: 'It's time our nation's public school children have the same options as their private school contemporaries' (Feller 2004). Similarly, then-Secretary of Education Rod Paige emphasized research suggesting that single-sex education can be particularly beneficial for 'underprivileged' children (Feller 2004). Underprivileged boys – and particularly boys of colour – were once again foregrounded in both verbal and visual representations of the 'boy crisis' – but in a way that cleared the way for single-sex initiatives everywhere, rather than specifically promoting programmes that adopted an intersectional approach to addressing the plight of economically and racially disadvantaged boys.

In this regard, it is particularly important to note the appropriation of a rhetoric of 'social justice' in the campaign for single-sex public education. In 2002, Dr Leonard Sax founded the National Association for the Advancement of Single Sex Public Education, a name that itself indicates a self-conscious effort to align the campaign with a broader project of racial justice.[14] Since 1992, Sax has become the movement's most visible media spokesman, and he frequently invokes the phrase 'social justice' when arguing that all parents – not just those who can afford private school tuitions – should have the opportunity to choose a single-sex environment for their children. In this way, the promise to provide elite educational opportunities to socially disadvantaged students is used to justify policies that segregate on the basis of sex. Once again, this sets up an intersectional dilemma, where to contest sex segregation leaves one vulnerable to the charge of denying educational opportunities to economically disadvantaged boys of colour. At the same time, one might also note the way in which the very idea of 'social justice' itself is being re-signified here – away from its strong association, two decades ago, with educational reform initiatives that specified racial and economic

14 The phrase 'the Advancement of' subsequently was dropped.

disadvantage as a primary cause of underachievement among African-American boys, to the current deployment of the term, which understands 'social justice' as a matter of insuring equality of 'choice' for children of all economic backgrounds.

This kind of manoeuvre reveals an important aspect of what we might think of as the political condition of intersectionality – where intersectionality refers not simply to the complexity of identity but to the distinctive political dilemmas engendered by the strategic mobilization of identitarian logics. In this case, an equivalence is established between African-American boys in particular and 'boys' as a universal class. The equivalence serves, on the one hand, to enable boys not traditionally associated with disadvantage to partake of a discourse of redress, one that is premised, often explicitly, on the claim that girls today have been overcompensated for past injustice while boys are now being 'left behind'. At the same time, in establishing this equivalence between the plight of boys of colour and boys as a class, the notion of 'social justice' is evacuated of meaning as it ceases to be identified with any particular social movement struggle.

Masculinities Studies and the Future of Intersectionality

Within the academy, growing recognition of 'multiple masculinities' has encouraged research that centres the voices and experiences of marginalized subjects. Undeniably, increased attention to the diverse masculinities associated with non-white, non-heterosexual male subjects has had a salutary effect not only in enriching our understanding of gendered identities, but also in correcting for the tendency to replicate patterns of social marginalization within the academic study of gender itself. By revealing the historical and cultural variability of ideals and norms of masculinity, multiple masculinities scholarship contributes to the de-naturalization and potentially de-stabilization of essentialized gender ideals by demonstrating the contingent relationship between masculine privilege and male bodies.

Outside of the academy, however, the politics of recognition have proven significantly more complicated. In drawing public attention to the distinctive challenges facing young men of colour, the proliferation of 'boy crisis' discourse has advanced an agenda promoting a highly traditional account of masculinity. In this case, recognition of intragroup differences among boys from different racial and economic backgrounds has been leveraged to justify and inoculate against political challenge policies – including sex-segregated classrooms – that re-entrench essentialist gender ideals.

The preceding discussion highlights the need for an understanding of intersectional politics that engages the political dynamics engendered not only by the neglect, but also by the recognition, of intragroup difference. Masculinities studies scholars have a particularly valuable contribution to make, I would suggest, in propelling intersectional analysis beyond its more traditional focus on silencing and marginalization as the primary means by which social inequality is produced and maintained.

Chapter 12
No Boy Left Behind? Single-sex Education and the Essentialist Myth of Masculinity[1]

David S. Cohen

Introduction

Single-sex public education is in the midst of drastic expansion in the United States. Despite Justice Scalia calling it 'functionally dead' in 1996 (*U.S. v. Virginia* [Scalia, J., dissenting]), ten years later single-sex education received the blessing of the U.S. Department of Education. Responding to language in the No Child Left Behind Act that encouraged states to experiment with single-sex education, the Department changed its Title IX regulations to permit single-sex education in much broader circumstances than had previously been allowed. Public schools have responded en masse, with 442 schools providing single-sex educational opportunities for the 2008/09 school year, compared to just three in 1995.

Amidst this expansion, calls for single-sex education of boys have been a major impetus for this change in educational policy. While girls and women were the impetus for enacting Title IX in 1972, the current drumbeat for increased single-sex educational opportunities has included a substantial amount of rhetoric about treating boys' problems seriously. And the reported problems are legion in the United States. Boys are dropping out of school more than girls (Laird et al. 2006). Boys are more likely to repeat a grade than girls (Freeman 2005). Boys are going to and completing college in smaller numbers than girls (Peter et al. 2005). Boys are disciplinary problems more than girls (Dinkes et al. 2007). Boys use more drugs and alcohol than girls (Freeman 2005). Boys constitute a higher percentage of developmentally disabled and learning-disabled students than girls (Holt et al. 2007, Freeman 2005). To be sure, some experts disagree with the story about boys that emerges from these numbers (Mead 2006, Von Drehle 2007), but most reform efforts that have focused on boys have relied on the trends that show boys suffering.

The troubling part of this growing concern is that a narrative about boys and masculinity has emerged that relies upon what I call the essentialist myth of masculinity. Because of all of their problems, what boys need, part of this narrative says, is to be separated from girls so they can learn on their own, in their own

1 A longer version of this chapter was first published in the *Indiana Law Journal*, 84, 135 (2009).

boy-friendly environment. Why do boys need this? Because, the essentialist myth of masculinity explains, by nature, boys are different from girls. And they are different from girls in ways that make educating both of them fairly and effectively in the same room difficult, if not impossible. Boys are distracted by the presence of girls. Boys are aggressive yet stoic. They learn best through competition and sports. They need firm men, not women, teaching them. Ultimately, they are completely different from girls. In order to teach boys and address these unique needs (but without doing anything to change them), advocates and proponents of the essentialist myth of masculinity maintain that, in schools, the sexes need to be segregated. In other words, we need single-sex education.

This chapter describes, dissects and critically analyses this narrative about boys, masculinity and single-sex education that has arisen in the United States over the past decade.[2] Understood from within the burgeoning sociological study of masculinities, a field that legal scholars are just beginning to utilize, the essentialist myth of masculinity that has accompanied single-sex education reforms produces distinct harms for boys and girls. With the strong anti-essentialist reading of Title IX and the Equal Protection Clause set forth here, I argue that the essentialist myth of masculinity is incompatible with sex equality. Ultimately, I conclude that legal protections should broadly prohibit schools from perpetuating gender essentialism and sex stereotyping, which is what schools do when they act in accordance with the essentialist myth.

Anti-essentialism and Masculinities

Feminist anti-essentialist theory provides a powerful framework for understanding men and masculinity. It teaches us that, even though a dominant, or hegemonic, notion of masculinity may exist, it cannot account for the multiple masculinities lived by boys and men.

Analysing masculinity from the perspective of the feminist anti-essentialist tradition is important for the same reasons it is important to analyse femininity from an anti-essentialist perspective. Essentialism incorporates the notion that all women, as members of the group women, necessarily have certain characteristics in common and that all men, as members of the group men, necessarily have other characteristics in common. Essentialism ignores differences among women based on other identity characteristics (Harris 1990) as well as, to take anti-essentialism a step further, basic differences of individual personhood. For instance, not all women fit into Carol Gilligan's (1982) mould of having a more caring moral foundation than men; ascribing such a quality to all women is empirically inaccurate (Hyde 2005) in a world of 'multiplicitous, shifting, socially constructed' identities (Frug 1992: 18). Furthermore, essentialist conceptions of gender tend to reinforce power

2 Similar issues have arisen elsewhere (Reichert and Hawley 2009, Smithers and Robinson 2006), but I focus here on the United States.

differentials between men and women as well as 'patriarchal assumptions about women as a group' (Higgins 1996: 99).

As anti-essentialism teaches us, defining masculinity risks essentializing masculinity and men (and thus femininity and women) (Connell and Messerschmidt 2005). Attaching substantive content to the term in the form of particular characteristics is thus problematic, as it is clear that masculinity is more complicated than just a description of what men do. The concept includes what those in power expect of men (or women) who want to access benefits and positions associated with men, and frequently those also associated with power (Pascoe 2007, Renold 2004).

Because of these difficulties, I find it much more useful to use the sociological concept of 'multiple masculinities'. 'Multiple masculinities' is the anti-essentialist notion that different people experience and live masculinity differently. Stated otherwise, there is no one masculinity that all men, or even most men, live (Connell 1996). R.W. Connell (2002a), perhaps the most influential theorist on masculinity, posits multiple masculinities among and within cultures, institutions, workplaces and peer groups. Individual men and women can also access and perform different masculinities at different points and sites in their lives, as individual masculine identity is not static over time or within different contexts (Connell and Messerschmidt 2005, Kimmel 1997a).

Although there is no one 'true' or essential masculinity, there are certain types of masculinity that are more visible and influential than others. 'Hegemonic masculinity', also theorized by Connell, is the dominant normative form of masculinity within any particular context:

> Hegemonic masculinity was distinguished from other masculinities, especially subordinated masculinities. Hegemonic masculinity was not assumed to be normal in the statistical sense; only a minority of men might enact it. But it was certainly normative. It embodied the currently most honored way of being a man, it required all other men to position themselves in relation to it, and it ideologically legitimated the global subordination of women to men. (Connell and Messerschmidt 2005: 832)

Thus, although boys and girls, men and women, live and experience different forms of masculinity within particular contexts, often one form of masculinity exerts the most pressure to conform to it. Hegemonic masculinity is usually associated with power and the subordination of both women and non-hegemonically masculine men (Renold 2005, McGinley 2007b). In traditionally male-dominated societies and institutions, there are certain characteristics that are more likely to be associated with hegemonic masculinity than others (Gilbert and Gilbert 1998: 48, Renold 2004: 251, Riggs 1999: 311). Among those characteristics are the themes from the narrative about boys and the need for single-sex schooling that I identify below: heteronormativity, aggression, activity, sports obsession, competitiveness, stoicism, and not being female or feminine.

Theorists have criticized the concept of hegemonic masculinity in various ways, including claiming that it is unclear in its substance (Hearn 2004). However, my working premise here is that the notion is nonetheless useful in understanding what conceptions of masculinity exist that exert normative force on people to conform. Though it may be impossible to fully describe such a masculinity in the abstract because of the wide variety of forces that influence its nature as well as global variances with respect to expectations of men (Beasley 2008a), some understanding of it can come from looking at the forces, such as the narrative about boys described here, that create and reinforce its hegemony. Before describing this hegemonic masculinity and arguing for a strong anti-essentialist reading of anti-discrimination law, the next section briefly describes the legal setting in which the narrative about masculinity and single-sex education has arisen in the US.

The Federal Law of Single-sex Education

For those not familiar with this area of law, it may come as a surprise that the U.S. Supreme Court has not had a *Brown v. Board of Education* (1954) 'separate is inherently unequal' (or even the opposite, 'separate is equal') moment for single-sex education. The Court has addressed some aspects of single-sex education, but it has not definitively stated one way or the other whether the Constitution forbids or allows public schools to separate students based on sex. Likewise, Title IX and its regulations have, until 2006, had an equivocal stance on single-sex education – allowing it, but only in very limited circumstances.

It is now a familiar principle of US constitutional law that government classifications based on sex are subject to a level of scrutiny lower than strict scrutiny but greater than rational basis analysis (*Craig v. Boren* 1976). But, of course, that has not always been the case, and the first litigation involving the constitutionality of single-sex education arose as the Supreme Court was sorting out how to address sex discrimination under the Equal Protection Clause. In that litigation, the Third Circuit found that Philadelphia's two sex-segregated 'academic' high schools posed no constitutional problems because both schools offered similarly excellent academic environments and enrolment was purely voluntary (*Vorchheimer v. Sch. Dist.* 1976). In the midst of the rapidly developing constitutional doctrine around sex discrimination, the Supreme Court took the case but affirmed by an equally divided vote, resulting in no published opinion on the constitutionality of single-sex education (*Vorchheimer v. Sch. Dist.* 1977).

The Supreme Court has not heard any other cases that present the issue of the constitutionality of single-sex education in elementary or secondary schools. But a high-profile Detroit case resulted in another constitutional ruling on the issue in the early 1990s. In that case, *Garrett v. Board of Education* (1991), a federal district court found unconstitutional three all-boys academies with an Afrocentric curriculum. The district court found that the plaintiffs challenging the sex segregation were likely to succeed on the merits of their constitutional claim because the school, while having an important justification for the special academies, could not justify excluding girls, who also had faced learning problems.

Garrett was the last federal court decision regarding a single-sex elementary or secondary school,[3] but two other Supreme Court cases have raised important issues relating to single-sex education in very specific higher-educational settings. In *Mississippi University for Women v. Hogan* (1982), the Supreme Court found unconstitutional Mississippi's women-only nursing school because the state did not have an 'exceedingly persuasive justification' for its sex-based admissions classification. Fourteen years later, in *United States v. Virginia* (1996), the Court found unconstitutional a state-run, all-male military academy, the Virginia Military Institute (VMI). Taking what it called a 'hard look' at generalized claims about the sexes, the Court found that the state's goal of educating 'citizen soldiers' by excluding all women, 'in total disregard for their individual merit', violated the constitutional equality guarantee. In neither case did the Court address the general issue of single-sex education.

Title IX (20 U.S.C. § 1681–88) prohibits sex discrimination in federally funded educational programmes. The statute specifically exempts admissions from its ambit, except in vocational, professional, graduate and public undergraduate schools. Thus, preschools, elementary schools, secondary schools and private undergraduate schools can, under the statute, have sex-segregated admissions.

Title IX's regulations (34 C.F.R. § 106.1–.71) spell out the requirements for single-sex classes in elementary and secondary schools. Originally, the regulations allowed segregation by sex in only a limited number of circumstances. However, in 2001, Congress included in the No Child Left Behind Act a provision that encouraged experimentation with single-sex schools (20 U.S.C. § 7215[a][23]). In 2006, the Department of Education released final regulations consistent with the new law that greatly expanded schools' opportunities to provide single-sex education opportunities (*Nondiscrimination on the Basis of Sex in Education Programs or Activities Receiving Federal Financial Assistance*, 71 Fed. Reg. 62,529 [25 October 2006]).

These new regulations require schools to have an 'important objective' in separating the sexes. The Department delineated only two objectives that qualify: a school district's desire to improve educational achievement through an 'overall established policy to provide diverse educational opportunities' or the district's desire to 'meet the particular, identified educational needs of its students.' The school has to be 'evenhanded' in implementing the objective, and the single-sex classes have to be 'completely voluntary.' For students of the other sex who are excluded from the single-sex class, the school does not have to provide a single-

---

3 At least three cases have been filed since the 2006 change in Title IX regulations. *Selden v. Livingston Parish School Board*, No. 3:2006cv00553 (M.D. La. filed 2 August 2006), settled. Two others are in active litigation. See *A.N.A. v. Breckinridge County Bd. of Educ.*, No. 3:08-cv-00004-CRS (W.D. Ky. filed 19 May 2008); *Jane Doe v. Vermilion Parish Sch. Bd.* (D. La. filed 8 September 2009).

sex class, but rather must provide only a 'substantially equal coeducational class … in the same subject'. The school district must periodically evaluate the single-sex classes to ensure that they 'are based upon genuine justifications and do not rely on overly broad generalizations about the different talents, capacities, or preferences of either sex'. The new regulations for single-sex schools, rather than individual classes within schools, have virtually the same requirements.

The Narrative of Essentialized Masculinity

While the above changes were taking place, people began to pay close attention to the issue of single-sex schooling. Among other justifications, such as educational diversity, the needs of girls, and perceived improved educational outcomes, the public's attention to boys and their seemingly particular needs and concerns played an important part in the changes.

In particular, while the Title IX regulatory change suggests that educational policy decisions based on gender stereotypes are discriminatory and prohibited, it is hard to find a coherent body of literature identifying and defining these stereotypes – particularly as they apply to males. With the development of all-male schooling opportunities under the blessing of the new regulations, the need to understand these damaging stereotypes is greatly increased. I thus describe the myth of essentialist masculinity that emerged from this narrative in an effort to fill that void.

Methodology

This section of the chapter details this narrative by breaking it down into the main characteristics associated with boys and masculinity. In laying out the assumptions and arguments of the narrative, I reference stories about boys and single-sex education from the mass media that have appeared during and following the change in federal law, when the debate over single-sex education was at its peak in the United States. I have also based the narrative on the popular books about boys that have contributed to this debate. Finally, to a lesser extent, the narrative also draws on the comments submitted to the Department of Education in support of the recent Title IX regulatory change.

These sources almost uniformly tell the same story: that school-aged boys naturally possess a dominant form of heterosexual masculinity and need to be taught differently as a result. Occasionally, the authors do mention that single-sex education can break down stereotypes; however, statements about breaking down stereotypes are inevitably followed by or appear at the end of a long discussion of the stereotypes discussed here. Also, the authors sometimes hedge their descriptions of boys with comments that indicate that most, but not all, boys are a certain way. That, indeed, is consistent with the overall point of my critique. What is problematic with these comments, regardless of any hedge, is that they appear within a dominant narrative about boys' separate needs and characteristics; thus, they contribute to the discourse described below about male and female essential differences and the resulting need for single-sex education.

Essentialized Masculinity in the Context of Single-sex Education

In explaining the problems boys face and the ways that single-sex education can address them, the narrative of masculinity that has emerged during and after the regulatory change is striking. The narrative tells the story that all boys possess a particular dominant kind of masculinity. Themes of heterosexism, aggression, activity, sports obsession, competitiveness, stoicism, and being anything but female or feminine dominate this narrative. There is very little attention paid to individualized or alternative masculinities, with much of the discussion assuming that all boys fit into one essentialized masculinity.

Heteronormativity

Feminist and queer theorists of all disciplines have long critiqued compulsory heterosexuality and heteronormativity, or when structures presume, normalize or force heterosexuality over other sexual identities. Conversely, sexual identities other than heterosexuality are devalued, shamed, and forcefully resisted (Rich 1986, Mandel and Shakeshaft 2000, Pascoe 2007). Particular to masculinity, boys are told that in order to be truly male they must be heterosexual because, in part, to be otherwise and to be attracted to males is something associated with being a girl (Gilbert and Gilbert 1998, Epstein 1997). Put more strongly, Catharine MacKinnon (2004: 1087) has argued that homophobia and the institution of compulsory heterosexuality are essential parts of hegemonic masculinity because it 'keep[s] women sexually for men and men sexually inviolable.'

In the single-sex narrative, this phenomenon is embodied by the discussion of 'distraction' (Campbell and Sanders 2002). In the literature reviewed here, it has two essential components: assuming that all boys are sexually attracted to girls, and assuming that all boys are not sexually attracted to other boys. Many of the comments to the Department of Education made both of these arguments, sometimes very forcefully.

Journalists writing about single-sex education also overplayed this argument. For instance, the *Boston Globe* wrote about the benefits of being less distracted for boys, claiming that boys will stay more focused on academics 'because there is no one to tease' (Sacchetti 2006: A1). Other journalists told a common tale: with girls in the classroom, boys are distracted and self-conscious; therefore, they lose interest in school (Libby 2007), they act out to impress the girls (Bach 2006), and they compete with one another for the attention of the girls (Wermers 2004). Without girls in the classroom, boys will no longer show off (Planas 2007, Pollack 1998: 261–2), sexuality and hormones will be removed from learning (Higgins 2006, Wascoe 2006), and boys will focus on academics (Gonzalez 2004, Flowers 2005).

Aggression

Traditional notions of masculinity posit boys as aggressive and as needing aggression from others (Levit 1996). Nancy Levit (2001) has reasoned that, in its decisions that assumed 'male sexual aggression' and approved of the 'gendered construct' of war and military combat, the Supreme Court has given credence to this notion that masculinity is aggressive. Within schools, the notion that boys are aggressive is powerful, as boys not seen as aggressive will be seen as 'wimps' or 'as either a girl or a homosexual' (James 2007: 126).

The same-sex education masculinity narrative proclaims that boys are naturally aggressive and schools need to adapt to that by separating them from girls who, naturally, are not. For example, Leonard Sax, the executive director of the National Association for Single-sex Public Education, an oft-cited voice in favour of single-sex education, writes that '[b]oys often employ aggressive behaviors playfully, as a way of making friends' (Sax 2006: 62–3). Christina Hoff Sommers explains to educators that 'natural male aggression is not something to be feared; it is normal and healthy' (Sommers 2000: 63). As a *Newsweek* commentary proclaimed, 'boys bond bloody' (Flowers 2005: 26).

The theme of aggression is particularly present in descriptions of African-American boys and their needs. Verna Williams (2004) has described some of the rhetoric of aggression and violence used in the media portrayals of young African-American men and their need for single-sex education. As a result, news coverage focuses on structure in schools, such as an *Ebony* article that stressed the need for discipline and strict rules for African-American male students (Robinson-English 2006).

Activity

The masculinity narrative also portrays boys as active, in the sense that they are always moving and fidgeting. Along with boys' aggression, this constant activity is one of the most recurring features of the narrative driving the need for single-sex education. As Abigail Norfleet James (2007: 49) – an educator who has written a book about sex differences and how to teach boys – wrote, 'the activity level of boys is the stuff of legend.'

The most common discussion of this trait comes in the form of criticizing regular coeducational schooling for keeping boys sitting still rather than playing outside during recess. Michael Gurian and Kathy Stevens wrote in *The Minds of Boys: Saving Our Sons from Falling Behind in School and Life* (2005), an important book in the single-sex education literature, about the value of 'boy energy', which leads to risk taking and the need for movement. Terry Neu and Rich Weinfeld (2007: 134–5), two therapists with a book on helping boys in school, made a similar argument: 'There is a biological need for boys to express themselves through motion and to find an outlet for competition'.

The popular media has picked up on this theme repeatedly. As David Brooks, the *New York Times* columnist, wrote in criticizing the educational status quo, 'young boys are compelled to sit still in schools that have sacrificed recess for test prep[aration]' (Brooks 2006: 12). The *Boston Globe* claims that 'normal behavior by boys [includes] the need to move around frequently' (Editorial 2006a: A10). One ABC story asked the question in its headline, *Can Boys Really Not Sit Still in School?* The story explains that boys need five to seven recesses per day, have a biological imperative to move, and like to roll their chairs around the room (Lewin 2006).

To address boys' need for activity, the single-sex education narrative tells how boys-only classrooms should encourage movement through the structure of the classroom. As one principal wrote in comments to the Department of Education, 'young boys … generally do well in rooms that are more kinetic, active. Males are often noisy when in groups, and classically desirable school behavior is, in general, harder for boys to maintain.' In *Education Week*, Leonard Sax (2005: 50) describes a boys-only classroom that resembled a 'can of worms' as follows: 'Some of the boys were standing, some were sitting; another boy was twirling in circles. But all of them were, in their own way, paying close attention'. Capturing the common thread here, a math teacher told the Associated Press that he achieves success because 'I don't expect them to sit still' (Associated Press 2006).

Sports Obsession

If there is any trait that most people would think is gendered, it would be obsession with sports. Masculinity and sports are often seen as inseparable, especially in the context of competitive athletics in schools (Parker 1996, Lesko 2000b, Pascoe 2007). School sports 'define[] a pattern of aggressive and dominating performance as the most admired form of masculinity' (Connell 2000: 159). Success at sports is almost seen as the equivalent to success at being masculine (Renold 2005). In the single-sex education narrative, sports obsession is the basis for the argument that boys will learn better than girls when a class incorporates sports examples, sporting events and sporting breaks; therefore, boys need to be separated from girls in order to benefit from this learning technique.

Based on the reporting about single-sex education, the examples of sport use in single-sex classes are bounded only by teachers' imaginations. Some schools incorporate sports into the substance of the academic lessons. A teacher in San Francisco has the boys play 'multiplication baseball' (DeFao 2007: A1). In New York, boys learned grammar by shooting a miniature basketball through a hoop each time they answered a question from their teacher (Gomstyn 2007). Other articles discuss the use of sports as a complement to the long school day. The *Chicago Tribune* describes a teacher who, '[w]hen it's time to change to a new lesson … lets one boy either take a shot at the basketball hoop nailed to a cabinet or putt a golf ball' (Banchero 2006: 1).

Competitiveness

Related to boys' sports obsession in the single-sex narrative is their need to be competitive rather than cooperative. According to a 2007 book on helping boys in school, the best way to teach boys is to bring more competition into the classroom and not punish boys for being naturally competitive (Neu and Weinfeld 2007). Michael Gurian and Kathy Stevens (2005) have a biological explanation for this competitiveness, saying that boys have a natural 'team instinct' that teachers must use in the classroom.

This message has thoroughly saturated the media coverage of single-sex education reforms. For instance, *USA Today* wrote that succeeding with boys requires 'making learning competitive' (Editorial 2006b: A12). Boys' classrooms could, according to *Newsweek*, have more 'timed, multiple-choice tests' to accommodate their competitive streak (Tyre 2005: 59). The Department of Education also heard this explanation in the comments. For instance, one principal who claimed to have researched the topic stated that boys learn best in a competitive environment: 'When boys are asked to work in collaborative groups, they are more likely to get off-task and not do their best work.'

Stoicism

Traditional masculinity allows little room for boys or men to be emotional. The central premise of Dan Kindlon and Michael Thompson's popular book *Raising Cain* (1999: xv) is that 'boys, beginning at a young age, are systematically steered away from their emotional lives toward silence, solitude, and distrust.' In their book about teaching boys, Neu and Weinfeld (2007: 11–12) describe the same: 'As a whole, our society teaches boys to suppress their feelings. As a result, boys don't have experience with and often don't feel comfortable exploring their emotions.'

The single-sex narrative includes this idea that boys are not in touch with their emotions and that schools should teach them accordingly. In an editorial explaining the need for single-sex schooling, *USA Today* tells the following story about two boys, one in a mixed-sex school and the other in a single-sex school: 'Emanuel's teacher asks the class to do things that aren't boy-friendly. His latest assignment: Build a "feelings chart" for *Little Red Riding Hood* showing who's happy or sad throughout the book. Anthony spends twice as much time on literacy skills, none of it describing "feelings"' (Editorial 2006b: A12).

This area in particular is one in which supporters of single-sex education rely on brain science to support their claims that boys process emotion less efficiently than girls. For instance, Leonard Sax (2006: 29) writes that neuroscience shows that '[a]sking a seventeen-year-old boy to talk about why he's feeling glum may be about as productive as asking a six-year-old boy the same question.' The public narrative rarely includes the challenges to the conclusions drawn from the scientific research (Barnett and Rivers 2004), instead stating that experts believe the 'worst thing a teacher can do … is ask a male student how he feels about a subject' (Davila 2004: H2).

Not Girls

In many ways, what is being described here is masculinity that is defined by that which is not female or feminine. Stated differently, this dominant masculinity requires the othering and subordination of femininity. Sociologists have long understood that dominant masculinity is defined by that which is not female (Jordan 1995, Renold 2004). Boys often associate femininity with negative traits such as weakness, incompetency, inferiority and disease (Renold 2005). Teachers sometimes reinforce this fear of the feminine when disciplining boys by saying they are 'acting like a girl' (Connell 2000: 158).

In the discussion of single-sex education, the narrative reflects a strong belief that boys and girls occupy completely separate worlds. William Pollack, in his book *Real Boys* (1998: 232), advocates for teachers to develop 'boy-specific classroom materials'. Leonard Sax (2006: 9) states in his book, 'many administrators and teachers don't fully appreciate that girls and boys enter the classroom with different needs, different abilities, and different goals.' Putting this belief into practice, one teacher of single-sex classrooms said, '[I]t is sometimes more effective posing problems for girls using shopping examples and for boys using sports' (Rivera 2006: A1).

An excellent example of this separate spheres ideology is in the reading lists that commentators advocate giving to boys as opposed to girls. Boys are said to need action-oriented story lines (Gewertz 2007, Kenning 2005); 'stories about superheroes, sports, wild animals, bugs, war and monsters, as well as gross or slapstick humor that appeals to boys' (Constable 2006: A7); books about fantasy and hunting – and that are, of course, not 'too "girly"' (Sellers 2006: B1); books about history and adventure (Mahoney 2006, Hawk 2006); stories about music, heavy equipment, cars and trucks (Bowler 2004); and books with graphics and visuals that contain 'spatial-kinesthetic action' or are 'technical and mechanical in content' (Gurian and Stevens 2005: 138–9).

Another common argument in the narrative is the claim that boys need to learn from men, not women, because they cannot relate to women within the 'feminized' learning environment. *The War Against Boys* by Christina Hoff Sommers (2000) blames the feminization of school, among other institutions, for oppressing or even ignoring boys. Gurian and Stevens claim that the American classroom – with its emphasis on reading, writing, and complex word making – is better suited for the female brain and 'is set up for problems with a number of boys and young men' (2005: 52). An editorial in the *Salt Lake City Desert News* described a 'female world of academia' that boys get lost in (Thomasson 2006: A11). One comment to the Department of Education blamed boys' educational failure on their being taught by women. One student candidly stated, 'If we have a boy teacher, we can learn better. He is someone we can depend on' (Quimby 2006: A1).

The Essentialist Myth of Masculinity's Effect in School

The essentialist myth of masculinity described above corresponds with a dominant hegemonic notion of masculinity that is theoretically problematic and empirically harmful to boys and girls alike.

Schools can influence gender construction in many different ways. They can do so in power relations, such as those between teachers and students; in the division of labour, or how boys and girls (or men and women) do different things within a school; in patterns of emotion associated with different positions within the school, such as the tough principal, the feeling drama teacher, or the heterosexual homecoming king and queen; and in symbolization through dress codes, language codes and curricular areas (Connell 1996, Weaver-Hightower 2003). Gender construction influences in the school can come from students, teachers and administrators (Weiler 2000, Jacklin and Lacey 1997). Outside influences, such as popular, media-based conceptions of boys' and girls' proper behaviour, can influence these actors' conceptions of gender (Connell 1996). Thus, schools function in two different roles in the construction of masculinity: first, through the actors within the school, they exert a very powerful pressure on boys to conform; and second, they serve as an important site for popular discourse about gender to be played out.

A school adopting the masculinity narrative described here in its gender regime tells students that masculinity should be a certain way. Even more powerfully, it tells boys that they must conform to this narrative in order to truly be a boy.[4]

Constructing this hegemonic masculinity, particularly one associated with dominant traditional masculinity,[5] harms several different groups of students in different ways. First, it harms those boys who do not perfectly fit within its constraints. Second, it harms girls and women. Third, it constrains all boys, whether or not they adopt the hegemonic masculinity. Each of these harms will be described in turn below.

Harm to boys who fail to fit within the constraints of hegemonic masculinity has been heavily theorized, studied and catalogued by researchers. Put simply, those boys who do not exhibit hegemonically masculine traits 'are subject to varying degrees of oppression from the hegemonic group' (Weaver-Hightower 2003: 480). Even worse, those who actually adopt non-hegemonic or alternative masculinities 'can incur high social and emotional costs' and are 'subordinated and pathologized' (Renold 2004: 249). Beyond the loss of self-esteem, this subordination and oppression can take the form of 'verbal and physical teasing, bullying, and harassment of lower-status students [such as] not-sufficiently masculine boys' (Lesko 2000a: xiv). In fact, gender theorists have explained that hegemonic masculinity often relies on such a dichotomy and tension because hegemony

4 As a result, the fact that the Title IX regulations require that single-sex schooling be entirely voluntary is irrelevant. When a school or school district creates an environment in which the message is that real boys are a certain way, even those boys not in the single-sex classes or school will get the message (Levit 2005).

5 The unique problems associated with traditional masculinity, such as stereotypical gender roles for women, might not be present with a different hegemonic masculinity. However, similar problems of forcing one view of masculinity onto a diverse group of boys and girls would still be raised under such circumstances. For example, if a school were to have as its hegemonic form of masculinity one that was gay, passive and noncompetitive, it would still present the problem of forcing one form of masculinity onto its students who did not fit within it. Thus, many of the issues raised here would still be present.

requires domination over non-hegemonic forms of masculinity (Renold 2005, Connell 2000).

The difficulties faced by boys who break the norm of heterosexuality are particularly illustrative of the harms facing boys who do not exhibit traditional hegemonic masculinity. Many researchers have described the peculiar harm experienced by those who break the norm of heterosexuality, one of the previously discussed components of the essentialist myth from single-sex education. 'Studies consistently report that gay and lesbian youth who depart from traditional norms of masculinity and femininity are often targets of violence and harassment in school because they do not conform to cultural ideals of what is considered "appropriately" male or female' (Mandel and Shakeshaft 2000: 77–8). Boys who do not exhibit stereotypically heterosexual traits – those who position themselves outside scripts of hegemonic masculinity – routinely report being teased, excluded, humiliated or bullied. Heteronormativity requires the stigmatization and oppression of homosexuality because homosexuality is perceived as threatening to young people's emerging sexuality. This stigma certainly exists in coeducational schools as well as single-sex schools. However, a school that switches to single-sex education by emphasizing heteronormativity can exacerbate the problem. This is true whether heteronormativity is emphasized directly or indirectly by acting in accord with the hegemonic masculinity narrative.

Second, in addition to harming boys who fail to display the hegemonic traits of heterosexuality and physical ability, this form of dominant hegemonic masculinity also harms girls and women. The hegemonic masculinity described here is consistent with traditional masculinity that relies on societal domination of women by men. In the context of social inequality between males and females, schools can reinforce those roles when they fail to challenge sexist ideology and culturally stereotypical roles for boys that can affect girls (Kruse 1992). As Mark Fajer (1992: 633) summarized, 'To be blunt, we can hardly expect that boys who learn that their peers who cry or play with dolls are sissies and faggots will grow into men interested in displaying sensitivity or in taking on child-care responsibilities.' Moreover, the hegemonic masculinity described here can lead to emotional and physical harassment of and violence against girls, similar to that described above for boys exhibiting non-hegemonic masculinity. The notion of femininity as the opposite of desirable hegemonic masculinity, one of the important traits of the single-sex narrative, leads to a conception that to be a boy means to dominate and control female bodies.

Third, as would be the case with the construction of any hegemonic masculinity, the masculinity narrative's assumption that all boys are the same and that their masculinity is static constrains all boys – those who adopt the hegemonic masculinity, those who actively and knowingly struggle against it, and everyone in between. When a particular notion of masculinity is presented as the model or assumed as universal, that notion 'fosters limited expressions of identity' for all boys (Mandel and Shakeshaft 2000: 98). This constricted notion of gendered behaviour is particularly problematic for boys because, unlike girls, they have not seen an expansion in the acceptable forms of behaviour associated with being a boy (Thorne 1993). In fact, because it is virtually impossible for any one boy to always live consistently with any narrative of hegemonic masculinity, most boys will struggle with living up to the ideal and may be teased, bullied or worse for not doing so (Renold 2005).

When this story of 'true' masculinity for boys is told in the context of a predominantly African-American school, the effects are more complex and more damaging. The dominant form of masculinity described here conforms in many ways with the historical construction of African-American masculinity outlined by Verna Williams (2004) in her review of the interrelatedness of sex and race segregation. In line with the story of male aggression told above, African-American males have been viewed as oversexed, dangerous and threatening (Williams 2004, Cooper 2006a). Proclaiming that they need to be sex segregated because of these characteristics furthers racial stereotypes and subordination for all African-American boys and men.

Given that the fixed hegemonic masculinity associated with single-sex education can be harmful, a normatively preferable understanding of gender identity would be one that is fluid and multiple – accepting difference and experimentation – and not reliant on the domination of those who do not exhibit particular traits nor linked to any particular expression of sexual identity. Boys trying to establish their gender identity would be able to 'draw on … "a full—and fully human—emotional palette"' (Barnett and Rivers 2004: 14). Without fear of harassment, pressure, identity confusion, emotional torture or physical violence, boys would be able to act and experiment in school according to their own desires without the need to conform to a masculinity that may or may not resonate with who they are.

Stated more broadly, this notion of masculinity and gender would divorce the concepts from biological sex. Both boys and girls would be free to draw on all forms of gendered identity rather than on merely the strict confines of masculinity and femininity. Particular characteristics, personality traits, and likes or dislikes would not have any connection to the presumed reproductive biology of a boy or a girl. Such traits and preferences would be evaluated as positives or negatives on their own, without the additional loaded baggage of whether they are appropriate for a boy or a girl. Such 'gender multiculturalism' (Connell 1996: 211–13) would avoid the problems that result from a strict notion of masculinity to which boys have to adhere.

Essentialized versus Multiple Masculinities: A Better Way for the Law

This broad notion of masculinity I support is not only normatively preferable – particularly in comparison to the essentialist myth that has accompanied the expansion of single-sex education – but adherence to it should also be an important goal of the law. In this section, I will first consider the expressive effects that the regulation and the creation of all-boys educational opportunities may have on entrenching the essentialist myth. I will also suggest the safeguards that must be taken to guard against these expressive effects. A strong jurisprudence may be the most effective way to excise policy decisions by school administrators that advance deeply essentialist ideas. Thus, I ultimately argue for strong interpretations of Title IX and the Equal Protection Clause, which will support a broad notion of masculinity and disfavour the hegemonic narrative described above.

The Expressive Harms of Title IX's New Regulation

Before looking at Title IX and the Constitution, it is important to be clear how the new Title IX regulation itself can work both to create and to entrench the essentialist myth of masculinity. A developed literature describes how a regulation that allows single-sex schooling and the actual creation of such schooling opportunities will increase the harmful application of the essentialist myth. In doing so, single-sex educational opportunities, especially those that employ the essentialist myth of masculinity in school policies and practices, may create serious problems under the regulation's prohibition of sex stereotyping.

Over the last decade, expressive law scholars have made great progress in explaining the ways in which law may reflect social norms in society (Geisinger 2002, Lessig 1995). A core of expressive theory describes how law works by changing beliefs. In line with these theories, the move to single-sex education for boys may significantly increase beliefs in the validity of the male stereotypes I described previously. Validation of the essentialist myth, in turn, will increase its use by the general public with a similar increase in harms identified previously. Validation of the essentialist myth will also affect policy built on the myth in both coeducational and single-sex settings. However, because all-boys educational settings will require consistent consideration of the ways in which males learn, validation of the myth is likely to have a greater effect in the context of single-sex education.

Both the new regulation and the subsequent creation of single-sex educational opportunities will affect what people believe about boys. In particular, both will likely increase individuals' certainty that the vision of boys that the essentialist myth promotes is objectively true. This reification happens through the mechanisms by which law influences belief. For those people who know of the movement to single-sex schooling and believe that it is based in part on the need to educate boys differently because of their different essential characteristics, the regulation coupled with single-sex educational opportunities will validate this pre-existing belief. Put simply, if someone believes that sex segregation of boys is based on the fact that boys are inherently different and thus need to be educated differently, the legal support of such schools will act as proof of the truthfulness of that underlying belief. Similarly, those who had not previously believed that boys are inherently different might assume such a belief based on the development of sex-segregated education. The move to single-sex schooling is thus likely both to reflect and further entrench the essentialist vision of boys, with the resulting harms that accompany such a result (Geisinger 2002). To the extent that the essentialist myth described above was a primary motivator of the move to single-sex schools, the resulting expressive effect would likely be large.

The regulation drafters certainly recognized that the regulation and the resulting educational opportunities may influence beliefs in existing stereotypes. As a result, the drafters expressly made an effort to ensure that such stereotypes do not form the basis of curricular or educational decisions. I have already argued that separation based on sex affects male stereotypes to the detriment of all men and boys who do not conform to the essentialist myth. Thus, arguably the mere creation of single-sex schooling opportunities for boys – with the resulting increased acceptance of the essentialist myth of masculinity – violates Title IX's regulatory requirement prohibiting the promotion of sex stereotyping. While this argument is admittedly tenuous, given that the purpose of the regulatory change was to allow the creation of single sex-educational opportunities, it is similarly clear that regulators are concerned about the effect the creation of such schooling opportunities will have on negative gender stereotypes. Thus, not all sex segregation in schools will be protected by the regulation. Educational policies, curricular developments, and any other element of single-sex educational opportunities that foster the essentialist myth of masculinity described previously would be subject to review as a violation of this regulatory restraint. As I will discuss in the next two sections, Title IX and the Equal Protection Clause also provide robust protection for individuals who claim that a specific school policy or curricula advances the essentialist myth.

Title IX's Anti-essentialism Thread

Title IX is a powerful tool against sex discrimination in schools (Cohen 2005). In several different ways, that power comes from its rejection of gender essentialism. In this section, I will sketch the basis for understanding Title IX as an anti-essentialist law and conclude that Title IX should provide strong grounds for rejecting educational practices that implement and further the essentialist myth of masculinity.

One of Title IX's overarching themes, from its enactment through its judicial applications today, is its rejection of essentialist gender roles. This theme was apparent at Title IX's inception in its treatment of vocational education. At the time Title IX was enacted, there was widespread discrimination, both overt and subtle, in vocational education in the United States (Shelton and Berndt 1974). Aware of this problem, in the text of Title IX, Congress specifically prohibited discrimination in vocational admissions (20 U.S.C. § 1681[a][1]), and the regulations mirrored that prohibition (34 C.F.R. § 106.35). In the proposed and actual changes to the regulations in 2004 and 2006 for single-sex education, the Department of Education did not alter the prohibition on discrimination in vocational education. Senator Birch Bayh, the sponsor of Title IX, complained about vocational school admissions on the Senate floor, stating that the schools were sex segregated because of discrimination and 'sex-role expectations' that guided women into stereotypical female careers and educational placements (118 Cong. Rec. 3936–37 [1972]). In strictly prohibiting discrimination in vocational education admissions and attempting to move beyond sex-role expectations in trade schooling, Congress instilled a powerful anti-essentialist thread within Title IX's requirements.

Anti-essentialism is apparent in other aspects of the design of Title IX as well. In the area of professional education, in the early 1970s, girls and women had difficulty dreaming of going into professional careers because the educational opportunities required to go down those paths – at the time strongly associated with men and masculinity – were closed or minimally accessible to them (118 Cong. Rec. 274 [1972]). Title IX has helped open these career paths to women (Walsh 1977: 268), and today women are very close to outnumbering men in professional school enrolment (National Center for Education Statistics 2007).

Title IX's application to athletic participation, one of the statute's biggest achievements, also demonstrates its anti-essentialist bearings. In the early 1970s, girls and women were not encouraged to play sports because it was not perceived to be a part of what it meant to be feminine. Title IX has radically changed that fundamental understanding of what it means to be a girl (National Collegiate Athletic Association 2007). In fact, Title IX has so transformed the sports and female disconnect that, absent a high level of proof, courts will no longer accept the position, advanced by many schools in the face of a Title IX challenge, that they do not have sports for girls or young women because girls and young women are simply not interested in athletics (*Neal v. Board of Trustees of the California State Universities* [1999]).

Another area where Title IX's strong anti-essentialist thread appears is in its protection against harassment based on gender nonconformity. Several fairly recent controversies involve students harassing another student for failure to display stereotypically masculine or feminine characteristics. The Department of Education's guidance to schools reflects this anti-essentialism by specifically stating that claims of harassment 'on the basis of the victim's failure to conform to stereotyped notions of masculinity and femininity' are covered under Title IX (Office of Civil Rights 2001: 3). When these cases have made it to court, judges have applied Title IX's anti-essentialism in their understanding of masculinity. For instance, one representative court wrote that Title IX protects against 'harassment based on the perception that [a student] did not fit his peers' stereotypes of masculinity' (*Montgomery v. Independent School District No. 709* [2000]).

Scholars have written that these 'gender nonconformity' Title IX claims reflect a concern with children being harassed because of 'their failure to conform to the gender norms assigned to their sex (*i.e.*, their degree of masculinity if they are male or [of] femininity if they are female)' (Varona and Monks 2000: 67–8). In other words, Title IX prohibits schools from taking action against a student because that student fails to live up to what others believe it means to be a boy or a girl. This rejection of essentialism with respect to gender expression fits within the statute's general anti-essentialism and, as a result, would prohibit schools from placing boys who do not fit within one aspect of the hegemonic narrative of masculinity in any disadvantageous position.

Ultimately Title IX is, in substantial part, a statute about anti-essentialism. Just as Title IX does not allow schools to assume that girls and women are not interested in sports, vocational schooling or professional careers, it should not tolerate schools experimenting with single-sex education based on the assumption that all boys possess the same characteristics or that all masculinity is the same.

Constitutional Norm against Sex Stereotyping

The guarantee of equality from the Equal Protection Clause can also be read, like Title IX, as strongly prohibiting essentialist notions of gender. Preventing sex-role stereotyping is a central basis of constitutional protections against sex discrimination. In the previously discussed cases involving single-sex education, much of the Court's concern was with overbroad stereotyping.

For instance, in *Mississippi University for Women v. Hogan* (1982), the case involving a male nurse attempting to gain admission to the all-female Mississippi University for Women, the Court wrote repeatedly that the Equal Protection Clause is concerned with the dangers of sex stereotyping. Justice O'Connor's opinion for the Court targeted policies that rely on 'archaic and stereotypic notions' about 'the roles and abilities of males and females' as unconstitutional (725). Mississippi's enrolment restriction was based on such an archaic stereotype because it 'perpetuate[d] the stereotyped view of nursing as an exclusively woman's job' (729). The Court noted that Mississippi's stated purpose in 1972 for establishing women-only colleges very clearly relied on 'archaic and overbroad generalizations' (730 n.16).

In the more recent *United States v. Virginia* (1996) decision, which required the Virginia Military Institute (VMI) to admit women, Justice Ginsburg wrote extensively about sex-role stereotypes. She wrote that 'supposed "inherent differences"' are prohibited as the basis of classification when they 'create or perpetuate the legal, social, and economic inferiority of women' (533–4). In response to Virginia's argument that women would not choose to be educated according to VMI's intense adversative method, the Court accepted that most women, like most men, would not choose this method of education. The Court concluded, however, that Virginia was prohibited from excluding the women who would choose this method – those that buck the stereotype of what women want in education. 'Generalizations about "the way women are," estimates of what is appropriate for *most women*, no longer justify denying opportunity to women whose talent and capacity place them outside the average description' (550). In both *Virginia* and *Hogan*, essentialist stereotyping about women was found to be unconstitutional. This concern about stereotyping permeates the other, noneducation equal protection cases as well (Franklin 2010).

This antistereotyping component of equal protection sex-discrimination jurisprudence has been closely studied by feminist legal theorists. Mary Anne

Case (2000: 1449) has argued that prohibiting stereotypes, rather than utilizing the formal analysis of intermediate scrutiny (that is, substantially related to an important governmental objective), has done the 'bulk of the work' in the Court's sex discrimination cases. She claims that the Court requires a 'perfect proxy' in order to sustain a sex classification: 'That is to say, the assumption at the root of the sex-respecting rule must be true of either all women or no women or all men or no men; there must be a zero or a hundred on one side of the sex equation or the other' (1449–50).

This antistereotyping principle has been loudly critiqued as insufficient. In particular, antisubordination feminist theorists have argued that, while the antistereotyping principle does the important work of making the government treat women fairly as individuals by preventing overbroad classifications, it overlooks the ways in which government actions beyond mere sex-role stereotyping perpetuate women's inferiority as a group (MacKinnon 1979, Brake 2001). Reva Siegel (2004: 1472–3) has explained the difference as follows:

> For many, the belief that anticlassification commitments are fundamental entails the view that our tradition embraces a particular conception of equality, one that is committed to individuals rather than to groups. On this account, the tradition's embrace of the anticlassification principle signifies its repudiation of an alternative conception of equal protection, the antisubordination principle: the conviction that it is wrong for the state to engage in practices that enforce the inferior social status of historically oppressed groups.

Antistereotyping and formal equality, Ruthann Robson (2002) has argued, does nothing more than assimilate women into the dominant and idealized male world that remains unchanged.

Yet it seems that these criticisms do not fully appreciate the power of a strong reading of the antistereotyping principle from the Supreme Court's decisions, especially as applied to institutions that construct the identity of men and dominant masculinity. At a minimum, the antistereotyping theory furthers core equal protection values of treating people as individuals, but taken further, it can also help to dismantle 'systemic gender hierarchy' and to reimagine a 'society without [patriarchy]' (Pillard 2007: 949).

If all imperfect stereotyped notions of how men and women are to act and be treated by government are prohibited by the Constitution – no matter how close they approximate reality – gender essentialism, from the particular treatment of individuals to institution-wide construction of group identities, would be constitutionally problematic. Rejecting gender essentialism as unconstitutional would work against heteronormativity, which is one of the important gender stereotypes in the single-sex narrative, and one stereotype that antistereotyping principles should, but frequently fail to, address. With the Supreme Court's repeated warnings that imperfect stereotypes are constitutionally suspect, it is not a difficult step to begin questioning how those stereotypes have emerged and how institutions have constructed them to seem natural. This endeavour, the central inquiry of this chapter, has been linked to poststructuralism, a theory that 'emphasizes the variety, complexity, and contingency of the discursive influences that shape subject formation' (Abrams 2000: 1437 n.52).

The value of this poststructuralist approach is the way that it would deconstruct the institutional influences on men and masculinity, rather than simply reward women who do not fit stereotypes about femininity (Williams 1989). Traditional approaches towards antidiscrimination do not take the principle of antistereotyping far enough and leave the ideals of men and masculinity untouched:

> The standard for assessing women's relative difference is men; those institutional policies, practices, and structures that have been created for men are seen as the aspiration for women who can prove they are 'really' just like men. Whether what has been established for men is beneficial for men or women—whether the norm is worth aspiring to or instead needs fundamental change—usually eludes the inquiry of the similarly situated model of equality. (Finley 1996: 1109)

But adopting the strong antistereotyping approach suggested here, one that attacks essentialist notions of masculinity, would go beyond traditional antidiscrimination principles by examining the 'underlying social norm' against which comparisons of women have been made: men and dominant masculinity (Finley 1996: 1109). Katherine Franke has called this a 'deeply radical move' that would separate masculinity from maleness and femininity from femaleness (Franke 1995: 87). When the law complies with essentialist notions of how men and women should behave, desire and feel, and allows institutions to build and construct those notions, the law is furthering sex-role stereotyping of men and women. Furthermore, it perpetuates the association of power – which has been traditionally masculine – with men and, by proxy, enforces and furthers a certain type of manhood. Removing this association helps spread power to nonconforming men and to women. This principle is consistent with a strong reading of the antistereotyping jurisprudence, one that understands how men's roles are just as stereotyped and socially constructed as women's.

Strongly interpreting this antistereotyping strand of equal protection doctrine, as suggested here, would call into question schools that adopt or further the essentialist myth of masculinity described above. As demonstrated earlier, the single-sex education narrative of what boys need stereotypes boys, and schools that participate in the discourse perpetuate a hegemonic masculinity that harms both boys and girls. This form of masculinity aligns with traditional masculinity that has oppressed girls and women and limited the identity construction of all boys and men. Because, as Katherine Franke has argued, the 'wrong of sex discrimination must be understood to include all gender role stereotypes whether imposed upon men, women, or both men and women' (Franke 1995: 8), the narrative's construction of this masculinity is the essence of sex stereotyping and sex discrimination, and Title IX and the Constitution should prohibit schools from acting upon or implementing it.

Conclusion

Boys-only education is a risky proposition. If done poorly, it can reinforce stereotypes and be a 'breeding ground' for sexism and misogyny (Finley 1996: 1119, Karpiak et al. 2007). When California experimented with single-sex education in the late 1990s, researchers found that the single-sex classrooms, particularly the boys-only classrooms, reinforced traditional notions of masculinity – portraying men and boys as 'tough, "rowdy," and most importantly, not girls or women' (Datnow et al. 2001: 52). But education experts have also devised and studied ways in which gender-conscious programmes within single-sex schooling can have the effect of breaking down stereotypes (Davies 2003, Sanford and Blair 2002). Thus, implementation is key in determining whether single-sex education reifies or breaks down stereotypes of masculinity.

The climate surrounding the recent changes to Title IX's regulations does not indicate that the expansion of single-sex education in the US is off to a good start in this regard. One of the justifications fuelling this expansion, as described here, relied on traditional stereotypes about boys and masculinity. Because, as essential characteristics, boys were heterosexual, aggressive, active, obsessed with sports, competitive, stoic and – above all else – not girls, schools needed to educate them apart from girls and to educate them differently.

This narrative of how boys are and what they need corresponds to a dominant hegemonic masculinity that harms both boys and girls, albeit in different ways. Boys who struggle with attaining the hegemonic version of masculinity suffer – from verbal taunts to emotional distress to physical abuse. Girls, especially in light of the masculinity narrative's overlap with traditional patriarchal masculinity, suffer at the hands of boys who are taught that girls are weak, different and alien. And all boys' individuality is stifled when they are told that there is only one way to be masculine. Sex stereotyping in this form, especially with its reification of powerful forms of masculinity, runs counter to strong readings of Title IX's anti-essentialism thread and the Constitution's protections against sex stereotyping.

Although there may be other reasons to reject single-sex education in its entirety, this chapter does not make those arguments. Rather, this chapter argues that the essentialist myth of masculinity and its harmful effects should be a warning for schools that implement single-sex education. In implementing sex segregation, schools must vigilantly work against this myth, both in the way they talk about and teach to boys. If schools do not heed this warning, Title IX and the Constitution should prohibit this essentialization of masculinity.

PART V
Work

Chapter 13
Masculinities and Disparate Impacts

Ann C. McGinley[1]

Introduction

Masculinities studies observe that there are multiple forms of masculinity: men of different races, classes and sexual orientations perform their masculinity in different ways and in relation to one another (Dowd 2008: 210, McGinley 2004). Masculinities theorists posit that gender is socially constructed; they consider how societal norms shape individual behaviour, how masculinities are imbedded in the structure of institutions, and how individuals and groups perform masculinities within those institutions (Connell 2005a, Kimmel 1997b, Martin 2003). While the term 'masculinities' has multiple meanings, as used in this chapter, it has three meanings that are relevant to work. First, it describes a complex social structure that is embedded in organizations and determines and reflects power relationships at work. Second, it refers to the construction of masculine identities at work through performance. Finally, the term describes a set of practices and the active engagement in these practices by men or women. The presence of masculine structures, performances and practices in the workplace creates barriers to entry and promotion and affects the terms and conditions of employment at work based on gender combined with race, national origin, class and other categories to which an individual belongs (McGinley 2004, 2008).

This chapter examines the disparate impact cause of action under Title VII of the 1964 Civil Rights Act, as a potential means of ameliorating the negative effects of masculinities in workplaces (*Civil Rights Act of 1964*). Title VII prohibits discrimination based on race, colour, national origin, religion and sex. Unlike disparate treatment causes of action under Title VII, a plaintiff alleging disparate impact need not demonstrate that the employer intentionally discriminated against the plaintiff (*Ricci* 2009). Rather, disparate impact law requires that the plaintiff prove that a facially neutral employment practice that is also neutral as to its intent causes an adverse disparate effect on a group protected by the statute (*Ricci* 2009). If the employer cannot demonstrate that the practice is job related and consistent with business necessity, the plaintiff will prevail (*Ricci* 2009). Even if the employer proves job relatedness, the plaintiff can still prevail if s/he proves

 A version of this chapter will appear in A.C. McGinley, *Through a Different Lens: Using Masculinities Theory to Interpret Title VII* (forthcoming NYU Press, 2014).

that there are less discriminatory alternatives available to the employer that the employer refused to adopt (*Ricci* 2009). Because masculinities are often invisible and rarely intentionally discriminatory, disparate impact is a proof structure that litigants may use successfully to challenge masculine employment structures, hiring and promotion requirements and practices that create a disparate effect on women and non-conforming men. The next part of this chapter examines masculinities theory and the presence of masculine practices in workplaces. The subsequent part explains the history and theory of disparate impact law and argues that Title VII disparate impact law can be interpreted to ameliorate or ban certain masculine structures, requirements and practices in workplaces that harm women and some men.

Masculinities and the Workplace

Western society views masculinity as a static, natural result of male biology. In this view, there is only one form of masculinity that results naturally from the male body. Society's view of masculinity is both descriptive and prescriptive. It is descriptive in that it concludes that men are naturally masculine. It is simultaneously prescriptive, because it assumes that all men *should* naturally *be* masculine and that they *should act* masculine, as society defines the term (Kimmel 1997b). The powerful 'hegemonic masculinity' is ordinarily white, heterosexual and middle class. While society may be unaware of its prejudices, the definition of masculinity varies depending on the race, class and ethnicity of the individual man (Kimmel 1997b). Prescriptions of hegemonic masculinity define only a small percentage of men as appropriately masculine and to the extent that individual men do not live up to society's concept of masculine identity and behaviour, they are not 'real men' (Kimmel 1997b). Masculinities theorists conclude that the prescriptions take their toll on men who engage in a constant struggle to prove their masculinity to other men in order to gain acceptance (Kimmel 1997b).

Work is a site where men engage in this struggle. Work constructs masculine identities through organizational and individual behaviour (Martin 2003). The organization assigns genders to jobs, and the expectations of persons doing those jobs are built upon a traditional division of labour in the family (Martin 2003). In both blue- and white-collar workplaces, the jobs that perform the primary and most respected work of the institution are gendered male. The jobs that serve the auxiliary role of helping the men are performed by females (McGinley 2009b). This division of labour reflects and reinforces the traditional roles of men and women in the family (Williams 2000). Masculinity prescriptions affect men of different races, ethnic backgrounds, classes and sexual orientations in different ways. The normative masculinity in the American workplace includes aggression, competition and anxiety (Kimmel 1997b). Although numerous masculinities exist in tension with one another, the powerful hegemonic masculinity is white, middle class and heterosexual (Kimmel 1997b). Masculinity is defined more by what it is not than what it is. The normative masculinity is not feminine. It is not homosexual (Karst 1991, Kimmel 1997b).

Some, but not all white, heterosexual men can fulfil the masculinity expectations of them. Men who either decide not to follow the prescriptions or because of their identities are unable to do so suffer significantly from the masculinity prescriptions. Men who do not conform to traditional white upper-middle-class notions of masculinity suffer discrimination and harassment at work, and often do not succeed as 'real men' do (McGinley 2008).

Just as white, heterosexual men must learn to construct their masculinity in the workplace through performances of expected behaviour, men of colour must perform their masculinity at work. Men of colour, however, may experience even greater difficulty complying with the prescriptions in part because of racial and ethnic stereotypes. To achieve acceptance by the predominately white workplace, black men, for example, should perform their masculinity less aggressively than their white colleagues to assuage the fears of whites around them (Cooper 2006a, Cooper 2009a). Asian men should perform their masculinity more aggressively than whites due to the stereotypes that Asians are weak, nerdy and feminine (Carbado and Gulati 2000). Latino men, especially those of Mexican national origin, suffer from stereotypes that describe them simultaneously as lazy and hardworking and that often see them as rigid, 'macho' in a negative way and unintelligent (Niemann 2001). While many of these stereotypes are changing, they also endure, and require Latinos to attempt to counteract them in their work behaviours (Weaver 2005). These identity performances require more work of men of colour in workplaces that value the hegemonic masculinity because they often contradict masculinity prescriptions held by their own racial groups, and an attempt to emulate 'white' characteristics is often seen as 'selling out'. For example, Chicanos may be regarded as 'skirt-wearing' and may be ostracized by their culture if they adopt less macho behaviours (Niemann 2001). Women of colour also suffer from these prescriptions. For example, Chicanas who resist the stereotype of the good submissive woman and attain higher education and compete in the workforce will have to exhibit more masculine traits than those expected of them in their culture. If they do, however, they may be regarded by their own community as bad women who have assimilated to the white American woman's culture and as 'traitors' to their own culture (Niemann 2001).

While certain men in white-collar workplaces engage in performances in order to construct their identities in fashions that are acceptable to the power structure, others construct their masculine identities through subversive or subordinated masculinities (Connell 2005a, Collinson 1988). These men resist the hegemonic form of masculinity and present a different, often more forceful or violent, form of masculinity. Examples of subversive masculinities include the hyper-masculinities performed in shop cultures described by David Collinson (Collinson 1988), in a police academy described by Anastasia Prokos and Irene Padavic (Prokos and Padavic 2002), and in Las Vegas residential construction described by Leticia Saucedo and Maria Cristina Morales (Saucedo and Morales 2010).

Collinson's ethnographic study reveals blue-collar workers who construct their masculinity by engaging in hyper-masculine performances. By contrasting their own hyper-masculinity with what they characterize as effeminate behaviour of management, the men actively resist their subordination by management (Collinson 1988). Humour gives them a sense of power and authority at work, permitting them to 'negate and distance' their managers. It also permits them to define their own work as masculine and to police the masculinity of those doing the shop work (Collinson 1988).

In '"There oughta be a law against bitches': Masculinity Lessons in Policy Academy Training', Anastasia Prokos and Irene Padavic detail a 'hidden curriculum' that is described more fully below, in the police academy. This 'hidden curriculum' includes hyper-masculine behaviour and harassment of their female colleagues; it teaches students that male police officers are superior to female officers and creates barriers to equal employment of the female recruits (Prokos and Padavic 2002).

Saucedo's study of illegal immigrant construction workers in Las Vegas finds that male workers enact their masculinities by individualism and a refusal to act collectively, adherence to the belief that only they are capable of doing their difficult work, and harassment of their female co-workers (Saucedo 2010).

The British shop workers, the male police officers in the policy academy, and the Latino construction workers construct their own forms of masculinity in resistance to the hegemonic forms of masculinity. They also subordinate others as they construct their masculinity, violently disparaging women and other men who do not live up to the ideals of masculinity. These examples demonstrate that masculinities are dynamic and that they are created through interaction with others and performance at work. Sometimes the interaction is between men; sometimes the men use the women as foils to construct their own superior masculinity.

As the harassment of the Latino construction workers and the 'hidden curriculum' in the police academy show, women suffer in workplaces from the masculinity prescriptions. These prescriptions not only cause harassment of women but also limit their career prospects because the most powerful jobs are often built around the male body and lived experience. Women are expected to exhibit femininity because of social stereotypes about women, but femininity is denigrated by society and in the more prestigious, better-paid and more powerful jobs in the workplace.

This chapter offers examples of masculinities at work and the social-science research that plaintiffs should use to prosecute a disparate impact claim under Title VII. Examples of masculinities that exist in the workplace having a disparate impact based on gender alone or combined with race, sexual orientation or national origin and class include 'up-or-out' promotion tracks for tenure or partnership, hidden curricula in training programmes, and aggressiveness or competitiveness as hiring or promotion qualifications. I discuss these different masculinities, their effect on workplaces, and how the law can be interpreted either to ban them or to ameliorate their effects. Before reaching this discussion, however, I describe the history and theory of disparate impact law.

Disparate Impact under Title VII and Masculinities

History and Theory of Disparate Impact Law

From Griggs to Wards Cove to the 1991 Civil Right Amendments

Title VII of the 1964 Civil Rights Act prohibits discrimination in employment based on race, colour, religion, national origin and sex.[2] While disparate impact language originally did not appear in the text of Title VII, soon after Congress passed the Civil Rights Act, activists and key personnel at all levels of the Equal Employment Opportunity Commission ('E.E.O.C.') recognized that a focus on intentional discrimination under Title VII would limit the statute's usefulness in combating racial inequalities in the workplace (Eskridge 1994: 24, 73, 78). In 1971, the United States Supreme Court unanimously adopted the disparate impact theory of discrimination in *Griggs v. Duke Power Co.* (*Griggs* 1971).

In *Griggs*, black employees demonstrated that high-school diploma and standardized test requirements for transfer to 'inside' operating jobs in the defendant's power plant had a disparate impact on black advancement in the company. The employer could not prove that the requirements had a 'demonstrable relationship to successful performance of the jobs for which [they were] used' (*Griggs* 1971: 431). Thus, the Court held that the black employees had established a violation of Title VII. The Court declared that the 'touchstone is business necessity' and assigned the employer with the burden of proving that 'any given requirement must have a manifest relationship to the employment in question' (*Griggs* 1971: 431–2).

Congress amended Title VII in 1972, but did not amend Title VII to overrule the *Griggs* ruling, clarifying that Congress had adopted the Supreme Court's view that disparate impact was a viable theory of recovery under Title VII. After 1972, the Court decided a number of disparate impact cases, clarifying and at times muddying the *Griggs* ruling. In *Dothard v. Rawlinson*, it applied disparate impact theory to practices causing discriminatory effects based on sex and struck down height and weight requirements for prison guards in Alabama (*Dothard* 1977). In *Watson v. Fort Worth Bank & Trust*, it held that plaintiffs may challenge subjective employment practices in hiring and promotions by using the disparate impact cause of action (*Watson* 1988). Despite the majority's expansion of disparate impact

---

2 It states: 'It shall be an unlawful employment practice for an employer – To fail or refuse to hire or to discharge any individual, or otherwise to discriminate against any individual with respect to his compensation, terms, conditions, or privileges of employment, because of such individual's race, color, religion, sex, or national origin; or to limit, segregate, or classify his employees or applicants for employment in any way which would deprive or tend to deprive any individual of employment opportunities or otherwise adversely affect his status as an employee, because of such individual's race, color, religion, sex, or national origin' 42 U.S.C. Sec. 2000e-2(a)(2000).

theory to subjective employment practices, a plurality of the Court in *Watson* laid the groundwork for a major change in the burden of persuasion. Before *Watson*, courts and commentators generally agreed that, once a plaintiff proved that an employment practice caused a disparate impact, the burden of persuasion shifted to the employer to demonstrate that the practice was job related and necessary to the business (*Dothard* 1977: 321, *Connecticut* 1982: 446–7). The plurality in *Watson*, however, argued that the plaintiffs should retain the burden of persuasion throughout, and advocated significantly reducing the employer's quality of evidence from business necessity to business justification (*Watson* 1988). The plurality's formulation soon gained a majority of the Court's support in 1989 in *Wards Cove Packing Co. v. Atonio* (*Wards Cove* 1989).

Wards Cove changed the law in three important aspects. First, it held that employees may not prove disparate impact by comparing statistics of two groups of employees within an employer's workforce. Rather, it was necessary to compare those in the job with the statistics of those in the qualified labour pool. Second, the Court held that the employees had to prove that a specific employment practice caused the disparate impact. Finally, following the plurality in *Watson*, the Court imposed the burden of persuasion on the plaintiff throughout and altered the defendant's rebuttal requirement to business justification (*Wards Cove* 1989).

There was substantial opposition to *Wards Cove* and to other Supreme Court opinions decided in 1989 that moved the interpretation of civil rights significantly to the right (McGinley 1993). As a result, Congress enacted the 1991 Civil Rights Act, which the President signed (*Civil Rights Act of 1991*). The 1991 Civil Rights Act clarified a number of issues concerning the disparate impact cause of action, but left others unresolved. It states in relevant portion:

> (A) An unlawful employment practice based on disparate impact is established under this title only if –
>
> (i) a complaining party demonstrates that a respondent uses a particular employment practice that causes a disparate impact on the basis of race, color, religion, sex, or national origin and the respondent fails to demonstrate that the challenged practice is job related for the position in question and consistent with business necessity; or
>
> (ii) the complaining party makes the demonstration described in paragraph (C) with respect to an alternative employment practice and the respondent refuses to adopt such alternative employment practice.[3]

3 42 U.S.C. Sec. 2000e-2(k)(1)(A). Paragraph (C) states: 'The demonstration referred to by subparagraph (A)(ii) shall be in accordance with the law as it existed on June 4, 1989, with respect to the concept of "alternative employment practice"', 42 U.S.C. Sec. 2000e-2(k)(1)(C).

Proving Disparate Impact after the 1991 Act

Proper Comparison Pool – Qualified Labour Pool There is general agreement after the 1991 Act that a plaintiff ordinarily may prove disparate impact through statistics by comparing the proportion of members of the protected class in the *qualified* labour pool with the proportion of members of the protected class in the employer's workforce. This concept was well established by the Supreme Court in a systemic disparate treatment case, *Hazelwood School District v. United States* (*Hazelwood* 1977), and clearly applies to disparate impact cases after the 1991 Civil Rights Act. The legislative history demonstrates little or no disagreement over the basic issue of comparing the employer's workforce with the qualified labour pool. Nonetheless, statistical proof may not be necessary or even convincing in cases where the plaintiffs argue that the terms and conditions of employment create a disparate impact on protected groups. Examples of this type of disparate impact case that include challenges to English-only rules by Latinos and to bathroom facilities by women will be discussed below.

There is another caveat to the general principle that plaintiffs should use statistics to compare the employer's workforce to the qualified labour pool. Where the plaintiffs allege that a particular qualification creates a disparate impact, the appropriate 'qualified' labour pool cannot be limited to those possessing the challenged qualification, or it would be impossible for the plaintiff to prove that the qualification itself causes the disparate impact. In *Griggs*, for example, the plaintiffs alleged that high-school diploma and intelligence test requirements created a disparate impact on blacks for operating positions at the defendant's plant (*Griggs* 1971). In order to determine whether there was a disparate impact on blacks imposed by these requirements, the Court looked at the difference in high-school graduation rates between whites and blacks in North Carolina, and evidence of a much higher pass rate for whites than for blacks on the required employment test (*Griggs* 1971: 431 n.6). It did not compare those in the employer's workforce with blacks possessing a high-school diploma and/or passing test scores. Likewise, in *Anderson v. Zubieta* (*Anderson* 1999), after the passage of the 1991 Act (*Civil Rights Act of 1991*), the plaintiffs, American citizens of Panamanian and Hispanic descent working in the Panama Canal Zone, alleged that rules paying workers less if they became citizens after a particular date had a disparate impact based on national origin (*Civil Rights Act of 1964*). Because the plaintiffs alleged that the timing of citizenship requirement caused the disparate impact, the United States Court of Appeals for the District of Columbia Circuit refused to include early citizenship in the definition of the qualified labour pool. To do so would 'effectively define disparate impact analysis out of existence' (*Anderson* 1999: 342).

Particular Employment Practices and Causation – Subjective Practices According to the 1991 amendments, the plaintiff has the burden of proving that a particular employment practice causes the disparate impact or that 'the elements of a respondent's decisionmaking process are not capable of separation for analysis.'

In the event that the process is not capable of separation, the entire process will be treated as one employment practice (*Civil Rights Act of 1991*: 42 U.S.C. Sec. 2000e-2[B][i]).

Burdens of Persuasion and Production The 1991 Civil Rights Act clearly overrules the *Wards Cove* allocation of the burdens of production and persuasion. The Act shifts the burden of persuasion – not merely the burden of production – to the defendant once the plaintiff has proven that the employer's practices cause a disparate impact on a protected group. The 1991 Act also amends the definition of exactly what the employer has to prove to rebut a showing of disparate impact. First, the plaintiff has the burden of proving a prima facie case by a preponderance of the evidence. Once this proof is made, the burden shifts to the defendant to prove that the challenged practice is 'job related for the position in question and consistent with business necessity' (*Civil Rights Act of 1991*: 42 U.S.C. Sec. 2000e[m]; 42 U.S.C. Sec. 2000e-2[k][1][A][i]). Members of Congress had difficulty reaching agreement on exactly what burden the defendant has, and there is varying interpretation of the meaning of the 1991 Act. Some argue that 'job-related' is a very general term that does not apply to the performance of the particular job. This interpretation seems to stretch reality. While it is clear that the Democrats did not get exactly the language they would have preferred in the Act, they did accomplish a burden of persuasion on the employer of job relatedness and consistency with business necessity. In fact, Congress reached a compromise that included a decision to allow some ambiguities to remain for the courts to resolve.

Less Discriminatory Alternative Employment Practices Although the 1991 Act makes it appear that plaintiffs may prove alternative employment practices *instead of* proving that a disparate impact exists, courts and commentators have uniformly interpreted this section to follow the three-step burden of production and persuasion that existed before *Watson* and *Wards Cove* were decided (*Albermarle* 1975). In those cases, after the defendant proves that the employment practice is performance related and/or a business necessity, the burden shifts back to the plaintiff to prove that an alternative employment practice exists that would have a less discriminatory effect on the protected group (*Albermarle* 1975). The 1991 Act requires that the plaintiff demonstrate the availability of the less discriminatory alternative and that the employer refused to adopt it.

Ricci v. DeStefano Before moving to the analysis of masculine structures, policies and practices that have a disparate impact on women applicants and employees, we should consider whether *Ricci v. DeStefano* (*Ricci* 2009) should affect a court's analysis. In *Ricci*, a disparate treatment case, one Hispanic and 17 white New Haven firefighters sued the City under Title VII, alleging that the City's failure to certify the results of promotional exams because of the race (predominately white) of the successful exam takers was illegal intentional race discrimination. The City defended the suit by offering evidence that the exam had a disparate impact on African Americans and Hispanics. The Supreme Court analysed the case as a battle between two conflicting theories under Title VII: disparate treatment and disparate impact. It held that the City was liable for intentionally throwing out the exam results because of the race of the successful candidates. A city under these circumstances could successfully defend if it had a strong basis in evidence to support the argument that it would lose a disparate impact suit brought by unsuccessful minority candidates. In this case, the Court held, that a strong basis in evidence was lacking (*Ricci* 2009). In reaching this conclusion, the Court emphasized that New Haven had hired an expert consultant to establish the test, which, in turn, got significant feedback from firefighters who were members of racial minorities. Thus, the Court concluded, the test was job related. The Court also emphasized that the City had created 'legitimate expectations' in the firefighters who studied hard and were successful in the test. Finally, the Court noted that it would be legitimate to take race into account while creating the assessment, but once the expectations had been created, and the test was job related, it was illegal to throw out the test results because of race. In essence, the Court created an incentive in employers carefully to consider the possible ramifications of giving the test or of using a different assessment mechanism before administering the test.

It is unclear whether *Ricci* would affect disparate impact law in challenges to 'up-or-out' structures, and to other masculine structures and policies described below. In *The New Disparate Impact*, Joseph Seiner and Benjamin Gutman argue that *Ricci* creates an affirmative defence for an employer who is unaware of the impact of the challenged policy (Seiner and Gutman 2010). This conclusion appears to be too broad, however, at least with reference to the situations I am addressing in this chapter. First, the structures and practices that I analyse below are not promotional exams. Unlike the exams in *Ricci*, the structures and practices I discuss contain subjective criteria whose application adversely affects the plaintiff's job opportunities and/or harassing behaviour that affects the terms or conditions of the plaintiffs' employment. Second, unlike in *Ricci*, the particular masculine structures, job requirements and policies that I address below do not create a zero–sum game. That is, if the courts conclude that they create a disparate impact on women, there would be no concomitant harm to men. Because there is no potential disparate treatment case, the strong basis in evidence test would not apply. Thus, it appears that the courts should not alter the traditional burdens of proof and production articulated by the 1991 Civil Rights Act, and the Court's conclusion that the firefighters' exam was job related and consistent with business necessity and that there was insufficient evidence of less discriminatory alternatives in *Ricci* should have little effect, if any, on the analysis of the cases presented below.

Using Disparate Impact to Challenge Masculinities in the Workplace

Structures Creating Barriers to Advancement and Retention

Masculinities in the workplace include structures that privilege men by designing work around male bodies and lifestyles. These structures create opportunities for men and barriers for women (Connell 2005a: 71, Lorber 1994: 81). Many of these structures are invisible because we are so accustomed to them that we assume their necessity without exploring plausible alternative structures that may have less of a gender effect. The disparate impact cause of action offers an opportunity to make these structures visible and to consider what these alternative structures may be (Connell 2005a, Lorber 1994). Particularly problematic for women's careers is the structuring of employment opportunities around the reproductive processes of men (Connell 2005a: 71–6). This structure has a negative effect on women because of biology and social prescriptions. Examples of structures that are vulnerable to disparate impact attacks are 'up-or-out' tenure and partnership tracks, found in academia and in law and accounting firms. These mechanisms place pressure on individuals to work extremely hard and long hours at a time in their lives when, because of biology and social circumstances, it is generally easier for men to do so than for women. Because of limited space, this chapter deals only with up-or-out tenure tracks, but the same argument should be used to invalidate partnership tracks.

'Up-or-out' Promotion Tracks 'Up-or-out' promotion tracks for tenure or partnership are gendered structures built around male bodies and lifestyles. Most universities have tenure-earning and non-tenure-earning jobs. Academic tenure-track jobs are more prestigious and better paid, and an employee holding tenure has greater job security than one without it. Tenure-earning jobs place a heavy burden on persons who are new to the academy, however. Ordinarily, the first five or six years' teaching, scholarly publications and service determine whether the candidate earns tenure. Tenure grants a faculty member the right to continue teaching and researching at the university unless the university establishes good cause for de-tenuring the individual. The purpose of tenure is to protect the individual's academic freedom to teach, research, freely discuss her subject matter and to provide a 'sufficient degree of economic security to make the profession attractive to men and women of ability' (AAUP 2006a). While this is a worthy goal because it furthers independent thought, research and teaching and it would be problematic to eliminate the job security afforded by tenure, the process of determining who receives tenure is inflexible and biased towards men's bodies and lifestyles (AAUP 2006b).

The disparate effect of tenure tracks on women is amplified by the long years of education and preparation for a tenure-track position, a period when it is inadvisable to take on the responsibilities of bearing and rearing children due to the intensive time commitment involved. Most universities require a PhD of faculty members; moreover, many academic institutions now require 'post-docs', fellowship years after the PhD (Wilson 2005: A10–12). Given that the average age of persons earning a PhD is 33 or 34 (Wolfinger et al. 2009a), that a post-doctoral fellowship takes at least an additional year, and that the tenure track itself lasts approximately six years, the pre-tenure years coincide roughly with the average professor's life from 34 to 40 years of age (Mason and Goulden 2004a). This age span presents few problems for men or women who do not aspire to having a family. For those who wish to have a family, however, men enjoy a distinct advantage over women, both socially and biologically.

The years studying for the PhD and the first five or six years in academic jobs coincide with prime childbearing age (Shrier and Shrier 2009). As women age, their fertility rates are reduced and their offspring become more vulnerable to genetic disorders. A woman who waits until she accomplishes tenure risks the possibility of never having children or of damage to her future offspring. Knowing this, some women delay or forego having children (Mason and Goulden 2004a). Those who have children have less time to devote to their research and teaching because of the physical difficulties of pregnancy, childbirth and post-partum periods. As a matter of biology, men, in contrast, do not suffer the choice between delaying or never having children and suffering from lower productivity.

When social factors are added to biological differences in bearing children, the disparate impact on women is great. The placement of a trial period early in a man's career benefits the man who heads a traditional family with a wife or partner who not only bears the children but also rears them. The wife's labour grants the husband the opportunity to focus on his career. Women in academia often lack similar support, and therefore suffer a disadvantage that is enhanced by the demanding, inflexible, short time lines of the 'up-or-out' tenure clock (Armenti 2004).

Moreover, society conceives of men as breadwinners, and men construct their masculine identities by competing in the workplace as breadwinners (Collinson 1988). The hard-driving competitive atmosphere reinforces the masculine self-concept of many men. Society reinforces men's belief that men benefit their families by working extremely hard, even if working long hours causes men to neglect their families (Wallace and Young 2008: 111).

Women are socialized differently from men (Wallace and Young 2008: 111). Society conceives of women as care givers. While society rewards a man who spends all his time at work for being a good family man (based on his ability to be a good breadwinner), society views a woman who spends the same amount of time working as harmful to the family rather than supportive of it (Williams 2000: 70).

Moreover, heterosexual women with children with equally demanding jobs to their partners are expected to and do spend more time with their families and working in the home (Hochschild 1989: 8–10, 271–8, Mason and Goulden 2004a, Wolfinger et al. 2008: 390, Wallace and Young 2008: 117, Shrier and Shrier 2009, Wolfinger et al. 2009b). At the same time, employers often view a woman who struggles to accommodate both the needs of her family and those of her workplace as not committed to work (Williams 2000: 70, Armenti 2004).

In lesbian partnerships and single-parent homes, the 'up-or-out' processes also present a problem. While academia can be more tolerant of non-traditional lifestyles, the tenure track structure is unforgiving with a disparate effect on women. The ability to do research at home draws many who have childcare and homecare responsibilities, but the tenure track forces those who have these responsibilities to work on a short and inflexible timetable that clashes with the biological clock of many women. Women exclusively bear children, and they are disproportionately represented among primary parents and childcare givers.

Evidence of the disparate effects of the tenure process on women is startling. Recent studies demonstrate that men with babies entering their households *within* five years of receiving their PhDs are 38 per cent more likely than their female counterparts to receive tenure (Mason and Goulden 2004a: 11). Moreover, only one in every three women who takes a tenure-track university job before having children will ever become a mother (Mason and Goulden 2004a: 12). Women with tenure are twice as likely as their male colleagues to be single twelve years after receiving their PhDs, and women who are married when they begin their academic careers are much more likely to be divorced or separated from their spouses than their male counterparts (Mason and Goulden 2004a: 12). These statistics measure both the biological and the social constraints on women who attempt to further a career in academia.

Perhaps more telling is the proliferation of adjunct teaching jobs in academia that are not tenure-track jobs. Academics holding these positions are second-class citizens. They have low pay, long hours, and little job security. These positions have increased as the percentage of women entering academia has increased. While 22 per cent of female faculty members hold these positions, only 11 per cent of male faculty members hold non-tenure-track academic positions (Wolfinger et al. 2009b). Mothers with children under six years old are 'disproportionately likely to have adjunct professorships', whereas women without young children hold these positions only at a slightly higher rate than their male counterparts (Wolfinger et al. 2009b: 1612). Research demonstrates that women who leave the tenure track to work in non-tenure-track positions are sometimes hired into tenure-track positions after their children grow, but many are not (Wolfinger et al. 2009b). The combination of gender and family formation clearly harms a woman's ability to succeed in traditional academic tenure-track positions that have a rigid 'up-or-out' structure.

In an 'up-or-out' situation, courts should permit plaintiffs to use a variety of types of evidence to establish a prima facie case of disparate impact. The law requires that a plaintiff prove that the employer uses a particular employment practice that causes a disparate impact on a protected group. Plaintiffs should attack the short 'up-or-out' track as the particular employment practice that causes the differential between the success rates of men and women at tenure time. As permitted in *Dothard v. Rawlinson*, they should present national statistics to prove their case (*Dothard* 1977). National statistics can demonstrate a significant difference in success rates for women and men in academia in achieving tenure.

The plaintiffs should also present evidence that an inflexible tenure track and a differential between men's and women's success rates exists in the plaintiff's workplace. They should supplement this evidence with social-science evidence that explains why the rigid 'up-or-out' track causes the differential. The social-science evidence should demonstrate not only the biological burdens women encounter when bearing children but also the extra social burdens shared by women with children who work outside of the home. This evidence should be sufficient for most courts to recognize the burdens that the 'up-or-out' process places on women's careers.

Some respondents will likely argue that the plaintiffs are attempting to hold the university responsible for societal discrimination rather than for its own discrimination. And, at least in the equal protection cases, the Court has made clear that societal discrimination does not justify a remedy based on a racial classification (*Wygant* 1986). The fact pattern in the 'up-or-out' cases, however, does not ask the Court to impose a gender- or race-based remedy. And, it is not significantly different from the fact pattern in *Griggs*. In *Griggs*, the Court held the employer responsible for testing mechanisms that screened out black employees who presumably failed the test because of an inferior education due to societal discrimination in imposing poor, segregated schools upon blacks. While the employer was responsible, it was not judged morally culpable. The Court saw the disparate impact cause of action as necessary to encourage employers to eliminate non-job-related employer practices that created barriers to blacks as a result of past discrimination against blacks in the society. Here, the plaintiffs would ask the courts to strike down a process that, without moral culpability of the employer, builds arbitrary barriers to women who have children or wish to have children.

Proof of a disparate impact on women would shift the burden to the employer to prove that the 'up-or-out' process is related to the job in question and consistent with business necessity. Whether a university employer could meet this burden is unclear. The university would likely argue that one of its core missions is research and that it is vital that a faculty member become seriously engaged in research early on in order to promote the faculty member's and the university's reputations. Similarly, good teaching is crucial to the university and the 'up-or-out' process allows the faculty to assure that the individuals engaged in the teaching and research mission of the university are excellent. Finally, the 'up-or-out' track allows the university to assure that the individuals' academic freedom is protected. Although a court might accept the university's defence, there are good reasons why it would not. The American Association of University Professors ('AAUP') recommends that universities and colleges adopt 'general policies addressing family responsibilities, including family care leaves and institutional support for child and elder care' and 'more specific policies, such as stopping the tenure track, that relate directly to pretenure faculty members who are primary or coequal caregivers' (AAUP 2006b: 220). It recommends that universities permit pretenure faculty caregivers to stop the tenure clock one year each for the birth or adoption of a child up to a maximum of two years total (AAUP 2006b: 223).

This recommendation would permit pretenure faculty members who have children to continue to work full time and draw full-time salaries while the tenure clock is stopped. An increasing number of universities and colleges have adopted this recommendation and other family-friendly policies (Pribbenow et al. 2010, Wilson 2008, University of Michigan Center for the Education of Women 2007). These include the universities of Michigan, Minnesota, Chicago, California, Massachusetts at Amherst and Wisconsin at Madison, as well as Duke, Vanderbilt and Princeton. While tenure may be job related and necessary to the business of academia, the short five-year track may not be.

Even if a court concludes that a short tenure track is job related and a business necessity, the plaintiff has the option of proving that there exists an alternative that has less discriminatory impact based on gender that will be equally effective in furthering the university's goals of promoting excellence in teaching and research and protecting faculty academic freedom. If the plaintiff demonstrates that the employer refused to adopt the alternative, the plaintiff will prevail. The plaintiff can demonstrate that an 'up-or-out' process that includes flexibility for parents (women and men) who have child-caring responsibilities would not undermine excellence in teaching and research. She would argue that the process should permit a more flexible tenure track, allowing faculty parents to remove themselves from the tenure track for breaks of 12 months or more when a family event such as a birth or adoption takes place. She would also point to prestigious universities that have adopted the AAUP's recommendation to stop the tenure track and that have not lost prestige or scholarship as a result.

While the faculty members who take breaks in the tenure track may not produce as much scholarship early in their careers, there may be a benefit to a longer tenure track in that the work produced is more careful and better done. The faculty member's teaching will likely improve because of less pressure to research under a rigid timetable. The faculty member could prove that women tend to have less linear careers than men and may become more productive later on in life as their children age (Shrier and Shrier 2009). The breaks in the tenure track may actually foster excellence by avoiding the burn out often experienced by older faculty members, post tenure. For all of this proof, it would be necessary to have solid research demonstrating that the alternative presented works to promote the objectives of the employer.

Research demonstrates that some universities and colleges apply the stop-the-tenure-clock policies more equitably than others. For example, while some schools do not require those stopping the clock to produce additional scholarship during the time period while the clock is stopped, others expect additional scholarship of the candidate, a practice that defeats the purpose of stopping the clock in the first place. Still others review a candidate negatively merely because he or she has stopped the tenure clock (Thornton 2005). Furthermore, in some institutions, the family-friendly policies are allocated only to those women who are perceived to be 'the best and the brightest' (Spalter-Roth and Erskine 2005: 19). These practices are not less discriminatory alternatives that should be adopted. Instead, the plaintiff should focus on those universities that apply the policies in equitable manners. Reference to programmes at these universities, especially if there are studies demonstrating that these processes are equally as effective in achieving the university's goal, would be particularly useful.

Training Programs with Hidden Curricula Masculinities studies may also reveal and recognize as harmful hidden (or not-so-hidden) messages sent to women in predominately male blue-collar environments. For example, In '"There oughta be a law against bitches": Masculinity Lessons in Police Academy Training', Anastasia Prokos and Irene Padavic describe an ethnographic study of the overt and hidden curricula of a police academy's training programme in a mid-sized city in the United States. While the overt curriculum taught gender equality, the hidden curriculum allowed men to construct their masculine identities in the police academy programme by distinguishing themselves from women in the programme, by treating women as outsiders, exaggerating gender differences, denigrating and objectifying women, and resisting powerful women with authority (Prokos and Padavic 2002: 447). Male instructors and students demonstrated that they considered themselves superior to the women by using gendered language and male-centric examples when describing how to do police work. Male students used the classrooms as male-bonding experiences. The men glorified violence and associated it with masculinity. They exaggerated the differences between men and women, denigrated women and the feminine, and resisted the authority of women instructors.

The authors concluded that the men created informal barriers between themselves and the women in order to counter the threat to their masculinity of women's entry into a male profession (Prokos and Padavic 2002: 454). They opined, 'Some male resistance stems from women's disruption of male bonding and the equation of masculine men with masculine work' (Prokos and Padavic 2002: 454). By their presence, women furthered the construction of masculinity by encouraging the men to engage in the process of resistance to women and 'femininity'. Male students and instructors used the women's presence to 'aid in their construction of divisions along gender lines' (Prokos and Padavic 2002: 454). The resistance helped the men to sustain the gender status quo (Prokos and Padavic 2002: 454). The authors concluded that the resistance may have been exaggerated because the male police academy instructors and students' identities connect with a particular type of masculinity that is associated with violence and control. 'Control over institutionalized violence is a core component of men's authority in western cultures. Thus, while police culture, like the culture of many other male-dominated occupations, defines itself through masculinity, it is perhaps the association not only with masculinity, but also with violence that leads men to resist women in policing' (Prokos and Padavic 2002: 455).

This study describes an employer practice – the requirement that recruits attend a training programme – that is neutral in that it overtly prohibits discrimination, but that actually has a disparate effect on women who attend the training. The authors state:

> [T]he hidden curriculum there taught recruits that dominant masculinity is necessary to performing their duties as cops. Women's presence at the academy facilitated these lessons by indicating the boundaries surrounding masculinity (accomplished through differentiation) and by highlighting masculinity's superiority over things not-masculine. Specifically, male students learned that it is acceptable to exclude women, that women are naturally very different from men and thus can be treated differently, that denigrating and objectifying women is commonplace and expected, and that they can disregard women in authority. For each of these lessons, male recruits learned accompanying strategies for excluding and antagonizing women, strategies that effectively communicated to women that they were not welcome as equals. (Prokos and Padavic 2002: 455)

While the study does not say whether women performed less well than men in the training programme or in their employment as cops as a result of the training programme, a showing of an adverse effect on hiring or promotional opportunities should not be necessary in order to tackle the programme through disparate impact theory. Although the Supreme Court has never confronted the issue of whether employees can attack employer practices by pointing to terms and conditions of employment that adversely affect a protected group, lower courts have held before and after the passage of the 1991 Civil Rights Act that litigants can employ disparate impact theory to attack terms and conditions of employment having an adverse effect under Section 703 (a)(1) of the Act[4] (*Lynch* 1987, *Garcia* 1993, *E.E.O.C. v. Premier Operator Services* 2000, *E.E.O.C. v. Beauty Enterprises* 2005, *Johnson* 2008).

In cases challenging English-only rules (*Garcia* 1993, *E.E.O.C. v. Premier Operator Services* 2000, *E.E.O.C. v. Beauty Enterprises* 2005) and the failure to provide clean restroom facilities (*Lynch* 1987, *DeClue* 2000, *Johnson* 2008), for example, courts have resisted the defence that a disparate impact cause of action can be brought only to attack barriers to hiring and promotions under 703(a)(2) of Title VII.[5] Moreover, the legislative history of the 1991 Civil Rights Act appears to presume that disparate impact litigation can challenge terms and conditions of employment.

4 Section 703 (a) (1) makes it illegal for employers '[t]o fail or refuse to hire or to discharge any individual, or otherwise to discriminate against any individual with respect to his compensation, terms, conditions, or privileges of employment, because of such individual's race, color, religion, sex, or national origin.'

5 That section makes it illegal for an employer 'to limit, segregate, or classify his employees or applicants for employment in any way which would deprive or tend to deprive any individual of employment opportunities or otherwise adversely affect his status as an employee, because of such individual's race, color, religion, sex, or national origin.'

Because the plaintiffs' challenge is that the terms and conditions of employment have an adverse effect on women, the plaintiffs would use their own testimony combined with social-science expert testimony of the harm caused by the training programme to demonstrate that the employer's practice has a disparate impact on women at work (*Lynch* 1987, *E.E.O.C. v. Premier Operator Services* 2000, *E.E.O.C. v. Beauty Enterprises* 2005). Statistics that prove a differential in success rates in the training programme between women and men would be helpful, but not necessary. When the challenge is to terms and conditions of employment, the best evidence may be the testimony of the plaintiffs, combined with expert testimony. In *Lynch v. Freeman*, for example, the plaintiff alleged that dirty portable toilets were a neutral employment practice having a disparate impact on women, and offered expert medical testimony as well as the testimony of female co-workers to support the claim. The lower court made a factual finding that unsanitary portable toilets disparately affected women because of the difference in men's and women's anatomy and because of women's need to use sanitary products. Nonetheless, the lower court held that the women would be able to ameliorate the condition themselves, and, therefore, their claim failed. The Sixth Circuit reversed, concluding that the showing of disparate impact was sufficient to shift the burden to the employer to prove its affirmative defence. The Sixth Circuit concluded that disparate impact claims can be used to challenge terms and conditions of employment, and that it was not always necessary to use statistics to prove a disparate impact. The Court accepted the women employees' testimony about the difficulty they had in using the toilets in a sanitary fashion and the expert medical testimony about the disparate effect the unsanitary conditions had on women workers (*Lynch* 1987). Likewise, in *Johnson*, the Court held that the plaintiff's testimony that the defendant provided no break time over a 12-hour shift to visit restrooms, that the male employees urinated over the side of the truck, and that she was told to urinate in the same manner, created a genuine issue of material fact as to whether the failure to provide break time and restrooms created a disparate impact on women (*Johnson* 2008).

In *E.E.O.C. v. Premier Operator Services*, the Court held that English-only rules created a disparate impact on bilingual Latino telephone operators hired to speak Spanish to clients on the telephone, but who were forbidden from speaking Spanish between the telephone calls and during breaks. The plaintiff class established that the rule caused a disparate impact on workers whose national origin was a Spanish-speaking country through the expert testimony of a linguist who interviewed members of the class and placed their experiences in the context of linguistic studies. The expert testified that native speakers unconsciously engage in 'code-switching' into their native language with other native speakers and that class members switched from one language to another unknowingly. Because this 'code-switching' was unconscious, speaking in Spanish did not constitute a preference. Nonetheless, Hispanic employees were subjected to risk of reprimand or losing their jobs based on their speaking Spanish inadvertently, and the English-only policy posed no such comparable risk to non-Hispanic employees (*E.E.O.C.*

v. Premier Operator Services 2000: 1069–71). The Court endorses this approach in *E.E.O.C. v. Beauty Enterprises*, where the Court states that the plaintiffs would have to prove a disparate impact through their own testimony and testimony of an expert on code-switching (*E.E.O.C. v. Beauty Enterprises* 2005:*11). Similar expert testimony concerning the effects of the hidden curricula in the police academy on women from masculinities experts should establish a disparate impact based on sex or gender, either alone or in combination with race, class, sexual orientation or gender identity.

Once the disparate impact is established, the burden of proof shifts to the defendant to demonstrate that the training programme is job related and consistent with business necessity. While the training programme is concededly job related and necessary to the business of policing, the plaintiffs attack the hidden curriculum that sends the message that women are inferior to their male colleagues; they do not attack the fact of training itself. It would be highly unlikely that the defendant could argue that the hidden curriculum is job related or consistent with business necessity. Nevertheless, if the court were to look at the entire training programme and conclude that it is job related and consistent with business necessity, the burden would shift to the plaintiffs to prove that a less discriminatory training programme was available to the defendant and the defendant refused to adopt it. This proof should not be difficult. There is no issue that the training programme, absent the hidden curriculum, would be less discriminatory and would be equally effective.

The defendant's responsibility for the hidden curriculum in the training is obvious. The hidden curriculum is part of a programme required for entry into the police force. If the employer claims that it is impossible to screen out the hidden gender bias in the curriculum, the employees would have a good argument that the employer condoned the instructors' and students' behaviours that were used by male students and instructors to resist the female students' presence, to establish superiority of men in the job, and to discourage women from continuing in the profession. The hidden curriculum also reifies a particular species of aggressive, heterosexual and, at times, violent masculinity over other types of masculinity. Students and instructors use terms such as 'pussy' to refer to non-masculine men, a term that refers in derogatory fashion to the women's body, and show students a film with a man dreaming about sexually available and attractive woman (Prokos and Padavic 2002). This behaviour, which is unrelated to the content of the training, not only threatens the dignity of the women, but also may have an adverse effect on men who do not ascribe to violent, aggressive sexuality because of their gender.

Police recruits may also have success attacking the training programme through a disparate treatment analysis, by arguing that the training programme created a hostile work environment for the women because of their sex. In order to make a prima facie case, they would have to demonstrate that the behaviour was severe or pervasive and that it occurred because of their sex (*Faragher v. City of Boca Raton* 1998). While the training programme should fit the hostile work environment model, and employees challenging the training programme should allege hostile work environment and disparate impact, there are some concerns about the hostile work environment case. Courts have aggressively granted summary judgment in hostile work environment cases, holding as a matter of law that the behaviour is insufficiently severe or pervasive to alter the terms or conditions of employment (Beiner 1999, Beiner 2005, McGinley 2008). Some courts may consider the training programme in this case to create a disparate impact on the women recruits while not reaching the level of a hostile work environment that is sufficiently severe or pervasive to alter the terms and conditions of employment. Moreover the different remedies provided in disparate treatment and disparate impact cases may justify different standards. Plaintiffs may collect punitive and compensatory damages in disparate treatment cases in addition to the equitable remedies traditionally granted including backpay, injunctive relief, declaratory relief, and attorneys' fees and costs (*Civil Rights Act 1991*). Punitive and compensatory damages are not available, however, upon a showing of disparate impact (*Civil Right Act 1991*). Thus, it would make sense for courts to hold employers liable in disparate impact in some cases where they are hesitant to find the employer liable for a hostile work environment.

Hiring and Promotion Qualifications Reflecting Hegemonic Masculinity: Competitiveness and Aggressiveness Masculinities research may also aide employees arguing that the employer's neutral hiring and promotion qualifications have a disparate impact based on the intersection of race and gender. That is, these qualifications, as interpreted by an employer through a stereotyped lens, will disparately affect the hiring and promotion opportunities of women or men who do not conform to the hegemonic view of masculinity, based on their gender and race. Consider the hiring of personnel to sell used cars. The employer's image of a used car salesman is a white man who acts in a competitive and aggressive fashion. Thus, the employer searching for new sales personnel may consider aggression and competitiveness as qualifications for the job. These qualifications are gender- and race neutral, but they will likely have a disparate effect on white women, women of colour and men of colour as well as on white men and men of colour who are perceived as effeminate. Identity studies tell us that because of stereotypes we expect different behaviours from diverse people. We expect white women to be less competitive and aggressive than their male counterparts, but we attribute anger to black women and expect them to be more aggressive than white women (McGinley 2009a). Nonetheless, in contrast to an aggressive and competitive white man who would likely receive a job offer, a black woman would likely not receive the offer if she manifests aggression and competitiveness because of the negative stereotype of black women as angry, dangerous and hypersexual. We expect black men to be threatening, violent, angry and aggressive, but we expect Asian men to be passive, quiet and effeminate (Cooper 2006a, Cooper 2009a, Carbado and Gulati 2000, Chen 1996). These stereotypes affect our perception of how a person behaves and distort the person in the eyes of the employer when matching the person to the stated qualifications of competitiveness and aggressiveness.

The stereotype that white women are passive and caring, unaggressive and uncompetitive is both descriptive and prescriptive. People believe that white women fit the stereotype; they also believe that white women *should* fit the stereotype. So, a white woman who applies for a job as salesperson will be presumed to be inadequately aggressive and competitive to do the job. If, however, she demonstrates aggression and competitiveness equal to the men applying for the job, because of the prescriptive stereotype, the employer will likely judge her differently for her failure to comply with the stereotypes of white women (Butler and Geis 1990, Foschi et al. 1994, Eagly and Karau 2002, Heilman et al. 2004). In this event, the interviewer will likely refuse to hire her exactly because she meets the job qualifications. Chicanas and other Latina women may have an even more difficult experience than white women. The good and bad woman stereotypes are particularly compelling in the Mexican–American community, so a Chicana who resists the stereotype of passive and submissive in the business world in order to prove that she can perform the job may risk disapproval not only of a potential employer but also of her community and even a threat to her own self-identity (Niemann 2001).

Unlike the stereotypes of white women, stereotypes of black women and men are descriptive, but are not prescriptive. Thus, the black man and black woman may have to play a role in order to defeat the negative stereotypes of danger, aggression and anger. A black man applying for the job who demonstrates equal competitiveness and aggression to that of the white male applicants because of the descriptive stereotypes of black males may be considered more aggressive and competitive than the white male applicants. He will likely not get the job because his aggressiveness and competitiveness make him appear to his interviewer as threatening (Carbado and Gulati 2000, Cooper 2006a, Cooper 2009a). Black women, although stereotypically considered aggressive, a quality that the job description may call for, may also be considered angry and dangerous and therefore unacceptable to the employer. She is in a double bind because to the extent she plays the 'good black woman' – the motherly Aunt Jemima type – she will likely not be considered appropriate for the job.

Asian men suffer from a 'good Asian' and 'bad Asian' stereotype of their own. Good Asian men are feminine and child-like, never aggressive. Bad Asian men are devious and violent (Chen 1996). In both cases, the stereotypes will make it very difficult for Asian men to compete for the job of car salesman.

Moreover, men and women of colour may adopt certain behaviours in order to compete more successfully with another oppressed group of colour. One example is the Mexican workers interviewed by David Karjanen, who, referring to Chicano workers' view of how black men exhibit their masculinity at work, noted, 'Mexican men see this [black] hypermasculinity as troubling to employers and, like Mexican women, reproduce employers' stereotypes of workers by distinguishing themselves from black men' (Karjanen 2008: 59).

Finally, individual men of colour may respond to the hegemonic ideal in different ways. Anthony Chen explained that the Asian American men he interviewed dealt with the hegemonic ideal by using four different coping methods, some of which actually reinforced the hegemony of white men. They engaged in compensation, deflection, denial and repudiation. Only the last coping method counters the hegemonic ideal and fights the oppression that the Chinese American men experienced. The other methods demonstrate that men who cannot reach the hegemonic ideal actually might encourage their own oppression and that of women (Chen 1999).

The stereotypes of white women and persons of colour will affect how they are viewed, how they respond to certain behaviours, and how those responses are interpreted. Thus, job or promotional requirements that are linked unconsciously or consciously to the dominant white male such as aggression and competitiveness are problematic.

Masculinities and other social-science studies can demonstrate that the qualifications of competitiveness and aggression required by the car dealership have a disparate impact on white women and persons of colour. In fact, these standards are based on the hegemonic white man as the measuring stick, and while they may predict success in white men, they are not the only qualities that predict success. Employers will presume that white, Asian and Latina women are not sufficiently competitive and aggressive. Those white women who demonstrate competitiveness and aggression that would be lauded in a white male salesman may be denied the job because they would be considered unlikeable (Heilman et al. 2004). A similar dynamic occurs with black men and women. Even though they may be exactly as aggressive and competitive as the ideal white male car salesman, stereotypes will cause a distorted perception of them. Thus, white women and men of colour may have to perform their identities in ways that make them more acceptable to the car dealership in order to attain the jobs (Carbado and Gulati 2000, Cooper 2006a, Cooper 2009a). But these performances are far from guaranteed as to their potential success and they are fraught with danger of harming the individual's standing in their communities and self-identity. The plaintiffs should be able to show through masculinities and other social-science research that establishing qualifications such as competitiveness and aggression creates a disparate impact on white women and persons of colour.

The employer will respond by attempting to demonstrate that aggressiveness and competitiveness are job related and consistent with business necessity. Because judges often state that they do not sit as 'super personnel officers', they may be likely to conclude that employers had made out the affirmative defence. This holding would shift the burden to the plaintiffs to prove that a less discriminatory alternative exists.

The opportunity to prove that a less discriminatory alternative exists may offer these plaintiffs a chance to demonstrate that, even without the characteristics such as competitiveness or aggression, a salesperson can perform the job well. In fact, men's attempts to prove their masculinity through aggression and competitiveness may lead to less, rather than more, productive work environments. Work by organizational experts Robin Ely and Debra Meyerson may aide plaintiffs in proving less discriminatory alternatives where the employer requires or tolerates masculine behaviours. In 'An organizational approach to undoing gender', Ely and Meyerson theorize that organizations have the capacity to 'undo gender' (Ely and Meyerson 2010). They studied the working environments of two oil rigs (the 'safety-first' oil rigs) whose management had adopted strong safety policies and compared them to the working atmospheres of oil rigs that had not adopted the safety policies (the 'conventional' oil rigs), as described by earlier studies. On the conventional oil rigs, the men showed off their physical prowess, idealized physical strength and likened weakness to being a woman, demonstrated bravado in the presence of physical dangers, projected images of sexual potency and technical competence, and displayed emotional detachment towards others. The men working on the safety-first rigs, in contrast, developed close interpersonal relationships, openly admitted their mistakes, and showed sensitivity toward others. Ely and Meyerson concluded that there was a transformation in the safety-first men that was caused by organizational practices and norms stemming from the safety initiative. The transformation was due to the (1) importance of contribution goals; (2) definition of competence with reference to task requirements, not an idealized image of masculinity; and (3) creation of a learning-oriented rather than a performance-oriented environment. Safety was the highest priority on the safety-first rigs, and the men knew it. Men were encouraged to show humility and to admit vulnerability, and the goal was not to prove one's competence but to learn how to do the job better. This initiative led to an 84 per cent decline in the accident rate and a simultaneous increase in productivity.

Ely and Meyerson's study, if it can be replicated in other workplaces, would suggest that eliminating negative masculine aggression and competition is a less discriminatory alternative because it improves relationships among workers and enhances productivity. Expert testimony by these researchers or by others who have made similar findings would help plaintiffs prove that there are less discriminatory, effective alternatives to aggressive, competitive behaviours.

Conclusion: Ameliorating Masculinities through Disparate Impact

This chapter proposes the use disparate impact theory under Title VII of the Civil Rights Act to challenge the presence of masculine structures and practices in workplaces that create barriers to women, men of colour, and gender non-conforming men. Because the harm done by masculine structures and practices is often invisible and unintentional, disparate impact theory, which holds employers responsible for facially neutral policies or practices that unintentionally create a disparate impact on protected groups, is a vehicle that may prove successful in attacking invisible but harmful structures and practices.

Chapter 14
Masculinities Narratives and Latino Immigrant Workers: A Case Study of the Las Vegas Residential Construction Trades[1]

Leticia M. Saucedo and Maria Cristina Morales[2]

Introduction

Masculinities theories explain that the norms governing how men behave perpetuate male-gendered social constructs (McGinley 2004: 368–70). These theories typically expose how masculinities narratives and behaviours sustain white, male hegemony. They also explain how individuals in subordinated positions utilize similar narratives to distinguish themselves from females (McGinley 2004: 364). In the subordination narratives, even though men have low status, they still maintain positions above women in a hierarchical structure.[3] After conducting a study of residential construction workers in Las Vegas, we observed this dynamic in the case of Latino immigrant workers, who are increasingly segregated into low-wage workplaces.

The Immigrant Construction Worker Study, a qualitative empirical study of immigrant construction workers employed in the Las Vegas residential construction industry, provides us with data on the narratives of immigrant male construction workers.[4] Over a two-year period, the authors interviewed over seventy male and female construction workers in Las Vegas, with the purpose of understanding the demographic changes in the residential construction industry and their effects on workers. We found that demographic changes resulting from the restructuring and

---

1 This chapter originally appeared in the Harvard Journal on Gender and the Law, vol. 33:2, Spring 2010.

2 Special thanks to all the workers who gave us their time and their viewpoints about their workplace conditions.

3 For a fuller discussion of masculinities theories, see *infra*, 'Masculinities Theories in General'.

4 The authors collaborated in an Institutional Review Board-approved study at the University of Nevada, Las Vegas entitled *Labor Demographics and Union Activity in the Las Vegas Construction Industry*. The study consisted of focus groups and interviews with union leaders and construction workers over a two-year period. For a detailed explanation of the study, see discussion *infra*, 'The Study'.

de-unionizing of the industry have given rise to a mostly male, 'brown-collar' residential construction industry (Catanzarite 2002: 301).[5] We also discovered that the restructuring of the residential construction industry in Las Vegas reflects a parallel trend: immigrant women's entry into the labour market in traditional labour and in non-traditional labour, such as construction (Foner 2005: 89–105, Hondagneu-Sotelo 2001). By analysing the workers' attitudes through the lens of masculinities theories, this chapter suggests that the existence of certain workplace structures explains male workers' treatment of women, both on and off the job. Our interview data suggest that immigrant men reinterpret their experiences in ways that elevate them above women in the workplace hierarchy.

There are few studies that theorize or analyse how masculinities narratives operate in the immigrant-worker context (Adib and Guerrier 2003: 430). The Immigrant Construction Worker Study reveals, in relevant part, that male immigrant workers develop their own masculinities narratives to explain their entry and assignment into non-unionized and segregated occupations within the residential construction industry in Las Vegas. These narratives reflect and track the masculinities narratives found in traditional Anglo blue-collar work (Paap 2006), even as they are invoked to justify jobs that now pay less and offer fewer benefits than when Anglo men held them (Rabourn 2008). This is an important contribution to the literature, because it engages class, immigration status and national origin in the analysis of how masculinities are perpetuated in low-wage workplaces. Masculinities theories explain the process of internalizing what otherwise seem natural or endemic gendered qualities and practices in the immigrant workplace (Paap 2006: 116, McGinley 2004: 364–5). If gendered practices are, in essence, responses to the structures that employers use to maintain low-wage, segregated jobs, we can start to focus on and identify what those structures might be. Ultimately, masculinities theories, by unmasking the operation of narratives, should facilitate holding employers accountable for their operation in the workplace.

The first part of this chapter discusses the Immigrant Construction Worker Study, as well as the employer structures that may have led to a demographic shift from blue-collar to brown-collar construction work in Las Vegas.[6] The second part explores masculinities theories in general, and then as they apply in the immigrant-construction-worker context. The third part discusses the advantages of viewing the dynamics of the immigrant workplace through masculinities theories. This part provides guidelines for the types of changes needed in the traditional judicial anti-discrimination doctrines in order for us to understand how discrimination might manifest itself in these workplaces.

5 Catanzarite (2002: 301) describes 'brown-collar occupations' as occupations with 'strong overrepresentations' of recent-immigrant Latino workers.

6 The term 'employer structures' refers to the workplace arrangements, terms or conditions that make brown-collar construction jobs qualitatively different from the blue-collar construction jobs previously held by unionized Anglo workers.

The Development of Brown-collar Construction Work in Las Vegas

The Study

In 2006 and 2007, we interviewed over seventy workers in the Las Vegas residential construction industry. In 2008, we travelled to Hidalgo, Mexico to interview former construction workers who had returned to Mexico after the construction boom in Las Vegas and other regions of the United States went bust. We sought information from workers about why and how they entered construction work, about workplace conditions, about the security of their jobs, and about their attitudes towards unionization. During the course of the study, we collected the data reported in this chapter regarding gendered perceptions of the work and the workplace among immigrant workers in residential construction. The masculinities in the immigrant construction workplace are worth scrutiny, because they demonstrate how much race, national origin and immigration status can affect the adoption of the general masculinities narratives in a specific context.

Along with our interviews with union leaders and construction workers, observation revealed that the residential construction industry is dominated by immigrant workers (Rabourn 2008: 15–17). The shift from Anglo to Latino immigrant labour has occurred over a period of years. It is apparent that employers sought out immigrant workers in part because of their willingness to take fewer benefits than unionized workers (Erlich and Grabelsky 2005: 425–6). As the numbers of immigrant workers in construction grew, employers changed the terms of their agreements with workers, most notably by transforming workplace arrangements from employment to independent contractor arrangements (Rabourn 2008: 15, Linder 2000). Masculinities narratives seemed to play an important role in revaluing the work that historically had been well paid.

We observed masculinities narratives operating at several levels in our discussions with immigrant workers. The extent to which workers internalized the ideology of male hegemony – even in low-wage positions – was noteworthy. Workers justified specific workplace terms and conditions by using masculinities narratives, which in turn made the workplace tolerable. In this chapter, we shall focus on masculinities narratives responding to the independent contractor arrangement, safety conditions and workplace dangers, and the workers' approaches to workplace grievances. A detailed focus on the narratives sheds light on an alternative to the traditional discrimination framework, which emphasizes employer state of mind or motive. Here, a focus on the dynamic created in the workplace allows us to think more broadly about how today's segregated workplaces occur, what role masculinities narratives play, and what role the legal system can have in changing the narratives.

The Independent Contractor Arrangement

Transnationally and domestically, employers have used independent contractor arrangements to reduce labour costs (Erlich and Grabelsky 2005: 428–9, Greenhouse 2007, Donahue, Lamare and Kotler 2007). Sociological studies in several disciplines have revealed that independent contractor or informal economic relationships exist in occupations where the worker has the least amount of power (Agustin 2007: 21–3, Rabourn 2008: 15, Cranford 1998). Thus, the employer may be signalling its strength in the labour market when it offers independent contractor employment arrangements; only employers who have leverage or power in bargaining can make such arrangements (Reskin and Roos 1990, Roediger 2007, Cranford 1998: 35–6). Employers save costs since they do not have to pay employment taxes, benefits, insurance, or workers' compensation benefits for such arrangements (Rabourn 2008: 16, Greenhouse 2007). Consequently, the worker pool shrinks to include only those who have little choice for alternate employment. The workers we interviewed accepted the independent contractor structure in part because they had no choice.

Our interviews revealed that immigrant residential construction workers in Las Vegas were, for the most part, hired as independent contractors, and were responsible for their own benefits, pensions, and workers' compensation. A union leader described the arrangement as follows:

> I don't know how they do it, but [employers] pay these guys and … these guys are responsible for their own taxes, their own social security. And they could do the job whenever they want and basically release them from the company, from any kind of liability because they're subcontracting supposedly, that work out to these guys [who] are not subcontractors. They don't have a licence but that's what they're calling them.[7]

These arrangements skirt the edges of legality (Greenhouse 2007, Donahue, Lamare and Kotler 2007). Workers are more likely misclassified employees of a subcontractor, who directs their work on a daily basis. Somehow, the arrangement seems natural in the construction industry – an inevitable evolution in a competitive housing market (Erlich and Grabelsky 2005: 426). The prior existence of union employment and of union–employer relations in the housing construction industry demonstrates, however, that the independent contracting arrangements in the current workplace regime are anything but inexorable (Erlich and Grabelsky 2005: 423–4). Had the unions succeeded in organizing the new wave of workers into the industry, the workplace relationship would mirror the employer–employee relationships in commercial construction, and even in the hospitality industry in Las Vegas. Both of these industries are typified by strong employee leverage, relatively higher wages, and fewer wage competition issues (Rabourn 2008: 9,

7 Interview with Joe, Union Leader, in Las Vegas, Nev. (20 June 2006).

Waddoups 2000: 346). The housing construction sector, devoid of effective union-organizing activity, has instead seen strong employer leverage over the terms and conditions of employment.

Because the independent contractor arrangement makes accountability for employer liability much more difficult, it can lead to worker exploitation in ways that a traditional employer–employee relationship cannot. The independent contractor relationship, for example, raises legal questions about who is ultimately liable for employment discrimination, wage disputes, and unfair labour practices (Zheng v. Liberty Apparel Co. Inc. [2003] 355 F.3d 61). The independent contractor arrangement has become acceptable among workers in part because of the narratives that immigrant workers appropriate to explain and justify the arrangement. Some of the workers we interviewed said they preferred the arrangement because of its flexibility and the possibilities for greater wealth accumulation under the arrangement. Masculinities narratives in this context – rather than deterioration in employment law enforcement or restrictive Supreme Court interpretation of labour laws – serve to justify the employees' lack of leverage. The narratives are not entirely accepted among workers. The female workers highly favoured unionization. Nonetheless, most of the workers' responses to independent contractor arrangements were interesting in their individualistic approaches to the relationships. Ultimately, as will be shown, the narratives play a substantial role in deflecting criticism about the exploitative nature of the independent contractor arrangement.

Piece-rate Wages

In addition to an independent contractor norm, the introduction of immigrant workers into the industry coincided with an increase in informal piece-rate wage arrangements. Indeed, workers explained that they are paid by the piece in many situations, depending on the whim of the subcontractor, who is himself paid on a contract basis for the work that his workers perform. An individual or a group of individuals will be paid per task and per house.[8] The subcontractor decides how much each worker will be paid and sometimes negotiates piece rates separately with each worker. One worker described the process as follows:

> Based on budget they give a series of houses or a certain amount of houses to a foreman. … [T]here are people who can make money with what the house pays because that worker brings his cousin, his neighbour, or his friend from Mexico and he puts them to work with him. And the foreman acts as if he doesn't notice anything. But it's good for them – those are the ghost workers. Who's paying? Well the other worker because he's producing more, more houses. For this reason he is paying that worker, but of course, he is not paying him that much because he's also paying the other worker.[9]

8 Interview with Deltorro, Construction Worker, in Las Vegas, Nev. (15 June 2007).

9 Interview with Timoteo, Paint Supervisor, in Las Vegas, Nev. (20 June 2006).

Union leaders we interviewed criticized the exploitative nature of the system:

> [A]ccording to the law, when one is working piece work one has a right to overtime. So what happens? [T]he superintendent or foreman comes and says on a Friday afternoon, he says 'Look,' he says, 'I need you to do this house. … I want it by Monday at ten in the morning.' That means [they have] to work late Friday, Saturday, and even Sunday. On Monday, he has to sandpaper it and turn it in. But what's the problem? … [What happens] is that they work with you, they work ten, fifteen hours. But the problem is that they put in seventy hours. Seventy hours but since they get paid by the piece, then they don't get paid overtime. But according to federal law, if you work seventy hours for piece work you have to get paid overtime, but they are not paying that. They do not pay like that. It's a huge exploitation.[10]

Piece-rate wages, although now prevalent in the industry, are not inevitable. When the work was unionized, it was paid on an hourly basis, and workers were entitled to, and often received, overtime pay and bonuses for their work. Assignment policies were governed by a union contract, which regulated the type of work that employees would be required to do, the safety and other conditions under which the work could be performed, and the wages and hours to be paid for such performance. A high level of deskilling has occurred in residential construction over the past few years (Rabourn 2008: 11), similar to the Taylorization processes evident in the manufacturing and service industries (Ritzer 2000: 181).

One union leader described the before-and-after structures, and how they have affected both the skill base and pay structures for residential construction workers:

> [E]mployers, over the last twenty years, have broken the craft down to where … you have a person who spackles and caulks paste board, that's all they do. They go house to house [and] do four or five or ten houses a day. And then maybe they're sent back to mask … But, generally, the opportunity for them to learn more or do more is really dependent on, you know, the foreman … if you got somebody that can prep ten houses in a day, why would you want him to start painting? 'This guy's making me money. I'm gonna keep him right where he's at.' … [T]hey broke the trade down to operations [and] really deflated … the salaries of these workers by doing that.[11]

This description shows large-scale industry changes undermining the traditional trade-union structure that encourages the development of a broader set of skills. Importantly, the growth of these piece-rate wage policies has created a set of jobs that no one but immigrant workers will take (Erlich and Grabelsky 2005: 426–7, Rabourn 2008: 15–16, Saucedo 2006). It reflects the shift in power towards

10 Interview with Joe, Union Leader, *supra* note 7.

11 Interview with Union Leader Focus Group, in Las Vegas, Nev. (20 June 2006).

employers in the evolution of construction jobs. The structures themselves gave rise to a masculinities narrative unique to the immigrant-worker context.

Safety Conditions

The biggest problems with both the independent contractor and the piece-rate wage systems are their effects on productivity, workplace conditions and, most importantly, safety on the job. The workers who complained reported not receiving satisfactory responses from employers to their safety concerns. For example, workers were not provided with adequate equipment when working with chemical solvents:

> I had to scrub ladders on Friday with lacquer thinner, a strong solvent. I began at 1 p.m. and our shift ends at 3 p.m., but an hour after I started, I started to get a headache and they gave me a regular mask. But what we need is a special mask with filters. But if we ask for that mask they say they don't have it and a regular mask will do.[12]

One worker, a woman, explained how her employer failed to provide adequate ladders:

> We don't have the right equipment to do the work … [F]or example, they make us move these really heavy ladders back and forth that are sometimes too heavy … These companies know that they can provide the adequate equipment that allows us to do our work more efficiently and what they have done is use … the same old equipment over and over again. When in fact they are not providing the safety conditions that they should be providing to help us all work efficiently.[13]

Male workers, on the other hand, tended to accept more personal responsibility for safety conditions on the job.[14] The differential perceptions about employer responsibility are key to understanding how women continue to be locked out of construction work. The immigrant masculinities narratives motivate men to accept more dangerous work conditions, while women tend to complain about them. The masculinities narrative does the work of preventing or hindering legitimate complaints, whether about safety, pay, working conditions, or a hostile work environment. As one female worker noted, 'If we go to the head of the company, we are seen as problematic and they say we go only to complain, and we are only looking for problems.'[15] Viewed from the complainant's perspective, masculinities operate to hinder the ability of an individual to step forward and try to improve

12 Interview with Women's Focus Group, in Las Vegas, Nev. (12 Dec. 2006).

13 Interview with Women's Community Forum, in Las Vegas, Nev. (12 Dec. 2006).

14 Interview with Worker Focus Group, in Las Vegas, Nev. (13 Sept. 2006).

15 Interview with Women's Focus Group, *supra* note 12.

working conditions on behalf of all. Those who complain – male or female – are classified as not up to the task, even if the task is itself unsafe. The norm of not complaining that accompanies hypermasculinity carries an even higher risk for immigrant workers. Because of their status, workers believed they had fewer rights than their Anglo or native-born counterparts. The belief that they had fewer rights dovetailed with a sense that complaints would not resolve workplace grievances.

Masculinities Operating in the Residential Construction Industry

In addition to the structural developments discussed earlier, the masculinities narratives discussed in this section are themselves structures that perpetuate gender-based barriers to opportunity. In one set of narratives, construction work is men's work – and more precisely, immigrant men's work. In a second narrative, immigrant men do not complain because they prefer to 'man up' in the face of tough conditions. In a third narrative, immigrant workers embody the traits of risk, ambition and ultimate reward, which are inherent in entrepreneurs. In the fourth narrative, immigrant men endure the risks of the job, just as they endure the risks of undocumented or immigrant status, because they are responsible family providers.

Interestingly, each of these narratives affects and is affected by the vulnerable immigration status of the men who operate in the construction industry. The workers tolerate exploitative work conditions because of their undocumented status, and it is, paradoxically, their ability to withstand such status-based conditions that makes them manly. It is as if the masculinities narratives elevate the stakes for success among the immigrant men who participate, while at the same time erecting barriers for those who refuse to participate. These narratives are explored in depth here, to explain how they operate to create barriers to employment for those who refuse to accept or do not fit into the images created by the narratives. This section explores general theories about masculinities and then applies them to the behaviours and attitudes expressed by the workers in our study.

Masculinities Theories in General

The term 'masculinities' refers to norms governing how men should behave in a given context. The study of masculinities is informed by the notion that our gendered identities and gender performances are socially constructed everywhere, including in the workplace (McGinley 2004: 368–70, Collinson 1992, Collinson and Hearn 2005, Willis 1979). They are invisible, however, because they seem so natural (McGinley 2004: 368–70, Willis 1979: 185). Masculinities shift over time and place; '[t]hey are historically, culturally, and temporally contingent' (Collinson and Hearn 2005: 295). Because they can change over time and place, 'their making and remaking is a political process affecting the balance of interests in society and the direction of social change' (Connell 2005a: 44). The contextual twist in the residential construction trades involves the transformation of the work composition from Anglo to immigrant workers. What was once a set of masculinities narratives and behaviours invoked by Anglo blue-collar workers is now adapted by immigrant workers to fit their own experience in the construction industry. The narratives themselves have changed just enough to accommodate the deterioration in the jobs and the change in demographic.

In the workplace, masculine norms are expressed within a hierarchy and are embedded into certain jobs and occupations (Cranford 2007: 411). Such norms as aggressiveness, competition and entrepreneurship become part of workplace culture at all levels (Bruni, Gherardi and Poggio 2005: 59). In the same space, several levels of hegemony and subordination can operate. So, for example, one worker who is subordinate to another group of workers can still invoke masculinities narratives that subordinate others (Maier and Messerschmidt 1998: 332–7).

Masculinities researchers note that the 'gendering of men only exists in the intersections with other social divisions and social differences' (Connell, Hearn and Kimmel 2005: 3). Masculinities are replicated in institutional structures, such as workplaces, where they shape and are shaped by the relationships developed within the institution, and where they influence terms such as pay, assignment practices, hiring practices, and workplace conditions. Masculinities scholar David Collinson (1992: 207) posits that, while individuals are shaped by institutional power structures, they are also agents in explaining and fitting themselves within those power dynamics. The power dynamic between employer and workers operates within the residential construction industry to create gendered definitions of who can do what kind of work, affecting co-worker and employer–employee relationships. Masculinities are not simply an inherent property of maleness, in other words. Instead, they are the processes – variable, ever changing, contextual and fluid – by which gender relations are played out and by which practices that create a gender hierarchy become established and replicated (Bruni, Gherardi, and Poggio 2005: 61). There may be different masculinities operating at the same time that workers utilize to fit themselves within the workplace hierarchy. In analyzing immigrant-construction-worker masculinities, we were influenced by the work of sociologists and theorists studying two types of masculinities: working-class 'blue-collar' masculinities and entrepreneurial masculinities. We saw strains of each in the immigrants' narratives.

'Blue-collar' Hypermasculinity

From the inception of masculinities studies, several scholars have analysed Anglo 'blue-collar' workplace masculinities and their effects on work relationships (Collinson 1992, Paap 2006, Blum 2000, Prokos and Padavic 2002, Willis 1979). In studying Anglo working-class culture in the manufacturing environment, sociologist Paul Willis (1979: 188) found that workers in dead-end jobs recreated their experiences and gave them positive, transformative meaning, in part to make their work lives tolerable. Willis observed that the workers developed a culture that embraced 'the sheer mental and physical bravery of surviving in hostile conditions, and doing difficult work on intractable materials' (1979: 189).

The narrative of the tough, brave, fearless male helped workers develop self-esteem, in addition to some measure of control over difficult, sometimes unbearable, working conditions. Willis terms this the 'mythology of the masculine reputation' (1979: 189, 196), or the way in which a difficult work environment is transformed into a bearable one by giving it significance beyond the work itself and instilling it with masculine requirements (1979: 196).

Willis's study concluded that workers express their place in the work hierarchy through a series of masculinities narratives that define worker solidarity through humour and language in the workplace, distrust of abstraction or of theory, and devaluing or denigrating the work of women, minorities, and non-manual workers, such as managers and professionals (1979: 196). In short, masculinities narratives helped blue-collar workers explain or make sense of their subordinated lives.

Sociologist Kris Paap (2006) recently studied masculinities among Anglo blue-collar construction workers, spending two years working on a construction site in the Midwest. Paap described the masculinities narratives among Anglo construction workers as structures that maintain a power hierarchy at the intersection of gender and race (2006: 25–7). The behaviours that Paap described among Anglo blue-collar workers are similar to those we uncovered within brown-collar work environments saturated with recently arrived immigrant workers. Her descriptions of the hypermasculine male narrative are especially relevant to what we call 'brown-collar masculinities', or narratives infused with the hypermasculine immigrant norms found among our interview subjects (2006: 133–4).

The hypermasculine male narrative explains 'manly man' behaviour on construction sites. Paap argues that the narrative that 'men are animals' gives workers permission to be rude, crude or unrefined on the job. Moreover, the narrative propels the expectation that, because they are animals, men will perform all sorts of tough, difficult and dangerous jobs (Paap 2006: 134–8). The narrative itself serves several purposes. First, it provides a cover for the use of slurs and politically incorrect behaviours, such as sexism, racism and homophobia, which would not be tolerated in other contexts. It excuses behaviour that is otherwise inappropriate outside the construction site. This is why the stereotypical image of men on a construction site is difficult to eradicate: hypermasculine behaviour becomes so embedded in the masculinities narrative that it seems natural or endemic to the prototypical construction worker's character (Paap 2006: 133–5).

Second, hypermasculinity acts as an affirmation of one's manhood or heterosexuality. It allows men to act out in the workplace in ways that would be unacceptable in less 'manly' contexts (Paap 2006: 134–5). Examples of hypermasculine behaviour include excessive competitiveness, aggressiveness, and overt hypersexual acts aimed at women (McGinley 2004: 365).[16]

---

16 Although not a focus of this chapter, it is worth noting that we observed evidence of this kind of behaviour in the immigrant construction workplace. Several of the women we interviewed described their experiences with co-worker sexual harassment. Interview

Third, just as in Willis's blue-collar study described above, hypermasculinity in the US construction context is the method by which working-class men value themselves and their otherwise undervalued jobs. Describing themselves as animals allows men to define themselves as less sophisticated and, at the same time, more masculine than their middle-class superiors (Paap 2006: 135). In other words, the 'identity of raw masculinity and real manhood is clearly a nonmonetary job benefit that the men can cash in on when they claim that they are "pigs" and "animals"' (Paap 2006: 136). Hypermasculine behaviours, in turn, allow construction workers to define themselves as 'natural workers', who are made to perform work that is physical, tiring, dangerous and manly (Paap 2006: 138). Anyone who complains about the abuse is not strong enough or manly enough to do the job (Paap 2006: 145). The narrative, then, operates as a self-policing or regulatory mechanism that screens for those who are not 'tough enough' (Paap 2006: 148).

Fourth, hypermasculinity gives rise to what Paap calls a 'Culture of No Complaints' among the workers, who individually may fear ridicule or ostracism if they cannot tolerate the tough conditions on the job (Paap 2006: 143–8). The Culture of No Complaints preserves a set of behavioural responses to the work environment, such as unsafe conditions, undesirable job tasks, and even harassment on the job (Paap 2006: 143–8). Workers are expected to put up with harsh conditions, and even harassment, because '[t]o complain about harassment and mistreatment … is to violate the widespread code of the industry' (Paap 2006: 145). Paap describes this culture as a structure in and of itself, supporting workplace norms that bar women from construction work:

> By imposing a Structure of No Complaints upon the construction workforce … pigness is able to protect the jobs for people who can 'handle' the environment – most often and most likely, people who look like or are related to the men working in the jobs already. (2006: 148)

The narrative relies on the corollary myth that individuals choose their jobs and career paths, and those who cannot tolerate the hypermasculine environment would naturally choose to be elsewhere (Paap 2006: 148). Hypermasculinity itself operates subliminally and at cross purposes to formal legal prohibitions on discrimination. Masculinities narratives blur the line between activities for which employers are responsible and those which are societal and therefore endemic to a worker's character. If hypermasculinity is a structure that helps employers maintain the job for the tough, hardened worker who can handle it, Paap argues,

> [P]igness is able to do informally what exclusionary laws and rules, discriminatory practices, and systematic violence did for many years but are no longer formally allowed to do. It is not that women … aren't *formally* and *legally*

---

with Carlotta, Construction Worker, in Las Vegas, Nev. (16 June 2007); interview with Nancy, Construction Worker, in Las Vegas, Nev. (13 June 2007).

> welcomed, it is simply that the men who chose to be construction workers are 'pigs' and that under the right conditions most women (and nonpig men) will choose to do something else somewhere else. Thus pigness serves companies as an *occupational gatekeeping* mechanism for women … without their having to hire or fire explicitly on these lines. (2006: 148, emphasis in original)

In other words, the narrative masks or hides the operation of employer practices that encourage discrimination by allowing the narrative to self-perpetuate.

Entrepreneurial Masculinities

Entrepreneurial masculinities in general assume that risk taking, leadership qualities, and a competitive spirit are attributes that are gendered male. Not only are entrepreneurship activities gendered, but so are the narratives used to sustain this type of economic activity. Entrepreneurial masculinities narratives appeal to ideas of freedom, success and individualism (Bruni, Gherardi and Poggio 2005: 59). They embody the heroic quality of the entrepreneur, one that evokes images of the rugged individualist, the risk taker, the leader and manager, the rational decision maker, and the competitor (Bruni, Gherardi and Poggio 2005: 59–60). Each of these, separate and together, has been packaged into a cultural narrative as masculine characteristics (Bruni, Gherardi and Poggio 2005: 59–60).

Entrepreneurial masculinities narratives incorporate elements that contrast with descriptions of employees in the workplace. For instance, the language of risk or the assumption of responsibility for others if something goes awry is a form of entrepreneurial masculinity (Bruni, Gherardi and Poggio 2005: 144).

The language of risk is used to describe the initial decision to start an enterprise, as well as subsequent decisions to expand (Bruni, Gherardi and Poggio 2005: 146–7). The narrative also involves the notion of reinvestment into the enterprise and concern for long-term planning involving the enterprise (Bruni, Gherardi and Poggio 2005: 148–9). As such, this narrative distinguishes the entrepreneur from the worker or the employee, who is concerned primarily with salary and less with efficiency or quality of production (Bruni, Gherardi and Poggio 2005: 149).

In the construction industry, entrepreneurship is one of the narratives that constructs masculinity in the workplace (Bruni, Gherardi and Poggio 2005: 57–60). 'The individual', 'choice' and 'the market' are the buzz words for explaining workplace arrangements – like independent contracting – in which the employee or contractor carries the vast majority of the risk of illness, injury, disability and market downturns (Connell 2005b: 76). As we shall show, for immigrant workers, the entrepreneur narrative ameliorates the harsh effects of downsizing, benefit loss, and reduction of safety-net benefits on men's self-image and self-respect.

The 'Brown-collar' Worker Masculinities

Interviews with both male and female immigrant construction workers revealed the operation of workplace masculinities. Although similar to the masculinities described above, brown-collar masculinities had distinct characteristics and impetuses.

The similarities between masculinities narratives in general and as they appear in the immigrant workplace give credence to masculinities theorists who argue that 'gendered power relations can simultaneously both change (in character) yet remain broadly the same (in structure)' (Collinson and Hearn 2005: 295). The fact that our female interviewees experienced several forms of discrimination from masculine behaviours in the immigrant workplace shows that masculinities narratives adapt to different cultural environments. Just as with the blue-collar workers described in Paap's study, brown-collar workers emphasize the masculine characteristics of their jobs as a way to build collective self-esteem about their work and to devalue the contributions of women in the workplace (Paap 2006: 148, Willis 1979: 196).

We identified four principal forms of masculinities that the interviewees described. The first is constructed around the narrative that brown-collar work is labour that no one else will do. In this narrative, the workers are proud that they are performing dangerous, difficult and physically demanding labour. This narrative responds to the changes in wage structures and assignment policies within the industry. Closely related, the second set of masculinities is constructed around hypermasculine behaviours, emphasizing the craft, skill and toughness required of the workers, even as the jobs themselves are deskilled. It responds, in part, to the piece-rate wage policies and safety conditions described earlier. As with Anglo blue-collar workers, the danger of the work is masked by a narrative that discourages complaints. The third set of masculinities, growing out of the independent contractor relationships with employers, is constructed around the idea of workers as entrepreneurs or businessmen in the making. It responds to the independent contractor arrangements prevalent in the residential construction industry. The fourth set of masculinities centres on the men as breadwinners, and on their masculinity in enduring the dangers of border crossing and undocumented status to get to their jobs in the United States. Each of these narratives is discussed in detail below.

No One Else Can/Will Do the Job

A form of masculinity is embedded in the claim that the jobs into which newly arrived immigrants are segregated are jobs that only immigrants will take. Male interviewees expressed the sentiment that they felt good about doing their jobs, because they worked hard to perform work that no native-born worker would do. They took pride in performing dirty, difficult, low-paying and dangerous jobs in construction and in tolerating the work conditions. One worker from an indigenous Mexican community noted,

> What happens is that the majority of us indigenous people, it does not matter what we earn, just as long as we earn something. Just as long as we have work,

> it does not matter if it's cheap. What interests us more is to stay active, to know that we will be getting paid at the end of the week, even if it's a small paycheck.[17]

The worker's assertion that the level of pay or the type of work does not matter implies a different attitude from one ascribed to native-born workers who do care about pay and working conditions. At the same time, the workers asserted that, even among immigrants, only a few can or will do these jobs. As one worker put it,

> Construction in and of itself is a very difficult job. There are many people who have worked in construction who are now working in casinos because you have food, a uniform, and you're in a shaded area, with air conditioner there. Regardless of what you earn in construction, it's a difficult job.[18]

Study interviewees expressed satisfaction that they were doing a job no one else could do, thus internalizing and valuing the sentiment heard in the public that immigrant workers took jobs no one else would take. This sentiment parallels that of the blue-collar construction workers studied by Paap, who carried with them an attitude of superiority at being able to do a job that their middle-class counterparts could not do (2006: 135–6). It also parallels the opinions of manufacturing workers in Willis' study, who disdained professionals and others who did not master a task by doing it (1979: 194). Interestingly, immigrant men felt pride in their work even though they understood that their jobs were devalued as work that no native-born worker would perform.

The masculinity expressed in 'doing a job nobody else will do' serves several purposes. First, it dignifies the otherwise dirty, difficult and undesirable aspects of a job. Second, as some masculinities theorists have suggested, it rationalizes the wage deterioration of the job (Willis 1979: 196–7, Zinn 1982: 39). A worker can rationalize taking a job that pays less if it somehow increases his status through masculinization (Willis 1979: 196–7, Zinn 1982: 39). This second aspect is important, because masculinities narratives compensate for the devaluation of a job once it becomes a 'brown-collar' job (Roediger 2007: 13–14, Catanzarite 2002, Kelley 1993: 101). Third, this narrative operates to maintain a gendered performative masculine identity in the workplace. When workers performed the role of the prototypical male construction worker, their performance suppressed others' complaints about working conditions. Employers desired those who performed to meet expectations of the hardworking, subservient and compliant employee. The idea that they do the work nobody else will do bolsters expectations about their hardworking character and about the conditions they will endure to continue to be the ones chosen to do that work (Carbado, Fisk and Gulati

17 Interview with Antonio, Construction Worker, in Las Vegas, Nev. (12 June 2007).

18 Interview with Worker Focus Group, *supra* note 14.

2007, Carbado and Gulati 2000).[19] As with hypermasculinity, this expression of masculinity encourages individual workers to take more risk and accept more dangerous conditions.

Hypermasculinity in the Brown-collar Context

The hypermasculine male stereotype continues to reproduce itself among immigrant workers. While the stereotype of the manly construction worker once had an Anglo, male face, the stereotype in the residential industry has taken on the face of the Latino immigrant.

Some of the workers we interviewed provided several examples of hypermasculinity among the men, in the form of sexual advances and sexual innuendos as well as in the form of attitudes about what kind of work was appropriate for men. Not only did men banter about sex and sexual activities in front of women, they also treated them as sexually loose women. Some of the women reported that they had to develop their own mechanisms of self-protection in reaction to men's comments about why they worked in construction.[20] One woman observed that the men she worked with questioned her morals simply because she decided to take a job in a male-dominated environment. Her frustration was evident:

> For the majority of the people, women who work in construction come from a bad background … I don't know why they have that idea of women in construction, but women don't work in construction … [merely] because they like men.[21]

Non-sexual forms of harassment took the form of opinions about what women could and could not do. Female construction workers provided several examples of sex-role stereotyping in the assessment of their work capabilities:

- [I]f we as women go and apply to the company, the response we get is, 'What do you know how to do?' … it's sort of this presumption that you don't know how to do this kind of work.[22]
- The problem is when the company doesn't have enough work … they give [women] the heaviest work so we can feel pressured to do it and if we tell them, 'How are we going to do it?', they say, 'Aren't you asking for

19 Here, we invoke the work of legal scholars Devon Carbado, Mitu Gulati and Catherine Fisk, who write about the power of workplace structures to define the performative identity of the worker through its workplace requirements. In the immigrant worker case, workers will keep their employment over the long term if they live up to the 'hard worker' stereotype established by the myth of the job nobody else will take. In contrast, those immigrant workers who complain about working conditions tend to lose their jobs over time.

20 Interview with Carlotta, *supra* note 16.

21 Interview with Women's Focus Group, *supra* note 12.

22 Interview with Women's Community Forum, *supra* note 13.

equality?' That is how they put pressure on us.[23]

- 'Unless we come in with a recommendation, what we see there are even barriers of entry and we go in and turn in an application to the company and as soon as we leave that application goes into the trash can.'[24]

The hypermasculinity was also manifested in the ways that men accepted unsafe tasks or worked in unsafe conditions without complaint. One male worker who built an unsafe wooden scaffold in order to get ahead with his production quota explained his disregard of safety in terms of productivity:

> That's why accidents occur more often, because there are no safety norms. They're just given a paper that talks about safety, but since you're there for production … the more you make, the better. … Yes, you sign it, but since you're working to get ahead and you want to get ahead the most you can do, for example, right here it's forbidden to make a wooden scaffold. However, in order to not fall behind we make it quickly out of wood and that's how we pass through there. And it's forbidden, but since you're working by production you have to get ahead; if not you don't make a good paycheck.[25]

His response was typical of men's responses to safety problems in the workplace. Safety was invariably balanced against the production and quota requirements of the piece-rate wage system now prevalent in the industry. The masculinities narratives encouraged a Culture of No Complaints in the brown-collar context, which was also evident in similar blue-collar environments discussed by Paap in her study (2006). In such a hypermasculine environment, only those who cannot 'man up' to the task will complain about the terms and conditions, including unsafe conditions, of the job.

By conceptualizing hypermasculinity as an endemic trait (rather than as a response to external workplace conditions), the narrative in the immigrant worker context devalues the humanity of the individual. After all, the more we associate the workers with their animalistic behaviours, the less we have to consider their human worth. In this sense, the narrative easily accommodates the concomitant racialization of the jobs in construction. As Paap notes with respect to Anglo blue-collar workers,

> To attribute animal status to a group is to remove them from the moral responsibility and consciousness of the nation. It is to mark them as a group whose interests, pain, and suffering are to be seen as bearing little relation to those of the general public. And under conditions of increasingly globalized market pressures, ongoing if not rising drives for profit, and increasingly tight

23 Interview with Women's Focus Group, *supra* note 12.

24 Interview with Women's Community Forum, *supra* note 13.

25 Interview with Worker Focus Group, in Las Vegas, Nev. (12 Dec. 2006).

> production schedules in the construction industry, this sort of cultural posturing might be all that the industry – and the public – needs to turn its attention and concerns elsewhere. (2006: 156–7)

Paap's observations equally apply to immigrant workers. In the immigrant-worker context, the hypermasculinity narrative is especially powerful and dangerous, because it compounds immigration and prosecution policies that make undocumented workers both invisible and vulnerable (Camayd-Freixas 2008). Not only is the work now assigned to the immigrant 'other', but ascribing animal-like qualities further separates the residential construction worker from the rest of the Las Vegas population. Removal from public consciousness facilitates exploitation both because employers can more easily ignore undocumented status if everyone is undocumented and because undocumented workers will complain less in order to avoid intrusive questions.

Entrepreneurial Masculinities in the Brown-collar Context

Immigrant workers have accepted the independent contractor arrangement because it is the only employment structure offered to them in the construction business (Cranford 1998: 25–6). The arrangement lacks the medical benefits, pension, workers' compensation, unemployment insurance, and higher wage structures of a traditional employer–employee relationship (Rabourn 2008: 15). It also frees the employer of tax liabilities, including the employer portions of Social Security and Medicare taxes (Greenhouse 2007). This trend towards independent contracting, despite bordering on illegality in some instances, has become a successful business model for trade employers (Rabourn 2008: 15–17).

In response, immigrant workers have created their own narratives about the benefits of the independent contractor arrangement, which parallel those of the entrepreneurial masculinities narratives described earlier. For instance, the independent contractor model afforded one worker the freedom and flexibility to accumulate money, plan for a future business in construction, and fulfil his dream of building towards the future:

> When one is under contract … there's more opportunity to make more money. Well, you make good money with a contract, because there is no set hours. You can work until you want. And with salary and hourly, you can only work the certain hours that they give you and you cannot work more hours.[26]

This narrative also mirrors the neoliberal entrepreneurial masculinities written about in the transnational context, which serve the function of dignifying jobs that are now contingent and unstable (Stone 2004: 67–72). In the immigrant construction worker context, the entrepreneurial masculinity narrative not only redignifies a job's status (raising it as a noble enterprise even though it is now

26 Interview with Deltorro, Construction Worker, *supra* note 8.

occupied by immigrant workers), it also dignifies the working conditions, the pay structures, and the relative inferiority and declining position of the job, providing the possibility of opportunity even as it transforms into a menial job. The workers envisioned themselves following the business model of the labour brokers who brought them into the business by utilizing social networks, family ties and friendships to build contracting crews (Erlich and Grabelsky 2005: 428). One worker described this subcontracting structure, highlighting the business aspect of the arrangement, even as he acknowledged its exploitative nature:

> I work for a company but directly I don't work for that company. I work for the sub-contractor and that sub-contractor tells me, 'Look, tomorrow you are going to the *Silverado Ranch*.' Then the next day he tells me, 'Now you are going somewhere else.' Then he gives me the price of a house but the company is giving him a higher price. He wins just because he moves me around and because I am new, illegal, fearful, without a passport, without transportation, and without tools.[27]

The entrepreneurial narrative is an example of how workplaces reflect the dynamic social relationships between employer and employee. The independent contractor arrangement was a fringe employment structure when unions were strong in the residential construction industry (Rabourn 2008: 11, 14). It has now surpassed union employment as the dominant employment arrangement in residential construction, in part because of employers' aggressive campaigns to de-unionize the industry (Erlich and Grabelsky 2005: 423–4, Linder 2000). The entrepreneurial narrative adapts easily to a restructured industry. It places a positive light on the changes in the industry that would otherwise be viewed as a defeat for a formerly unionized, higher-paying workforce. Entrepreneurship in the immigrant workplace was viewed as the path to upward mobility for the risk-taking, aggressive and ambitious worker. The alternate narrative of collective empowerment was not deemed attractive or even possible.

Masculinities in Rights Perception, Immigration Status, and Family-provider Status

In addition to masculinities narratives, immigration status is a reason why workers do not seek to challenge their working conditions in the brown-collar environments. Restrictive immigration policies and laws create the conditions for exploitation that native-born workers do not experience. The spectre of raids and deportations in the brown-collar workplace adds to the danger of the job (Erlich and Grabelsky 2005: 427). As a group, the men feel powerless to enforce whatever workplace rights they might have or to protect themselves from scrutiny about their immigration status. The response among men is to construct narratives for themselves that incorporate their journey into the United States. Their ability to withstand dangers upon crossing the border bolsters the claim that they can handle

27 Interview with Worker Focus Group, *supra* note 14.

whatever dangers they face in the workplace and justifies the decision to take jobs that nobody else will take. Interwoven among the stories the workers shared was a sense that they had endured much pain, difficulty and hardship to arrive in the United States as undocumented workers. One interviewee noted that he had to walk several days 'in the desert during night and day, hungry, cold, thirsty.'[28] The workers focused on enduring their treatment on the job because of their undocumented status. If they could endure the dangers of the border crossing, they could endure tough working conditions including, if need be, limited workplace rights, all for the sake of supporting their families.

The story that we saw emerging from our series of interviews was two fold: first, the workers had endured a tremendous amount of danger and personal suffering to cross the border; and second, they had endured both the border-crossing difficulties and workplace exploitation because they had families to support. The overall endurance story provides a justification for tolerating poor workplace conditions. In other words, poor workplace treatment is tolerable compared to what the worker had to endure to get into the United States. Enduring exploitation because of their undocumented status was just one more set of difficulties that came with crossing the border illegally to support their families. This narrative is unique because of its peculiar application to border-crossing culture. While they understood that their exploitation stemmed from their undocumented status, they accepted the conditions that arose from the status because they took ownership of the situations they now found themselves in. Listening to the stories, it was almost as if the workplace exploitations were an expected part of the overall difficulties the workers voluntarily accepted when they crossed the border. The deliberate acceptance of the status gave the workers agency and some level of empowerment over their situation. Even though they had grievances, they endured.

A related masculinities narrative, the family-provider narrative, provided the rationale for enduring much of the difficult work imposed on our interviewees. As one worker noted, 'There were times when I … had to leave my house at 6 in the morning and I would get home at 11 at night. Sometimes we'd work twelve and a half hours. … We all come here [for] our families.'[29] Another worker explained that he did work that '[o]nly Latinos' did, even though he did not like the work, in order to support his family in Mexico.[30]

In contrast, many of the female workers we interviewed struggled to accept the endurance narrative. Instead, they voiced complaints openly and persistently on the job. The women themselves viewed their subordination in terms of *both* immigration status and gender, as demonstrated by one interviewee's assessment:

> [W]hat they see is and what they think is that because we're immigrants, because we're women and because we are Latinas they can exploit us and they

28 Interview with Samuel, Construction Worker, in Las Vegas, Nev. (15 June 2007).

29 Interview with Tony, Construction Worker, in Las Vegas, Nev. (5 June 2007).

30 Interview with Samuel, Construction Worker, *supra* note 28.

> can step all over us and that we are not going to do something about this. But [complaining openly shows] them that we can actually do something about [our work conditions].[31]

While the women we interviewed were offended by the treatment enough to seek redress, the men accepted it as part of their role as responsible family providers.

Changing the Narratives: Opportunities for Empowerment

Employers benefit from the masculinities narratives to the extent that these narratives provide for a stable, complacent workforce. Moreover, employers benefit to the extent that they can remove themselves from direct liability for harassment or a hostile work environment. The narratives uphold the myth that hypermasculinity is endemic to the workers themselves. Employers can easily say that it is reasonable to expect the type of hypermasculinity experienced in the immigrant workplace because such behaviour is in the nature of immigrant construction workers. If employers create the conditions that spark the development of masculinities narratives and the concomitant behaviours that workers engage in to maintain gender superiority, what kinds of leverage can the law and alternative narratives generate to change employer practices?

Sociologists have posited that organizational changes can disrupt the existing structures and their narratives, allowing men and women to both perceive themselves differently and work together to reshape the workplace dynamic that creates the dominant masculinities narrative (Ely and Meyerson 2010). In this section, we shall discuss some of those disruptive narratives and the employer's role in their development. We are assuming an employer's will to change the narratives in this section. We fully acknowledge, however, that some force outside capitalism – such as legislative change or stronger agency enforcement – will need to incentivize employer will. In the following section, we shall analyse some of the ways that the law can encourage or force employers to develop the conditions for alternate narratives in the workplace. We shall also discuss how, given the external legal institutional incentives, alternate narratives can start to change the workplace.

Shifting the Narratives

Organizational theorists Robin Ely and Debra Meyerson have developed a theory describing how employers and organizations can change their processes to emphasize how alternative identities are important to the life of the organization. After studying workplace dynamics in an offshore oil platform operation – a stereotypically hypermasculine work environment – they found that the employer's emphasis on safety and performance changed the way that men enacted their

31 Interview with Women's Community Forum, *supra* note 13.

male identities in the workplace (2010: 2, 39, 44). The focus on the masculine nature of the job had forced workers to act defensively for themselves, rather than proactively to meet the company's overall goals (2010: 49–50). In contrast, Ely and Meyerson found that a company-wide initiative focusing on safety created a set of norms and practices that 'released men from the performance of masculinity commonly associated with dangerous work' (2010: 27). These practices and norms 'served to decouple idealized images of masculinity and definitions of competence so that proving masculinity did not render men competent. Instead, practices and norms legitimated the expression of vulnerability as an element of competence by linking such expressions to core work requirements' (2010: 46).

Specifically, practices and norms that emphasized the importance of working together to meet broader goals, driven by larger concerns, such as a team or social ideal, enabled workers to release concerns over 'self-image goals' for the broader organizational good (Ely and Meyerson 2010: 46). These practices, in turn, resulted in more positive relational processes (2010: 52). In other words, masculinities performed in the service of work-related goals, rather than in service of individual or collective self-worth, operate to benefit those within the workplace more than the defensive use of masculinities to construct the self in the workplace (2010: 52). It was the change in organizational practices and norms that elicited the change in individual worker behaviour (2010: 56). Once safety became a real and stated priority over production and profit, the men felt secure in letting go of masculinities narratives that encouraged individualism, risk taking, aggressiveness and danger (2010: 2, 27). Organizational practices that signalled to workers that they were part of a larger community communicated the importance of workers within the organization (2010: 44–5). Practices that communicated the company's preference for workers who learned from mistakes and worked well in teams decoupled masculinities narratives from notions of competence (2010: 31–5).

An example of a disruptive practice, therefore, involves the decoupling of masculinity from the requirements of the job. To the extent that the employer incentivizes workplace practices that distance masculinities behaviours from success on the job, all workers will feel more ownership of and take a stake in the success of the employer's business. In the oil rig scenario, for example, an emphasis on a knowledge culture that emphasized reflecting on the relative successes or failures of implementing alternative systems decreased workers' reliance on masculinities and defensive behaviours (Ely and Meyerson 2010: 31–5). This change to knowledge and reflection from production and individualism fostered a more collaborative and inclusive environment for all workers. In the immigrant construction context, an alternative narrative might involve rewarding workers for collaborative, team-based approaches to potentially dangerous conditions. Compensating team-based approaches to safety, rather than, or in addition to, compensating individuals on a piece-rate basis might encourage workers to think more reflectively about carrying heavy ladders, or building safe scaffolds more efficiently.

Ely and Meyerson (2000) concluded from a separate study of gender dynamics that deconstructing the way that work privileges men and how men sustain that privilege will expose where seemingly neutral practices and policies have a gendered effect. In the immigrant construction context, one practice is the deskilling of jobs. Deskilling invites masculinities narratives that overcompensate for decreased satisfaction, the contingent nature of the work, the increased repetitiveness, or the decreased wages (Stone 2004: 92). These narratives include the myth that no one else will do the job, the hypermasculinity narrative, and the provider narrative. One possible set of changes that employers can consider is to reduce the amount of deskilling taking place in occupations within low-wage workplaces. This change would involve creating more worth and less rigidity in the tasks assigned to a particular job. It would likely also require de-emphasizing productivity and profit, and emphasizing the overall value of the worker as part of a larger team of tradespeople. Some of the women we interviewed spoke about the difficulty of learning new skills on the job, precisely because the tasks in each trade had become so compartmentalized. They were told that they could not learn new skills because they were not suited for them. Union leaders also commented on how the compartmentalized nature of the work made it difficult to build expertise in workers who, historically, had amassed several types of skills within a trade. The deskilled nature of the work made it much less appealing to union workers who were accustomed to practising several skills as part of their jobs. Thus, changing the employer practice of deskilling and compartmentalizing work would make it more desirable and less vulnerable to the wage- and condition deterioration that elicits masculinities narratives.

Another practice and narrative example is that of the independent contractor, who is solely responsible for his failures, leaving employers and their structures unaccountable. Immigrants and women are especially vulnerable to and harmed by this construction of the worker, because it exploits workers who have few resources with which to self-insure when things go wrong.

A narrative that disrupts the myth that the independent contractor model leads to upward mobility centres on workers leveraging their collective bargaining or organizing strength. The idea that workers have to collect their strength in order to bargain for better conditions runs directly counter to the independent contractor model of work. In this narrative, workers are not small businessmen, but rather have a more traditional employer–employee relationship, in which the employer has the upper hand as long as workers are divided. The organizing narrative emphasizes connections among workers, as well as connections between workers and employers. Employer practices that may contribute to the disruptive, alternate narrative include an emphasis on safety, community building, and stating a broader company mission than short-term production and profit maximization. In this narrative, the employer is responsible for the welfare of the workers, rather than the workers being responsible for themselves. The employer provides the safety net of benefits that were traditionally part of the job when it was held by unionized workers. The employer is held accountable for workplace accidents and therefore is incentivized to avoid them. In this narrative, immigrant workers can gain leverage, because they are active and engaged members of the polity, who can voice their concerns without fear of removal from the polity. In the immigrant context, because of the implication of immigration status (or lack thereof), this narrative is different from the traditional union-organizing narrative. It necessarily includes organizing for the rights of immigrants outside the workplace as well as inside. Its success in changing employer practices necessarily depends on the effectiveness of organizing efforts in garnering legal status for the undocumented in the workforce.

The Role of the Legal System

What can the law or the legal system do to encourage the development of these alternative narratives in the workplace? Assuming that employers are responsible for workplace conditions from which masculinities narratives arise, the legal system should hold employers accountable and should incentivize change. Stronger enforcement of existing labour and employment laws could accomplish a narrative shift, much in the same way it occurred on Ely and Meyerson's oil rig operation (2010). In addition, focusing on the narrative as a structure provides a different perspective on use of an anti-discrimination framework to change the narrative.

Stronger Enforcement of Existing Laws

Stronger enforcement of workplace laws could disrupt masculinities narratives and at the same time generate the development of alternative narratives. In residential construction, conditions described by our interviewees involved changes in the employer–employee relationship, pay disputes, safety issues, and sexual harassment, in addition to the deterioration of jobs that interviewees attributed in part to their immigration status. The workers responded with masculinities narratives that made the workplace seem more tolerable, at least for men. If employer practices changed to accommodate enforcement, however, the masculinities narratives would themselves shift, much as Ely and Meyerson documented in their oil-rig study, precisely because the narrative would no longer fit the reality of the workplace (2010). The independent contractor arrangement, for example, requires some level of buy-in from the workers who accept the arrangement. In this case, the buy-in was facilitated by several masculinities narratives, including the entrepreneurial narrative and the narrative that only immigrant workers would take these jobs. If the federal Department of Labor (DOL) or state labour agencies enforced employee classification requirements through inspections of residential construction worksites, employers would have difficulty proving that their workers were, in fact, independent contractors and not employees as defined by state or federal statute (U.S. v Silk [1947], 331 U.S. 701). Labour agency investigations could reveal that the workers are, in fact, employees who have been misclassified as independent contractors (Greenhouse 2007). The distinction is important because independent contractors do not have access to the safety-net benefits available to employees. Nor do independent contractors have the protection of anti-discrimination laws, safety standards, or laws governing collective bargaining. If the workers are actually employees and adjudicated as such, however, the entrepreneurial narrative that legitimizes the arrangement might give way to the alternate narrative of workers who need to collaborate to gain leverage with an employer and seek the protections of labour and employment laws. Interestingly, undocumented status has increasingly begun to factor into workplace protections for workers in much the same way that independent contractor status affects terms of employment. Courts have considered a worker's immigration status, for example, in determining proper remedies for employment violations under the National Labor Relations Act and in lost wages calculations in workplace accident or workers' compensation cases (Hoffman [2002], 535 U.S. 137, Veliz [2003], 313 F. Supp. 2d 1317). The similar treatment of undocumented and independent contractor status, in terms of workplace protections, is difficult to ignore in the low-wage workplace, where workers are already so poorly protected. The proliferation of masculinities narratives surrounding the independent contractor arrangement makes the arrangement seem that much more inevitable. Stronger enforcement would necessarily disrupt the perception of inevitability.

Another example of the possibility of narrative shifts exists around the piece-rate wage structure in the industry. As we saw from our interviews, the piece-rate wage structure was also imbued with the entrepreneurial masculinities narrative. Workers did not think of their work in terms of overtime pay, because they did not consider themselves employees. As with misclassification cases, strong DOL or private enforcement, along with stiff penalties for wage violations, would change both employer practices and the narrative.

A third example revolves around safety conditions. Stronger enforcement of OSHA standards, and more frequent onsite investigations, fines and enforcement orders would incentivize safer worksite behaviour. No longer would the narratives of the family provider, the hypermasculine male, or the entrepreneur fit the reality of a workplace that values safety over profit.

Of course, stronger enforcement of workplace laws alone will not protect immigrant workers, especially undocumented workers. Stronger enforcement must be accompanied by a path for legalizing workers who cooperate with enforcement investigations. Arguably, one such legalization vehicle is available in the form of a U visa for egregious workplace violations. U visas are available to victims of certain crimes, including workplace criminal activity. A U visa can be a path to permanent legal residency and citizenship. Accordingly, regulations governing U visas can and should clarify that they are available for workers who cooperate with labour agencies investigating workplace violations in situations where the agency finds that the employer (in this case, the local industry) has purposefully structured jobs to attract the most vulnerable workers in the labour market (in this case, undocumented workers) (Saucedo 2008a).

Changes in Anti-discrimination Doctrine

In the anti-discrimination context, the existence of masculinities narratives should raise red flags about the possibility of workplace discrimination. The traditional anti-discrimination frameworks, however, would not easily capture as discriminatory employer practices such as the independent contractor arrangement, the piece-rate arrangement, or other exploitative conditions the workers described.

Indeed, these workplace arrangements may not be considered discriminatory under disparate impact or disparate treatment frameworks. Leticia Saucedo has written elsewhere about the limitations of the anti-discrimination frameworks to capture such exploitative conditions (Saucedo 2006, 2008b). In short, the traditional frameworks focus on employer actions – such as practices or policies – that are themselves discriminatory. In a disparate treatment framework, the plaintiff must demonstrate differential treatment. To establish a prima facie case, the plaintiff must show: (i) that she was a member of a protected class; (ii) that she was qualified for a particular position; (iii) that she was passed over for the position despite her qualifications; and (iv) that the employer continued to hold the position open after rejecting the plaintiff (McDonnell Douglas [1973], 411 U.S. 792). Implicit in this proof is the differential treatment that the doctrine requires. In a disparate impact framework, the plaintiff must show that an employer's facially neutral policy or practice had a significant disparate impact on the basis of race, colour, religion, sex or national origin, and that the employer cannot demonstrate that the challenged practice is job related and consistent with business necessity (Civil Rights Act of 1991 [2006]). Again, the plaintiff must show that a particular policy or practice or employer action was the cause of the disparate impact. In each of these traditional frameworks, then, the legal issues focus on whether there was an employer action or series of actions that the plaintiff can isolate as the cause of the differential treatment or impact. In the case of the brown-collar workplace, however, an employer could conceivably point to all kinds of factors outside of employer action that contribute to workplace discrimination. The traditional frameworks allow for this kind of speculation about who is responsible for the altered terms and conditions of employment for a class of workers, because the burden remains heavily on the plaintiff to show the connection between the employer practice and the discrimination. So, for example, female workers may be victims of societal bias or immigrations laws that subordinate them based on how the economy prices their work. The employer, therefore, would have a defence because no particular employer policy or practice creates these conditions.

In an alternate discrimination framework, the focus would be on the dynamic created between the employers' structuring of the job and the employee's response. This dynamic is itself a structure, as legal scholar Tristin Green has noted in her work (Green 2007: 857). Green argues that 'workplace dynamics' themselves must be considered in determining whether the employer is discriminating in the way it sets up its workplace arrangements (Green 2003: 92). In such a non-traditional framework, the context and the dynamic created between employer and workers in the workplace could lead to the conclusion that discrimination has occurred. Under this framework, employers who target particular workers for a set of jobs at the bottom of the economic ladder encourage altered terms and conditions by requiring the very performance that they elicit from their workers. In the immigrant construction trades context, subservience, flexibility, and conformance to an independent contractor and piece-rate system, are all attributes that employers seek and immigrant workers provide. The very masculinities that workers use to bring value to their work in dynamic response to their work conditions further subjugate them and their female counterparts in the workplace. The drawback of this approach is that it would require more explanation among, within and around the contours of the existing frameworks, which insist on identifying particular employer actions. The alternative framework describes what is happening much more aptly and at the same time provides an alternative proof mechanism for a showing of discrimination that would not otherwise be obvious. The alternative framework would, in other words, explain just how the dynamic between employer and worker, which includes the development of the masculinities narratives, can be discriminatory.

Conclusion

Masculinities theories illuminate how employer practices can foster, exacerbate and take advantage of discriminatory and exploitative conditions. Uncovering the masculinities narratives present in the immigrant workplace, and placing them in the context of employer structures and arrangements, reveals just how discrimination and exploitation manifest themselves in the immigrant workplace and what role workers play in the perpetuation of such conditions. In the case of the Immigrant Construction Worker Study in Las Vegas, employer structures such as the independent contractor arrangement and piece-rate wages elicited the masculinities responses that we observed. The effects of such responses are demonstrated in gendered responses to workplace safety, to perceptions of rights in the workplace, to workers' perceptions about their entrepreneurial character, and to hypermasculinity and pride over doing the difficult work in construction.

The workers' responses to workplace conditions provide us with opportunities to see how an alternative set of structures and their accompanying narratives can empower workers. Sociological studies demonstrate how masculinities narratives can be disrupted. Employers who change their practices can change the underlying narratives and behaviours that perpetuate masculine workplace environments.

Why would an employer want to disrupt a narrative that they perceive as encouraging productivity, profit maximization, and a smooth-running operation? One response is that external incentives might force employers to change their practices. This is where the legal system plays a crucial role. Enforcement of existing laws goes a long way towards creating employer incentives for change in the immigrant workplace. Focusing on the dynamic created by employer structures, moreover, captures more effectively the discriminatory nature of employer practices. Each of these legal system interventions should result in change. Masculinities theories, by exposing how practices are related to workplace dynamics, can facilitate change in the immigrant workplace. Ultimately, masculinities theories deserve a place in the further investigation of these types of workplaces so that we can continue to formulate more effective ways to improve their conditions.

PART VI
Family

Chapter 15
On Masculinities, Law and Family Practices: A Case Study of Fathers' Rights and Gender[1]

Richard Collier

Introduction

The relationship between law and masculinity is a topic marginal to much mainstream legal scholarship. Even at international conferences and symposia concerned with law, gender and sexuality it remains rare, still, to find workshops specifically focused on this subject. Nonetheless, there are signs that things are changing. Writing in 1995, in the book *Masculinity, Law and the Family*, I observed how, at the time, there had been few texts that took as the specific object of study the relationship between masculinity and *law* (Collier 1995). This is no longer the case, and over the past fifteen years or so a rich picture has emerged within law and society scholarship of the 'man' or, more accurately, the 'men' of legal discourse. A now substantial body of research has unpacked the ways in which ideas about men and gender have been understood, constructed, or otherwise depicted in law. This work raises important questions about many aspects of social life, as well as about the variable and contested meanings that attach to gender. Events such as the 'Masculinities and the Law' workshop, from which this collection is drawn, held at Emory Law School in September 2009, and the symposium on 'Feminist Perspectives in Masculinities' held at Harvard Law School in March 2010, are indicative of a field of study that, in recent years in particular, has developed rapidly. More legal scholars are seeking, in diverse areas of law, and via a range of methods, to reconsider how ideas about masculinities inform and circulate in law and policy debates within specific jurisdictions (see, for example, Dowd 2010, McGinley 2004, Cooper 2009a, 2006a, Collier 2010b, 2009, 1998, Cooper and McGinley 2012, Thomson 2008).

In a sense, with regard to the development of a critical engagement with masculinity, law has 'lagged behind' other disciplines. This is despite longstanding calls on the part of feminist legal scholars for legal studies to ask 'the man question' (Ferguson 1993, May et al. 1996), to engage with masculinity (O'Donovan 1993:

1 This chapter presented a revised version of material contained in R. Collier, Fathers' Rights, Gender and Welfare: Some Questions for Family Law, *Journal of Social Welfare and Family Law* 31(4) (2009), 357–71, and selected themes discussed in R. Collier, *Men, Law and Gender: Essays on the 'Man' of Law*, London: Routledge, 2010. I am grateful to the publishers for permission to revise and republish this work here.

88) as part of a 'discursive attempt to stop the depiction of women as "the problem"' (Thornton 2004: 12) and for law to deflect

> the objectifying gaze from women and Indigenous people to benchmark masculinity and heterosexuality, as well as 'whiteness' [as part of] an attempt to disrupt the conventional orderings of modernity within legal texts. (Thornton 2004: 15; see also Middleton 1992)

At the same time, a now-voluminous body of interdisciplinary theoretical and empirical research, termed variously the new sociology or critical study of men and masculinities, has sought, in different ways and from a variety of perspectives, to explore the gender of men in an explicitly pro-feminist manner. The scale of the contemporary literature on masculinities is demonstrated by the sheer number of books, articles and research reports on the topic, as well as the existence of dedicated encyclopaedias and extensive bibliographic databases (for an introduction see Connell 2005a, 2002a, Kimmel 2005b, Flood et al. 2007, Kahn 2009, Whitehead 2002). Significant social, economic and cultural shifts, meanwhile, have served to question the contemporary meaning of masculinity in complex and often contradictory ways (Kimmel and Messner 2010). As the author of one recent introduction to the subject notes, '[i]ssues surrounding men and masculinities have become "hot politics" in late capitalist societies … [T]he new focus on [questions about] men's identities [and practices] has been a consequence of structural changes … interacting with the social and political effects of feminism' (Ashe 2007: 1).

I have sought elsewhere to track the lineage and distinctive political, intellectual and institutional influences that have shaped this work on masculinities, and consider its broader implications for studies of law and gender (see Collier 2010a, 2010b). Developments in relation to third-wave/anti-essentialist and materialist feminism, intersectionality, queer theory, and sociological and socio-legal work around 'personal life' (Smart 2007), in particular, I have argued, raise important questions about the concept of masculinity in developing understanding of the relationship between law, men and gender. There are signs, at the time of writing, that work on masculinities and law, as it is evolving within different jurisdictions, is marked by subtle differences in terms of the frameworks adopted and focus of analysis. This is the case notably with regard to engagements with, and deployment of, the concept of hegemonic masculinity (see further on this idea Beasley 2008a, Elias and Beasley 2009, Hearn 2004, Howson 2005, Spector-Mersel 2006, Donaldson 1993, Hall 2002). In relation to work in North America and Europe, for example, contrasting welfare regimes and distinctive legal–political systems (Hearn and Pringle 2006) shape these contemporary engagements with masculinity and law in a number of ways. Different social, economic and policy contexts (see COMAB 2009) inform the way studies of masculinities and law integrate discussion of issues such as class, race and ethnicity.

This chapter focuses on one particular area of law, Family Law, and, more specifically, the subject of fathers' rights politics within the jurisdiction of England and Wales. However, the issues raised, I shall argue, have general application for studies of law and masculinity. I wish to use this reading of fathers' rights as a 'case study' for how an understanding of contemporary legal debates can gain much from a richer, more nuanced engagement with the masculinities literature. Indeed, I shall contend, questions raised by the study of masculinities can reshape and add texture to understandings of fathers' rights politics, doing so, importantly, without losing sight of the issues of power central to feminist work in this area (Smart 2006b). An amalgam of social, economic and cultural change, alongside the embedding in law of models of formal equality and ideas of gender neutrality, has profoundly reshaped a legal–political terrain based on a particular set of beliefs about men and masculinities. Interrogating how debates about fathers' rights connect to a 'new politics of masculinity' reveals significant features of broader 'crisis tendencies', if not 'historical collapse of the legitimacy of patriarchal power' (Connell 2005a: 85) that have arisen around gender relations in late modern societies. Set in the context of contemporary debates about law and gender, the direction of feminist legal scholarship, and what it might mean to transcend the boundaries of law (Fineman 2010b), the time is propitious to reassess what it means to speak, in this area, of a relationship between masculinity and law.

Setting the Scene

In the light of the above, how might fathers' rights, law and masculinities be approached? Writing from the field of social policy, Brid Featherstone notes in her 2009 book *Contemporary Fathering* how 'given the symbolic weight and often the centrality of fathering practices for everyday lives', to some extent 'men and masculinities scholars have vacated the field [of fathers' rights politics] and left a vacuum for the conservatives to fill' (Featherstone 2009: 110). In the field of Family Law scholarship, meanwhile, there has been a questioning over the past decade of the way assumptions about rationality and emotion inform legal policy around separation. The 'missing ingredient' within debates around divorce and the welfare of the child, it has been argued, has all too often been the underlying *emotional* agenda between disputants (Barnett 2009b, Vallance-Webb 2009). Importantly, the reality of separation for many parents, linking to recent literature on the idea of the new responsible divorcing subject (Boyd 2005, Reece 2003, van Krieken 2004), can sit uneasily with the dominant images of 'good', 'reasonable' mothers and fathers to be found in legal policy (Barnett 2009a, Collier 2009, Kaganas and Day Sclater 2004).

These arguments draw attention to the complex grounding of interpersonal conflict within individual biography (Day Sclater and Richards 1995), the situated, structural and material contexts in which individuals live. Such readings align with a resurgence of interest in affect and emotion within legal scholarship (Abrams 2005,

Huntington 2010), as well as chiming with recent sociological work that has sought to highlight the complexity and diversity of the ways families are constituted and change at various stages throughout the life course (Smart 2007). These debates provide the backdrop for the re-reading of fathers' rights to follow, in which I shall argue there is a pressing need to see 'beyond … images of "safe family men", angry fathers and "implacably hostile mothers"' (Barnett 2009b: 141). These ideas have circulated widely in recent debates around separation and fathers' rights. Looking closer at the interconnections between law and masculinities, however, raises questions about gender and welfare in the context of those difficult cases where the courts have had to deal with fathers and mothers who, in a term the judges have used in England and Wales, appear 'vengeful' in their relations with the other parent (Vallance-Webb 2008).

Family Law and the Politics of Fathers' Rights

There exists now a considerable international research base concerned with fathers' rights groups, the arguments advanced by, and the impact of, a diverse range of fathers' organizations. The case for legal studies to take fathers' rights seriously does not need repeating (see Crowley 2008a, 2009b, Gavanas 2004b, Rhoades 2002, Flood 2004, Boyd 2009, 2004, Wallbank 2005, Featherstone 2009: ch. 7, Collier 2009, 2005, Smart 2006a, 2004). There is no one fathers' rights group, no one kind of fathers' rights activist. Indeed, the very idea of a fathers' movement based on a primary appeal to legal rights should be treated with a considerable degree of caution (Crowley 2008a, Collier 2010b: ch. 7). It is difficult to generalize about the impact of fathers' groups on legal debates without taking into account the specificities of different legal systems (Collier and Sheldon 2006a). Nonetheless, across jurisdictions, a vocal, visible and, in terms of strategy, increasingly militant fathers' rights movement has, in recent years, been widely credited with, to varying degrees and in different ways depending on country, influencing the direction of Family Law reform (Collier 2010b: ch. 7, Collier and Sheldon 2008: ch. 5, Diduck and Kaganas 2006: 561).

A central theme within much social policy, sociological and legal scholarship on this issue has been that men's collective mobilization around law is deeply problematic, not least for women and children. Fathers' groups have sought, critics suggest, to 'refashion and reposition fatherhood in the legal and cultural imaginary' in regressive ways (Smart 2006a: 123). In some accounts, fathers' rights claims in the legal arena are seen as part of a strategy for the maintenance of power, emblematic of a wider social, cultural and legal backlash against feminism, as well as the embodiment of problematic assumptions about masculinity. Fathers' groups, legal scholars have suggested, appear trapped in their engagement with law by a central commitment to formal legal equality and to a model of the private (hetero)-sexual family (Fineman 2004, 1995, Collier 2005), a visioning of post-separation parenting profoundly out of step with the (gendered) realities of care (Lewis 2005, Smart and Neale 1999; Fineman 1995).

A closer look at the relationship between law and masculinities, however, casts light on this terrain of fathers' rights politics and, in particular, how it relates to the issues of emotion, gender and welfare noted above. In the following two sections, I shall first look at the relevance of key themes within the recent literature on masculinities for approaching fathers' rights. I shall proceed, secondly, to reconsider the messages that law itself sends about the role of the father, and paternal masculinity, both in the context of post-separation parenting and in a more general sense.

Law and Masculinities: A Snapshot of a Growing Field

Paying attention to the complexity and diversity of practices within the category of men, an issue of heightened concern in recent masculinities scholarship, does not in itself, Ashe (2007) contends, mean evading questions of power or accountability. There has been a move within work on masculinities to call, rather, for a more nuanced account of men's identities, highlighting the need to engage with the way ideas about, for example, emotion, memory, intimacy, love and commitment can inform social experiences within discrete contexts around law. Thus, it has been argued, reducing a complex social development (such as the rise of fathers' rights groups) to a unitary cause (say, a backlash to feminism) offers little 'in terms of conceptual clarity or theoretical usefulness' (Ashe 2007: 159). This is the case whether in terms of understanding the changing nature of gendered subject(s) within the legal arena or, as feminist scholars have argued, the double-edged and often unintended consequences of law reform itself (Fineman 2004, 1995, 1991). It is revealing in this regard, therefore, how two of the leading writers on masculinities recognize in their 2005 reappraisal (and broad defence) of the concept of hegemonic masculinity that 'the internal complexities of masculinities' is an issue that 'has only gradually come into focus as a research issue' (Connell and Messerschmidt 2005: 852). Moreover, they suggest, 'without treating men as objects of pity, we should recognise that hegemonic masculinity does not necessarily translate into a satisfying experience of life' (Connell and Messerschmidt 2005: 852: see further Beasley 2008a, Howson 2005).

With regard to gender and welfare, writing on the relationship between rationality and emotion in the context of men's mental health, Jane Garde questions how contemporary ideas about masculinity intersect with men's own subjective experiences, or degrees, of power, and powerlessness. Thus, she notes, if men have

> more personal and socio-political power [than women and] can enforce on others their constructions and perceptions of reality, and enjoy material advantages … it would … seem reasonable to assume that males have fewer, less severe and more personalized psychological problems, and that they would easily avail themselves of psychotherapeutic services should the need arise. (Garde 2003: 6)

A wealth of research suggests, however, that this is far from the case (see further Robertson 2007), and research on fathers' rights groups similarly reveals that gender differences in relation to the psychological and sociological dynamics of separation remain significant within family justice processes (Crowley 2008a, Collier 2010b: ch. 7).

In looking closer at this issue a discernible, and significant, shift can be detected in the study of masculinities towards a greater recognition of 'the internal complexities of masculinities' and the way men's lives and motivations may be marked by gendered investments and commitments experienced as fluid and contradictory within particular, situated contexts. Rejecting the idea that there exist essential male identities among those people who are identified within particular societies as 'men', contemporary work on masculinities, interlinked to developments at the interface of third-wave/anti-essentialist feminism (Dowd and Jacobs 2003), and queer theory, has been marked, rather, by a growing recognition of the complexity of the gendered subject. In relation to law, for example, I have argued elsewhere (2010a) that individual men's responses to social changes do not map in any straightforward way either to dominant cultural associations between masculinity and rationality nor to political–legal assumptions about the 'reasonable' parent in the process of separation (the very assumptions that recent work in Family Law has itself sought to critique). The situated, and often contradictory, investments individuals can have in gender categories at particular moments – noting how experiences of masculinity themselves change throughout the life course – can usefully be seen *as* effects of power while, at the same time, having the potential to produce oppositional practices and resistances (Ashe 2007). Masculinity, as a marker of social identity (connected in some way to feeling oneself to be, or to be seen by others as, 'a man'), has been produced and sustained by discourses of sexuality and gender interwoven and rooted within the dualistic configurations that pervade liberal legal thought.

In questioning gender categories as contingent, discursive, and of variable significance, it remains possible to locate ideologies and beliefs about men and masculinity that remain socially powerful and experientially significant (see Connell and Messerschmidt 2005). However, tracking to the above concerns in Family Law about the centrality of emotion, these developments within sociological studies of masculinity raise intriguing questions, I shall argue below, about how assumptions concerning welfare and gender interconnect in the legal field. In the case of fathers' rights, a rather different question, one that I explore in the following section, concerns the messages that *law* itself has sought to communicate about fatherhood. In what sense do traditional forms of masculinity, whether or not conceptualized as hegemonic or patriarchal, cut across, in the ethical values they have historically been associated with, ideas of (relational) autonomy and interconnectedness in a sense at the heart of the interdependent relationships and inevitable dependencies with which Family Law is concerned? (Herring 2009, Fineman 2004) What does it mean, in law, and in terms of ideas of masculinity, to be a 'good father'?

The 'Good Father' in Law: An Example from England and Wales

In relation to fatherhood, Sally Sheldon and I argue in the book *Fragmenting Fatherhood: A Socio-legal Study* (Collier and Sheldon 2008), the role of law has been much more ambiguous and contradictory than any reading of fathers' rights as 'backlash' to feminism would suggest. It is possible to detect, across diverse areas of law and legal regulation, a broader and multi-layered transformation in ideas about men's parenting and, more specifically, the emergence in law of a new normative model of responsible fatherhood that embodies a particular *kind* of heterosexual masculinity. This model of masculinity, importantly, is markedly different in significant respects from the ideas about men and manhood, employment, sexuality, care, gender and rationality that informed earlier beliefs about fatherhood. As Fineman astutely observes, 'law's desire for gender neutrality and ideals of egalitarianism', alongside related assumptions about gender convergence, has played a key role in the creation of a 'new set of norms for fatherhood' in law (Fineman 2004: 195). The simultaneous political and policy reconstruction of fatherhood as a particular kind of social problem and object of intervention for law, meanwhile, in turn raises important questions about the changing 'nature of fatherhood and … transformation of the role of the father in response to changing expectations, norms and practices' (Fineman 2004: 195).

Discussion of the relationship between fatherhood and law has become a significant feature of wider debates in the UK about how a reconfiguration of gender relations has reshaped ideas about equality, responsibility, autonomy and welfare in law (see, for example, Bridgeman et al. 2008, Fineman 2004, Wallbank et al. 2009, Hunter 2009). These issues must be set against the backdrop of significant changes in the messages law has sought to radiate about what being a 'good father' entails, whether in relation to the role of fathers in birth (Fatherhood Institute 2010), fathers' negotiations of work and care commitments, or relationship to post-separation parenting (Collier and Sheldon 2008: ch. 5). This reconstruction of the 'good father' in law has drawn on a nexus of interrelated developments: changes in the scope and function of Family Law in promoting equality, a rethinking of the role of the father in child welfare and development, and the proliferation of expert knowledge about parenting. What has resulted in legal policy in England and Wales are class-mediated ideas about (post-liberal) parental responsibility based on a problematic, gender-neutral model of rationality (Reece 2003, Gillies 2005) and framed by the rise of intensive parenting cultures (Bristow 2009, Furedi 2003) that have constituted some, but not other, parents as a social problem. These developments inform debates about fathers' rights in the legal arena in a number of contradictory ways, a point of importance in considering the cultural and political resonance of contestations around fathers' groups within contact and residence law.

The Messages Law Sends I: Fathers Matter

On one level, fathers' articulation of legal claims via what Carol Smart has referred to as a simultaneous language of rights/justice and ideas about men's care, capacity to care and children's welfare (Smart 2006a) is not surprising. Economic and cultural changes have reshaped ideas about fatherhood and intimacy (Dermott 2008) and the ethical basis of men's relationships with children in such a way that appeals to formal gender equality and men's capacity to care map to broader cultural ideas about what fathers are 'for'. Looking closer at the arguments advanced by fathers' groups in the legal arena, this can be narrowed down to two specific developments. First, and central to a broader reconstruction of the welfare of the child within family policy, the father–child dyad has been positioned as of equal importance to that of the mother–child dyad. Bound up with an acceptance within legal policy debates of the psychological importance of knowing (genetic) Truth (Smart 2007), a 'geneticisation of fatherhood' has been traced across diverse areas of law (Collier and Sheldon 2008: 225–6), involving greater importance being ascribed to the genetic link between men and children. Second, the economic and social benefits of 'engaged fathering' have been stressed in a policy paradigm that over the past decade or so in the UK, at least until 2010 and the election of the Conservative-Liberal Coalition Government and subsequent austerity politics, focused increasingly on the role of fathers in terms of social investment in children (see further Featherstone 2009, Featherstone and Trinder 2001, Lister 2006).

The result has been a significant reshaping of the relationship between fathers and their children in social and legal policy over this period. Debates in England and Wales about the reform of the law relating to unmarried fathers and birth registration (DWP 2009, Sheldon 2009) and the 'rolling out' of Parental Responsibility (as a distinct legal concept) to more and more fathers exemplify this repositioning of the father–child dyad in particularly clear ways. *Fathers matter* and fathers do and should have a direct vertical relationship with their children unmediated by the child's mother. This argument can be taken further. Interlinked to the above, Family Law has also seen an acceptance on the part of legal policy makers, politicians and judges that law has a profound *symbolic* power in signalling ratification of the parental role and formal gender equality. This symbolic role has been explicitly recognized by the courts in recent case law around the allocation of Parental Responsibility Orders (Reece 2009) and Shared Residence under the Children Act 1989. Various judicial statements have noted, for example, how the allocation of PR involves questions of status and 'official approval' (Reece 2009: 202) that fathers might understandably, and reasonably, seek to obtain.

Set in such a context, fathers' activists, seeking precisely such a relationship with their children, can be seen as highly attuned to what law is saying about the importance of fathers, about formal gender equality and gender neutrality in parenting. These arguments also track, within the UK, to the heightened political resonance of rights discourse following the Human Rights Act 1998 (Eekelaar 2006). Mediated by a heightened policy concern with individual responsibility and a self-help parenting culture aligned to powerful neo-liberal economic imperatives (Furedi 2003), turning to law, and evoking legal rights, can be seen as broadly in keeping with the kinds of messages law is communicating about what it means to be a good father.

The Messages Law Sends II: Masculinities and the Importance of Context

If we look closer, however, at the ideas about men and masculinity circulating within law, there is a considerable degree of ambiguity within legal policy in England and Wales as to whether, and in what way, families 'need fathers'. In some contexts, certainly, the message is clear – fathers matter (Featherstone 2009). In others, however, different models of gender-neutral parenting are at play, as in, for example, the parenting provisions relating to assisted reproduction contained in the 2008 Human Fertilisation and Embryology Act (Collier and Sheldon 2008: 237–8, McCandless and Sheldon 2010). In this area, the replacing in law of the 'need for a father' with a need for supportive (gender-neutral) parenting has been interpreted by some, not least parts of the British media, as an assault on the institution of fatherhood, indicative of a fragmentation of the heterosexual family. Digging deeper, in some contexts – in particular, Family Law – law is marked, Scourfield and Drakeford (2002) suggest, by a broadly optimistic ideal of the 'new' caring father, aligned to core beliefs, as above, about gender convergence and formal gender equality. In others, however, notably the field of criminal justice policy, legal debates are informed not by appeals to gender-neutrality and gender convergence but by ideas about the essentialist nature of men's parenting and the importance of paternal masculinity (what is distinctive, for example, about the fathering role, not least in relation to the socialization of boys). In the latter area, in particular, rather different ideas about class, race and ethnicity have historically informed dominant constructions of what fathers are 'for'.

There is, therefore, no one model of the father role and paternal masculinity circulating in legal policy debates, a point of considerable importance when we look closer at the relationship between emotion, welfare and separation. In terms of dominant models of rationality and 'being reasonable' in Family Law, further tensions and contradictions appear in the messages law sends about what being a good father entails. John Eekelaar observes in the book *Family Law and Personal Life* how a reconfiguration of rights and responsibilities in Family Law has resulted in the policy demand for something more than simply meeting legal obligations (Eekelaar 2006: 128). The truly responsible, rational subject should 'exercise restraint within their legal rights' and show an awareness of the potential consequences of their actions (Featherstone 2009: 144). Being neutral, that is, is not enough – to be responsible entails seeing what is best for the child (in this case, avoiding conflict) and acting accordingly. With regard to being responsible in dealing with separation, fathers' rights activists have been variously described by critics as engaging in an often obsessive pursuit of legal action through the courts, psychologically 'stuck' in conflict, 'vengeful' (Vallance-Webb 2008) in the making of an appeal to 'my rights'. Yet, on the one hand, law is communicating clear messages about the legitimacy of such action as a result of the way ideas about fatherhood, rights and equality have been transformed within the legal and cultural arena. On the other hand, as above, to *be* rational and reasonable is to desist from the inappropriate pursuit of legal rights through the courts. This whole area is thus fraught with contradictions that, I have argued elsewhere (2010a, 2010b), in terms of understanding these gendered dynamics, the concept of hegemonic masculinity does not provide us a handle with to begin to explore this complexity of how law connects to shifting ideas about men and gender.

In the next section, I shall focus on the connections between emotion, welfare and gender in debates about fathers' rights and law. Turning to questions of masculinity, I argue, throws considerable light on the above issues and illustrates why studies of law and gender need to incorporate a more complex account of the gendered male subject and an appreciation of the interconnected, interrelated and interdependent nature of the lives of women, children and men.

Emotion, Welfare and Separation

How do issues about masculinity relate to the contemporary terrain of fathers politics? The campaigns directed at law reform by fathers' rights groups in the UK, in particular the highly visible demonstrations of a group called Fathers 4 Justice from 2002 to 2008 (see further Collier 2010b: ch. 7, 2009, 2005, Jordan 2009), have been wide ranging. Looking closer, the protests that occurred embody and, at the same time, appear the antithesis of contemporary ideas about normative masculinity, as well as what it means to *be* rational, responsible and reasonable in engaging with law. In some respects, these protests are quintessentially masculine, involving, for example, a 'heroic' climbing of public buildings, a deployment of a male body enmeshed with appeals to danger, risk, physicality and struggle (and indeed, violence and the threat of violence). There has been a gendered dimension, in particular, to the targeting of certain women ministers and judges (see Jordan 2009). From this perspective, the campaign of civil disobedience exemplified by Fathers 4 Justice illustrates a distinctive gendered, embodied and hyper-masculine performative practice within public space, a form of 'protest masculinity'; indeed, a distinctive 'masculinity practice'.

At the same time, however, looking beyond surface images of 'superheroes' and 'safe family men', of 'angry' and 'hysterical' fathers, these fathers' protests also deal directly in and make visible ideas about men's health, welfare and emotion, and the importance of the affective domain referred to above. This involves ideas about masculinity that stand in a profoundly ambivalent relation to the beliefs about what it means to be a good father contained in law, as above, supposedly hegemonic ideas about masculinity itself (Collier 2010b: ch. 1; Beasley 2008a), and now dominant beliefs about what it means to be a rational and reasonable subject within family policy. These points require clarification in terms of understanding how ideas about masculinity circulate in these debates.

Conflict, Men's Health and Gender

The representation of emotion, pain, anger and loss deployed by fathers' groups speaks to an affective domain that cuts across traditional ideas about masculinity and gendered ideas of rationality and autonomy in a number of ways. For critics of fathers' rights, the idea of the good non-residential father in law entails assumptions about responsibility that contrast markedly with what is required, legally and culturally, of the residential mother. Meanwhile, men showing emotion, crying tears or otherwise, is an issue that has tended to attract a redemptive value culturally not accorded to women (Showalter 1987). What is made visible here, however, all too clearly, is precisely the underlying emotional agenda between the disputants discussed above, the presence of pain, anger and loss, the experiential dimensions of separation. This, in turn, connects to how ideas about masculinity inform understandings of law, rationality and welfare in this context.

In what way is masculinity relevant here? Studies from a range of sources indicate that the experience of depression and other health problems is common for those involved in high-conflict disputes, in the case of some non-resident fathers the very men more likely to become involved in fathers' groups (Gouldstone 2008). Findings of ill health and depression are consistent with what is known about the vulnerability of the divorcing population generally (Woodall and Woodall 2007). The presence of court proceedings or a live dispute (Trinder et al. 2006: 85, Trinder and Kellett 2007: 30), in particular, can be detrimental to the mental health of women and men, with prolonged conflict having a significant impact on parental well being. As a 2007 study of separated parents in England and Wales put it, both parents and children can face

> [s]ignificant difficulties, with fraught or tenuous contact, conflicted and distrustful parental relationships, very limited shared decision-making [and] high levels of dissatisfaction with arrangements and numerous contact problems. *It is ... no surprise that this translates into high levels of adult and child distress*. (Trinder et al. 2006: 39, my emphasis)

The growing literature on fatherhood and masculinity suggests, however, that particular issues pertaining to men's health and gender also come into play here. It is known, for example, within the vast scholarship on men's health, friendship networks, and experiences of loss and belonging over the life course, that men's responses to personal problems can take distinctive gendered forms. This raises questions about the interconnections between masculinity and, for example, ideas about vulnerability, cultural assumptions about men's reluctance to seek help (Wheeler 2003), relationship to depression (McVeigh 2010), therapeutic intervention (Millar 2003), and so forth. In relation to post-separation life, and recognizing the diversity of men's family practices therein, studies of fathers' groups suggest fathers' experiences can be marked by a wide range of gendered behaviour, each of which draws, in different ways, on ideas about and facets of contemporary masculinity.

For some men the process and aftermath of separation can involve a heightened focus on physical exercise, 'perfecting' the desirable male body. For other separated fathers, in contrast, the dynamics of separation, and beyond, involves higher levels of engagement in unhealthy, risky behaviour – for example, alcohol or drug use – and susceptibility to mental illness. In a context in which the question of men's violence generally has, critics suggest, been systematically marginalized in the name of promoting the 'harmonious divorce', it is revealing how a representation of acute despair and, at times, suicide has played a significant part within some fathers' campaigns.

Each of the above issues connects to masculinity in a number of ways. A recurring theme within the masculinities literature concerns the way ideas about male maturation have historically involved circumventing emotionality, vulnerability and openness. The process of becoming 'a man', at its simplest, requires control over an inner world in ways that correlate dominant cultural forms of (notably heterosexual) masculinity with a suppression of emotion, denial of vulnerability, and proscribing of any sharing of inner experiences. These are ideas that may well have changed, and be changing, in highly significant respects (if not in others) in terms of contemporary culturally normative ideas about masculinity. However, Garde (2003: 14) observes, commenting on the relationship between men and mental health, one result of the operation of a distinctive ideology of masculinism can be that 'the depth of psychic injury accrued from damaging external realities [is] denied or underestimated' by many men. In seeking to progress an engagement with 'the material and psychological manifestations of social realities' (Garde 2003: 14), and in much the way advocates of the 'emotional turn' in Family Law suggest is desirable, Garde proceeds to challenge gendered assumptions about whether men do, in fact, have 'fewer, less severe and more personalized psychological problems' (2003: 14).

These issues, not least around depression, take on particular importance in the context of divorce and separation, in relation to which powerful ideas of normative masculinity, and of the paternal role, shape in distinctive ways how men negotiate what can be a difficult life transition. One aspect of men's gendered response to separation, in particular, has implications for debates around fathers' rights, law and contact. This involves what research suggests is, for many men, a significant reappraisal of past relationships with children, a desire to 'make up' for what has been (or might in time be) lost and to be a 'better' kind of separated dad. This maps to a key feature of the model of paternal responsibility circulating in family policy noted above, whereby it is argued that men should, legally and culturally, take on such responsibility. It also connects to arguments within recent sociological work around fatherhood and intimacy (Dermott 2008), suggesting that the loss of intimacy experienced by many separated and divorced men can for some '(re)create a sense of loneliness and emotional isolation' in ways that raise particular 'questions for men about gendered identity and emotional expressiveness' (Robertson 2007: 98). Such emotions, importantly, contemporary research on fathers' rights groups (Crowley 2008a) suggests then find an outlet via participation in fathers' organizations in ways that link men's distinctive gendered practices to an intensification of what Smart has termed the 'micro-politics' of contact (Smart 2006b).

At issue, therefore, are not just questions of men's physical and psychological health but also an emotional response to separation that leads some men to review previous patterns of behaviour, in particular their role as fathers and the quality of the relationship they have had with their children. This results for some fathers in a higher prioritizing of family ties and emotional expressiveness that takes the form of the articulation of rights claims in the legal arena. The problem, of course, is that from the perspective of many mothers this is deeply problematic ('he wants to do this now, but he did not when we were together'). Yet, I have suggested, in making sense of these debates, a reading of masculinities, emotion and welfare can inform understandings of separation as a process involving the constitution of a particular *kind* of gendered identity as a father.

In the context of recent attempts to reposition the emotional domain within debates about the welfare of the child in Family Law, such an engagement with the psychological and sociological dynamics of separation leads us to further consider how these issues of emotion are dealt with (or not dealt with) in family justice processes. This is an issue, I argue in the following and penultimate section of this chapter, that has policy implications for law.

Policy: Masculinity, Becoming Involved, and 'Being Reasonable'

Evidence emerging from international research on fathers' rights groups indicates that many men, and some women, turn to organizations in order to access practical and emotional assistance at a time when they are experiencing psychological distress (Crowley 2008a, Jordan 2009). What is motivating participation, that is, is a desire to benefit from services it is felt would otherwise be unavailable, including information about statute and case law, the legal process, and an opportunity to discuss, in a safe supportive setting, personal and health issues (Collier 2010b: ch. 7). It is important to remember in this regard that, certainly in the UK, there is at present very limited provision available to support and engage non-resident fathers. Articulating a rights-based equality claim in the legal arena is not, necessarily, the primary motivation in becoming or remaining involved in such a group.

In such a context, some fathers' groups and parenting organizations, notably those with charitable status, have developed a significant service function involving the provision of advice and support to separated parents, women and men, at a national and local level. In the UK, Families Need Fathers remains the most obvious and high-profile example of this kind of body, balancing a campaigning/political role with this support function. There also exist under the radar, however, a diverse range of smaller, local-based groups providing similar advice and assistance (Featherstone 2009: 111). These points are important, for they shed light on the question of what the connections between emotion, gender and law can tell us about contemporary fathers' rights politics, and the relationship between masculinity and law outlined at the beginning of this chapter.

Looking closer at why participation in fathers' rights groups might be subjectively experienced as valuable, connecting to emotional need at a time of distress, the work of the sociologist Esther Dermott provides insight. Contemporary fatherhood, Dermott suggests, can usefully be understood as an intimate relationship in such a way as to allow for 'an emphasis on the aspects of male parenting that fathers themselves view as most significant: emotions, the expression of affection, and the exclusivity of the reciprocal father–child dyad' (Dermott 2008: 143). Fatherhood, Dermott argues, is increasingly centred for many men

> on a personal connection at the expense of participation in the work of childcare; because caring activities flow from an emotional connection rather than in themselves constituting the fathering role, the practicalities of 'intimate fatherhood' are fluid and open to negotiation … Understanding this special quality of contemporary fatherhood is necessary in order to move *beyond narrow formulations of fathers, either as failing to contribute to, or as sidelined from, contemporary family life*. (Dermott 2008: 143, my emphasis)

Dermott suggests that the way separation is presently experienced by men is bound up with changing ideas about masculine identity and, importantly, culturally normative expectations about fathers, including those contained in law of the kind outlined above.

Two further points are pertinent in this regard. First, what is now generally positioned as a traditional, as opposed to the 'new' father discourse, not least in relation to the breadwinner role of men in families, is something research suggests remains resonant for considerable numbers of men and women, as well as children, in constituting contemporary ideas about what a good father entails. This is not to downplay the extent of change in men's family practices. It is, however, to highlight how this debate is marked not just by change but also by continuity. It also raises the important question of the agency of women and children, something often overlooked in accounts of fathers' rights politics that fail to address the interconnected nature of men's and women's personal lives. As Stuart Aitken observes (2005), in a way that links to Dermott's analysis, so much discussion of the institution of fatherhood has not embraced questions of fathering as a daily emotional, intimate practice, with little theory or empirical data existing on how the 'spaces' of fatherhood are produced, situated and gendered.

Second, a potential source of men's anger in the process of separation would appear to be located in these gendered dynamics of a move from a situation in which both parents may have colluded in maintaining a belief in gender equality in parenting prior to separation. This is an anger that finds expression, Smart (2006b) suggests, for some men at least, via an engagement in fathers' rights politics. In linking these two themes, it becomes possible to see how the heightened profile of fathers' rights in recent years has emerged at a complex nexus of social, economic, cultural and political change. These are changes marked by profound contestations about the content and role of law in regulating personal lives, by conflicting beliefs about gender, parenting cultures, and the implications of shifting relationships between women, men and children for understandings of equality. This reading of masculinities and law suggests, in short, that contemporary debates about fathers' rights are more complex and multi-layered than any simplistic deployment of ideas of 'safe fathers' and 'implacably hostile mothers', or 'vengeful' unreasonable parents, would indicate.

Concluding Remarks

This chapter has explored selected aspects of how issues around emotion, masculinity and welfare interconnect to the psychological dimensions of separation. I have argued that it is important to recognize the significance not only of what fathers rationally think in terms of shaping their behaviour but also what they emotionally feel and desire (see also Haywood and Mac an Ghaill 2003). This entails addressing the gendered dimensions and psychological complexity of the way parents can be moving in different directions, in asynchronous ways, during the course of separation, experiencing possibly contradictory emotions within what is, for the vast majority, a significant and often emotionally painful life transition (Douglas 2008). Looking more closely at the gendered aspects of this process, and beyond surface representations of men's invulnerability and protest masculinity, what comes to light is the need for a gender-sensitive relevant account of the dynamics of conflict in this area. This would be an account, importantly, grounded in men's, women's and children's actual experiences of family practices and, indeed, of the legal system, not in idealized and essentialist beliefs about masculinity.

The arguments of fathers' rights groups align, and yet simultaneously sit uneasily, with contemporary ideas about fatherhood and gender contained in law. I have not sought to depict a simple, causal account of men internalizing traditional ideas of masculinity nor of fathers as in any sense straightforward 'victims' of gender 'roles'. Conceptual work in the field of masculinities and law has moved far beyond such models and has sought to integrate a new complexity to understanding of the gendered male subject (for discussion, Collier 2010b; Cooper and McGinley 2012; Dowd 2010). It is intriguing to ask, however, given evidence that overall levels of distress appear broadly similar for both men and women involved in court proceedings (Trinder et al. 2005: 106), why this anger should be expressed in different forms. Certainly, an ambivalence to femininity, avoidance of emotion and devaluing of affective phenomena – and the desire to be in control of situations, to 'take action' – can be seen as key features of gendered ideologies that still shape masculine identities in a number of ways, remembering here that masculinity is 'in the making' throughout the life course. Yet to interpret generalized responses to conflict via simple gendered divisions in terms of how men and women internalize distress, I have argued, can miss what parents share and the groundings of such conflict within individual life histories.

The issues discussed in this chapter have bearing, ultimately, not just on the dynamics of individual disputes in the field of Family Law, but also on how the relationship between law and masculinity is approached in a more general sense, a central theme of this collection and the workshop on which it is based. Taking masculinity seriously in this context raises questions about the nature of individual and collective investments in identity politics. It is misleading, I have argued, to see the heightened political and cultural prominence of fathers' rights groups simply in terms of the manifestation of anti-women sentiment on the part of certain men, or as somehow straightforwardly anti-feminist. There is undoubtedly a strong element of such attitudes within parts of the fathers' rights movement. However, the interests at stake here and being contested in the legal field cut across men and women in complex ways. They involve, for example, not just biological mothers and fathers but also second partners, husbands, wives, grandparents and wider kin and, importantly, children, whose voices are so often absent in these debates. This heightens the importance of questioning how emotions and gendered social experiences are dealt with (or not dealt with) in law (contrast Nussbaum 2004, Douglas 1993), the many dimensions, conscious and unconscious, that shape personal action.

In this chapter, part of a broader project concerned with how ideas about masculinities have been constituted in law (Collier 2010a, 2010b), I have argued that it is important to recognize how social relations and structures beyond families can impact on individual experiences of parenthood and parenting cultures. This is why contemporary work exploring shifting ideas about intimacy, relationality and autonomy raises such important questions about changing configurations of gender, care and welfare in law. Law is just part, albeit a significant part, of how rights, responsibilities and family practices are experienced and take on subjective meaning for individuals. Family lawyers will miss much, therefore, if the rise of fathers' rights activism is dismissed as no more than a reactionary, minority, marginal activity. Equally, the study of law and masculinity has much to gain from incorporating a more complex and multi-layered account of the gendered subject, recognizing the interconnected nature of the lives of women, children and men (Smart 2007). Public policies based on outmoded stereotypes of both sexes, certainly, are unlikely to address the real problems that parents, whether resident and non-resident (Peacey and Hunt 2008), can face in dealing with divorce and separation. Indeed, they are more likely to create barriers to communication if informed by increasingly outdated gendered assumptions about the lives of women and men. At issue in contemporary debates about fathers' rights are the complex interconnections between law and economic, social and cultural shifts that, taken together, have transformed normative beliefs about fathers, fatherhood and paternal masculinities. What is happening connects directly to substantive changes in the law within specific jurisdictions, as above, shifting ideas of intimacy, emotion and welfare, as well as a realignment of social solidarities that is far more complex than the simple idea of men's 'gender protest' would indicate to be the case.

Chapter 16

Taking Custody of Motherhood: Fathers' Rights Activists and the Politics of Parenting[1]

Jocelyn Elise Crowley

Introduction

What makes a good father in contemporary American society? And more importantly, can good fathers effectively 'mother' their children? Without a doubt, over the past several decades, the cultural imagery surrounding what it means to be a fully participatory father has dramatically shifted (Burgess 1997; Coltrane 1989; Hobson and Morgan 2002; Ranson 2001). Instead of the ideal father being simply the breadwinner of the family, this 'new father' combines earning a living with the day-to-day care of his children (Pleck 1987). In other words, not only does he work full time, but he also is present at his children's birth, goes to school conferences, does their laundry, and prepares their meals. This 'new father' is, in fact, just like any other modern mother.

While this recent paternal imagery has been extremely powerful, scholars have also noted that fathers' actions have yet to meet this emerging ideal. While their contributions to child care have been increasing over time, particularly since the 1980s, fathers still lag behind mothers in terms of the amount of parental work they perform on a regular basis (Ahmeduzzaman and Roopnarine 1992; Aldous, Mulligan and Bjarnason 1998; Sandberg and Hofferth 2001; Sayer, Bianchi and Robinson 2004). In fact, in one of the most recent and comprehensive studies that explored this division of responsibility issue in 2000, Bianchi, Robinson and Milkie (2006, 116) found enormous gaps in paid and unpaid work between the sexes, with women allocating 12.9 hours per week to child care, and men only completing 6.5 hours on this task.

Nevertheless, despite the fact that real-world practices have yet to catch up to the new cultural ideal of fatherhood, fathers' rights groups have seized upon this

1 This chapter originally appeared in the Mother issue of *WSQ: Women's Studies Quarterly* 37: 3&4 (Fall/Winter 2009), published by the Feminist Press at the City University of New York, USA. WSQ is an interdisciplinary forum for the exchange of emerging perspectives on women, gender, and sexuality since 1972. For more information, visit http://www.feministpress.org/wsq.

compelling imagery in making their political claims. Fathers' rights organizations, composed primarily of white, middle-class men, have grown in number in recent years in order to challenge the legal system that they must confront when their families dissolve. One of their most prominent assertions is that the family law system, specifically through its child custody procedures that tend to physically place children with their mothers, denies them the opportunity to effectively personify their 'new father' roles.

This chapter explores precisely how fathers' rights groups have tapped into the cultural symbolism of the 'new father'. More specifically, it delves into how these activists express themselves as equally capable caregivers as mothers and how they present a critique of custody determination processes that, they argue, prevent them from realizing the full manifestation of their parental identities. This analysis proceeds as follows. First, I describe the research context involving the rise of fathers' rights groups in the United States. Second, I detail the research methodology involving content analysis of 103 in-depth interviews of fathers' rights activists across the United States in 2003. Third, I present the results of the analysis, and finally, I conclude with a discussion about how the custody system could be reformed to honour the difficulty of carework performed by either sex.

Research Context

The fathers' rights movement in the United States began to grow quite rapidly during the 1980s. In many ways, the groups that formed across the 50 states have the same grievances with respect to family policy as those organizations that were being started all across the globe at the same time, such as in Canada (Bertoia and Drakich 1993; Boyd 2003; Boyd 2006; Kenedy 2004), the United Kingdom (Collier 1995; Collier 2006; Collier and Sheldon 2006b), Sweden (Eriksson and Pringle 2006) and Australia (Flood 1998; Flood 2004; Flood 2006). While it is difficult to pinpoint the exact number of fathers who belong to the American groups – some have suggested that they contain about 10,000 members in total – they have structured their membership-based units in ways designed to maximize their policy influence (Crowley 2008a, 37). That is, since family policy tends to be determined at the state level in the United States, most fathers' rights organizations are state-based institutions with local branches, such as Pennsylvania's Families' and Children's Equality (FACE) and Wisconsin Fathers for Children and Family (WFCF), or national organizations with state chapters, such as the Children's Rights Council (CRC).[2]

Wherever they are located and whatever their form, fathers' rights groups provide their members with three main benefits when they join: (1) legal information regarding their family dissolution case, (2) emotional support, and (3)

2 The inclusion of these particular groups is meant for illustrative purposes only, as all of the groups that were analysed in this study were guaranteed confidentiality.

public policy advocacy (Crowley 2006). In terms of public policy reform, which is the focus of this analysis, fathers' rights activists across the board charge that once their families break up, they lack certain parental rights (Clatterbaugh 2000; Coltrane and Hickman 1992; Fineman 1991; Williams and Williams 1995). Their grievances revolve around two critical areas: child support and child custody policy (Crowley 2003). For fathers' rights groups, these two issues are highly interlinked. Activists complain that policymakers force them to pay exorbitant amounts of child support to the mothers of their children, who typically receive primary physical custody. However, these payments would not be necessary at all, argue these men, if the child custody system were reformed in a way to automatically give fathers equal time with their children.

Across the United States, judges make custody determinations for dissolving families. There are two types of joint custody at stake. *Joint legal custody* refers to a partnership between parents over the major decisions that they must make regarding their children's well-being; *joint physical custody* refers to equally shared living arrangements for the involved children. Although joint legal custody is fairly common in the United States, joint physical custody is not and therefore is the focus of fathers' rights groups concerns. While there are no state-level statistics available that permit more regional geographic comparisons, there are several national measures related to custody that are collected by the Census Bureau. More specifically, the Census' Current Population Survey (CPS) routinely asks respondents where their children are living at the time of the data collections. According to the CPS, in 2005, approximately 84 per cent of all custodial parents were mothers, while only 16 per cent were fathers (Grall 2007, 3). When probed about their more formal custody arrangements, only about 28 per cent of these custodial parents reported having some type of joint legal or joint physical custody order in place.[3]

Given these statistics that overwhelmingly favour the mother in terms of child placement, fathers' rights groups have begun a concerted effort to publicize what in their view are the faulty methods utilized by judges in supervising custody proceedings. Throughout the early part of this country's history, American courts viewed children as property, and therefore, in the rare cases of family dissolution that occurred, tended to place children with the most important property owner: the father. At the turn of the century, however, American society began to view children no longer as property, but rather as unique individuals with special developmental needs of their own. These special demands were seen as requiring one-on-one, interpersonal cultivation, a process that only mothers could adequately direct. Hence, until the mid-twentieth century, the courts upheld what came to be known as the 'tender years' doctrine, and overwhelmingly placed children from separating families with their mothers (Ellis 2000; Luepnitz 1982).

With the emergence of the women's movement that took place during the 1960s and 1970s, however, states gradually removed any references to maternal

3 See Table 9 at http://www.cenus.gov/hhes/www/childsupport/chldsu05.pdf [accessed: 31 December 2008].

preferences in their custody codes and instead replaced them with the 'best interest of the child' standard (May 2001). This standard was designed to be broad, with judges taking into consideration a variety of factors in making their placement decisions, including each child's physical, emotional, mental, religious and social needs. However, exactly because of this extremely extensive and nebulous framework, fathers' rights activists contend, judges have become rogue public servants who routinely ignore with impunity the value that fathers bring into their children's lives.

Methodology

In order to most effectively map out the complaints of fathers' rights groups against the current custody system, I turned to the words of the members themselves through in-depth interviewing, as other scholars studying family policies have done in the past (Arendell 1995; Waller 2002). As part of a larger project on the fathers' rights movement in the United States, I first attempted to map out the population of groups in existence. Since no complete population count exists – and groups are somewhat difficult to identify since they emerge and decline quite rapidly – I utilized the internet rather than printed directories to locate these organizations. In order to qualify as part of the sampling frame, these organizations had to have regular, in-person meetings of their members; online-only organizations, blogs, attorney referral sites and other news-related sites were excluded. As a result of this initial search, I secured a potential pool of 50 groups located across the United States. After I contacted each group leader to ask for permission to study the group, 26 organizations agreed to participate, including seven from the north-east, eight from the mid-west, nine from the south, and two from the west.[4] Out of the 24 that did not participate, four simply declined, two had ceased meeting in person when contacted, 14 did not respond, and four no longer had functioning contact information.

After I interviewed each group leader, I notified potential respondents via e-mail lists, postings on websites, sign-up sheets, and referrals about the possibility of participating in the study. This snowball sampling technique was necessary because the organizations themselves often do not keep updated membership lists on record. The maximum number of interviews I obtained from one group was 20, while the minimum was only one. In the end, I secured a total of 158 interviews and conducted them during the summer of 2003. Each in-depth interview was completed on the telephone, and lasted for approximately one hour. I asked respondents questions in six areas, including: (1) Demographics,

4 These 26 groups constitute the total of each respondent's primary affiliation. Some were members of multiple groups at one point in time – belonging to other groups in this study or, in most case, groups that I did not have permission to study. Counting these second and third affiliations would bring the total group involvement by these respondents to 34.

(2) Group Patterns of Recruitment and Goals, (3) Relationship with Past Partners, (4) Relationships with their Children, (5) Political Behaviour, and (6) Challenges Related to Leadership (asked of leaders only). These interviews were then professionally transcribed.

In terms of collecting their views on custody, I asked each respondent the following questions: 'Some people have said that child custody and visitation laws are unfair. Do you agree or disagree with this statement?' Out of the total of 158 interviews conducted, 103 respondents spoke about child custody (with the remainder primarily focusing on visitation law in their answers); these 103 interviews served as the data for the analysis conducted here. Previous research suggested possible thematic categories that could emerge (Crowley 2008a); I then used standard content analysis methods with the software programme Atlas.ti to code each response as either falling into one of these categories (described below), or into an 'other' category if the member offered a different type of custody complaint.

Results

Table 16.1 provides descriptive statistics on the sample of 103 fathers' rights activists included in this analysis. The mean age of the same was 46, and activists had, on average, two children. The majority were divorced/separated (52) rather than married (42) or widowed/single (9). Men dominated these groups, at 90 total, although some women, 13 here, join as new wives, girlfriends and relatives of men experiencing child support and child custody issues. A handful of women also affiliate as child advocates or as non-custodial parents (Crowley 2009a). In terms of race, most were white, at 90 members, and in terms of education, 64 members had at least a bachelor's degree or more. With respect to occupation, 86 members were employed in white-collar jobs, and the sample as a whole divided about equally in terms of partisan identifications (40 Republicans, 25 Democrats, 37 Independents, and one other).

In their critique of the child custody system, fathers' rights activists maintain that the processes that are currently in operation in terms of determining child placement work against them in several fundamental ways. More specifically, they lodge three unique critiques of custody adjudication procedures as they currently exist in the United States. These criticisms include their belief that custody processes are: (1) Anti-child; (2) Excessively Interventionist; and (3) Excessively Biased towards Women's Interests.

Custody Processes are Anti-child

One of the most stinging complaints that fathers' rights activists press against current custody determination processes is that they are decidedly anti-child in outlook. Even though judges are supposed to use the 'best interest of the child' standard when making their decisions, fathers' rights activists charge that they

Table 16.1 Socio-demographic characteristics of the fathers' rights group members

Socio-demographic characteristics	Fathers' rights group members
Current marital status	
Married	42
Divorced/separated	52
Widowed/single	9
Gender	
Male	90
Female	13
Race	
Caucasian	89
Black	8
Hispanic	1
Asian	1
Multiple/unspecified	2
Refuse	2
Education	
High school diploma/GED	9
Associate's degree/some college or vocational training	30
Bachelor's degree	34
Graduate degree (master's, doctorate or professional)	30
Employment	
White collar	86
Blue collar	11
Retired	4
Unemployed/student/volunteer	2
Political party identification	
Republican	40
Democrat	25
Independent	37
Other/no response	1
Region	
Northeast	29
Mid-west	48
South	22
West	4
Mean age	*46*
Mean number of biological children	*2*
Sample size	*103*

neglect to consider several important needs of children, who, in their view, must have a paternal figure in their lives in order to fully flourish.

The first need of all children, according to fathers' rights activists, relates to parent–child bonding time. The research on children in joint custody situations does show that children in these particular arrangements spend more time with both parents and move more frequently between houses than children in sole custody situations (Amato and Gilbreth 1999; Ferreiro 1990; Kline et al. 1989; Lee 2002). However, the scholarship on the quality of these relationships is much more mixed. Donnelly and Finkelhor (1992), for example, examined how various custody arrangements impact affection and support transmitted from parents to children; they found no relationship between joint physical custody and higher absolute levels of these measures of emotional communication. In contrast, other scholars have argued that bonds do become strengthened in circumstances of joint physical custody, especially between fathers and children (Shapiro and Lambert 1999). However, it is difficult to know whether these results are the product of improved access and contact or the joint custody arrangement itself. In addition, these benefits are likely to be erased in cases of high-conflict families (Kline, Johnston and Tschann 1991; Maccoby et al. 1993).

Despite these somewhat mixed research findings, fathers' rights activists argue that judges do not consider the special bond that children must form with their fathers from the day that they are born in order to fully thrive. Edmund, a 49-year-old divorced father of a six-year-old daughter, considered himself to be very lucky. He had a joint physical custody arrangement with his ex-wife. However, he committed himself to working with his local fathers' rights group because he wanted all men to be as fortunate as he was in his case. In this instance, Edmund appealed to judges to consider the precious months that are critical for fathers and babies to interact:

> You miss so much [when you don't have joint custody], especially when a child is real young. You miss that and that bond is not there. You almost have to be with that child. Like me, since I get her 50 per cent of the time, you know, I see that growth. I see those changes. I see her losing her teeth. I see the different things that she is going through. To me, not being able to [see her] … [I would] miss so much about that child and that child doesn't get attached to you. It is like when a baby is born, if you don't bond with that child, you are never going to bond with that child and that child is never going to bond with you. I think that happens throughout the child's life. – Edmund

Other fathers' rights activists were not as convinced as to the importance of an early father–child bond as to the centrality of a father figure in a child's life as that child ages. Vic, a 44-year-old remarried man of a 14-year-old son, asserted that judges do not take into account that, as their children enter adolescence, they need their fathers even more strongly than before:

> This is my own personal opinion on this. I think the mother is the best for child care when a child is developing from an infant … When you have a baby … and you've got a room full of men and women, when you bring that baby into that room, the women go right over there. They have to look at it and interact with the baby and the men won't. As the child grows up a little more, the attraction isn't there with the women, but the men have an attraction to try and teach that child, especially … when they have an ability to learn. So I think that when a couple goes through a divorce, the reward is given to the mother because the mother makes the best parent for the child's beginning and I think that's okay. But later on in life, and this is in my own situation with my 14-year-old son, as they develop into teenagers and they develop into their own sense of self, that's when the father's contribution kicks in. – Vic

As this quote demonstrates, Vic maintained that mothers and fathers bond with their children at different points during their development. To him, fathers need to interweave themselves into their children's lives as they get older, but unfortunately, the courts tend to ignore this important relationship when they overwhelmingly place children with their mothers.

The second need fathers' rights activists maintain that the courts ignore relates to positive developmental outcomes for children; to these men, fathers play critical roles in their children's maturation processes. Here again, however, the research is mixed as to the benefits of joint physical custody in producing this beneficial result. On the one hand, scholars have noted that children in joint living arrangements have higher self-esteem and a better outlook on their families' dissolution than children in sole custody situations (Bauserman 2002; Bender 1994). They also do not report feeling 'torn' between their parents, as some joint custody opponents fear, and they tend to look back at their childhood experiences as adults with a sense of closure (Fabricius and Hull 2000). On the other hand, if there is a high degree of tension between the separating parents, joint custody can be disastrous for children, harming them emotionally and behaviourally over the long run (Johnston, Kline and Tschann 1989).

Again, though, despite these mixed research findings, fathers' rights groups tend to argue that joint physical custody is always best for all children's developmental progress. One way this theme emerged is though fathers' rights activists' claim that current custody procedures are 'anti-child' because they prevent children from benefiting from the experiences of both parents in their daily lives, thereby hindering their growth. Malik, a 41-year-old remarried father of two children, a boy of 15 and a girl of 12, made this point explicitly when he cited the work of fathers' rights activist and author Dr Warren Farrell on the importance of both parents contributing to the well-being of their children.

> [Child custody laws are unfair in that] the children end up growing up with one parent. [Author] Warren Farrell used this example which is good. In an intact family when you have mom and dad in the family, there is always this tension

> between the parents; the two together make better decisions than one alone. He gives an example where the child may want to climb the tree and mom says no, you can't climb the tree, which can protect the child from a fall. But the child doesn't learn to take any risks, so the father says go ahead and climb the tree. The tension between those two creates a better situation for the child. If you have one parent, you have one perspective for the child. They get short changed. – Malik

While Malik condemned what he viewed as the courts' lack of consideration of the distinct contributions that both parents make to the development of their children's character, Brent expressed his concern over the custody system's dismissal of paternal involvement in a child's emotional development. Brent was twice divorced and a currently remarried 45-year-old father of two adult children – one young man and one young woman – in their early twenties. While he was able to have a lot of contact with his son growing up, for a variety of reasons he remained estranged from his daughter. In his view, this lack of contact with his daughter hindered her emotional maturation:

> Well, it takes two people to make [a child], [and] it takes two people to raise one; that's why we come in pairs. My, it's interesting. My son, who had a lot of contact with me and his mother – and I was very careful not to run his mom down – … my son's emotional development in many ways is much better than my daughter's in spite of the fact that she is the older of the two. He has a more balanced view of the world whereas my daughter, I call her 'the little general'. There are … very great differences in the basic functioning of their emotional lives. Having a lot of contact with both parents is extremely important to these kids. – Brent

Similar to Malik's comments, Brent expressed remorse over the fact that his daughter did not receive the proper 'balance' from both parents that she needed to develop a more well-rounded view of the world. Instead, in Brent's view, she approached her life with much more rigidity than he preferred, and as a result would continue to suffer from this developmental stunting throughout her adult life.

Custody Processes are Excessively Interventionist

The second area of concern for fathers' rights activists in the area of child custody relates to what they view as the excessive intervention of the courts in their lives. This type of intervention manifests itself in a variety of ways, but all results in fathers feeling as if they are at the whim of a very capricious, judicially based process.

For some fathers, their objection to excessive intervention centres on their sense that any type of custody action by the courts is simply unconstitutional. Sean, 56 years old, compared the fatherly relationship that he had with the son produced by his first marriage to his current situation, where he barely sees his six-year-old son and his four-year-old daughter because of a bitter break-up with their mother, his third wife:

> My oldest son, the one who is [now] 25, when his mother and I split, we had equal joint custody. She moved about four blocks away; I had my son a week, then she had him a week. We lived in the same school district; he could ride his bike between us. I would pick him up from school on Wednesday and I would keep him until the following Wednesday morning when I dropped him off at school. This way there was none of this waiting-on-the-doorstep kind of stuff. No confrontation between parents … I could remain active in his education and monitor his homework and his tests and his health, all phases of his life. Under the current situation [with my two youngest children], I am no longer a parent. I have relinquished my Constitutional right to be a parent … I have no Constitutional rights; they were just summarily taken from me because I am a man. – Sean

Ethan, a 44-year-old father of an 11-year-old daughter, made the same Constitutional claim somewhat more succinctly:

> From the Constitution, the state is not to interfere with parental rights unless there is a compelling reason, which to me would be, say, if you're a crack addict. But the state interjects itself in the family when it does not have the authority to do so. It violates the Constitution … You shouldn't need to fight to be a parent; you should just be a parent. – Ethan

Like many other activists in fathers' rights groups, Sean and Ethan took their rights to be full parents as inherent in the Constitution. They, in essence, felt no civil rights protections from the document that was supposed to protect their freedoms as United States citizens.

On a more practical but no less spirited level, fathers' rights activists also critique what they view as excessive intervention in the form of judges' beliefs in their own omnipotence in resolving custody disputes. Here, Leon, twice divorced with a 10-year-old son and an eight-year-old daughter, complained about how judges use their authority to impose their will upon all families that enter their courtrooms.

> Basically, what you've got is a system where one person – the judge – is judge, jury [and] executioner, and that's not the way the legal system is to be set up … Every judge is biased in some way or another. The whole system is as biased here as it is in Saudi Arabia. Over there the father will get custody; over here the mother will … A judge is not a jury of our peers. Judges are lawyers. What we are saying is the best people to decide how to raise our children are lawyers.

> I think a lot of people do object to that. Lawyers are not the best people to raise their children. The best people to raise their children are parents. – Leon

Kip, a 49-year-old twice-divorced father of three daughters, ages 22, 15 and 13, echoed a similar complaint when he argued that it was impossible for judges to make any type of serious custody decision within the short period of time in which they meet a family:

> I know of people who have custody of their kids who should never be allowed near a child again. I also know people who get to see their kids once every two weeks who should have been given custody. Again, each case has to be taken individually and that's a shortcoming of our judicial system. You have a judge who in 30 minutes is supposed to decide who's going to be a parent and who is not. I would not want that job. I could not sleep at night having that job and knowing the effect it would have on kids' lives. Granted, someone has to do it, but to me, it's kind of ludicrous to ask someone to make that decision in 30 minutes with very little knowledge. – Kip

Kip recognized that judges face an uphill battle when they are asked to make decisions in these types of cases. However, he also maintained that the court system could do a better job than permitting one person, a judge, to evaluate what might be the best living arrangements for children whom they do not know.

In response to criticisms like these, over the past several decades, the custody system has opened up the decision-making process to many types of experts who can help judges make their final placement rulings. For example, in some cases, courts might rely on mental-health evaluators to generate recommendations regarding the best interests of the children. These mental-health evaluators, also known as custody or forensic evaluators, undertake intensive studies of a family in order to produce a formal report to the court. They can conduct interviews with all those individuals who are responsible for the well-being of the involved children, including but not limited to doctors, teachers, babysitters, and others (Gould 1998; Stahl 1994). In addition to these types of evaluators, the courts can also appoint guardians ad litem or attorneys for the child (Mason 1999). Guardians ad litem are not necessarily attorneys; instead, their job is to protect the interests of the children in all custody proceedings, and they might be social workers or psychologists. Attorneys for the child, in contrast, are lawyers involved in these proceedings as agents for the children; they directly articulate the children's wishes to the court.

Yet, while designated to be helpful players in presenting information to the courts, these experts do not necessarily command the deference of judges. In fact, in numerous cases, fathers' rights activists such as Jorge, a 45-year-old father of a 10-year-old daughter, maintained that the judges viewed these expert statements as only somewhat relevant to their decision-making process:

> We brought in a custody expert [to help decide our case] … The gentleman in his testimony indicated that he had done 300–500 custody evaluations. In spite of this, the judge did not go along with what his recommendation was … The judge said that he'd been sitting on the bench for 17 years, but the judge saw us for three days of testimony (total number of hours, let's see 2, 5, and maybe a total of 7 hours). The custody evaluator followed us for close to two years and probably interacted with us for tens of hours. Who do you think is going to have a better idea of what went on with the case? … The judge in his testimony even admitted that he didn't read the custody evaluator's recommendations although they were provided for him well in advance. – Jorge

Ricardo, a three-times divorced father of five children, echoed this perspective:

> In custody situations, guardians ad litem and psychologists … may all come in and testify to the fact that the father is the best parent and the children should be with the father; then the judge will go against everything and give custody to the mother. There is a profound bias there and everybody knows it, but with the discretion they give the family court judges and the fact that in very few states individuals are allowed jury trials in divorces, there is no way to get away from that bias. – Ricardo

Both Jorge and Ricardo felt disappointed that the court system, which was designed to help them, actually ended up causing them more desperation. The professionals who were supposed to assist them raised their spirits; however, the judges used their power to summarily dismiss their claims and rule against them as fathers.

In addition to their complaints that the Constitution was not being followed, as well as that individual judges acted as if they were omnipotent, other fathers' rights activists pointed to the greed of lawyers as the main motivation for excessive state intervention in their lives. The more conflict that is generated by attorneys, according to fathers' rights activists, the more hours lawyers can bill for their services. Joanna, a divorced mother of four, argued that the entire adversarial custody system was established so that lawyers can make more money off family dissolution:

> The attorneys try to make it a win/lose [situation], [like] somebody is going to win the children; they are like an award. I think [that this is] because attorneys, by nature, are adversarial and greedy. The American society is greedy. The more money attorneys can bill through conflict, the more heartache they create and the more really everyone suffers … The more a system can be matter of fact without the competition and tug of war, the more rational it will be. I think that would eliminate parents [fighting] … I've totally depleted my retirement. It has just been haemorrhaging because of attorney fees. – Joanna

According to Joanna and other fathers' rights activists, profit making off custody disputes has become so commonplace that any new initiatives that attempt to create the best situation for all family members will be met with massive resistance. In this pessimistic view, the custody system will never suspend those activities from which it profits.

Custody Processes are Excessively Biased towards Women's Interests

The third barrier preventing fathers from assuming joint physical custody of their children, according to fathers' rights activists, is that the current processes in place are too biased in favour of women. These activists maintain that these biases can assume many forms, but all result in fathers receiving far less custody than they deserve.

One of the ways this bias emerges is when judges, in the view of fathers' rights activists, penalize men for the division of household labour that they assumed when the family was still together. Burt, a twice-divorced 47-year-old father of three daughters who later remarried, argued that decisions made in the context of a unified family as to who would do more child care have no relevance to decisions that need to be made now that the family is split apart:

> Many judges say, 'I'm going to try to preserve the relationships that [the family] had before [it broke up].' What you had before, [however], was maybe dad working and mom staying home; that is not going to happen after divorce. [Custody decisions] need to reflect the new relationship. The trade-offs that parents make when they are married are different after they are divorced. A man may be more inclined to work more hours to provide for his family when he's married, but if he does that after he's divorced, when does he get to see his children? – Burt

Like others in fathers' rights groups, Burt voiced his frustration over the courts' inability to understand that a family break-up is an opportunity to divide childcare responsibilities in new ways.

Other men in fathers' rights groups pointed to pro-female bias in what they viewed as the court system's overly sympathetic attitude to women's allegations of domestic violence. Many fathers' rights activists vigorously campaign against what they see as the rise in false allegations of abuse, which they maintain are simply weapons used against them in order to strip their custody rights away (Crowley 2009b). For example, Daniel, 44 years old, had an extremely volatile relationship with his ex-wife while they were raising their young son. After she accused him of domestic violence – a charge that he denied – he soon saw the relationship with his son fall apart:

> My wife accused me of domestic violence, which was not true … We got in an argument that night. She threw a drill down on the floor and [after] I went to put

> it down in the basement, I came upstairs. She was on the phone and when the police came, the police asked me what happened. I said we had an argument. They interviewed her; she was at a neighbour's house. She claimed that I spit food at her, which was not true. And she claimed that I was going to kill myself, which was not true. I represented myself in court and that's where my downfall was … I loved my wife very much and I trusted her. I represented myself [in court] and when I went to court, I saw she had an attorney and she had the woman from the domestic violence [shelter] there … But through that she was able to get me taken out of my house … She has told my son that I hit him and that I don't love him – that I hate him. She did some pretty awful things. My son was five years old at the time … Then I had to take my anger management class and that was six months. Then I had to take a parenting class and I think that was 13 weeks … [Then] I had to take an individual anger management [class] and yet my [ex-wife] didn't have to take anything. – Daniel

Artie, a 42-year-old father of two sons and one daughter, echoed a similar view to that of Daniel, but focused his attack on the Violence Against Women Act (VAWA), originally passed in 1994 and later reauthorized in 2000 and 2005. At the time of its initial passage, VAWA embodied a broad-ranging federal stance against violence, and included funding for shelters, training for police officers and judges related to violence, reporting requirements for schools and police, and the establishment of violence awareness programmes across the United States (Dragiewicz 2008). While VAWA has earned widespread support among women's advocates, fathers' rights activists have argued that the law systematically oppresses men by transforming all fathers into potential criminal abusers:

> There is a federal law … called the Violence Against Women Act … In layman's terms, as translated as I understand it, is if a woman feels threatened in a domestic situation, she can call the police and have a man arrested based on that allegation without investigation and the police have a duty to act. There is no such law for men. That was written for the National Organization for Woman who campaigned for Bill Clinton … I have been personally affected by that federal law, here locally. Any time my ex-wife gets mad at me, which is all the time, she can just call 9-1-1 and say, I feel threatened, I'm a woman, I demand protection under the Violence Against Women Act … I've been arrested … She demands [to know] where I'm going to be, what I'm doing with the kids … For people who haven't been through it, [they] don't know what the heck I'm talking about. – Artie

For fathers' rights activists like Daniel and Artie, the custody system has been captured in a very detrimental way by domestic violence interest groups. These organizations have wrongly, in their view, persuaded judges that women are almost always blameless when there are allegations of violence, leaving fathers to carry the burden of unjustified guilt simply by accident of their sex. Inevitably, then, when judges ultimately consider the question as to which parent should get custody, they almost always select the mother.

Criticizing another form of pro-female bias, fathers' rights activists also complain that the system creates a power imbalance between the sexes after a family break-up, and that judges intentionally give more power to women because they see them as more stable parents. Tomas, a 31-year-old father of three young children, articulated his concerns the following way:

> I think [current custody law] gives more power to the person who holds the children. I'll have to beg and plead to see my kids for a few hours here or there, and she'll say, well, it is not your weekend. There have been a couple of times when I didn't have to work on a Friday and I wanted to spend the day with my boys so they didn't have to be in daycare while she is at work … She said I couldn't have them. I shouldn't have to wait until my weekend to see my kids.
> – Tomas

Others argue that the system is so biased against them that a mother has to have a horrible character flaw or be engaged in an illegal activity in order not to obtain custody. On this point, Lukas, a 43-year-old divorced father of three daughters, made the case that, even if mothers behave in a negative fashion, judges consistently view them as the more capable parent:

> The mother is automatically looked at as the one who is the nurturer and primary caregiver and therefore the courts automatically … 9 times out of 10, I would say award custody to her. The man has to fight like hell to get any type of visitation. You go through all kinds of mental … evaluation programmes where you actually see a psychiatrist and you are evaluated as to whether or not you are going to be a good parent and be able to see your child. It is tough fight for a man, it really is, to get any type of custody unless the mother was arrested for drug possession and was under the influence or maybe caught prostituting herself. It would have to be something devastating for the father to get custody.
> – Lukas

In either case, according to Tomas and Lukas, judges' decisions almost uniformly place the mother in the dominant position when it comes to caregiving rights. This bias, according to fathers' rights activists, means men have to beg, plead and cajole their way into their own children's lives.

Finally, fathers' rights activists also charge that custody procedures favour women because the system is intended to channel the most money to them in the post-dissolution family context. Devin, 35 years old, was the father of two sons under the age of three. One of these sons was a non-marital child whom he had when he was briefly separated from his wife. Of course, since he ultimately reconciled with his wife, the courts required that he pay child support to the non-marital child's mother. With this judicial decision, Devin complained that the courts were compelling him into participating in an income redistribution scheme with which he did not agree:

> Right now custody is the ticket to the free paycheck. The more custody time someone gets … the more she makes … the problem is this … I'm not a woman-hater … don't get me wrong … [but] why is it that women are going to make money off of that? If they both have the child the same amount of time and they both make the same amount of money, how can you tell me that she should get money for this? It's asinine, is the only way to describe it. – Devin

For Devin, the easy way out of this predicament would be to award both parents more equal physical custody. However, according to Devin and fathers' rights activists like him, because of the court's favouritism towards women in terms of protecting them financially, mothers almost always receive primary physical custody.

Conclusions

As this chapter has clearly demonstrated, fathers' rights groups take great umbrage at the treatment of men as parents in cases of familial dissolution. Through their own words, these activists have criticized a multi-layer, child custody determination system that, in their view, does not take their role as competent parents seriously enough. More specifically, they argue that the current methods for determining the physical placement of minors is anti-child, excessively interventionist, and overly biased towards women. Because of the deficiencies in the system, fathers' rights activists maintain, once their families break apart, they no longer have the ability to effectively parent their children. They, in other words, no longer have the opportunity to either 'father' or 'mother'.

There is, however, a potential solution to these fathers' concerns. Judges relying on the best interest of the child standard, as described above, take into account many factors when they determine where to place children after a familial dissolution. Fathers' rights activists complain that the standard's very vagueness leads to unequal outcomes between the sexes. One potential solution might be the replacement of the best interest of the child standard with a new set of guidelines that could help rectify these inequities over the long run, and a key contender that suits this purpose is the primary caregiver model. Simply put, the primary caregiver model gives priority custodial preference to those parents who have played the most significant role in their children's lives prior to the family's dissolution (Boyd 2003). Activities that might count as parental involvement include economic provision, attending the children's school and extra-curricular activities, preparing meals, doing laundry, meeting with paediatricians, and so forth.

The primary caregiver standard on its face is gender neutral, although undoubtedly, given the current division of child care labour within the majority of

American homes, women would still be granted physical custody more often than men. However, if this standard were uniformly adopted across all of the states, it would have the power to dramatically influence behaviour towards a more egalitarian set of parental responsibilities. More specifically, if both mothers and fathers know that, if they break up, judges will utilize this standard in awarding child custody, both sexes would be motivated to strive for equality in both the paid labour market and in undertaking unpaid childcare duties. In other words, once this standard is in place, while parents are still together, mothers may invest more time in the paid labour market, and fathers may invest more time in the unpaid work of household and child care. Ultimately, if the couple dissolves, both mothers and fathers would logically have an equal chance of securing physical custody. In this world, both parents would then have the opportunity to 'mother' both before and after dissolution, undoubtedly to the developmental and emotional benefit of children living all across the country.

Chapter 17
To Be Male: Homophobia, Sexism, and the Production of 'Masculine' Boys

Clifford J. Rosky

This chapter is about the relationship between homophobia and sexism in family law. By conducting an empirical analysis of custody and visitation cases, it shows that stereotypes about the children of lesbian and gay parents are both sexist and homophobic. In some cases, the relationship between homophobia and sexism becomes especially obvious, when stereotypes explicitly conflate the sexual orientation, gender identity and gender roles of children and parents. By looking more closely, however, we can find more subtle evidence of this relationship in a much wider range of cases, wherever stereotypes of the children of lesbian and gay parents appear.

In masculinities studies, the relationship between homophobia and sexism is most often theorized in terms of 'hegemonic masculinity', the dominant concept of masculinity within particular cultures (Connell and Messerschmidt 2005). Among others, Michael Kimmel has observed that hegemonic masculinity is principally defined in negative terms, as that which is neither 'female' nor 'homosexual' (Kimmel 1997b, Pleck 1980). In this field, masculinity is portrayed as a confluence of sexism and homophobia – a collection of essentialist distinctions between 'male' and 'female', on the one hand, and 'straight' and 'gay', on the other hand. In this respect, masculinities studies follows a long line of feminist and queer theorists who have observed connections between sexism and homophobia (Valdes 1995a, Koppelman 1994, Sedgwick 1993, Law 1988, MacKinnon 1983).

In most legal disputes over lesbian and gay parenthood, however, the relationship between sexism and homophobia has been ignored. Opponents of lesbian and gay parenthood have claimed that 'children' should not be exposed to the 'homosexual lifestyle', and they have urged people to choose between homosexuality and parenthood; advocates have called such claims 'homophobic' and 'heterosexist', and they have urged legislatures and courts to reject them. In both camps, the terms of the debate have remained neutral with regard to sex: fathers have been lumped together with mothers; sons have been lumped together with daughters. As a result, the influence of sexism on legal disputes over lesbian and gay parenthood has been left unexplored.

For the most part, the US legal scholarship on lesbian and gay parenthood reflects a similar framework. If sexism has had any influence in disputes over lesbian and gay parenthood, legal scholars have apparently overlooked it. Over the past several decades, lawyers and law professors have written dozens of articles about homosexuality and parenthood, in which they have generally argued for pro-gay reforms to family law. In most of these articles, lesbian mothers and gay fathers have been considered together, and the legal problems that they face have not been distinguished (Harding 2010: 8). While several scholars have written articles specifically about lesbian mothers (Dalton 2003, Velte 2001, Robson 2000, Boyd 1998, Polikoff 1996, Peltz 1995, Ronner 1995, Robson 1994, Sella 1991, Polikoff 1990, Polikoff 1986, Hunter and Polikoff 1976), only a few have written specifically about gay fathers (Spitko 2005, Hollandsworth 1995, Rush 1993), and almost none have separately theorized the obstacles confronted by these two groups of parents.[1] In this body of scholarship, moreover, no one seems to have considered the influence of the child's sex on disputes over lesbian and gay parenthood.[2]

This chapter argues that sexism influences the expression of homophobic stereotypes about the children of lesbian and gay parents. On a general level, it challenges a paradigm that seems to ignore the influence of sexism, or pretend that sexism has no influence at all; on a specific level, it focuses on the influence of maleness – on fathers and sons – a subject that has generally been neglected by lesbian, feminist and family law scholars. By conducting a comparative analysis of reported family law opinions, the chapter shows that the children of lesbian and gay parents are subjected to stereotypes in custody and visitation cases that are both sexist and homophobic – influenced by both the parent's sex and the child's sex. By taking account of the complex relationship between homophobia and sexism, the chapter aims to develop a more compelling case for lesbian and gay families – a case that vindicates the developmental interests of children, in addition to the parental interests of lesbians and gay men.

The argument proceeds in two parts. The first part is based on my analysis of a collection of almost 200 family law opinions, which represents every custody and visitation case involving a gay, lesbian or bisexual parent and a heterosexual parent reported in the United States since the 1950s. The part begins with a description of my methodology for collecting and analysing these cases, and a brief consideration of how legal and social norms have developed in this field during the relevant time

---

1 The tendency of legal scholars to lump together lesbian mothers and gay fathers is nicely captured by the following title: 'Lesbian (and Gay) Custody Claims: What Difference Does Difference Make?' (Boyd 1998). The title refers to the difference between queer and heterosexual parents. Although the article is primarily based on cases involving lesbian mothers, the author does not distinguish cases involving gay fathers.

2 In her recent book, *Regulating Sexuality: Legal Consciousness in Lesbian and Gay Lives*, Rosie Harding briefly considers the influence of the child's sex on similar stereotypes that appear in a related context. Based on a series of in-depth interviews, she shows that counsellors who serve lesbian and gay parents in assisted reproduction clinics have applied different stereotypes about boys and girls raised by lesbian mothers and gay fathers (2010: 132–4).

period. Next, it lays out the focus of my analysis – the stereotype that children raised by lesbian and gay parents are likely to develop homosexual fantasies, engage in homosexual behaviour, and identify as gay, lesbian or bisexual.

By comparing how often this stereotype appears in cases involving fathers, mothers, sons and daughters, I illustrate that homophobia is influenced by sexism in both obvious and subtle ways. In general, this stereotype is influenced by the child's sex: it is applied more often to sons than daughters. In particular, however, the stereotype is influenced by the relationship between the child's sex and the parent's sex: it is applied most often to sons raised by gay fathers, slightly less often to sons and daughters raised by lesbian mothers, and almost never to daughters raised by gay fathers. By drawing upon relevant literature on homophobia, sexism, and the psychology of child development, and taking a closer look at each group of cases, I reveal the underlying assumptions about childhood sexual and gender development that have produced this hierarchy of sexual development concerns. A close reading of this pattern of stereotypes betrays hetero-patriarchal assumptions about the need to secure the role of 'masculine' fathers in the development of 'masculine' boys.

In responding to these stereotypes, the US legal academy has cited a large body of empirical studies claiming that children raised by lesbian and gay parents are 'no different' from children raised by heterosexual parents. As I explain in the second part of this chapter, however, the reliability of these claims has not withstood independent review. In 2001, two sociologists published a comprehensive meta-analysis of the best-designed studies, in which they found that researchers had overlooked significant differences in the sexual and gender development of children raised by lesbian and gay parents.

To date, most advocates for lesbian and gay parents have responded to these provocative findings by downplaying or ignoring them. In his 2003 article, however, Carlos Ball took the academy's first, courageous step towards confronting these findings. Rather than downplaying the data, he both entertained and defended the possibility that children raised by lesbian and gay parents were more likely to violate traditional sex stereotypes. In this article, however, Professor Ball was not willing to entertain the possibility that such children were more likely to engage in homosexual behaviour or identify as lesbian, gay or bisexual.

In this chapter, I push Ball's argument one step further: I argue that the state has no legitimate interest in discouraging children from being lesbian, gay or bisexual, and that any attempt to distinguish between homophobic and sexist stereotypes is unnecessary and unhelpful. Based on my empirical analysis of custody and visitation cases, I claim that homophobia and sexism are inextricably intertwined in stereotypes about the children of lesbian and gay parents. As a result, any strategy that specifically targets sexist stereotypes – as distinguished from homophobic stereotypes – is likely to be futile, and any victory against sexism is unlikely, and may well be short-lived. Because homophobia and sexism are connected, conflated and collapsed in this context, opponents will readily shift from one discourse to the other, and neither stereotype will fall by itself.

The chapter concludes by suggesting that, sooner or later, we shall have to launch a coordinated attack against both of these forces, in which the battle is joined on both fronts. If we mean to redefine what it is to be male, ultimately we must be prepared to defend not only a boy's right to be feminine and a girl's right to be masculine, but any child's right to be lesbian, gay or bisexual.

Like Father, Like Son: Homophobia, Sexism, and the 'Production' of Masculine Boys

> Feminism … has a theory of power: Gender is sexualized as sexuality is gendered.
>
> – Catherine MacKinnon (1983: 635)

This empirical study of disputes over lesbian and gay parenthood is based on my analysis of a collection of 191 reported judicial opinions from 171 family law cases. To the best of my knowledge and effort, the collection includes every custody and visitation case involving a lesbian, gay or bisexual parent and a heterosexual parent reported in the United States between 1950 and 2007, when the empirical phase of the study concluded.[3] To build this database, I systematically gathered all of the reported opinions available in Westlaw, Lexis, casebooks and law reviews.[4] The collection consists exclusively of cases in which a man and a woman were married, had at least one child together, were divorced, and entered into custody or visitation proceedings; at some point in these cases, one of the parents was identified as gay or lesbian to the court. In such cases, litigants and experts have often claimed that a parent's homosexuality has had an 'adverse effect' on a child, and judges have often considered such claims in determining the 'best interests' of the child.

Of course, social understandings of homosexuality and parenthood have changed dramatically in the US since the 1950s, and to some extent, the laws of custody and visitation have changed with them. Over the last half century, US courts have gradually adopted a more liberal approach towards a parent's homosexuality in custody and visitation cases. In some early cases, courts had articulated a 'per se' rule against custody and visitation claims made by lesbian

3 My search did not reveal any relevant opinions reported before 1952. This fact is likely explained by the limitations of Westlaw and Lexis archives, which do not include a wide range of cases reported before 1945. In addition, in early cases, litigants and judges were profoundly reluctant to make any explicit references to homosexuality in custody and visitation cases.

4 In particular, I would like to thank Kimberly D. Richman of the University of San Francisco for generously sharing her collection of family law opinions involving LGBT parents. I supplemented Richman's list (Richman 2009) with my own research by conducting additional Westlaw and Lexis searches and checking citations in cases, casebooks, law review articles and internet sources.

and gay parents, holding that homosexuality was inherently inconsistent with parenthood as a matter of law (*Roe v. Roe*, Va. 1985, *Evans v. Evans*, Cal. 1960). In the last twenty-five years, the majority of US states have abandoned the per se rule in favour of a 'nexus' test (Eskridge and Hunter 2004). Under the nexus test, a parent's homosexuality is not a sufficient ground to revoke or limit the parent's custody or visitation rights, unless one parent proves that the other parent's homosexuality has an 'adverse effect' on the child.

As many scholars have observed, the shift from a per se rule to a nexus test represents a measure of progress for lesbian and gay parents (Yoshino 2002, Rubenstein 1997); today, the concept of 'homosexual parenthood' is no longer a contradiction in terms. Yet the nexus test has not eliminated homophobia from custody and visitation cases. Because the 'best interest of the child' standard is notoriously vague, many courts have continued to presume that when a parent exposes a child to the 'homosexual lifestyle' – for example, by coming out to the child, spending time with other gay men or lesbians, displaying same-sex affections, or living with a same-sex partner – the parent's homosexuality has an adverse effect on the child (Wald 2006).

In such disputes, litigants, experts and judges have expressed a long list of stereotypes about lesbian and gay parents, which have been well catalogued by lawyers, law professors and social scientists (Patterson 1992, Flaks 1994, *Harvard Law Review* 1989). Courts have suggested, for example, that gay men are likely to be child molesters, and thus, that a gay father is likely to sexually abuse his own child (*J.L.P.(H.) v. D.J.P.*, Mo. 1982).

In recent years, however, such stereotypes have appeared less often in custody and visitation cases (Rosky 2009), and the battle over lesbian and gay parenthood has shifted into the field of child sexual development (Stacey and Biblarz 2001, Bailey et al. 1995). More than anything else, lesbian and gay parents are now portrayed as 'recruiters' and 'role models' – people who actively or passively encourage children to become homosexual.[5] In some cases, courts have suggested that lesbian and gay parents will 'indoctrinate' children by exposing them to pro-gay events or media – for example, parades and rallies, weddings and churches, magazines and books, conferences and lectures, and radio and television programmes (*Hertzler v. Hertzler*, Wy. 1996). More often, however, courts have suggested that children will 'identify' with and 'imitate' lesbian and gay parents who model homosexual behaviour – for example, by coming out to a child, living with a same-sex partner, or displaying same-sex affections in front of a child (*Dailey v. Dailey*, Tenn. 1981).

Although recruiting and role modelling concerns are phrased in slightly different terms, they are based on the same underlying stereotypes about children raised by lesbian and gay parents – namely, that such children are likely to develop homosexual

5 In *Regulating Sexuality*, Rosie Harding shows that similar stereotypes have been articulated by counsellors serving lesbian mothers at assisted reproduction clinics (2010: 132–3).

fantasies, engage in homosexual behaviour, and identify as lesbian, gay or bisexual. Whether or not these concerns have any factual basis, they draw support from two popular, conventional assumptions about the process of sexual development, which can be traced back to the work of Sigmund Freud (1937, 1905): first, the notion that, during early childhood, children have both homosexual and heterosexual tendencies, and second, the notion that, during adolescence, they develop sexual desires, behaviours and identities based on models provided by adults, especially parents (Stockton 2010). By keeping children away from lesbian and gay parents, courts have sought to establish 'a proper atmosphere for young, pliable minds' in which children are shielded from 'any course of conduct that might influence them to develop homosexual traits' (*Black v. Black*, Tenn. 1988: 2–3).

To examine whether stereotypes about the sexual development of children have been influenced by the parent's sex and the child's sex, this part compares how often they have appeared in cases involving fathers, mothers, sons and daughters. Based on the distribution of stereotypes in these four groups of cases, the first section derives a hierarchy of concerns about childhood sexual development that have been expressed by litigants, experts and judges. By drawing upon relevant literature on homophobia, sexism, and the psychology of child development, and taking a closer look at each group of cases, subsequent sections reveal the underlying assumptions about childhood sexual and gender development that have produced this particular hierarchy of concerns.

The method has both qualitative and quantitative elements, as it involves reading rhetoric, counting cases, and theorizing explanations. The approach imposes a handful of intrinsic limitations, three of which I shall emphasize here.[6] First, I recognize that reported opinions are not representative of unreported opinions, appeals are not representative of trials, and neither appeals nor trials are representative of mediations, settlements or uncontested divorces, which are far more numerous. Second, I emphasize that, by focusing strictly on explicit stereotypes, I have taken a conservative approach to my rhetorical analysis. I include only references to stereotypes that appear in the text of opinions, rather than those that might be inferred from factual circumstances or ambiguous remarks. Finally, I note that, because I am working with a complete set of opinions rather than a representative sample, I do mean to suggest that my findings can be generalized.[7]

---

6 For a more complete explanation of the method and its limitations, see Rosky 2009.

7 In quantitative terms, the question of whether my findings are 'statistically significant' has no meaningful answer. The relevant question is not whether the differences that I observe are *significant* but whether they are *meaningful* – that is, whether they are large enough to be regarded as a pattern or trend rather than the random influence of a few anomalous cases. For the purposes of this study, I have defined a difference to be presumptively meaningful when it is based on a disparity of at least three cases, and thus could not have been produced by one or two outliers. Under this definition, all of the differences identified in this chapter qualified as presumptively meaningful – although, as I indicate in the text, some were more meaningful than others. See Rosky 2009: 276, 299.

Recruiting, Role Modelling, and the Sexual Development of Boys

Since the 1950s, sexual development stereotypes were raised by litigants and witnesses in about 28 per cent (48 of 171) of all reported custody and visitation cases, and they were accepted by judges in about 90 per cent (43 of 48) of these cases. These stereotypes appeared most often in southern and midwestern states, such as Alabama, Tennessee, Ohio and Missouri, and during the late 1980s and late 1990s, in the midst of national backlashes against lesbian and gay rights.[8] About half of the stereotypes appeared in the remaining states and about half appeared during other time periods. In the ten years between 1997 and 2007, these stereotypes continued to appear in ten reported cases, including one case published in 2007 (*Holmes v. Holmes*, Ark. 2007).

If we break down these cases based on the parent's sex and the child's sex, we can begin to see interesting patterns that illuminate the influence of sexism on these stereotypes. Comparing cases involving fathers and mothers, it initially appears that the expression of sexual development stereotypes is not influenced by the parent's sex at all. Sexual development stereotypes are applied equally often to the children of fathers and mothers – in exactly 28 per cent (14 of 50) of the cases involving gay fathers and about 28 per cent (34 of 121) of the cases involving lesbian mothers.

Given that these are stereotypes about the sexual development of *children*, however, it is not surprising that the child's sex has a more obvious influence upon them than the parent's sex. Comparing cases involving sons and daughters, we can see that sexual development stereotypes were applied to sons 49 per cent more often than they were applied to daughters – specifically, in about 38 per cent (20 of 52) of the cases involving sons and about 26 per cent (16 of 62) of the cases involving daughters.

Based on this pattern of stereotypes, it seems that litigants, experts and judges generally expressed greater concerns about the sexual development of boys than the sexual development of girls. Needless to say, this hierarchy of concerns was not explicitly acknowledged in the reported opinions: no one in these cases claimed, for example, that it was more important or more challenging to discourage homosexuality in boys.

By breaking down the cases by both the parent's sex and the child's sex, we can begin to see the influence of sex on the expression of sexual development stereotypes in more detail. The following matrix (Table 17.1) shows how often sexual development stereotypes appeared in four groups of cases defined by the parent's sex and the child's sex: (1) cases involving gay fathers and sons; (2) cases

8 The first backlash was triggered by the public's awareness of the risk of HIV infection and the scope of the AIDS epidemic (Shilts 2007, Engel 2006). The second backlash was triggered by the public's response to *Baehr v. Lewin* (Hawaii 1993), a case in which the Hawaii Supreme Court signalled that it was likely to strike down the state's law that prohibited same-sex couples from marrying.

involving lesbian mothers and daughters; (3) cases involving lesbian mothers and sons; and (4) cases involving gay fathers and daughters.

Table 17.1 Distribution of sexual development stereotypes by the parent's sex and the child's sex

	Fathers	Mothers
Sons	50% (9/18)	32% (11/34)
Daughters	10% (2/20)	33% (14/42)

By breaking down the cases in this manner, we can see that the parent's sex does influence the distribution of these stereotypes after all. It is not simply that litigants, experts and judges were more concerned about the sexual development of boys. Rather, they were concerned about particular relationships between parent and child, which were shaped by particular pairings of the parent's sex and the child's sex.

Based on this pattern of sexual development stereotypes, we can identify the following hierarchy of concerns expressed by litigants, experts and judges in custody and visitation cases:

1. They were *most* concerned about gay fathers raising gay sons: this stereotype appeared in half (9 of 18) of the cases involving fathers and sons.
2. They were *slightly less* concerned – but still quite concerned – about lesbian mothers raising lesbian daughters: this stereotype appeared in one third (14/42) of the cases involving mothers and daughters.
3. They were *equally* concerned about lesbian mothers raising gay sons: like the second stereotype, this one appeared in about one third (11/34) of the cases involving mothers and sons.
4. They were *least* concerned – indeed, hardly concerned at all – about gay fathers raising lesbian daughters: this stereotype appeared in only two cases – one tenth (2/20) of the cases involving fathers and daughters.

Above all, the differences between the last group of cases and the first three groups seem to be most meaningful:[9] litigants, experts and judges were five times more concerned about gay fathers raising gay sons than gay fathers raising lesbian daughters; similarly, they were three times more concerned about lesbian mothers raising gay sons or lesbian daughters than gay fathers raising lesbian daughters. The following sections explore what underlying, conventional assumptions about childhood sexual and gender development have produced this particular hierarchy of concerns.

9 For a quantitative definition of the term 'meaningful', see supra note 7.

Identification: Like Parent, Like Child

It is not difficult to understand why sexual development stereotypes were so prevalent in cases where the parent's sex and the child's sex were the same. In cases involving fathers and sons, the stereotypes reflect the assumption that boys are more likely to identify with male role models; in cases involving mothers and daughters, the stereotypes reflect the assumption that girls are more likely to identify with female role models. Whether or not these assumptions are sound, they draw support from the wisdom of two common proverbs – 'like father, like son' and 'like mother, like daughter' – which suggest that children typically take after parents of the same gender. More specifically, they draw support from many psychological theories of sexual development, which generally suggest that children typically form a bond of 'identification' with parents of the same gender – that is, boys normally identify with fathers and girls normally identify with mothers (Kaplan and Sedney 1980: 180).

In most of the sexual development cases, courts did not explicitly analyse the relationship between the parent's sex and the child's sex, so the significance of this bond was not often acknowledged. In a few cases, however, courts explicitly suggested that children are more likely to imitate parents of the same gender in the course of denying custody to lesbian and gay parents. In *Bennett v. O'Rourke* (Tenn. 1985: 3), for example, the court noted that 'the homosexual parent and the minor child are both female'; in denying the mother custody of her daughter, the court explained, 'we consider this factor particularly important because of the increased chance of role-modeling.' In *Glover v. Glover* (Ohio 1990: 164), when the court rejected the testimony of the father's expert witness, it expressed similar concerns about sons raised by gay fathers: 'Although studies showed that children raised by lesbian mothers were not affected by the custodial parent's sexual preference, [the expert] admitted no such research was available for male children raised by homosexual fathers.' In a similar vein, opponents of lesbian and gay parenthood have often claimed that '[p]arents are important as role models for their children of the same gender because children learn to be adults by watching adults' (Wardle 1997: 860–61).

Gender Identity Disorder: Lesbian Mothers, Effeminate Sons

The question remains, however, why the sons of lesbian mothers were often viewed so differently from the daughters of gay fathers. If the children of gay fathers were stereotyped so differently along gender lines, why were the children of lesbian mothers stereotyped so equally across gender lines? Why would litigants, experts and judges be so concerned about the possibility that the sons of lesbians might be gay, and so unconcerned that the daughters of gay men might be lesbian?

Answers to these questions can be developed from a brilliant essay by Eve Kosofsky Sedgwick, 'How to Bring Your Kids up Gay: The War on Effeminate Boys' (1991/1993). Sedgwick's essay is a classic text of queer theory, and it deserves a place in the canon of masculinities studies as well. As Sedgwick explains, the modern war over the sexual development of boys has been played out in the evolution of two theories of childhood sexual development that have been adopted by mainstream psychologists during different periods. The first is an old theory of why homosexuality develops in boys, which was closely associated with the diagnosis of homosexuality as a mental disorder. The second is a new theory of why effeminacy develops in boys, which is closely associated with the diagnosis of gender identity disorder of childhood, and the old theory of why homosexuality develops in boys. By briefly reviewing the evolution of these theories, we can develop a more specific understanding of why litigants, experts and judges expressed heightened concerns about lesbian mothers raising gay sons.

In *Woodruff v. Woodruff* (N.C. 1979: 776), a psychologist testified that there was 'a substantiated theory that a male child, raised by an extremely domineering mother, may pursue a homosexual lifestyle.' In the postwar era, this theory was popularized by psychologists who diagnosed homosexuality as mental disorder – specifically, an arrested form of sexual development. Citing clinical observations and psychological studies, these so-called 'conversion' therapists claimed that male homosexuality most often developed in boys raised by mothers who were 'domineering', 'harsh' or 'close-binding' and fathers who were 'weak', 'absent' or 'detached' (Socarides 1978: 183–4, Bieber et al. 1972: 79–81, 114). During this period, most psychologists believed that this family dynamic would cause a boy to identify with the 'wrong' gender – that is, with his mother instead of his father – and develop 'effeminate' traits, including a sexual attraction towards other males. For many years, this theory both informed and reflected the conventional wisdom that boys raised by 'smothering' mothers grow up to be 'sissies', 'fairies' or 'mama's boys' (Green 1987). Although some psychologists proposed similar theories about female homosexual development in this era, none gained widespread acceptance among mainstream psychologists (Goldstein and Horowitz 2003).

Based on this theory of homosexuality, therapists often sought to 'convert' male patients to heterosexuality by 'curing' them of maternal influences and effeminate traits. In the early 1970s, however, this theory of homosexuality came under attack, as a growing number of psychologists and gay rights activists began to view homosexuality as a normal and healthy form of sexual development. In 1973, the American Psychiatric Association (APA) voted to remove 'homosexuality' from the *Diagnostic and Statistical Manual of Mental Disorders* (DSM), indicating that psychologists should no longer diagnose or treat homosexuality as a mental disorder. For the next several years, the APA's decision was met with strong opposition from a substantial minority of APA members, including several prominent conversion therapists. By the 1990s, however, the APA's view had been embraced by every major mental health association in the United States. Today, the practice of conversion therapy has been thoroughly marginalized, and the theory that blames domineering mothers for the development of gay sons has been widely debunked (Yoshino 2002).

This is not to say, however, that the underlying logic of the theory has not been abandoned – not even by mainstream psychologists. In 1980, when the diagnosis of 'homosexuality' was officially removed from the DSM, a new diagnosis known as 'Gender Identity Disorder of Childhood' (GIDC) was added. As Sedgwick and others have noted, the new theory of GIDC is similar to the old theory of homosexuality in at least three ways: (1) it is specifically concerned with the development of effeminacy in boys; (2) it blames mothers for fostering effeminacy in boys; and (3) it links effeminacy in boys to homosexuality in gay male adolescents and adults (Zucker and Spitzer 2005, Wilson 1998, Sedgwick 1993). Once we spell out the nature of these similarities, it will be easier to see why litigants, experts and judges have been so willing to believe that lesbian mothers will raise gay sons.

First, like the old diagnosis of homosexuality, the new diagnosis of GIDC was specifically concerned with the gender development of boys. As Sedgwick explains (1991: 20), although the DSM's original diagnosis of GIDC was 'nominally gender-neutral', it was 'actually highly differentiated between boys and girls', insofar as it established a much lower threshold for diagnosing the disorder in boys. Under the DSM's guidelines, a girl could be treated for GIDC only in the rare case in which she denied that she was anatomically female (for example, 'she is biologically unable to become pregnant', 'she will not develop breasts', or 'she has no vagina') or asserted that she was anatomically male (for example, 'she has, or will grow a penis'). A boy, by contrast, could be treated for asserting merely that 'it would be better not to have a penis' or that 'his penis or testes are disgusting' – or alternatively, if he displayed 'a preference for either cross-dressing or simulating female attire, or … a compelling desire to participate in the games and pastimes of girls' (APA 1980: 256–66).

Even today, under the DSM's most recent version of the diagnosis, boys may still be treated for 'dressing in girl's or women's clothes', using '[t]owels, aprons, and scarves … to represent long hair or skirts', adopting the 'mother roles' when 'playing "house"', and playing with '[s]tereotypical female-type dolls, such as Barbie.' Alternatively, even if boys do not display stereotypically feminine behaviour, they may still be treated for displaying an aversion towards 'rough-and-tumble play' and rejection of 'stereotypical boy's toys', games and activities, such as 'cars', 'trucks' and 'competitive sports' (APA 1994: 533, 537). The DSM's focus on boys is only exacerbated by the secondary literature, which is almost exclusively preoccupied with the diagnosis and treatment of effeminate boys (Sedgwick 1993, Coates and Zucker 1988).

Second, like the old theory of homosexuality, the new theory of GIDC blames mothers for fostering effeminacy in boys. Although the DSM does not specify the causes of GIDC, the secondary literature speculates that effeminacy develops when mothers give boys too much attention and fathers fail to 'validate' boys 'as masculine'. In this account, '[m]others … have nothing to contribute to [the] process of masculine validation … any involvement is overinvolvement; any protectiveness is overprotectiveness' (Sedgwick 1991: 23). Much like conversion therapists, GIDC theorists often reserve the harshest criticisms for mothers who display any 'tolerance' for effeminacy in sons.

Finally, the DSM acknowledges that, for most boys, a diagnosis of GIDC is little more than a precursor to homosexuality in adulthood. 'By late adolescence or adulthood,' the DSM reports, 'about three-quarters of boys who had a childhood history of Gender Identity Disorder report a homosexual or bisexual orientation, but without concurrent Gender Identity Disorder' (APA 1994: 536).

In light of these similarities, some observers have claimed that the APA's introduction of the new diagnosis of GIDC was a 'backdoor maneuver' to reinstate the old diagnosis of homosexuality as a mental disorder (Zucker and Spitzer 2005: 32, Mass 1990: 214). Whether or not they are correct, the similarities between the two theories can hardly be doubted. Both theories are specifically concerned with the development of effeminacy and homosexuality in boys, and both theories blame a surplus of mothering and a deficit of fathering for inhibiting the development of 'masculine' boys.

In custody and visitation cases, the theory of GIDC has played a significant role in the expression of sexual development stereotypes about sons raised by lesbian mothers. In 55 per cent (6 of 11) of the cases where such stereotypes appeared, litigants, experts and judges expressed concerns about the development of 'gender identity' or 'masculine roles' in boys, in addition to the development of homosexuality in boys.[10] In 83 per cent (5 of 6) of these cases, gender identity and gender role stereotypes were accepted by judges. By sharp contrast, gender development stereotypes appeared in only 7 per cent (1 of 14) of the cases involving mothers and daughters, and none (0 of 50) of the cases involving gay fathers. Among all the cases, the term 'masculine' appeared three times – all in cases involving sons raised by lesbian mothers – while the term 'feminine' did not appear at all. In other words, gender development stereotypes were applied almost exclusively to sons raised by lesbian mothers.

In *Dailey v. Dailey* (Tenn. 1981: 394), the court cited a psychologist's view that it would be 'preferable' to raise Rusty, a four-year-old boy, in 'a normal relationship wherein males and females adhere to their roles' rather than in 'a homosexual relationship involving a mother in a submissive role' because 'homosexuality is a learned trait and it would be very difficult for Rusty to learn and approximate sex role identification from a homosexual environment.' Based on this testimony, the court transferred custody to the father and allowed the mother overnight visitation on alternating weekends. On appeal, the custody order was affirmed. Although neither the mother nor the father had challenged the visitation order, it was reversed sua sponte by the appellate court. After reciting the expert's testimony, the court

10 In these cases, litigants, experts and judges generally conflated the concepts of 'gender identity' and 'gender roles' (Ball 2003). This conflation is not surprising, in light of the DSM's tendency to interpret a child's failure to conform with traditional gender roles as symptomatic of gender identity disorder – especially when such non-conformity is exhibited by boys.

reasoned that the mother's behaviour 'could provide nothing but harmful effects in the [boy's] future life.' Based on this finding, the court prohibited overnight visits with the mother as well as any visits in the presence of the mother's live-in partner.

In *Lundin v. Lundin* (La. 1990: 1275), the court cited a psychologist's concerns that if a two-year-old boy were raised by his lesbian mother, he may not learn 'masculine and female' roles, which the psychologist referred to as 'sex appropriate roles'. 'I would be concerned,' the psychologist explained, 'if the role models were confused so that a child would not understand or know that this was not typical or usual or to be expected.' The court awarded primary custody to the father, based on a specific finding that 'the child is of an age where gender identity is being formed.'

In *Pleasant v. Pleasant* (Ill. 1993: 637–9), the trial court questioned the mother 'extensively' about a visit in which she took Jimmie, a ten-year-old boy, to march with her friends in a 'gay and lesbian pride parade.' After asking whether the parade was an appropriate environment for Jimmie and whether it had any effect on his sexual orientation, the judge asked if there were men who were not masculine in the parade. When the mother answered that there [were] no 'unmasculine' men in the parents' group with which she walked, the judge argued with her about the presence of so-called 'unmasculine' men.

In restricting the mother's visitation rights, the trial court cited a psychiatrist's testimony that, if Jimmie continued to spend extended, unsupervised visits with his mother, he 'might not develop a gender identity and may be confused about what it is to be a male.' Based on this testimony, the court found that Jimmie had a 'gender identity problem' and that 'having Jimmie in the presence of gays and lesbians was endangering his gender identity and morals.' After reviewing the expert's testimony, the appellate court reversed the trial court's visitation restrictions, finding that 'there is no evidence that Jimmie has a gender identity problem.'

In some cases, gender development stereotypes were raised more obliquely than others: litigants, experts and judges expressed concerns that closely tracked the DSM's diagnosis of gender identity disorder in boys, without explicitly referring to the boy's 'gender identity' or his understanding of 'masculine' roles. In *Holmes v. Holmes* (Ark. 2007: 484), for example, the court observed that Zachary, a seven-year-old boy, would 'not participate in organized sports despite [his father's] efforts to get him involved.' To support a transfer of custody, the boy's father testified that 'he did not approve of [the mother's] lifestyle and believed that he had a right to raise Zachary in a heterosexual environment.' In addition, the father expressed concerns 'about how much Zachary cried and about his lack of desire to play sports', and the father's friend testified 'that Zachary was whiney and did not like to be rambunctious.' The mother acknowledged that 'Zachary was afraid of getting hurt', but she insisted that he 'was not a whiner'; moreover, she argued, 'the evidence that Zachary whines and does not like to play sports is of no consequence.' The trial court transferred custody to the father, based on a finding that Zachary's 'exposure to [his mother's] sexual partners was detrimental to [his] welfare.' The court's order was affirmed on appeal.

In light of these pervasive concerns about the 'masculinity' of boys, one might wonder how courts would respond to lesbian mothers who present themselves as 'butch' or 'masculine' before family law judges. Although this subject has never explicitly been mentioned in any custody or visitation cases, one neglect case suggests that, for homophobic judges, a 'masculine' woman cannot serve as an acceptable substitute for a father. In *In re Breisch* (Pa. 1981: 817), the court suggested that, even though a lesbian mother had adopted a 'masculine' persona, she was still not capable of raising Joey, her four-year-old son. Based on testimony that '[t]he mother is a lesbian who effects a masculine appearance, wears men's clothing, and has a masculine oriented mental status', the court found that she had exposed Joey 'to a chaotic and harmful home life.' In this proceeding, the court transferred custody to the local child protection agency, and the court's order was affirmed on appeal.

Hetero-patriarchy: 'Fatherless' Daughters

As some scholars have observed, sexual development stereotypes about boys raised by lesbian mothers reflect not only the prevailing psychology of the times, but much older, much broader concerns about boys raised by 'fatherless' families, or families that lack 'strong' male role models (Harding 2010; Stacey and Biblarz 2001). Although these concerns were originally a product of the early industrial era (Lamb 2000, Pleck 1997, LaRossa 1997), they have continued to spawn controversies over single motherhood in the contemporary United States (Bosman 2008, Kreisberg 2006, Blankenhorn 2005).

The analogy between lesbian mothers and single mothers may seem far-fetched, but it is made frequently by opponents of lesbian and gay parenthood. Lynn Wardle (1997: 859–60), for example, has criticized lesbian mothers by invoking studies of children raised by single mothers. Defending the importance of fatherhood, he has argued that 'father love and mother love are different kinds of love', because only father love provides children with the following benefits: 'First, it provides them with a father's physical protection. Second, it provides them with a father's money and other material resources. Third, and probably most importantly, it provides them with what might be termed paternal cultural transmission: a father's distinctive capacity to contribute to [children's] identity, character, and competence.'

Although critics of 'fatherless' families profess generic concerns about the impact of fatherlessness on 'children', they seem to be especially focused on the impact on boys (Harding 2010). In the landmark marriage case of *Goodridge v. Department of Public Health* (Mass. 2003: 1000), three justices objected to the recognition of same-sex marriage on the ground that such unions 'raise[] the prospect of children lacking any parent of their own gender.' Although the justices initially stated this objection in gender-neutral terms, they promptly slipped into the classic trope of fatherless boys: 'For example,' they explained, 'a boy raised by two lesbians as his parents has no male parent. … [T]he child himself might invoke gender as a justification for the view that neither of his parents understands him, or that they 'don't know what he is going through', particularly if his disagreement or dissatisfaction involves some issue pertaining to sex.'

In light of these specific concerns about 'fatherless' families, it seems clear that developmental stereotypes about boys raised by lesbian mothers are patriarchal: they imply that every family should have a father, because only a man can raise 'masculine', heterosexual boys. In *Pleasant v. Pleasant* (Ill. 1993: 639), the trial court explained why gay fathers do not fit the bill: when boys are exposed to men who are 'unmasculine', they are likely to become 'unmasculine'. They may fail 'to develop a gender identity', and thus, 'be confused about what it is to be a male.' Thus, the stereotypes are not only patriarchal, but hetero-patriarchal (Valdes 1995a): under this framework, boys raised by gay fathers lack 'strong' male role models, so they are viewed as 'fatherless' – just like boys raised by lesbian mothers. In short, '[t]he stereotype of gay men as effeminate … is the basis for questions of whether gay men can be appropriate male role models for children (especially boys)' (Harding 2010: 133).[11]

What about girls raised by gay fathers? We have now analysed three of the four groups of cases, so only one group of cases remains. There were only two cases in which litigants, experts or judges expressed stereotypes about gay fathers raising lesbian daughters, and neither case yields any meaningful insights. In *Gottleib v. Gottleib* (N.Y. 1985), one judge invoked a generic need for 'proper identification' between the 'parents' and the 'child', rather than a gender-specific need for identification between fathers and daughters. In *J.P. v. P.W.* (Mo. 1989), the court did not directly express any sexual development stereotypes, but it quoted two such stereotypes from other opinions.

In this context, the silences seem to say more than the stereotypes. In a similar context, Rosie Harding has observed that 'the issue of whether a gay man would be able to raise a girl and the issue of appropriate female role models' are not often raised in discussions of lesbian and gay parenting (2010: 133). The same can surely be said of custody and visitation cases: in 85 per cent (17 of 20) of the cases involving daughters and gay fathers, there were no references to the sexual or gender development of girls.

Even without any text to guide us, we can guess why litigants, experts and judges may not have been too concerned about the 'gender identity' of girls raised by gay fathers. If they were anything like the trial judge in *Pleasant*, they would have viewed gay men as 'unmasculine' – that is, not only homosexual, but effeminate – so they would have assumed that gay fathers would raise feminine daughters.

---

11 In Harding's interviews of lesbian and gay parents, she recounts one interview with a gay man named Michael who seemed to have internalized this stereotype. During his interview, he explained that, when he considered the possibility of becoming a father, he expressed concerns about whether he is 'capable of raising a man', in light of his 'mannerisms' (2010: 132). He then poignantly observes that he 'couldn't come up with the answer to whether that was myself or whether that was society telling me that.'

While this explanation is an interesting point of departure, it does not provide a wholly satisfying account of the absence of stereotypes in these cases. After all, our culture includes other conventional stereotypes about girls who lack 'strong' male role models. In the literature on 'fatherless' families, commentators often claim that girls without fathers are likely to be 'wayward' or 'promiscuous', bearing children out of wedlock as teenagers (Wardle 1997). In cases involving gay fathers, the opportunity for deploying this stereotype seems especially clear. The same commentators who have stereotyped 'fatherless' girls as promiscuous have often stereotyped gay men as promiscuous. If litigants, experts and judges had drawn a link between these two stereotypes, we would expect them to express concerns that gay fathers would raise promiscuous daughters.

The fact remains, however, that these stereotypes did not appear in any of the custody or visitation cases involving gay men (or lesbians) with daughters. Litigants, experts and judges expressed no concerns about gay fathers raising promiscuous daughters, and they expressed very few concerns about gay fathers raising lesbian daughters in general. Apparently, they believed that gay fathers were 'strong' enough role models for daughters, even if they were not 'strong' enough role models for sons. In these cases, '[t]he question of appropriate female role models does not appear to be an issue – or at least has not received anywhere like the amount of attention that has been focused on concerns about appropriate male role models' (Harding 2010: 133).

I can think of only one principle that would explain this belief, and it is derived from the hetero-patriarchal framework itself: if litigants, experts and judges considered masculinity to be more valuable than femininity – that is, if they adhered to a male-supremacy principle – then they would generally be more concerned about securing the role of 'masculine' fathers in the production of 'masculine' sons.[12]

As we have seen in the cases, this principle has ironic implications for both fathers and sons: once masculinity is held to be more valuable than femininity, it becomes more important to maintain and more costly to lose – more precious and therefore more fragile (Faludi 1999, Kimmel 1994). Litigants, experts and judges must work harder to make boys into men and fathers into patriarchs; they must intervene more often in families, and earlier in life, in order to secure the production of 'masculine' boys.

12 On the surface, it may appear that this distinction can be explained away by the average age of children in custody and visitation cases. In general, most of these cases involve toddlers, and cases involving teenagers are exceedingly rare. As a result, it may well be that litigants, experts and judges were less concerned about gay fathers raising promiscuous daughters because the girls were still too young to be sexually active. The gap in this account, however, is that it begs the question of why litigants, experts and judges did not apply the same principle to sons raised by gay and lesbian parents. The fact that litigants, experts and judges were willing to intervene earlier in the sexual development of boys suggests that they considered male heterosexuality to be more valuable than female heterosexuality, as I argue in the text.

Against Homophobia, Against Sexism: Defending the Production of Gay Sons and Lesbian Daughters

> To begin to theorize gender and sexuality as distinct though intimately entangled axes of analysis has been … a great advance of recent lesbian and gay thought. There is a danger, however, that that advance may leave the effeminate boy once more in the position of the haunting abject – this time the haunting abject of gay thought itself.
>
> – Eve Kosofsky Sedgwick (1991: 20)

Drawing upon my empirical findings, this part develops a critique of the US legal academy's attempts to rebut stereotypes about the children of lesbian and gay parents. In responding to these stereotypes, legal scholars have cited a large body of empirical studies on the sexual development of children raised by lesbian and gay parents. In this literature, '[v]irtually all of the published research claims to find no differences in the sexuality of children reared by lesbigay parents and those raised by nongay parents', and more generally, no 'significant differences' of any kind (Stacey and Biblarz 2001: 162). In a recent review of the empirical data, the American Academy of Pediatrics reported that '[n]o differences have been found in the gender identity, social roles, or sexual orientation of adults who had a divorced homosexual parent (or parents), compared with those who had divorced heterosexual parents' (Perrin et al. 2002: 342). As both sides of the debate have observed, the 'unanimity' among scholars, lawyers and activists on this subject has been truly 'remarkable' (Stacey and Biblarz 2001: 160, Wardle 1997: 837).

In the first two sections below, I develop the claim that the 'no difference' argument suffers from a straightforward weakness: it is based on a questionable view of the empirical data. If anything, early studies seem to suggest that role-modelling stereotypes may be empirically valid: children raised by lesbian and gay parents may be less likely to adopt traditional gender roles, more likely to develop homosexual fantasies, and more likely to engage in homosexual behaviour, than children raised by heterosexual parents. If this hypothesis is validated by future studies, it will raise a profound philosophical and tactical dilemma for the LGBT equality movement.

As a rule, however, most advocates for lesbian and gay parents have responded to these provocative findings by downplaying and ignoring them. The third section highlights one of the rare exceptions to this rule: in a pathbreaking article (2003), Professor Carlos Ball both entertained and defended the possibility that children raised by lesbian and gay parents were more likely to violate traditional sex stereotypes. In this article, however, Professor Ball was not willing to entertain the possibility that such children were more likely to engage in homosexual behaviour or identify as lesbian, gay or bisexual. In the final section, I argue that Ball's distinction between stereotypes about sexual development and gender development is unhelpful. In this context, at least, stereotypes about sexual development and gender development are inextricably intertwined, and thus, our attack against them must be coordinated.

Lynn Wardle: Attacking 'No Differences'

Since the late 1990s, the US legal academy's 'no differences' paradigm has come under attack from opponents of lesbian and gay parenthood. In 'The Potential Impact of Homosexual Parenting on Children' (1997), Lynn Wardle argued that the legal scholarship on lesbian and gay parenthood was written in a 'propagandistic style' and based on a 'very unreliable' body of empirical studies, which he claimed were tainted by methodological and analytical flaws. Most significantly, Wardle claimed that pro-gay researchers and advocates have misrepresented the data produced by studies of lesbian and gay parenthood. Properly understood, he argued, the data 'provide[] a basis for serious concerns about potential detrimental effects upon children raised by gay or lesbian parents.' Like most of today's opponents of lesbian and gay parenthood, Wardle was chiefly concerned with the potential impact of lesbian and gay parents on children's sexual development: 'The most obvious risk to children from their parents' homosexual behavior suggested by the current studies relates to the sexual development of the child. Both theory and empirical studies indicate the potential that disproportionate percentages of children raised by homosexual parents will develop homosexual interests and behaviors' (852).

To bolster his argument, Wardle expressed several concerns about the findings of lesbian and gay parenting studies. To a remarkable extent, he shared the concerns expressed by litigants, experts and judges in custody and visitation cases. In his view, one study indicated that more than 10 per cent of the sons of gay men identified as gay in adulthood, another suggested 'a link between a daughter's sexual behavior and fantasy and her mother's homosexual behavior' (849), and yet another reported that 'boys raised by homosexual mothers may have a lower self-image regarding masculinity' (853–4). In other words, Wardle expressed specific concerns about gay fathers raising gay sons, lesbian mothers raising lesbian daughters, and lesbian mothers raising 'unmasculine' sons. He did not, by contrast, express any developmental concerns about daughters raised by gay fathers. Like other opponents of lesbian and gay parenthood, Wardle invoked the literature on 'fatherless' families, analogizing the children of lesbian mothers to the children of single mothers.

Judith Stacey and Timothy Biblarz: Acknowledging Differences

In the ten years since it was published, Wardle's article has played to mixed reviews in the US. While the article has been cited favourably by judges in custody and adoption cases, it has been rejected by most legal scholars, who overwhelmingly support lesbian and gay parenthood. For present purposes, however, the reaction of two sociologists is most relevant. In 2001, Judith Stacey and Timothy Biblarz published an article in the *American Sociological Review*, in which they asked,

'(How) Does the Sexual Orientation of Parents Matter?' The answer, they argued, is that the sexual orientation of parents matters 'somewhat more' than pro-gay researchers have acknowledged.

The article offers profound insight into the ways that ideology and fear have shaped the popular, academic and legal debates over lesbian and gay parenthood, so it is worth describing Stacey and Biblarz's argument in some detail. From the start, the authors emphasized that they were sympathetic to the case for lesbian and gay parenthood, and more generally, to the case for the equal treatment of gay men, lesbians and bisexuals. They were sharply critical of Wardle's arguments against lesbian and gay parenthood, including his analogy between lesbian and 'fatherless' families.

Stacey and Biblarz reluctantly agreed, however, with Wardle's suggestion that 'ideological pressures constrain intellectual development in this field.' 'In our view,' they explained, 'it is the pervasiveness of social prejudice and institutionalized discrimination against lesbians and gay men that exerts a powerful policing effect on the basic terms of psychological research and public discourse on the significance of parental sexual orientation.' 'Because anti-gay scholars seek evidence of harm,' they concluded, 'sympathetic researchers defensively stress its absence' (160).

After surveying the empirical data on lesbian and gay parenthood, Stacey and Biblarz reported a controversial result: they claimed that researchers have 'downplayed' evidence that the children of lesbian and gay parents were actually different from the children of heterosexual parents, out of legitimate fears about how such evidence would be used by opponents of lesbian and gay parenthood. Moreover, the authors claimed that researchers have been 'hesitant to theorize' about how the 'no differences' paradigm could be squared with any of the prevailing theories of sexual and gender development (160).

To analyse the empirical data, Stacey and Biblarz gathered twenty-one studies of lesbian and gay parenthood published between 1981 and 1998, which they considered the 'best equipped to address sociological questions about how parental sexual orientation matters to children' (167). After conducting an independent review, they found statistically significant differences concerning the sexual and gender development of the children of lesbian and gay parents – differences that they claimed had been downplayed and ignored by the researchers who conducted the studies.

The key findings were related to 'children's gender preferences and behavior' and 'children's sexual preferences and behavior' (168–71). With respect to children's gender development, Stacey and Biblarz relied on five studies of the children of lesbian mothers (Steckel 1987, R. Green et al. 1986, Golombok, Spencer and Rutter 1983, Hotvedt and Mandel 1982, Hoeffer 1981). Analysing these studies, they found that the daughters of lesbian mothers 'more frequently dress, play, and behave in ways that do not conform to sex-typed cultural norms' and held 'higher aspirations to nontraditional gender occupations … such as doctor, lawyer, engineer, and astronaut.' With respect to sons of lesbian mothers, the authors found mixed results. 'On some measures, like aggressiveness and play preferences', they found that 'the sons of lesbian mothers behave in less traditionally masculine ways than those raised by heterosexual single mothers.' '[O]n other measures, such as occupational goals and sartorial styles', they did not find any statistically significant differences between the two groups of sons (168).

With respect to children's sexual development, Stacey and Biblarz relied upon two 'intergenerational' studies – one study of the adult children of lesbian mothers (Tasker and Golombok 1997) and one study of the adult sons of gay fathers (Bailey et al. 1995). Of the two studies, the authors emphasized the first, which they regarded as one of the best designed of the twenty-one studies that they reviewed.

Reviewing the first study, Stacey and Biblarz found that the children of lesbian mothers were more likely to engage in homosexual behaviour than the children of heterosexual mothers, and even when they had not engaged in homosexual behaviour, they were more likely to entertain the possibility of doing so. These children were not, however, more likely to identify as gay, lesbian or bisexual.[13] Reviewing the second study, the authors found that the adult sons of gay fathers reported 'a moderate degree of parent-to-child transmission of sexual orientation' (171). These sons, in other words, were more likely than others to identify as gay or bisexual.[14]

With respect to other aspects of child development, Stacey and Biblarz generally confirmed the other researchers' conclusions that 'no significant differences' existed in the 'self-esteem', 'psychological well-being' and cognitive ability of the children of lesbian and gay parents. 'The few significant differences found,' they added, 'actually tend to favor children with lesbian mothers' (171). Based on this review of the empirical data, they argued: 'Most of the differences in the findings … cannot be considered deficits from any legitimate public policy perspective. They either favor the children with lesbigay parents … or represent "just a difference" of the sort democratic societies should respect and protect' (177). For these reasons, they concluded, 'there is no evidentiary basis for considering parental sexual orientation in decisions about children's "best interest"' (176).

Carlos Ball: Defending Gender Differences

The Stacey and Biblarz article caused quite a stir in debates over lesbian and gay parenthood. It was widely reported in the popular press when it was published,

13 This year, however, Stacey and Biblarz published a follow-up meta-analysis in which they found new evidence that the daughters of lesbian mothers were less likely to identify as heterosexual, based on a 2006 working paper by Bos et al. (Biblarz and Stacey 2010). In addition, a more recent study has produced evidence that such girls are more likely to identify as bisexual (Gartrell et al. 2010).

14 This finding has not been replicated in subsequent studies, which show significant differences in the influence of a parent's sexual orientation on boys and girls (Biblarz and Stacey 2010, Gartrell et al. 2010).

and it has been frequently quoted in cases, casebooks and law review articles in subsequent years.

The US legal academy's response to the article has been a case study in the politics of lesbian and gay parenthood, and a testament to the article's claim that 'ideological pressures constrain intellectual development in this field' (160). Opponents of lesbian and gay parenthood have welcomed the article, which they cite as conclusive proof that gay men and lesbians should not be granted custody, visitation, adoption or marriage rights. Among advocates, however, the reaction has been much more guarded. In law review articles, legal scholars have generally downplayed the article's finding that there were 'differences' between the children of lesbian and gay parents and the children of heterosexual parents. If they refer to the article at all, they typically cite only the conclusion that there were 'no differences' that could be considered 'deficits' – without acknowledging that the authors found significant differences in children's gender and sexual development.

In this literature, only one scholar has squarely confronted the legal implications of the article's controversial findings. This exceptional scholar is Carlos Ball, the legal academy's chief critic of Lynn Wardle's arguments against lesbian and gay parenthood. In 'Lesbian and Gay Families: Gender Nonconformity and the Implications of Difference' (2003), Ball considered whether the findings presented by Stacey and Biblarz could justify laws prohibiting adoptions by lesbian and gay couples.

Rather than insisting that the differences observed by Stacey and Biblarz were not significant, Ball acknowledged that they marked a 'turning point' (692) in the debate over lesbian and gay parenthood. 'As a practical matter,' he conceded, 'it is not likely that … state policy makers, judges, or the opponents of lesbian and gay families will soon view differences associated with gender and sexual preferences and behavior as irrelevant' (697, 705) to determinations of children's best interests. 'It is therefore necessary,' he resolved, 'to explore some of the policy and legal implications of the differences noted by Stacey and Biblarz' (702).

For the sake of argument, Ball assumed that the article's findings about children's 'gender related differences' were not only 'plausibl[e]' but would be 'confirm[ed]' by future studies (704). In other words, he assumed that, when children are raised by lesbian and gay parents, they are less likely to conform to traditional gender roles. 'Daughters of lesbians and gay men,' he conceded, 'may be more interested in "masculine" clothing or in careers that have traditionally been the prerogative of men', and 'the sons of lesbians and gay men may be less interested in sports or more interested in nurturing' (723).

Ball argued, however, that, even if these findings were confirmed, they could not provide a legitimate basis for laws prohibiting adoptions by lesbian and gay couples, because laws based on sex stereotypes violate the Equal Protection Clause of the US Constitution. Quoting the Supreme Court's decision in *United States v. Virginia* (U.S. 1996), Ball reasoned that laws cannot be justified by 'fixed notions concerning the roles and abilities of males and females' (733) or 'overbroad generalizations about the different talents, capacities, or preferences of males and females' (742).

In light of the 'no differences' paradigm of debates over lesbian and gay parenthood, and the legal academy's tendency to ignore the relationship between homophobia and sexism in this field, Ball's argument is both refreshing and courageous. Although his claims were specifically tailored to adoption laws, they could be extended to custody and visitation cases with one minor adjustment: in custody and visitation cases, it is not a statute that is based on gender stereotypes but a court's determination of a child's best interests.

Based on the analysis of these cases in the first part, we are in a position to see that Ball's willingness to defend gender development differences could be especially useful to lesbian mothers raising sons, who so often confront stereotypes about the formation of the boy's 'gender identity' and his adoption of 'masculine' roles. Rather than conceding that boys should be 'masculine' – 'no different' than boys raised by 'masculine' fathers – lesbian mothers could invoke the constitutional prohibition against sex stereotypes, insisting that the state has no legitimate interest in the production of 'masculine' boys.

Carlos Ball: Ignoring Sexual Differences

In one respect, however, Ball's argument is surprisingly limited: it is expressly confined to stereotypes about children's gender development; it does not address stereotypes about children's sexual development at all.

In reviewing the Stacey and Biblarz article, Ball drew a sharp distinction between the article's findings on 'gender behavior and preferences' and 'sexual behavior and preferences'. For the sake of argument, he was willing to concede the empirical controversy over children's gender development, so that he could 'focus fully on the implications of difference in this area, and in particular on the effects of such difference on the equality claims [of] lesbian and gay parents' (704–5). He was not, however, willing to concede the empirical controversy over children's sexual development – not even for the sake of argument.

Ball argued that the evidence on gender development had reached 'a minimum threshold of plausibility', but he claimed that the evidence on sexual development was not 'anywhere near' such a 'minimum threshold' (702). On this ground, he refused to entertain the notion that the children of lesbian and gay parents might be more likely to develop homosexual fantasies, engage in homosexual behaviour, or identify as lesbian, gay or bisexual. Above all, he emphasized that the evidence on sexual development was based on 'only one study' and contradicted by 'many studies', whereas the evidence on gender development was 'found in multiple studies.' He warned that '[w]e should be careful before we reach any conclusions, even tentative ones, regarding the transmissibility of sexual orientation from parents to children based on only one study of roughly twenty-five children of lesbian mothers.' '[W]hatever conclusions are reached from only one study,' he continued, 'are likely to be so speculative so as to be both useless and dangerous' (703).

This is not the place, and I am not the person, to resolve a long-standing dispute over the empirical data on lesbian and gay parenthood. While I have a few qualms about Ball's view of the data, I shall not dwell on the empirical controversy here.[15] For present purposes, I shall focus on the strategic implications of Ball's analysis for advocacy on behalf of lesbian and gay parenthood.

In custody and visitation cases, lesbian and gay parents do not have the luxury of avoiding 'dangerous' speculations about sexual development – or at least, they cannot avoid them by invoking Ball's sharp distinction between the empirical data on gender development and sexual development. As Francisco Valdes (1995a) has observed, our legal system often conflates sex, gender and sexual orientation in order to facilitate discrimination against 'queers, sissies, dykes, and tomboys.' Because litigants, experts and judges conflate sexual orientation with gender identity and gender roles, they also conflate sexual development stereotypes with gender development stereotypes. This dynamic is especially apparent in cases involving boys raised by lesbian mothers, the only cases in which gender development stereotypes have actually appeared. As a result, we cannot pick our battles here, even as a strategic matter. In order to challenge gender development stereotypes effectively, we must challenge sexual development stereotypes as well.

In custody and visitation cases, the overlap between gender development stereotypes and sexual development stereotypes was nearly perfect. In all but one (7 of 8) of the cases in which parents were subjected to stereotypes about gender development, they were also subjected to stereotypes about sexual development. In several of these cases, the two concerns were so thoroughly connected, conflated and collapsed that it was not possible to say which one influenced the other or even to distinguish them from each other.

Recall that in *Dailey v. Dailey* (1981), a psychologist testified that it would be 'preferable' to raise Rusty, a four-year-old boy, in 'a normal relationship wherein males and females adhere to their roles', because 'homosexuality is a learned trait and it would be very difficult for Rusty to learn and approximate sex role identification from a homosexual environment.' In *M.J.P. v. J.G.P* (Okla. 1982), a psychiatrist described the 'sexual identity' of the mother's six-year-old boy as 'masculine'. In *Lundin v. Lundin* (1990), the court cited a psychologist's concerns that, if a two-year-old boy were raised by his lesbian mother, he may not learn 'masculine and female' roles, which the psychologist described as 'sex appropriate roles'. In response to the court's question about the boy seeing his mother and her partner sharing a bed, the psychologist testified: 'I would be concerned if the role models were confused so that a child would not understand or know that this' – that is, the mother's homosexuality – 'was not typical or usual or to be expected.' Finally, in *Pleasant v. Pleasant* (1993), the trial court expressed concerns about a ten-year-old boy's 'sexual orientation' and 'gender identity problem', and the court repeatedly described gay men as 'unmasculine'.

The phenomenon is by no means unique to custody and visitation cases. In *Lofton v. Secretary of Department of Children and Family Services* (11th Cir. 2004: 818, 822), the plaintiffs argued that Florida's law prohibiting adoptions

15 For a more thorough critique of Ball's argument, see Rosky 2009.

by gay men and lesbians was unconstitutional. In defence of the law, the state claimed that 'dual-gender parenting' plays 'a vital role … in shaping sexual and gender identity and in providing heterosexual role modeling.' In upholding the law, the district court relied upon the state's interest in providing 'proper gender role modeling' and promoting 'proper gender identification', while the appellate court relied upon the state's interest in providing 'heterosexual role models.'

In fact, the phenomenon is not even limited to court cases – it comes up often in the scholarship on lesbian and gay parenthood. Lynn Wardle's (1997) work, for example, leaves little question that his concerns about gender development are both linked to and derived from his concerns about sexual development. For Wardle, 'the most obvious risk to children from their parents' homosexual behavior suggested by the current studies relates to the sexual development of the child.' He has argued at length, in several places, that 'children raised by homosexual parents will develop homosexual interests and behaviors.' By contrast, he has spared only two sentences in one article to express concerns about the 'masculinity' of boys and the 'cross-dressing' of girls, in the midst of a list of other concerns about the sexual development of children raised by lesbian and gay parents.

In light of the ubiquitous conflation of gender development stereotypes with sexual development stereotypes, I am concerned that Ball's limited defence of gender development differences may fall on deaf ears – especially in cases involving gay fathers raising sons, and lesbian mothers raising daughters, where sexual development stereotypes are most prevalent. Among opponents of lesbian and gay parenthood, concerns about gender development are rarely expressed by themselves, and they are often expressed as synonyms or euphemisms for concerns about sexual development. By overlooking the relationship between sexism and homophobia, Ball seemed to impose an unnecessary limitation on the scope of his argument – a limitation that, in my view, prevented him from hitting his mark.

To some extent, Ball may have been concerned about asking too much of judges: in order to advocate on behalf of lesbian and gay children, one must make a more ambitious argument, which depends on a much broader extension of existing case law. There is no question that, under today's equal protection jurisprudence, it is significantly easier to challenge sexist stereotypes than homophobic stereotypes. Although recent decisions from the California, Connecticut and Iowa supreme courts are promising (*Varnum v. Brien*, Iowa 2009, *In re Marriage Cases*, Cal. 2008, *Kerrigan v. Commissioner of Public Health*, Conn. 2008), federal courts have widely rejected the claim that discrimination against gay men and lesbians is 'inherently suspect'.[16]

In some cases, this trade-off may not be required: as we saw in the first part of this chapter, even when judges do not articulate stereotypes about gender development, they sometimes indicate explicitly sex-based stereotypes about

16 In *Perry v. Schwarzenegger* (Cal. 2010), a federal court struck down California's Proposition 8. In doing so, however, the judge applied rational basis review, expressly avoiding the question of whether sexual orientation classifications are 'suspect'.

sexual development – especially in cases involving a gay or lesbian parent and a child of the same sex. In *Bennett v. O'Rourke* (1985), for example, the court's ruling was based explicitly on the 'increased chance of role-modeling' because 'the homosexual parent and the minor child [we]re both female.' In such cases, the parent might challenge these stereotypes by invoking the Supreme Court's holding in *United States v. Virginia* (1996) that state action may not be based 'on fixed notions concerning the roles and abilities of males and females.'

Such cases are already rare, however – and if lesbian and gay parents begin challenging judges who articulate sex-based stereotypes, these cases are likely to become even rarer. Sooner or later, a gay or lesbian parent will be stereotyped as a recruiter or a role model and the judge's assumptions about the parent's sex and the child's sex will not be expressed in his ruling.[17] In these cases, parents and advocates will have to make difficult choices, and the argument for lesbian and gay parenthood will have to stand or fall by itself.

Conclusion

The choices facing lesbian and gay parents are not easy to make, but the options are fairly straightforward. On the one hand, we could insist that the sons and daughters of lesbian and gay parents are 'no different' – no more likely to be homosexual, no less likely to be heterosexual – than the children of heterosexual parents. On the other hand, we could acknowledge that they may well be different, but we can insist that a child's homosexuality is 'just a difference' – the kind of difference that a democracy should 'respect and protect' (Stacey and Biblarz 2001). By confronting the fear of parent-to-child transmission, we stand not only to win greater protections for lesbian and gay parents, but to challenge the ubiquitous 'fantasy that gay and lesbian youth do not exist' (Ruskola 1996).

Without the support of sex discrimination laws, the route to progress may well be slower, but the argument would not be wholly without precedent. In *Romer v. Evans* (U.S. 1996), the Supreme Court held that, under the Equal Protection Clause, a state's actions may not be based solely on 'animus' towards gay men and lesbians. More recently, in *Perry v. Schwarzenegger* (Cal. 2010: 1003), a federal trial judge applied the principle of *Romer* in a novel and promising

17 This consequence is one of the costs of focusing legal argument on the use of explicit stereotypes, which is well known to civil rights scholars and lawyers in other contexts. By challenging explicit stereotypes, one may effectively 'teach' litigants, experts and judges to avoid making such references in future cases. To some people, a world in which people no longer articulate anti-gay stereotypes may seem like an obvious improvement, but it would not necessarily be a better world for gay and lesbian parents. The literature on implicit bias warns that, even when people no longer rely explicitly on stereotypes, they may continue to rely implicitly on stereotypes. In comparison to explicit bias, implicit bias is considerably more difficult to detect and resist (Bodensteiner 2003).

manner: in striking down California's Proposition 8 – a state law that prohibits same-sex couples from marrying – the judge found that the law was based on the 'fear that exposure to homosexuality would turn children into homosexuals' and the assumption that 'parents should dread having a gay or lesbian child.' These fears, the judge reasoned, were 'completely unfounded' – not because a child's sexual orientation cannot be influenced or changed, but because a child's sexual orientation is legally irrelevant. The notion that children should be discouraged from being lesbian, gay or bisexual, the judge suggested, was nothing more than a form of homophobia – a kind of 'animus' against lesbian, gay and bisexual people, which may no longer serve as a legitimate justification for our country's laws.

I do not mean to predict that in the short run, lesbian and gay parents will win more custody and visitation cases by adopting this argument, invoking the principle of *Romer* to challenge a judge's conventional, strongly held beliefs about childhood sexual development. In light of the constitutional protections historically afforded to lesbians and gay men – and the pervasive, enduring hysteria surrounding the sexuality of children – such a prediction would be hopelessly naïve. In the short term, it does not seem likely that many judges will be persuaded by this argument – especially those who are already inclined to rule against lesbian and gay parents based on sexist and homophobic stereotypes.

Nor do I mean to suggest casually that lesbian and gay parents should advance a long-shot claim for the long-term good, without regard to the profound interests at stake in custody and visitation cases. When lesbian and gay parents confront homophobia and sexism in such cases, they are asked to balance the fight for a parent-child relationship against the broader fight for lesbian and gay parenthood. In such circumstances, strategic decisions are painful and difficult. I have no magic recipes for making such trade-offs; I leave them to individual parents and lawyers to make for themselves.

But scholars are another matter. As academics, we have an obligation to make claims that are not only useful but truthful, and we have the freedom to develop arguments that may not be advanced or adopted for years. My hope is that sooner or later – the sooner, the better – parents, lawyers and judges will be ready to stand up not only for the idea that gay men and lesbians can be parents, but for the idea that children should be free to love who they love, be who they are, and become the kind of adults who they want to become.

Bibliography

Abrams, K. 1993. Gender in the Military: Androcentrism and Institutional Reform. 56 *Law and Contemporary Problems* 4, 217.

Abrams, K. 2000. Afterword: Critical Strategy and the Judicial Evasion of Difference. 85 *Cornell Law Review*, 1426.

Abrams, K. 2005. Legal Feminism and the Emotions: Three Moments in an Evolving Relationship. 28 *Harvard Journal of Law and Gender* 2, 325.

Access to Classes and Schools. 34 C.F.R. § 106.34(b)(1)(i)(A)(B)(2006).

Adib, A. and Guerrier, Y. 2003. The Interlocking of Gender with Nationality, Race, Ethnicity and Class: The Narratives of Women in Hotel Work. 10 *Gender, Work, and Organization* 4, 413.

Adler, K. 2006. The Women of Hamas, Islam Protects US. Qnatara.de [online]. Available at: http://www.qantara.de/webcom/show_article.php/_c-651/_nr-10/i.html [accessed: 7 January 2013].

Agustin, L.M. 2007. *Sex at the Margins: Migration, Labour Markets, and the Rescue Industry*. Zed Books.

Ahmed, S. 2006. *Queer Phenomenology: Orientations, Objects, Others*. Duke University Press.

Ahmeduzzaman, M. and Roopnarine, J.L. 1992. Sociodemographic Factors, Functioning Style, Social Support, and Fathers' Involvement with Preschoolers in African–American Families. 54 *Journal of Marriage and the Family* 3, 699.

Aitken, S. 2005. The Awkward Spaces of Fathering, in *Spaces of Masculinities*, edited by K. Horschelmann and B. van Hoven. Routledge.

Albermarle Paper Co. v Moody [1975] 422 U.S. 405.

Alden, C. 2002. Making Old Soldiers Fade Away: Lessons from the Reintegration of Demobilized Soldiers in Mozambique. 33 *Security Dialogue* 3, 341.

Aldous, J., Mulligan, G.M. and Bjarnason, T. 1998. Fathering over Time: What Makes the Difference? 60 *Journal of Marriage and the Family* 4, 809.

Alexander, M.J. 1994. Not Just (Any)Body Can Be a Citizen: The Politics of Law, Sexuality and Postcoloniality in Trinidad and Tobago and the Bahamas. 48 *Feminist Review* 5, 15.

Alison, M. 2009. *Women and Political Violence: Female Combatants in Ethno-national Conflict*. Taylor & Francis.

Alleman, T. and Muraskin, R. 1993. *It's a Crime: Women and Justice*. Prentice Hall.

Allen, L. 2006. 'Looking at the Real Thing': Young men, Pornography, and Sexuality Education. 27 *Discourse* 1, 69.

Alperovitz, G. and Daly, L. 2008. *Unjust Deserts: How the Rich are Taking our Common Inheritance*. New Press.

Alvanou, M. 2007. *Palestinian Women Suicide Bombers: The Interplaying Effects of Islam, Nationalism and Honor Culture*. Strategic Research and Policy Centre, National Defense College, IDP, 5.

Amato, P.R. and Gilbreth, J.G. 1999. Nonresident Fathers and Children's Well-being: A Meta-analysis. 61 *Journal of Marriage and Family* 3, 557.

American Association of University Professors. 2006a. 1940 Statement of Principles on Academic Freedom and Tenure with 1970 Interpretive Comments, in *Policy Documents and Reports*, 10th edn. American Association of University Professors.

American Association of University Professors. 2006b. Statement of Principles on Family Responsibilities and Academic Work, in *Policy Documents and Reports*, 10th edn. American Association of University Professors.

American Association of University Women. 1992. *How Schools Shortchange Girls: The AAUW Report*. Marlowe & Company.

American Bar Association and National Bar Association. 2001. Justice By Gender: The Lack of Appropriate Prevention, Diversion and Treatment Alternatives for Girls in the Justice System [online]. Available at: http://www.abanet.org/crimjust/juvjus/girls.html [accessed: 6 September 2010].

American Psychiatric Association. 1980. *Diagnostic and Statistical Manual of Mental Disorders*, 3rd edn. American Psychiatric Association.

American Psychiatric Association. 1994. *Diagnostic and Statistical Manual of Mental Disorders*, 4th edn. American Psychiatric Association.

Amnesty International. 2005. The Impact of Guns on Women's Lives [online]. Available at: http://www.amnesty.org/en/library/info/ACT30/001/2005/en [accessed: 3 January 2013].

Amnesty International. 2008. Iran: Women's Rights Defenders Defy Repression [online]. Available at: http://www.amnesty.org/en/library/asset/MDE13/018/2008/en/63dd8933-e16d-11dc-9135-058f98b1fb80/mde130182008eng.pdf [accessed: 7 January 2013].

An Acte for the Punysshement for the vice of Buggerie, 1533–34, 25 Hen. 8, c. 6 (Eng.).

Anderson v Zubieta [D.C. Cir. 1999] 180 F.3d 329.

Anisi, F. 2005. Dokhtaran Zeytoon. 159 *Payam Zan* [online]. Available at: http://www.hawzah.net/hawzah/Magazines/MagArt.aspx?MagazineNumberID=4165&id=26106 [accessed: 7 January 2013].

Ansoumana v Gristede's Operating Corp. [S.D.N.Y. 2003] 255 F. Supp. 2d 184.

Aplon, J. 2008. *Post-conflict Peacebuilding: Connecting Research and Policy*, Acting Deputy Director, Office of Department Transition Initiatives, Agency for International Development, U.S. Department of State, Presentation at the Program on States and Security at the Ralph Bunche Institute for International Studies, 25 January.

Armenti, C. 2004. Women Faculty Seeking Tenure and Parenthood: Lessons from Previous Generations. 34 *Cambridge Journal of Education* 1, 65.

ARCSHS [Australian Research Centre in Sex, Health and Society]. 2003. Sex in Australia. LaTrobe University.

Arendell, T. 1995. *Fathers and Divorce*. Sage.

Arie, S. 2010. Male Circumcision. Circumcision: Divided We Fall. 341 *British Medical Journal*, c4266.

Armacost, B.E. 2004. Organizational Culture and Police Misconduct. 72 *George Washington Law Review* 3, 453.

Arnold, G. 2004. *Social Movement 'Success': The Battered Women's Discourse and Institutional Change*. Paper presented at the American Sociological Association Annual Meeting, San Francisco, California, 13–17 August [online]. Available at: http://www.allacademic.com//meta/p_mla_apa_research_citation/1/0/9/1/1/pages109112/p109112-1.php [accessed: 24 March 2010].

Ashe, F. 2007. *The New Politics of Masculinity: Men, Power and Resistance*. Routledge.

ASHR. 2003 [online]. Available at: http://www.ashr.edu.au/ [accessed: 31 May 2013].

Associated Press. 2006. More Grade Schools Test Single-sex Classrooms: Federal Change Expected that will See Trend Grow Further. *MSNBC* [online]. Available at: MSNBC.com [accessed: 6 July 2006].

Auvert, B.D. et al. 2005. Randomised, Controlled Intervention Trial of Male Circumcision for Reduction of HIV Infection Risk: The ANRS 1265 Trial. 11 *PLoS Medicine* 2, e298, doi:10.1371/journal.pmed.002098.

Ayandey-e R. 2006. Sokhangoy-e Setad-e Pasdasht Nehzat-e Jahani-e Islam: Esteshhadiyoon Iran ta Pirooziy-e Hatmiy-e Hezbullah dar Lobnan Baghi Khahand Moond (A Spokesman for the Islamic World Movement of Martyrs Stewardship Committee: Martyrdom Seekers will remain in Lebanon until the Definite Victory of Hezbollah). *Ayanday-e Roshan*, 16 July [online]. Available at: http://www.bfnews.ir/vdci.vayct1aywbc2t.txt [accessed: 7 January 2013].

Bach, M. 2006. Same Sex Classes Get High Marks. *Flint Journal*, 8 January.

Baehr v. Lewin [Hawaii 1993] 852 P.2d 44.

Bailey, C. et al. 2007. Male Circumcision for HIV Prevention in Young Men in Kyushu, Kenya: A Randomised Controlled Trial. 369 *Lancet*, 643.

Bailey, J. 1995. Sexual Orientation of Adult Sons of Gay Fathers. 31 *Developmental Psychology* 1, 124.

Baird, S., McIntosh, C. and Ozler, B. 2010. Schooling, Income, and HIV Risk: Experimental Evidence from a Cash Transfer Programme. XVIII International AIDS Conference; Vienna, Austria; 18–23 July [online]. Available at: http://pag.aids2010.org/session.aspx?s=70#2 [accessed: 21 January 2013].

Ball, C. 2003. Lesbian and Gay Families: Gender Nonconformity and the Implications of Difference. 31 *Capital University Law Review* 4, 691.

Ball, N. and van de Goor, L. 2006. Disarmament, Demobilization and Reintegration: Mapping Issues, Dilemmas and Guiding Principles. Relief Web [online]. Available at: http://reliefweb.int/sites/reliefweb.int/files/resources/17

0A4EF22D909FB1852572030052EFBE-cling-ddr-aug2006.pdf [accessed: 3 January 2013].

Banchero, S. 2006. Boys in One Class, Girls in the Other, *Chicago Tribune*, 5 November.

Bardaglio, P. 1999. 'Shameful Matches': The Regulation of Interracial Sex and Marriage in the South before 1900, in *Sex, Love, Race: Crossing Boundaries in North American History*, edited by M. Hodes. New York University Press.

Barker, G. and Ricardo, C. 2005. *Young Men and the Construction of Masculinity in Sub-Saharan Africa: Implications for HIV/AIDS, Conflict, and Violence*. Social Development Papers: Conflict Prevention & Reconstruction, Paper no. 26, World Bank [online]. Available at: http://www-wds.worldbank.org/external/default/WDSContentServer/WDSP/IB/2005/06/23/000012009_20050623134235/Rendered/PDF/327120rev0PAPER0AFR0young0men0WP26.pdf [accessed: 3 January 2013].

Barker-Benfield, B. 1975. Sexual Surgery in Late-nineteenth-century America. 5 *International Journal of Health Services* 2, 279.

Barnett, A. 2009a. The Welfare of the Child Re-visited: In Whose Best Interests? Part I *Family Law*, 50.

Barnett, A. 2009b. The Welfare of the Child Re-visited: In Whose Best Interests? Part II *Family Law*, 135.

Barnett, R. and Rivers, C. 2004. *Same Difference: How Gender Myths are Hurting our Relationships, our Children, and our Jobs*. Basic Books.

Barrow, S. and Dalton, P. 1997. *The Rough Guide to Reggae: The Definitive Guide to Jamaican Music from Ska through Roots to Bashment*, Jonathan Buckley edition. Rough Guides Ltd.

Bartlett, K.T. 1974. Pregnancy and the Constitution: The Uniqueness Trap. 62 *California Law Review*, 1532.

Bartlett, K.T. 1990. Feminist Legal Methods. 103 *Harvard Law Review* 829, 871.

Bartlett, K.T. 2000. Cracking Foundations as Feminist Method. 8 *American University Journal of Gender, Social Policy, and the Law* 1, 31.

Bastick, M. 2008. *Integrating Gender in Post-conflict Security Sector Reform*. Geneva Centre for the Democratic Control of Armed Forces: Policy Paper no. 29. DCAF.

Bauserman, R. 2002. Child Adjustment in Joint-custody versus Sole-custody Arrangements: A Meta-analytic Review. 16 *Journal of Family Psychology* 1, 91.

Baylies, C. 2000. Perspectives on Gender and AIDS in Africa, in *AIDS, Sexuality and Gender in Africa: Collective Strategies and Struggles in Tanzania and Zambia*, edited by C. Baylies and J. Bujra. Routledge.

Baylies, C. and Bujra, J. 2000. Responses to the AIDS Epidemic in Tanzania and Zambia, in *AIDS, Sexuality and Gender in Africa: Collective Strategies and Struggles in Tanzania and Zambia*, edited by C. Baylies and J. Bujra. Routledge.

Bayliss, J. and Smith, S. 2001. *The Globalization of World Politics: An Introduction to International Relations*, 3rd edn. Oxford University Press.

BBC. 2002. Female Bomber's Mother Speaks Out, 30 January [online]. Available at: http://news.bbc.co.uk/2/hi/middle_east/1791800.stm [accessed: 7 January 2013].

BBC News. 2008. In a HARDtalk interview shown on 20th May 2008, Stephen Sackur talks to Jamaica's Prime Minister Bruce Golding [online]. Available at: http://news.bbc.co.uk/2/hi/programmes/hardtalk/7410382.stm [accessed: 8 January 2013].

BBC Persian. 2005. 'Amadegi-e' Dokhtran-e Zeytoon dar Tehran baray-e Amaliat-e Enhetrai Aleyhe Israel (The Readiness of the Daughters of Olive in Tehran to Carry Out Suicide Operations against Israel), 20 April [online]. Available at: http://www.bbc.co.uk/persian/iran/story/2005/04/050420_mf_olivegirls.shtml [accessed: 7 January 2012].

Beasley, C. 2005. *Gender & Sexuality: Critical Theories, Critical Thinkers*. Sage.

Beasley, C. 2008a. Rethinking Hegemonic Masculinity in a Globalizing World. 11 *Men and Masculinities*, 86.

Beasley, C. 2008b. The Challenge of Pleasure: Re-imagining Sexuality and Sexual Health. 7 *Health Sociology Review*, Special Issue: Re-imagining Preventive Health – Theoretical Perspectives 4, 151.

Beasley, C. 2009. Is Masculinity Studies Increasingly the 'Odd Man Out'?: Considering Problems and Possibilities in Contemporary Gender/Sexuality Thinking, in *GEXcel Work in Progress Report: Volume 6, Deconstructing the Hegemony of Men and Masculinities*, edited by Alp Biricik and Jeff Hearn. GEXcel.

Beasley, C. 2011. Libidinous Politics: Heterosex, 'Transgression', and Social Change. 26 *Australian Feminist Studies* 67, 25.

Beasley, C. and Bacchi, C. 2007. Envisaging a New Politics for an Ethical Future: Beyond Trust, Care and Generosity towards an Ethic of Social Flesh. 8 *Feminist Theory* 3, 279.

Beasley, C., Brook, H. and Holmes, M. 2012. *Heterosexuality in Theory and Practice*, Advances in Feminist Studies and Intersectionality. Routledge.

Becker, M. 1987. Prince Charming: Abstract Equality. 1987 *Supreme Court Review*, 201.

Becker, M. 1992. The Politics of Women's Wrongs and the Bill of 'Rights': A Bicentennial Perspective. 59 *University of Chicago Law Review*, 453.

Bederman, G. 1995. *Manliness and Civilization: A Cultural History of Gender and Race in the United States 1880–1917*. University of Chicago Press.

Beiner, T.M. 1999. The Misuse of Summary Judgment in Hostile Environment Cases. 34 *Wake Forest Law Review* 1, 71.

Beiner, T.M. 2005. *Gender Myths v. Working Realities: Using Social Science to Reformulate Sexual Harassment Law*. New York University Press.

Bell, C. 2000. *Peace Agreements and Human Rights*. Oxford University Press.

Bell, D. and Binnie, J. 2000. *The Sexual Citizen: Queer Politics and Beyond*. Polity.

Bell, K. 2005. Genital Cutting and Western Discourses on Sexuality. 19 *Medical Anthropology Quarterly*, 125.

Bender, W.N. 1994. Joint Custody: The Option of Choice. 21 *Journal of Divorce and Remarriage* 3/4, 115.

Bennett v. O'Rourke [Tenn. Ct. App. Nov. 5, 1981] 1985 WL 3464.

Berdal, M.R. 1996. Disarmament and Demobilisation after Civil Wars: Arms, Soldiers and the Termination of Armed Conflicts, in *ADELPHI Paper 303*. International Institute for Strategic Studies.

Berer, M. 2007. Male Circumcision for HIV Prevention: Perspectives on Gender and Sexuality. 15 *Reproductive Health Matters* 29, 45.

Berer, M. 2008. Male Circumcision for HIV Prevention: What about Protecting Men's Partners? 16 *Reproductive Health Matters*, 171.

Berrebi, C. 2007. Evidence about the Link between Education, Poverty and Terrorism among Palestinians. 13 *Peace Economics, Peace Science and Public Policy* 1, 1.

Bertoia, C. and Janice, D. 1993. The Fathers' Rights Movement: Contradictions in Rhetoric and Practice. 14 *Journal of Family Issues* 4, 592.

Bianchi, S.M., Robinson, J.P. and Milkie, M.A. 2006. *Changing Rhythms of American Family Life*. Russell Sage Foundation.

Biblarz, T. and Stacey, J. 2010. How does the Gender of Parents Matter? 72 *Journal of Marriage and Family* 1, 3.

Bieber, I. et al. 1972. *Homosexuality: A Psychoanalytical Study*. Vintage.

Black v. Black [Tenn. Ct. App. Mar. 10, 1988], 1988 WL 22823.

Bland, L. 1981. The Domain of the Sexual: A Response. 39 *Screen Education*, 56.

Blankenhorn, D. 1995. *Fatherless America: Confronting Our Most Urgent Social Problem*. Basic Books.

Blum, D. 1998. *Sex on the Brain: The Biological Differences between Men and Women*. Penguin.

Blum, J.A. 2000. Degradation without Deskilling: Twenty-five Years in the San Francisco Shipyards, in *Global Ethnography: Forces, Connections, and Imaginations in a Postmodern World*, edited by M. Burowoy. University of California Press.

Bodensteiner, I. 2003. The Implications of Psychological Research Related to Unconscious Discrimination and Implicit Bias in Proving Intentional Discrimination. 73 *Missouri Law Review* 1, 83.

Bonner, K. 2001. Male Circumcision as an HIV Control Strategy: Not a 'Natural Condom'. 9 *Reproductive Health Matters* 18, 1.

Bosman, J. 2008. Obama Calls for More Responsibility from Black Fathers. *New York Times*, 16 June.

Bowler, M. 2004. School to Test All-boy Classes Experiment: Teachers and Parents at Twin Ridge Elementary Hope that Allowing for Gender Differences will Improve Learning. *Baltimore Sun*, 24 May.

Boyd, S.B. 1998. Lesbian (and Gay) Custody Claims: What Difference does Difference Make? 15 *Canadian Journal of Family Law* 1, 131.

Boyd, S.B. 2003. *Child Custody, Law, and Women's Work*. Oxford University Press.

Boyd, S.B. 2004. Backlash against Feminism: Canadian Custody and Access Reform Debates of the Late Twentieth Century. 16 *Canadian Journal of Women and Law* 2, 255.

Boyd, S.B. 2005. Review Essay: Being Responsible in the New Family Law. 1 *International Journal of Law in Context* 2, 199.

Boyd, S.B. 2006. Robbed of their Families? Fathers' Rights Discourses in Canadian Parenting Law Reform Processes, in *Fathers' Rights Activism and Law Reform in Comparative Perspective*, edited by R. Collier and S. Sheldon. Hart.

Boyd, S. 2009. Is Equality Enough? Fathers' Rights and Women's Rights Advocacy, in *Rethinking Equality Projects in Law: Feminist Challenges*, edited by R. Hunter. Hart.

Bradley, L. 2002. *Reggae: The Story of Jamaican Music*. Grove Press.

Brady, E. 2009. Gays to Boycott Jamaica Tonight. Village Voice, 15 April [online]. Available at: http://blogs.villagevoice.com/runninscared/2009/04/gays_to_boycott.php [accessed: 8 January 2013].

Brake, D. 2001. The Struggle for Sex Equality in Sport and the Theory behind Title IX. 34 *University of Michigan Journal of Law Reform*, 13.

Brandt, A.M. 1978. Racism and Research: The Case of the Tuskegee Syphilis Study. 6 *Hastings Center Report*, 21.

Branigan, T. and Travis, A. 2007. Straw Moves to Ban Incitement against Gays. *The Guardian* [online]. Available at: http://www.guardian.co.uk/uk/2007/oct/09/gayrights.immigrationpolicy [accessed: 8 January 2013].

Bridgeman, J., Lind, C. and Keating, H., eds. 2008. *Responsibility, Law and the Family*. Ashgate.

Brilmayer, R. L. 1993. Inclusive Feminism, 38 *New York Law School Law Review* 377, 383.

Bristow, J. 2009. *Standing up to Supernanny*. Societas.

Brizendine, L. 2007. *The Female Brain*. Broadway Books.

Bronfenbrenner, U. 1979. *The Ecology of Human Development: Experiments by Nature and Design*. Harvard University Press.

Brooks, D. 2006. The Gender Gap at School. *New York Times*, 11 June.

Broom, D. 2008. Hazardous Good Intentions? Unintended Consequences of the Project of Prevention. 17 *Health Sociology Review* 2, 129.

Brown v. Board of Education [1954] 347 U.S. 483.

Brown, K. and Hauswedell, C. 2002. Burying the Hatchet: The Decommissioning of Paramilitary Arms in Northern Ireland, in *Initiative on Conflict Resolution and Ethnicity* 22, Bonn International Centre for Conversion, Brief no. 22.

Bruni, A., Gherardi, S. and Poggio, B. 2005. *Gender and Entrepreneurship: An Ethnographical Approach*. Routledge.

Buel, S. 2003. Effective Assistance of Counsel for Battered Women Defendants: A Normative Construct. 26 *Harvard Women's Law Journal* 217, 296.

Bujra J. and Mkake, S.N. 2000. AIDS Activism in Dar es Salaam: Many Struggles; a Single Goal, in *AIDS, Sexuality and Gender in Africa: Collective Strategies and Struggles in Tanzania and Zambia* edited by C. Baylies and J. Bujra. Routledge.

Bureerong v Uvawas [1996] 922 F. Supp. 1450.

Burgess, A. 1997. *Fatherhood Reclaimed: The Making of a Modern Father.* Vermilion.

Burke, A. 2002. Rational Actors, Self-defense, and Duress: Making Sense, Not Syndromes, Out of the Battered Woman. 81 *North Carolina Law Review* 211, 220.

Burke, A. 2007. *Beyond Security, Ethics and Violence: War against the Other.* Routledge.

Butler, D. and Geis, F.L. 1990. Nonverbal Affect Responses to Male and Female Leaders: Implications for Leadership Evaluations. 58 *Journal of Personality and Social Psychology* 1, 48.

Butler, J. 1990. *Gender Trouble: Feminism and the Subversion of Identity.* Routledge.

Cahn, N. 1991. Civil Images of Battered Women: The Impact of Domestic Violence on Child Custody Decisions. 44 *Vanderbilt Law Review*, 1041.

Cahn, N. et al. 2011. *On the Frontlines: Gender, War and the Post-conflict Process.* Oxford University Press.

Califia, P. 1996. Feminism and Sadomasochism, in *Feminism and Sexuality: A Reader*, edited by S. Jackson and S. Scott. Edinburgh University Press.

Camayd-Freixas, E. 2008. Raids, Rights and Reform: The *Postville* Case and the Immigration Crisis. 2 *DePaul Journal of Social Justice* 1, 1.

Campbell, D. 2005. Sex Lessons Planned for All Children. *The Observer*, 4 December.

Campbell, P. and Sanders, J. 2002. Challenging the System: Assumptions and Data behind the Push for Single-sex Schooling, in *Gender in Policy and Practice: Perspectives on Single-sex and Coeducational Schooling*, edited by Amanda Datnow and Lee Hubbard. RoutledgeFalmer.

Capers, B. 2007. Reading Back, Reading Black. 35 *Hofstra Law Review* 8, 101.

Carbado, D.W. 1999. Introduction: When and Where Black Men Enter, in *Black Men on Race, Gender, and Sexuality*, edited by D. Carbado. New York University Press.

Carbado, D.W. 2000. Men in Black. 3 *Journal Gender, Race and Justice* 2, 427.

Carbado, D.W. 2002. (E)racing the Fourth Amendment. 100 *Michigan Law Review* 5, 946.

Carbado, D.W. and Gulati, M. 2000. Working Identity. 85 *Cornell Law Review* 5, 1259.

Carbado, D.W. and Gulati, M. 2003. What Exactly is Racial Diversity? 91 *California Law Review* 4, 1149.

Carbado, D., Fisk, C. and Gulati, M. 2007. Foreword: Making Makeup Matter. 14 *Duke Journal of Gender Law and Policy* 1, 1.

Carby, H. 1986. On the Threshold of the Women's Era: Lynching, Empire, and Sexuality in Black Feminist Theory, in *Race, Writing and Difference*, edited by H.L. Gates, Jr. Chicago University Press.

Cardwell, J. and Cardwell, P. 1996. The African AIDS Epidemic. 274 *Science America* 3, 62.

Carmody, M. 2005. Ethical Erotics: Reconceptualising Anti-rape Education. 8 *Sexualities* 4, 465.

Carreiras, H. 2006. *Gender and the Military: Women in the Armed Forces of Western Democracies*. Routledge.

Case, M.A. 1995. Disaggregating Gender from Sex and Sexual Orientation: The Effeminate Man in the Law and Feminist Jurisprudence. 105 *Yale Law Journal* 1, 1.

Case, M.A. 2000. 'The Very Stereotype the Law Condemns': Constitutional Sex Discrimination Law as a Quest for Perfect Proxies. 85 *Cornell Law Review*, 1447.

Catanzarite, L. 2002. Dynamics of Segregation and Earnings in Brown-collar Occupations. 29 *Work and Occupations* 3, 300.

Center for Disease Control and Prevention. 2006. Understanding Intimate Partner Violence, Fact Sheet 2006 [online]. Available at: http://www.cdc.gov/ncipc/dvp/ipv_factsheet.pdf [accessed: 21 January 2013].

Central Intelligence Agency. 2009. The World Factbook 2009, Central America and the Caribbean: Jamaica [online]. Available at: https://www.cia.gov/library/publications/the-world-factbook/geos/jm.html# [accessed: 8 January 2013].

Centre for the AIDS Programme of Research in South Africa. 2010 [online]. Available at: http://caprisa.org/joomla/index.php/component/content/article/1/226 [accessed: 1 November 2010]. Chamallas, M. 1999/2003. *Introduction to Feminist Legal Theory*. Aspen Publishers.

Chamallas, M. 2005. Women and War: A Critical Discourse: Panel Two – Women Warriors. 20 *Berkeley Journal of Gender Law and Justice*, 338.

Chamallas, M. 2012. *Introduction to Feminist Legal Theory*, 3rd edn. Wolters Kluwer.

Chambers, D. et al. 2004. Peer Regulation of Teenage Sexual Identities. 16 *Gender and Education* 3, 397.

Chancy, M.J.A. 2008. Subversive Sexualities: Revolutionizing Gendered Identities. 29 *Frontiers: A Journal of Women's Studies* 1, 51.

Chemerinsky, E. 2001. An Independent Analysis of the Los Angeles Police Department's Board of Inquiry Report on the Rampart Scandal. 34 *Loyola Los Angeles Law Review* 2, 545.

Chen, A.S. 1999. Lives at the Center of the Periphery, Lives at the Periphery of the Center: Chinese American Masculinities and Bargaining with Hegemony. 13 *Gender & Society* 5, 584.

Chen, C.H. 1996. Feminization of Asian (American) Men in the U.S. Mass Media: An Analysis of The Ballad of Little Jo. 20 *Journal of Communication Inquiry* 2, 57.
Chi Chi LaRue. 2010 [online]. Available at: www.safesexishotsex.com [accessed: 31 October 2010].
Chin, G.J. and Wells, S.C. 1998. The 'Blue Wall of Silence' as Evidence of Bias and Motive to Lie: A New Approach to Police Perjury. 59 *University Pittsburgh Law Review* 2, 233.
Chodorow, N.J. 1994. *Femininities, Masculinities, Sexualities: Freud and Beyond.* University Press of Kentucky.
Civil Rights Act of 1964 [2010] 42 U.S.C. §§ 2000e et seq.
Civil Rights Act of 1991 [2010] 42 U.S.C. §§ 2000e et seq.
Clark, K.M. 1996. *Fostering a Farewell to Arms: Preliminary Lessons Learned in the Demobilization and Reintegration of Combatants*. USAID.
Clatterbaugh, K. 1990. *Contemporary Perspectives on Masculinity, Men, Women, and Politics in Modern Society*. Westview Press.
Clatterbaugh, K. 2000. Literature of the U.S. Men's Movements. 25 *Signs: Journal of Women in Culture and Society* 3, 883.
Cloutier, K.M. 2008. Marching Toward War: Reconnoitering the Use of All Female Platoons. 40 *Connecticut Law Review*, 1535.
Coalition on Men and Boys (COMAB). 2009. *Man Made: Men, Masculinities and Equality in Public Policy*. COMAB.
Coates, S. and Zucker, K. 1988. Gender Identity Disorders in Children, in *Second Handbook of Clinical Assessment of Children and Adolescents*, edited by C. Kestenbaum and D. Williams. New York University Press.
Cochrane Database of Systematic Reviews 2009; (2):CD003362, doi: 10.1002/14651858.CD003362.pub2.
Cockshut, R.W. 1935. Circumcision. 2 *British Medical Journal*, 764.
Cohen, C. 1999. *Boundaries of Blackness*. University of Chicago Press.
Cohen, D. 2005. Title IX: Beyond Equal Protection. 28 *Harvard Journal of Law and Gender*, 217.
Cohen, D. 2009. No Boy Left Behind?: Single-sex Education and the Essentialist Myth of Masculinity. 84 *Indiana Law Journal* 1, 135.
Cohen, D. and Vandello, J. 1998. Meanings of Violence. 27 *Journal of Legal Studies* 2, 567.
Colleluori, S. and Powell, B. 2012. How ALEC is Quietly Influencing Education in Georgia. MediaMatters [online]. Available at: http://mediamatters.org/research/201205090007 [accessed: 9 May 2012].
Collier, R. 1995. *Masculinity, Law and the Family*. Routledge.
Collier, R. 1998. *Masculinities, Crime and Criminology*. Sage.
Collier, R. 2005. Fathers 4 Justice, Law and the New Politics of Fatherhood. 17 *Child and Family Law Quarterly*, 511.
Collier, R. 2006. The Outlaw Fathers Fight Back: Fathers' Rights Groups, Fathers 4 Justice and the Politics of Family Law Reform – Reflections on the UK

Experience, in *Fathers' Rights Activism and Law Reform in Comparative Perspective*, edited by R. Collier and S. Sheldon. Hart.

Collier, R. 2009. Fathers' Rights, Gender and Welfare: Some Questions for Family Law. 31 *Journal of Social Welfare and Family Law* 4, 357.

Collier, R. 2010a. Masculinities, Law and Personal Life: Towards a New Framework for Understanding Men, Law and Gender. 33 *Harvard Journal of Law and Gender* 2, 431.

Collier, R. 2010b. *Men, Law and Gender: Essays on the 'Man' of Law*. Routledge.

Collier, R. and Sheldon, S., eds. 2006a. *Fathers' Rights Activism and Law Reform in Comparative Perspective*. Hart.

Collier, R. and Sheldon, S. 2006b. Fathers' Rights, Fatherhood, and Law Reform: International Perspectives, in *Fathers for Justice? Fathers' Rights Activism and Legal Reform in Comparative Context*, edited by R. Collier and S. Sheldon. Hart.

Collier, R. and Sheldon, S. 2008. *Fragmenting Fatherhood: A Socio-legal Study*. Hart.

Collinson, D.L. 1988. 'Engineering Humor': Masculinity, Joking and Conflict in Shop-floor Relations. 9 *Organizational Studies* 2, 181.

Collinson, D.L. 1992. *Managing the Shopfloor: Subjectivity, Masculinity and Workplace Culture*. W. de Gruyter.

Collinson, D.L. and Hearn, J. 2005. Men and Masculinities in Work, Organizations, and Management, in *Handbook of Studies on Men & Masculinities*, edited by M.S. Kimmel, J. Hearn and R.W. Connell. Sage.

Coltrane, S. 1989. Household Labor and the Routine Production of Gender. 36 *Social Problems* 5, 473.

Coltrane, S. and Hickman, N. 1992. The Rhetoric of Rights and Needs: Moral Discourse in the Reform of Child Custody and Child Support Laws. 39 *Social Problems* 4, 400.

Combes, J. and Hinton, T. 2005. Making Choices: Young People and Pregnancy in Tasmania. Final Report, Department of Health and Human Services, Tasmania, June.

Conaghan, J. 2009. Intersectionality and the Feminist Project in Law, in *Intersectionality and Beyond: Law, Power and the Politics of Location*, edited by E. Grabham et al. Routledge-Cavendish.

Connecticut v Teal [1982] 457 U.S. 440.

Connell, R.W. 1987. *Gender and Power: Society, the Person, and Sexual Politics*. Stanford University Press.

Connell, R.W. 1994. Psychoanalysis on Masculinity, in *Theorizing Masculinities*, edited by H. Brod and M. Kaufman. Sage.

Connell, R.W. 1996. Teaching the Boys: New Research on Masculinity, and Gender Strategies for Schools. 98 *Teachers College Record*, 206.

Connell, R.W. 2000. *The Men and the Boys*. Polity.

Connell, R.W. 2002a. *Gender*. Polity.

Connell, R.W. 2002b. The History of Masculinity, in *The Masculinity Studies Reader*, edited by R. Adams and D. Savran. Blackwell.
Connell, R.W. 1995/2005a. *Masculinities*. Allen and Unwin/University of California Press.
Connell, R.W. 2005b. Globalization, Imperialism, and Masculinities, in *Handbook of Studies on Men & Masculinities*, edited by M.S. Kimmel, J. Hearn and R.W. Connell. Sage.
Connell, R.W. and Messerschmidt, J.W. 2005. Hegemonic Masculinity: Rethinking the Concept. 19 *Gender & Society* 6, 829.
Connell, R.W., Hearn, J. and Kimmel, M.S. 2005. Introduction, in *Handbook of Studies on Men & Masculinities*, edited by M.S. Kimmel, J. Hearn and R.W. Connell. Sage.
Constable, A. 2006. Colorado School's Changes Boost Boys' Test Scores. *Santa Fe New Mexican*, 10 December.
Constantine-Simms, D. ed. 2000. *The Greatest Taboo: Homosexuality in Black Communities*. Alyson Publications.
Cooke, M. 2008. Deploying the Muslimwoman. 24 *Journal of Feminist Studies in Religion* 1, 91.
Coombs, M.I. 1992. Outsider Scholarship: The Law Review Stories. 63 *University of Colorado Law Review*, 683.
Cooper, C. 1995. *Noises in the Blood: Orality, Gender and the 'Vulgar' Body of Jamaican Pop Culture*. Duke University Press.
Cooper, C. 2004. *Sound Clash: Jamaican Dancehall Culture at Large*. Palgrave Macmillan.
Cooper, F.R. 2006a. Against Bipolar Black Masculinity: Intersectionality, Assimilation, Identity Performance and Hierarchy. 39 *University of California Davis Law Review* 3, 853.
Cooper, F.R. 2006b. The 'Seesaw Effect' from Racial Profiling to Depolicing: Toward a Critical Cultural Theory, in *New Civil Rights Research: A Constitutive Approach*, edited by B. Fleury-Steiner and L.B. Nielsen. Ashgate.
Cooper, F.R. 2009a. Our First Unisex President?: Black Masculinity and Obama's Feminine Side. 86 *Denver University Law Review* Special Issue, 633.
Cooper, F.R. 2009b. 'Who's the Man?': Masculinities Studies, Terry Stops, and Police Training. 18 *Columbia Journal of Gender and Law* 3, 671.
Cooper, F.R. 2010. Masculinities, Post-racialism, and the Gates Controversy: The False Equivalence between Officer and Civilian. 11 *Nevada Law Journal* 1, 1.
Cooper, F.R. 2012. The King Stay the King: Masculinities and Capitalism in *The Wire*, in *Masculinities and the Law: A Multidimensional Approach*, edited by F.R. Cooper and A.C. McGinley. New York University Press.
Cooper, F.R. and McGinley, A.C. 2012. *Masculinities and the Law: A Multidimensional Approach*. New York University Press.
Coovadia, H. et al. 2009. The Health and Health System of South Africa: Historical Roots of Current Public Health Challenges, 374 *The Lancet*, 817.
Corea, G. 1985. *The Hidden Malpractice*. Harper Colophon.

Cornell, D. 1991. *Beyond Accommodation: Ethical Feminism, Deconstruction, and the Law*. Rowman & Littlefield.

Cornwall, A. and Jolly, S. eds. 2006. Sexuality Matters. 37 *IDS Bulletin: Institute of Development Studies* 5.

Craig v. Boren [1976] 429 U.S. 190, 197.

Cranford, C. 1998. Gender and Citizenship in the Restructuring of Janitorial Work in Los Angeles. 16 *Gender Issues* 4, 25.

Cranford, C. 2007. 'It's time to leave machismo behind!': Challenging Gender Inequality in an Immigrant Union. 21 *Gender & Society* 3, 409.

Crenshaw, K. 1989. Demarginalizing the Intersection of Race and Sex: A Black Feminist Critique of Antidiscrimination Doctrine, Feminist Theory and Antiracist Politics. *University of Chicago Legal Forum*, 139.

Crenshaw, K. 1991. Mapping the Margins: Intersectionality, Identity Politics, and Violence against Women of Color. 43 *Stanford Law Review* 6, 1241.

Criminal Law Policy Unit Ministry of Justice. 2010. Offences of Stirring Up Hatred on the Grounds of Sexual Orientation, Circular 2010/05 [online]. Available at: http://webarchive.nationalarchives.gov.uk/20100505212528/http://www.justice.gov.uk/publications/docs/circular-05-2010-sexual-orientation-stirring-up-hatred.pdf [accessed: 8 January 2013].

Crimp, D., ed. 1988. *AIDS: Cultural Analysis/Cultural Activism*. MIT Press.

Crowley, J.E. 2003. *The Politics of Child Support in America*. Cambridge University Press.

Crowley, J.E. 2006. Organizational Responses to the Fatherhood Crisis: The Case of Fathers' Rights Groups in the United States. 39 *Marriage and Family Review* 1/2, 99.

Crowley, J. 2008a. *Defiant Dads: Fathers' Rights Activists in America*. Cornell University Press.

Crowley, J. 2008b. On the Cusp of a Movement: Identity Work and Social Movement Identification Processes within Fathers' Rights Groups. 28 *Sociological Spectrum* 6, 705.

Crowley, J. 2009. Cambridge Police Department Incident Report # 90051272 [online]. Available at: http://www.thesmokinggun.com/archive/years/2009/0723092gates1.html [accessed: 9 October 2009].

Crowley, J.E. 2009a. Conflicted Membership: Women in Fathers' Rights Groups. 79 *Sociological Inquiry* 3, 328.

Crowley, J.E. 2009b. Fathers' Rights Groups, Domestic Violence, and Political Countermobilization. 88 *Social Forces* 2, 723.

Dahl, R. 1982. *Dilemmas of Pluralist Democracy: Autonomy vs. Control*. Yale University Press.

Dailey v. Dailey [Tenn. Ct. App. 1981] 635 S.W.2d 391.

Dalton, S. 2003. From Presumed Fathers to Lesbian Mothers: Sex Discrimination and the Legal Construction of Parenthood. 9 *Michigan Journal of Gender and Law* 2, 261.

Daniels, C.R. et al. ed. 1997. *Feminists Negotiate the State*. University Press of America.

Darby, R. 2003. The Masturbation Taboo and the Rise of Routine Male Circumcision: A Review of the Historiography. 36 *Journal of Social History*, 737.

Darby, R. 2005. *A Surgical Temptation: The Demonization of the Foreskin in Britain*. University of Chicago Press.

Darvill, W. and Powell, K. 2007. *The Puberty Book*, 4th edn. Hodder.

Das, V. 2000. *Critical Events: An Anthropological Perspective on Contemporary India*. Oxford University Press.

Datnow, A. et al. 2001. *Is Single Gender Schooling Viable in the Public Sector? Lessons from California's Pilot Program*. Education Resources Information Center.

Davies, B. 2003. Working with Primary School Children to Deconstruct Gender, in *Boys and Girls in the Primary Classroom*, edited by Christine Skelton and Becky Francis. Open University Press.

Davila, V. 2004. Expert Says Boys, Girls Learn Differently. *San Antonio Express-News*, 21 January.

Davis, G. 2001. Homophobia Remains High. *Jamaica Gleaner* [online]. Available at: http://www.jamaica-gleaner.com/pages/gay/homophobia.html [accessed: 8 January 2013].

Day Sclater, S. and Richards, M. 1995. How Adults Cope with Divorce – Strategies for Survival. *Family Law*, March, 143–7.

de Jonge, G. 2004. Youth, Crime and Juvenile Justice in the Netherlands. 4 *Journal of the Institute of Justice and International Studies*, 25.

DeClue v Central Illinois Light Company [7th Cir. 2000] 223 F.3d 434.

DeFao, J. 2007. Single-gender Education Gains Ground as Boys Lag. *San Francisco Chronicle*, 18 June.

Deleuze, G. and Guattari, F. 1980/1987. *A Thousand Plateaus: Capitalism and Schizophrenia Vol. 2*, translated by Brian Massumi. University of Minnesota Press.

Dermott, E. 2008. *Intimate Fatherhood: A Sociological Analysis*. Routledge

DeYoung, M. 2001. Sexuality: Histories, Behaviors, and Lifestyles that Impact Unit Readiness and Cohesion, in *Women in the Military*, edited by R.J. Simon. Transaction Publishers.

Didcock, B. 2005. How Jamaican Stars Turned from One Love to Homophobia and Violence. *Sunday Herald* [online]. Available at: http://sunday-herald.vlex.co.uk/vid/jamaican-turned-homophobia-violence-66078124 [accessed: 8 January 2013].

Diduck, A. and Kaganas, F. 2006. *Family Law, Gender and the State: Text, Cases and Materials*, 2nd edn. Hart.

Dinkes, R. et al. 2007. *Indicators of School Crime and Safety: 2006*. National Centre for Education Statistics.

Diprose, R. 2008. Biopolitical Technologies of Prevention. 17 *Health Sociology Review* 2, 141.

Doherty, J. 2009. Forum Sought on Race, Police: Harvard Professor's Arrest Spurs Syracuse Civil Rights Group's Push for Dialogue. *The Post-standard*, 2 August.

Dokhtaran Zeytoon [online]. Available at: http://www.rasekhoon.net/subject/show/1088/--/ [accessed: 7 January 2013].

Donahue, L.H., Lamare, J.R. and Kotler, F.B. 2007. Employee or Independent Contractor? Misclassification Comes at a Price (ILR Impact Brief #18) [online]. Available at: http://digitalcommons.ilr.cornell.edu/briefs/28/ [accessed: 23 April 2010].

Donaldson, M. 1993. What is Hegemonic Masculinity? 22 *Theory and Society*, 643.

Donnelly, D. and Finkelhor, D. 1992. Does Equality in Custody Arrangements Improve the Parent–Child Relationship? 54 *Journal of Marriage and the Family* 4, 837.

Donnelly, E. 2007. Constructing the Co-ed Military. 14 *Duke Journal of Gender Law and Policy*, 829.

Dorraj. M. 1997. Symbolic and Utilitarian Political Value of a Tradition: Martyrdom in the Iranian Political Culture. 59 *The Review of Politics* 3, Non-Western Political Thought, 489.

Dothard v Rawlinson [1977] 433 U.S. 321.

Doucet, A. 2006. *Do Men Mother? Fathering, Care and Domestic Responsibility*. University of Toronto Press.

Douglas, A. 2008. Transitions: The New Norm. Paper presented at 'Putting Children First' Conference, London, 16 October [online]. Available at: www.cafcass.gov.uk/idoc.ashx?docid=e07ff5e5-9c26-4937-af60-ff10764c1a01&version=-1 [accessed: 25 April 2009].

Douglas, M. 1993. Emotion and Culture in Theories of Justice. 22 *Economy and Society* 4, 501.

Dowd, N.E. 2000. *Redefining Fatherhood*, 1st edn. New York University Press.

Dowd, N.E. 2008. Masculinities and Feminist Legal Theory. 23 *Wisconsin Journal of Law, Gender, and Society* 2, 201.

Dowd, N.E. 2010. *The Man Question: Male Subordination and Privilege*, 1st edn. New York University Press.

Dowd, N.E. and Jacobs, M.S. 2003. *Feminist Legal Theory: An Anti-essentialist Reader*, 1st edn. New York University Press.

Dowd, N., Levit, N. and McGinley, A.C. 2012. Feminist Legal Theory Meets Masculinities Theory, in *Masculinities and the Law: A Multidimensional Approach*, edited by F.R. Cooper and A.C. McGinley. New York University Press.

Dowsett, G.W. and Couch, M. 2007. Male Circumcision and HIV Prevention: Is There Really Enough of the Right Kind of Evidence? 15 *Reproductive Health Matters*, 33.

Dozor, R. 1990. Routine Neonatal Circumcision. 22 *American Family Physician*, 820.

Dragiewicz, M. 2008. Patriarchy Reasserted: Fathers' Rights and Anti-VAWA Activism. 3 *Feminist Criminology* 2, 121.

Duggan, C. et al. 2008. Reparations for Sexual and Reproductive Violence. 2 *International Journal of Transitional Justice* 2, 192.

Duh, S.V. 1991. *Blacks and AIDS*. Sage.

Dunivin, K.O. 1997. Military Culture A Paradigm Shift, Maxwell Paper no. 10. Air War College [online]. Available at: http://www.au.af.mil/au/awc/awcgate/maxwell/mp10.pdf [accessed: 22 March 2010].

Dunn, S.E. 2009. The Military Selective Service Act's Exemption of Women: It's Time to End It. 1 *Army Law*, 18–19.

DWP. 2009. Joint Birth Registration: Promoting Parental Responsibility Cm 7160 [online]. Available at: http://www.dwp.gov.uk/jointbirthregistration/ [accessed: 25 February 2010].

E.E.O.C. v Beauty Enterprises, Incorporated [D. Conn. 2005] 2005 WL 2764822.

E.E.O.C. v Premier Operator Services [N.D. Tex. 2000] 113 F. Supp. 2d 1066.

Eagly, A.H. and Karau, S.J. 2002. Role Congruity Theory of Prejudice toward Female Leaders. 109 *Psychological Review* 3, 573.

Eagly, A.H., Johannesen-Schmidt, M.C. and Van Engen, M. 2003. Transformational, Transactional, and Laissez-faire Leadership Styles: A Meta-analysis Comparing Women and Men. 129 *Psychological Bulletin* 4, 569.

Eagly, A.H., Makhijani, M.G. and Klonsky, B.G. 1992. Gender and Evaluation of Leaders: A Meta-analysis. 111 *Psychological Bulletin* 1, 3.

Easy on the Eye. 2010 [online]. Available at: www.easyote.co.uk [accessed: 31 October 2010].

Echols, A. 1983. The New Feminism of Yin and Yang, in *Powers of Desire: The Politics of Sexuality*, edited by Anne Snitow et al. Monthly Review Press.

Echols, A. 1984. The Taming of the Id: Feminist Sexual Politics 1968–83, in *Pleasure and Danger: Exploring Female Sexuality*, edited by Carol Vance. Routledge.

Editorial. 1889. 5 *Daniel's Texas Medical Journal*, July.

Editorial. 2006a. Boy Trouble. *Boston Globe*, 2 October.

Editorial. 2006b. Single-sex Schools Can Work. *USA Today*, 29 March.

Eekelaar, J. 2006. *Family Law and Personal Life*. Oxford University Press.

Ehrenreich, N. 2002. Subordination and Symbiosis: Mechanisms of Mutual Support between Subordinating Systems. 71 *University of Missouri Kansas City Law Review* 2, 251.

Ehrlich, E. 1936. *Fundamental Principles of the Sociology of Law*. Transaction Publishers.

Elias, J. and Beasley, C. 2009. Hegemonic Masculinity and Globalization: Transnational Business Masculinities and Beyond. 6 *Globalizations* 2, 281.

Eliot, L. 2009. P*ink Brain, Blue Brain: How Small Differences Grow into Troublesome Gaps – and What We Can Do About It*. Houghton Mifflin.

Ellis, E.M. 2000. *Divorce Wars: Interventions with Families in Conflict.* American Psychological Association.

Ely, R.J. and Meyerson, D.E. 2000. Advancing Gender Equity in Organizations: The Challenge and Importance of Maintaining a Gender Narrative. 7 *Organizations* 4, 589.

Ely, R.J. and Meyerson, D.E. 2010. An Organizational Approach to Undoing Gender: The Unlikely Case of Offshore Oil Platforms. 30 *Research in Organizational Behaviour*, 3.

Engel, J. 2006. *The Epidemic: A Global History of AIDS.* HarperCollins.

Epstein, D. 1997. Boyz' Own Stories: Masculinities and Sexualities in Schools. 9 *Gender and Education*, 105.

Epstein, D. and Renold, E. 2005. Introduction (Special issue on Carol Vance's *Pleasure and Danger*). 8 *Sexualities* 4, 387.

Epstein, D. et al. 1998. Schoolboy Frictions: Feminism and 'Failing' Boys, in *Failing Boys? Issues in Gender and Achievement*, edited by D. Epstein et al. Open University Press.

Eriksson, M. and Pringle, K. 2006. Gender Equality, Child Welfare and Fathers' Rights in Sweden, in *Fathers' Rights Activism and Law Reform in Comparative Perspective*, edited by R. Collier and S. Sheldon. Hart.

Erin, C. and Ost, S., eds. 2007. *The Criminal Justice System and Health Care.* Oxford University Press.

Erlich, M. and Grabelsky, J. 2005. Standing at a Crossroads: The Building Trades in the Twenty-first Century. 46 *Labor History* 4, 421.

Esacove, A. 2010. Love Matches: Heteronormativity, Modernity and AIDS Prevention in Malawi. 24 *Gender & Society* 1, 83.

Eschle, C. 2001. *Global Democracy, Social Movements, and Feminism.* Westview Press.

Escola de Cultura de Pau. 2009. DDR 2009: Analysis of Disarmament, Demobilisation and Reintegration (DDR) Programmes in the World during 2008. Escola de Cultura de Pau [online]. Available at: http://escolapau.uab.cat/img/programas/desarme/ddr/ddr2009e.pdf [accessed: 3 January 2013].

Eskridge, W. and Hunter, N. 2004. *Sexuality, Gender, and the Law.* Foundation Press.

Eskridge, W.N., Jr. 1994. *Dynamic Statutory Interpretation.* Harvard University Press.

Esposito, J.L. 2003. *Unholy War: Terror in the Name of Islam.* Oxford University Press.

European Union Press Release. 2006. Winkler: Conflicts Cannot be Resolved Using Arms. European Union, 26 June [online]. Available at: http://www.eu2006.at/en/News/Press_Releases/June/2606WinklerUN.html [accessed: 3 January 2013].

Evans v. Evans [Ct. App. 1960] 8 Cal. Rptr. 412.

Evans, D. 1993. *Sexual Citizenship: The Material Construction of Sexualities.* Routledge.

Eyer, K.R. 2011. That's Not Discrimination: American Beliefs and the Limits of Anti-discrimination Law. 96 *Minnesota Law Review*, 1275.

Fabricius, W.V. and Hull, J. 2000. Young Adults' Perspectives on Divorce Living Arrangements. 38 *Family and Conciliation Courts Review* 4, 446.

Fajer, M. 1992. Can Two Real Men Eat Quiche Together? Storytelling, Gender Role Stereotypes, and Legal Protection for Lesbians and Gay Men. 46 *University of Miami Law Review*, 511.

Faludi, S. 1999. *Stiffed: The Betrayal of the American Man*. William Morrow.

Faragher v. City of Boca Raton [1998] 524 U.S. 775.

Fariba, A. 2005. Dokhtaran Zeytoon. *Payam Zan*, no. 159 [online]. Available at: http://www.hawzah.net/hawzah/Magazines/MagArt.aspx?MagazineNumberID=4165&id=26106 [accessed: 7 January 2013].

Farzaneh, M.M. 2007. Shi'i Ideology, Iranian Secular Nationalism and the Iran–Iraq War (1980–1988). 7 *Studies in Ethnicity and Nationalism* 1, 86.

Fatherhood Institute. 2010. *Fathers and Family Health in the Perinatal Period*. Fatherhood Institute.

Fausto-Sterling, A. 2000. *Sexing the Body: Gender, Politics and the Construction of Sexuality*. Basic Books.

Featherstone, B. 2009. *Contemporary Fathering: Theory, Policy and Practice*. Policy Press.

Featherstone, B. and Trinder, L. 2001. New Labour, Families and Fathers. 21 *Critical Social* 4, 534.

Feld, B.C. 1999. *Bad Kids: Race and the Transformation of the Juvenile Court*, 1st edn. Oxford University Press.

Feller, B. 2004. Federal Officials to Loosen Limits on Same-sex Public Schools. *The Associated Press*, 3 March, BC cycle.

Felter, E. 1997. A History of the State's Response to Domestic Violence in the United States, in *Feminists Negotiate the State: The Politics of Domestic Violence*, edited by C.R. Daniels. University Press of America.

Fenner, H.S. 2001. Either You Need These Women or You Do Not: Informing the Debate on Military Service and Citizenship, in *Women in the Military*, edited by R.J. Simon. Transaction Publishers.

Ferguson, K.E. 1993. *The Man Question: Visions of Subjectivity in Feminist Theory*. University of California Press.

Ferreiro, B.W. 1990. Presumption of Joint Custody: A Family Policy Dilemma. 39 *Family Relations* 4, 420.

Fine, C. 2010. *Delusions of Gender: How Our Minds, Society, and Neurosexism Create Difference*. W.W. Norton.

Fine, M. et al. 1997. (In)Secure Times: Constructing White Working-class Masculinities in the Late 20th Century. 10 *Gender & Society* 6, 52.

Fineman, M.A. 1991. *The Illusion of Equality: The Rhetoric and Reality of Divorce Reform*, 1st edn. University of Chicago Press.

Fineman, M.A. 1995. *The Neutered Mother, the Sexual Family, and Other Twentieth Century Tragedies*. Routledge.

Fineman, M.A. 2000. Cracking the Foundational Myths: Independence, Autonomy, and Self-sufficiency. 8 *The American University Journal of Gender, Social Policy & the Law* 1, 13.

Fineman, M.A. 2004. *The Autonomy Myth.* New Press.

Fineman, M.A. 2005. Feminist Legal Theory, 13 *American University Journal of Gender, Social Policy, and the Law*, 13.

Fineman, M.A. 2008. The Vulnerable Subject: Anchoring Equality in the Human Condition. 20 *Yale Journal of Law & Feminism* 1, 1.

Fineman M.A. 2010a. The Vulnerable Subject and the Responsive State. 60 *Emory Law Journal*, 251.

Fineman, M.A., ed. 2010b. *Transcending the Boundaries of Law: Generations of Feminism and Legal Theory*. Routledge.

Fink, A.J. 1989. Newborn Circumcision: A Long-term Strategy for AIDS Prevention. 82 *Journal of the Royal Society of Medicine*, 695.

Finley, L. 1996. Sex-blind, Separate but Equal, or Anti-subordination? The Uneasy Legacy of *Plessy v. Ferguson* for Sex and Gender Discrimination. 12 *Georgia State University Law Review*, 1089.

Finley, L.M. 1986. Transcending Equality Theory: A Way Out of the Maternity and the Workplace Debate. 86 *Columbia Law Review*, 1118.

First World Congress for Sexual Health. 2007 [online]. Available at: www.sex-sydney-007.com/callabstracts.htm [accessed: 31 October 2010].

Flaks, D. 1994. Gay and Lesbian Families: Judicial Assumptions, Scientific Realities. 3 *William and Mary Bill of Rights Journal* 1, 345.

Fletcher, R. 2005. Reproducing Irishness: Race, Gender, and Abortion Law. 17 *Canadian Journal of Women and the Law* 2, 365.

Flood, M. 1998. Men's Movements. 46 *Community Quarterly*, 62.

Flood, M. 2004. Backlash: Angry Men's Movements, in *The Battle and Backlash Rage On: Why Feminism Cannot be Obsolete*, edited by S.E. Rossi. Xlibris Press.

Flood, M. 2006. Separated Fathers and the Fathers' Rights Movement. Paper presented at Feminism, Law, and the Family Workshop, at Law School, University of Melbourne.

Flood, M. 2008. Bent Straights: Diversity and Flux among Heterosexual Men, in *Intimate Citizenships: Gender, Subjectivity, Politics*, edited by E.H. Oleksy. Routledge.

Flood, M. et al., eds. 2007. *The International Encyclopaedia of Men and Masculinities*. Routledge.

Flowers, C. 2005. With No Boys to Ogle, We Had Time to Learn, *Newsweek*, 24 October.

Foner, N. 2005. *In a New Land: A Comparative View of Immigration*. New York University Press.

Foschi, M., Lai, L. and Sigerson, K. 1994. Gender and Double Standards in the Assessment of Job Applicants. 57 *Social Psychology Quarterly* 4, 326.

Foucault, M. 1978. *History of Sexuality*. Vintage.

Foucault, M. 1980. *Power/Knowledge: Selected Interviews and Other Writings, 1972–1977*, edited by Colin Gordon. Harvester.

Foucault, M. 1981. *The History of Sexuality*, Part I. Penguin.

Foucault, M. 1982. The Subject and Power. 8 *Critical Inquiry*, 777.

Fox, M. and Thomson, M. 2005. Short Changed?: The Law and Ethics of Male Circumcision. 13 *International Journal of Children's Rights*, 157.

Fox, M. and Thomson, M. 2010. HIV/AIDS and Circumcision: Lost in Translation. 36 *Journal of Medical Ethics*, 798.

Fox, M. and Thomson, M. 2012. The New Politics of Male Circumcision: HIV/AIDS, Health Law and Social Justice. 32 *Legal Studies*, 255.

Fox, M. and Thomson, M. 2013. Realising Social Justice in Public Health Law. 21 *Medical Law Review* 2, 278.

Franke, K.M. 1995. The Central Mistake of Sex Discrimination Law: The Disaggregation of Sex from Gender. 144 *University of Pennsylvania Law Review*, 1.

Franke, K.M. 2009. Theorizing Yes: An Essay on Feminism, Law and Desire, in *Feminist and Queer Legal Theory: Intimate Encounters, Uncomfortable Conversations*, edited by M.A. Fineman et al. Ashgate.

Franklin, C. 2010. The Anti-stereotyping Principle in Constitutional Sex Discrimination Law. 85 *New York University Law Review*, 83.

Freeland, E.H. 1900. Circumcision as a Preventative of Syphilis and Other Disorders. II *British Medical Journal*, 1869.

Freeman, C. 2005. *Trends in Educational Equity of Girls & Women: 2004*. National Centre for Education Statistics,

Freud, S. 1905. Three Essays on the Theory of Sexuality, in *The Standard Edition of the Complete Psychological Works of Sigmund Freud*, edited by Sigmund Freud et al. Hogarth Press.

Freud, S. 1937. Analysis Terminable and Interminable, in *The Standard Edition of the Complete Psychological Works of Sigmund Freud*, edited by Sigmund Freud et al. Hogarth Press.

Frug, M. 1992. *Postmodern Legal Feminism*. Routledge.

Fullwood, S. The Greatest Taboo: An Interview with Delroy Constantine-Simms. Africana.com [online]. Available at: http://www.hartford-hwp.com/archives/45a/758.html [accessed: 8 January 2013].

Furedi, F. 2003. *Therapy Culture: Cultivating Vulnerability in an Uncertain Age*. Routledge.

Fussell, P. 1983. *Class: A Guide through the American Status System*. Touchstone.

Garcia v Spun Speak [9th Cir. 1993] 998 F.2d 1480.

Garcia, S.G. and Goldman, L. 2004. *Understanding Successful Condom Use in the Dominican Republic: Frontiers Final Report*. Population Council, Regional Office for Latin America and the Caribbean.

Garde, J. 2003. Masculinity and Madness. 3 *Counselling and Psychotherapy Research* 1, 6.

Garibaldi, A. 1992. Educating and Motivating African American Males to Succeed. 61 *The Journal of Negro Education* 1, 4.

Garrett v. Board of Education [E.D. Mich. 1991] 775 F. Supp. 1004.

Garth, B. and Sterling, J. 1998. From Legal Realism to Law and Society: Reshaping Law for the Last Stages of the Social Activist State. 32 *Law & Society Review* 409, 434.

Gartrell, N. et al. 2010. Adolescents of the U.S. National Longitudinal Lesbian Family Study: Sexual Orientation, Sexual Behavior, and Sexual Risk Exposure. *Archives of Sexual Behavior* [online]. Available at: http://www.springerlink.com/content/d967883qp3255733/fulltext.pdf [accessed: 31 May 2013].

Gatens, M. 1996. Through a Spinozist Lens: Ethology, Difference, Power, in *Deleuze: A Critical Reader*, edited by P. Patton. Blackwell.

Gates, E. 2009. My Daddy the Jailbird. *The Daily Beast* [online]. Available at: http://www.thedailybeast.com/blogs-and-stories/2009-07-22/my-daddy-the-jailbird/ [accessed: 5 December 2011].

Gates, Jr., H.L., ed. 1986. *Race, Writing and Difference*. Chicago University Press.

Gavanas, A. 2004a. Domesticating Masculinity and Masculinizing Domesticity in Contemporary U.S. Fatherhood Politics. 11 *Social Politics* 2, 247.

Gavanas, A. 2004b. *Fatherhood Politics in the United States: Masculinity, Sexuality, Race and Marriage*. University of Illinois Press.

Geisinger, A. 2002. A Belief Change Theory of Expressive Law. 88 *Iowa Law Review*, 35.

General Accounting Office. 1998. Gender Issues: Information on DOD's Assignment Policy and Direct Ground Combat Definition [online]. Available at: http://www.gao.gov/archive/1999/ns99007.pdf [accessed: 22 March 2010].

Gerami, S. 2003. Mullahs, Martyrs, and Men: Conceptualizing Masculinity in the Islamic Republic of Iran. 5 *Men and Masculinities* 3, 257.

Gettleman, J. 2009. Symbol of Unhealed Congo: Male Rape Victims. *New York Times*, 5 August [online]. Available at: http://www.nytimes.com/2009/08/05/world/africa/05congo.html?_r=0 [accessed: 3 January 2013].

Gewertz, C. 2007. Black Boys' Educational Plight Spurs Single-gender Schools. *Education Week*, 20 June, 1.

Gibson, S. 2007. The Language of the Right: Sex Education Debates in South Australia. 7 *Sex Education* 3, 239.

Gilbert, R. and Gilbert, P. 1998. *Masculinity Goes to School*. Routledge.

Giller, O. 2004. Patriarchy on Lockdown: Deliberate Indifference and Male Prison Rape. 10 *Cardozo Women's Law Journal*, 659.

Gillies, V. 2005. Meeting Parents' Needs? Discourses of 'Support' and 'Inclusion' in Family Policy. 25 *Critical Social Policy*, 70.

Gilligan, C. 1982. *In a Different Voice: Psychological Theory and Women's Development*, 1st edn. Harvard University Press.

Gilman, S. 1988. AIDS and Syphilis: The Iconography of Disease, in *AIDS: Cultural Analysis/Cultural Activism*, edited by D. Crimp. MIT Press.

Gilreath, S. 2007. Sexually Speaking: 'Don't Ask, Don't Tell' and the First Amendment after *Lawrence v. Texas*. 14 *Duke Journal of Gender Law and Policy*, 962.

Glover v. Glover [Ohio Ct. App. 1990] 586 N.E.2d 159.

Goldman v Weinberger [1986] 475 U.S. 503.

Goldstein, E. and Horowitz, L. 2003. *Lesbian Identity and Contemporary Psychotherapy: A Framework for Clinical Practice*. Analytic Press.

Goldstein, J.S. 2001. *War and Gender: How Gender Shapes the War System and Vice*. Cambridge University Press.

Gollaher, D.L. 1994. From Ritual to Science: The Medical Transformation of Circumcision in America. 28 *Journal of Social History*, 5.

Golner, J. 1993. An Overview of Legal Controls on Human Experimentation and the Regulatory Implications of Taking Professor Katz Seriously. 38 *Saint Louis University Law Journal*, 63.

Golombok, S., Spencer, A. and Rutter, M. 1983. Children in Lesbian and Single-parent Households: Psychosexual and Psychiatric Appraisal. 24 *Journal of Child Psychology and Psychiatry*, 551.

Gomstyn, A. 2007. 24 Volunteer for Boys-only Classes at Ramapo Freshman Center. *Journal News*, 30 May.

Gonzalez, B. 2004. Boys, Girls Separated in Poway. *South Dakota Union-Tribune*, 18 September.

Goodnough, A. 2009. Harvard Professor Jailed; Officer is Accused of Bias. *New York Times*, 21 July.

Goodridge v. Department of Public Health [Mass. 2003], 798 N.E.2d 941.

Gordon, L. 1990. The New Feminist Scholarship on the Welfare State, in *Women, the State, and Welfare*, edited by L. Gordon. University of Wisconsin Press.

Gottleib v. Gottleib [N.Y. Sup. Ct. 1985], 108 A.D.2d 120.

Gould, J.W. 1998. *Conducting Scientifically Crafted Child Custody Evaluations*. Sage.

Gouldstone, S. 2008. Family Law Survey Update. 82 *McKenzie: The National Magazine of Families Need Fathers* 5.

Government of Jamaica Ministry of Justice. 2005a. *Offences Against the Person Act*, § 76, L.N. 111/2005 [online]. Available at: http://www.moj.gov.jm/laws/statutes/Offences%20Against%20the%20Person%20Act.pdf [accessed: 8 January 2013].

Government of Jamaica Ministry of Justice. 2005b. *Offences Against the Person Act*, § 79, L.N. 111/2005 [online]. Available at: http://www.moj.gov.jm/laws/statutes/Offences%20Against%20the%20Person%20Act.pdf [accessed: 8 January 2013].

Grall, T. 2007. *Custodial Mothers and Fathers and Their Child Support: 2005*, Current Population Reports. U.S. Census Bureau. P60-234.

Grand Rapids Press. 2008. Dick and Jane Read – Just Not Together. *Grand Rapids Press*, 2 September.

Gray, H. et al. 2007. Male Circumcision for HIV Prevention in Young Men in Rakai, Uganda: A Randomised Trial. 369 *Lancet*, 657.

Green, L.W. et al. 2010. Male Circumcision and HIV Prevention: Insufficient Evidence and Neglected External Validity. 39 *American Journal of Preventive Medicine* 5, 479.

Green, R. 1987. *The Sissy Boy Syndrome and the Development of Homosexuality*. Yale University Press.

Green, R. et al. 1986. Lesbian Mothers and their Children: A Comparison with Solo Parent Heterosexual Mothers and their Children. 15 *Archives of Sexual Behavior*, 167.

Green, T. 2003. Discrimination in Workplace Dynamics: Toward a Structural Account of Disparate Treatment Theory. 38 *Harvard Civil Rights–Civil Liberties Law Review* 1, 91.

Green, T. 2007. A Structural Approach as Antidiscrimination Mandate: Locating Employer Wrong. 60 *Vanderbilt Law Review* 3, 849.

Greenhouse, S. 2007. Investigating Mislabeling of Workers. *New York Times*, 9 June.

Griggs v Duke Power Company [1971] 401 U.S. 424.

Gruber, A. 2007. The Feminist War on Crime. 92 *Iowa Law Review*, 741.

Gruber, J.E. and Morgan, P. 2005. *In the Company of Men: Male Dominance and Sexual Harassment*. Northeastern University Press.

Guerny, J. du and Sjoberg, E. 1999. Interrelationship between Gender Relations and the HIV/AIDS Epidemic: Some Possible Considerations for Policies and Programs, in *Health and Human Rights: A Reader*, edited by J.M. Mann et al. Routledge.

Gurian, M. 2002. *Boys and Girls Learn Differently!: A Guide for Teachers and Parents*. Jossey-Bass.

Gurian, M. 2003. *The Wonder of Girls: Understanding the Hidden Nature of Our Daughters*. Atria.

Gurian, M. and Stevens, K. 2005. *The Minds of Boys: Saving our Sons from Falling Behind in School and Life*. Jossey-Bass.

Gurian, M., Stevens, K. and Daniels, P. 2009. *Successful Single-sex Classrooms*. Jossey-Bass.

Hafez, M.M. 2006. *Manufacturing Human Bombs: The Making of Palestinian Suicide Bombers*. US Institute for Peace.

Hafez, M.M. 2007. Martyrdom Mythology in Iraq: How Jihadists Frame Suicide Terrorism in Videos and Biographies. 19 *Terrorism and Political Violence* 1, 95.

Hage, G. 2003. *Against Paranoid Nationalism: Searching for Hope in a Shrinking Society*. Pluto.

Hagman, L. and Nielsen, Z. 2002. *A Framework for Lasting Disarmament, Demobilisation, and Reintegration of Former Combatants in Crisis Situations*, International Peace Academy Workshop Report, New York, 12–13 December [online]. Available at: http://www.ipacademy.org/media/pdf/publications/framework_for_ddr.pdf [accessed: 3 January 2013].

Halberstam, J. 1998. *Female Masculinity*. Duke University Press.

Hall, S. 2002. Daubing the Drudges of Fury: Men, Violence and the Piety of the 'Hegemonic Masculinity' Thesis. 6 *Theoretical Criminology*, 35.

Halley, J. 2008. *Split Decisions: How and Why to Take a Break from Feminism*. Princeton University Press.

Halley, J., *sub nomine* Halley, I. 2009. Queer Theory by Men, in *Feminist and Queer Legal Theory: Intimate Encounters, Uncomfortable Conversations*, edited by M.A. Fineman et al. Ashgate.

Hamber, B. 2006. 'We Must Be Careful How We Emancipate Our Women': Shifting Masculinities in Post-Apartheid South Africa, 10 October [online]. Available at: http://www.brandonhamber.com/publications/Paper%20Careful%20how%20we%20emancipate.pdf [accessed: 3 January 2013].

Hamber, B. 2007. Masculinity and Transitional Justice: An Exploratory Essay. 1 *International Journal of Transitional Justice* 3, 375.

Hamshahri. 2004. Defa-e Janan-e az Harim Haram (Protecting the Shrines with Their Lives), no. 3395, May [online]. Available at: http://www.hamshahri.org/hamnews/1383/830311/Irshahr/_darsh.htm [accessed: 14 November 2010].

Hand, E. 1949. Circumcision and Venereal Disease. 60 *Archives of Dermatology and Syphilology*, 345.

Handrahan, L. 2004. Conflict, Gender, Ethnicity and Post-conflict Reconstruction. 35 *Security Dialogue* 4, 429.

Hanna, C. 1998. The Paradox of Hope: The Crime and Punishment of Domestic Violence. 39 *William and Mary Law Review*, 1505.

Harcourt, B. 2009. Henry Louis Gates and Racial Profiling: What's the Problem? Social Science Research Network [online]. Available at: http://ssrn.com/abstract=1474809 [accessed: 5 December 2011].

Harding, R. 2010. *Regulating Sexuality: Legal Consciousness in Lesbian and Gay Lives*. Routledge.

Harris, A.P. 1990. Race and Essentialism in Feminist Legal Theory. 42 *Stanford Law Review* 3, 581.

Harris, A.P. 2000. Gender, Violence, Race, and Criminal Justice. 52 *Stanford Law Review* 4, 777.

Harris, C.I. 1996. Finding Sojourner's Truth: Race, Gender, and the Institution of Property. 18 *Cardozo Law Review* 2, 309.

Harrison, C. 2008. Creating a National Feminist Agenda: Coalition Building in the 1970s, in *Feminist Coalitions: Historical Perspectives on Second-wave Feminism in the United States*, edited by S. Gilmore. University of Illinois Press.

Harrison, L. and Hillier, L. 1999. What should be the 'Subject' of Sex Education? 20 *Discourse* 2, 279.

Harvard Journal of Law and Gender. 2010. 33 *Symposium: Feminist Perspectives on Masculinities* 2.

Harvard Law Review. 1989. Developments in the Law: Sexual Orientation and the Law. 102 *Harvard Law Review*, 1629.

Hasso, F.S. 2005. Discursive and Political Deployments by/of the 2002 Palestinian Women Suicide Bombers/Martyrs.81 *Feminist Review, Bodily Interventions*, 23.

Hawk, F. 2006. Put Strategies to Good Use for Boys. *Post & Courier*, 20 April.

Hawkesworth, Mary. 2003. Congressional Enactments of Race–Gender: Toward a Theory of Raced–Gendered Institutions. 97 *American Political Science Review* 4, 529.

Haywood, C. and Mac an Ghaill, M. 2003. *Men and Masculinities: Theory, Research and Social Practice*. Open University Press.

Hazelwood School District v United States [1977] 433 U.S. 299.

Hearn, J. 1996. Is Masculinity Dead? A Critique of the Concept of Masculinity, in *Understanding Masculinities*, edited by M. Mac an Ghaill. Open University Press.

Hearn, J. 2004. From Hegemonic Masculinity to the Hegemony of Men. 5 *Feminist Theory* 1, 49.

Hearn, J. and Pringle, K. 2006. *European Perspectives on Men and Masculinities*. Palgrave Macmillan.

Heath v Perdue Farms, Inc. [D. Md. 2000] 87 F. Supp. 2d 452.

Hechinger, S.R. 2011. Juvenile Life Without Parole: An Antidote to Congress's One-way Criminal Law Ratchet? 35 *New York University Review of Law & Social Change* 408, 494.

Hedonism Resorts. 2011 [online]. Available at: http://hedonismresorts.com/ [accessed: 15 January 2011].

Heilman, M.E., Fuchs, A.S. and Tamkins, M.M. 2004. Penalties for Success: Reactions to Women who Succeed at Male Gender-typed Tasks. 89 *Journal of Applied Psychology* 3, 416.

Heise, L. 1997. Violence, Sexuality and Women's Lives, in *The Gender/Sexuality Reader: Culture, History, Political Economy*, edited by R. Lancaster and M. Di Leonardo. Routledge.

Heise, L. and Elias, C. 1995. Transforming AIDS Prevention to Meet Women's Needs: A Focus on Developing Countries. 40 *Social Science and Medicine*, 931.

Helfer, L.R. 2002. Overlegalizing Human Rights: International Relations Theory and the Commonwealth Caribbean Backlash against Human Rights Regimes. 102 *Columbia Law Review*, 1832.

Hellsten, S.K. 2004. Rationalising Circumcision: From Tradition to Fashion, from Public Health to Individual Freedom – Critical Notes on Cultural Persistence of the Practice of Mutilations. 30 *Journal of Medical Ethics*, 248.

Henry, K. and Evans, T. 2007. No Compassion for Dancehall. *Jamaica Gleaner* [online]. Available at: http://www.jamaica-gleaner.com/gleaner/20071007/ent/ent2.html [accessed: 8 January 2013].

Henry, R. 2006. Jamaican Music is a Multi-billion Business, but Tax Avoidance High. *Jamaica Observer* [online]. Available at: https://www.jamaicaobserver.com/news/97063_Jamaican-music-is-a-multi-billion-business--but-tax-avoidance-high [accessed: 8 January 2013].

Hernandez-Cortez v Hernandez [D. Kan. 2003] 2003 WL 22519678.

Herring, J. 2009. Autonomy and Family Law, in *Rights, Gender and Family Law*, edited by J. Wallbank, S. Choudhry and J. Herring. Routledge-Cavendish.

Hertzler v. Hertzler [Wy. 1996] 908 P.2d 946.

Hickey, A.M. 2006. The Sexual Savage: Race Science and the Medicalization of Black Masculinity, in *Medicalized Masculinities*, edited by D. Rosenfeld and C.A. Faircloth. Temple University Press.

Higgins, L. 2006. Legislators Push to Allow All-boy, All-girl Schools. *Detroit Free Press*, 15 June.

Higgins, T. 1996. Anti-essentialism, Relativism, and Human Rights. 19 *Harvard Women's Law Journal*, 89.

Higgins, T.E. 2004. Why Feminists Can't (or Shouldn't) Be Liberals. 72 *Fordham Law Review* 5, 1629.

Hilpern, K. 2008. Ending it All. *The Guardian*, 24 September.

Hing, J. 2012. Bobby Jindal, Using ALEC Playbook, Radically Reshapes Public Education. *ColorLines* [online]. Available at: http://colorlines.com/archives/2012/04/bobby_jindal_using_alec_playbook_signs_education_reform_overhaul.html [accessed: 23 April 2012].

HIV Incidence, Behaviour and Communication Survey. 2008 [online]. Available at: http://avert.org/safricastats.htm [accessed: 21 January 2013].

Hobson, B. and Morgan, D. 2002. Introduction: Making Men into Fathers, in *Making Men into Fathers*, edited by B. Hobson. Cambridge University Press.

Hochschild, A. 1989. *The Second Shift*. Viking.

Hockey, J. et al. 2007. *Mundane Heterosexualities: From Theory to Practice*. Palgrave Macmillan.

Hodes M., ed.. 1999. *Sex, Love, Race: Crossing Boundaries in North American History*. New York University Press.

Hodges, F.M. 2005. The Antimasturbation Crusade in Antebellum American Medicine. 2 *Journal of Sexual Medicine*, 722.

Hoeffer, Beverly. 1981. Children's Acquisition of Sex-role Behavior in Lesbian-mother Families. 51 *American Journal of Orthopsychiatry*, 536.

Hoffman Plastic Compounds, Inc. v NLRB [2002] 535 U.S. 137.

Holland, J. et al. 1992. Risk, Power and the Possibility of Pleasure: Young Women and Safer Sex. 4 *AIDS Care* 3, 273.

Holland, J. et al. 1998. *The Male in the Head: Young People, Heterosexuality and Power*. Tufnell Press.

Hollandsworth, M. 1995. Gay Men Creating Families through Surro-gay Arrangements: A Paradigm for Reproductive Freedom. 3 *American University Journal of Gender, Social Policy, and the Law* 2, 183.

Holmes v. Holmes [Ark. Ct. App. 2007] 255 S.W.3d 482.

Holt, E. et al. 2007. *Timing and Duration of Student Participation in Special Education in the Primary Grades*. National Centre for Education Statistics.

Hondagneu-Sotelo, P. 2001. *Domestica: Immigrant Workers Cleaning and Caring in the Shadows of Affluence*, 2nd edn. University of California Press.

Hotvedt, M.E. and Mandel, J. Barclay. 1982. Children of Lesbian Mothers, in *Homosexuality, Social, Psychological, and Biological Issues*, edited by W. Paul. Sage.

Howarth, J.W. 2002. Executing White Masculinities: Learning from Karla Faye Tucker. 81 *Oregon Law Review* 1, 183.

Howson, R. 2005. *Challenging Hegemonic Masculinity*. Routledge.

Hughes, Z. 2009. The Gates Arrest: Racism? Not so Much. Classism? You Bettcha. *The Huffington Post*, 30 July [online]. Available at: http://www.huffingtonpost.com/zondra-hughes/the-gates-arrest-racism-n_b_246647.html [accessed: 5 December 2011].

Human Rights Watch. 2004a. *Between Hope and Fear: Intimidation and Attacks against Women in Public Life in Afghanistan*. Human Rights Watch.

Human Rights Watch. 2004b. Hated To Death: Homophobia, Violence and Jamaica's HIV/AIDS Epidemic [online]. Available at: http://www.hrw.org/en/node/11894/section/14 [accessed: 8 January 2013].

Hunter, N. and Polikoff, N. 1976. Custody Rights of Lesbian Mothers: Legal Theory and Litigation Strategy. 25 *Buffalo Law Review* 3, 691.

Hunter, R. ed. 2009. *Rethinking Equality Projects in Law: Feminist Challenges*. Hart.

Huntington, C. 2010. Embracing the Affective Family. 33 *Harvard Journal of Law and Gender*, 321.

Hurst, J.W. 1950. *The Growth of American Law: The Law Makers*. Little, Brown and Company.

Hurst, J.W. 1977. *Law and Social Order in the United States*. Cornell University Press.

Hutchinson, D. 1997. Out Yet Unseen: A Racial Critique of Gay and Lesbian Legal Theory and Political Discourse. 19 *Connecticut Law Review*, 561.

Hutchinson, D. 1999. Ignoring the Intersection of Race: Heteronormativity, Critical Race Theory and Anti-racist Politics. 47 *Buffalo Law Review* 1, 1.

Hutchinson, D. 2000. 'Gay Rights' for 'Gay Whites'?: Race, Sexual Identity, and Equal Protection Discourse. 85 *Cornell Law Review* 5, 1358.

Hutchinson, D.L. 2001. Identity Crisis: 'Intersectionality,' 'Multidimensionality,' and the Development of an Adequate Theory of Subordination. 6 *Michigan Journal Race & Law* 285, 307.

Hyde, J.S. 2005. The Gender Similarities Hypothesis. 60 *American Psychologist*, 581.

Hylton, M.O. 1991. Parental Leaves and Poor Women: Paying the Price for Time Off. 52 *University of Pittsburgh Law Review*, 475.

Ibrahim, F. 2009. Al-Shahada: A Centre of the Shiite System of Belief, in *Dying for Faith, Religiously Motivated Violence in the Contemporary World*, edited by M. Al-Rasheed and M. Shterin. I.B. Tauris.

Immigration and Nationality Act [2006] 8 U.S.C. §§ 1255, 1324a.

Imrie, J. et al. 2007. Biomedical HIV Prevention – and Social Science. 370 *Lancet*, 10.

In re Breish [Pa. Super. Ct. 1981], 434 A.2d 815.

In re Marriage Cases [Cal. 2008], 183 P.3d 384.

Ingham, R. 2005. 'We Didn't Cover that at School': Education against Pleasure or Education for Pleasure? 5 *Sex Education* 4, 375.

Ingraham, C. 2008. *Heterosexuality: A Reader*. Routledge.

International Gay and Lesbian Human Rights Commission. 2009. Jamaica: Don't Boycott Us! [online]. Available at: http://www.iglhrc.org/cgi-bin/iowa/article/takeaction/partners/888.html [accessed: 10 August 2009].

Introvigne, M. 2009. Of 'Cultists' and 'Martyrs': The Study of New Religious Movements and Suicide Terrorism in Conversation, in *Dying for Faith, Religiously Motivated Violence in the Contemporary World*, edited by M. Al-Rasheed and M. Shterin. I.B. Tauris.

Irvine, J.M. 2000. Doing it with Words: Discourse and the Sex Education Culture Wars. 27 *Critical Inquiry*, 58.

J.L.P v. D.J.P. [Mo. Ct. App. 1982] 643 S.W.2d 865.

J.P. v. P.W. [Mo. Ct. App. 1989], 772 S.W.2d 786.

Jacklin, A. and Lacey, C. 1997. Gender Integration in the Infant Classroom: A Case Study. 23 *British Education Research Journal*, 623.

Jackson, S. 1999. *Heterosexuality in Question*. Sage.

Jagose, A. 1996. *Queer Theory: An Introduction*. New York University Press.

Jamail, D. 2009. Going AWOL for Post Traumatic Care. *Pacific Free Press*, 12 December.

James, A.N. 2007. *Teaching the Male Brain: How Boys Think, Feel and Learn in School*. Corwin Press.

James-Johnson, A. 2007. Fort Lauderdale Church Faces Furor for Starting Gay Congregation in Jamaica. *South Florida Sun-Sentinel*, 29 May.

Jan, T. 2009. No Charge, but Gates Case Seethes. *Boston Globe*, 22 July.

Jenkins, A. 1990. *Invitations to Responsibility: The Therapeutic Engagement of Men who are Violent and Abusive*. Dulwich Centre Publications.

Jenkins, K. 2006. Constitutional Lessons for the Next Generation of Public Single Sex Elementary and Secondary Schools. 47 *William and Mary Law Review* 6, 1953.

Jewkes, R.K. et al. 2010. Intimate Partner Violence, Relationship Power Inequity, and Incidence of HIV Infection in Young Women in South Africa: A Cohort Study. 376 *The Lancet*, 41.

Johnson v AK Steel Corporation [S.D. Oh. 2008] 2008 WL2184230.

Johnson, P. 2005. *Love, Heterosexuality and Society: Sociological Perspectives on Love and Heterosexuality*. Routledge.

Johnston, J.R., Kline, M. and Tschann, J.M. 1989. Ongoing Postdivorce Conflict: Effects on Children of Joint Custody and Frequent Access. 59 *American Journal of Orthopsychiatry* 4, 577.

Joint United Nations Programme on HIV/AIDS. 2007. New Data on Male Circumcision and HIV: Policy and Programme Implications [online]. Available at: http://www.who.int/hiv/mediacentre/MCrecommendations_en.pdf [accessed: 21 January 2013].

Joint United Nations Programme on HIV/AIDS and WHO. 2009. *AIDS Epidemic Update*. December.

Jordan, A. 2009. Dads aren't Demons, Mums aren't Madonnas: Constructions of Fatherhood and Masculinities in the (Real) Fathers 4 Justice Campaign. 31 *Journal of Social Welfare and Family Law*, 419.

Jordan, E. 1995. Fighting Boys and Fantasy Play: The Construction of Masculinity in the Early Years of School. 7 *Gender and Education*, 69.

Kaganas, F. and Day Sclater, S. 2004. Contact Disputes: Narrative Constructions of 'Good' Parents. 12 *Feminist Legal Studies* 1, 1.

Kahn, J.S. 2009. *An Introduction to Masculinities*. Wiley-Blackwell.

Kang, J. 2005. Trojan Horses of Race. 188 *Harvard Law Review*, 1489.

Kanneh, K. 1996. Sisters under the Skin: A Politics of Heterosexuality, in *Feminism and Sexuality: A Reader*, edited by S. Jackson and S. Scott. Edinburgh University Press.

Karjanen, D. 2008. Gender, Race, and Nationality in the Making of Mexican Migrant Labor in the United States. 35 *Latin American Perspectives* 1, 51.

Kaplan, A. and Sedney, M. 1980. *Psychology and Sex Roles*. Little, Brown.

Karpiak, C. et al. 2007. University Students from Single-sex and Coeducational High Schools: Differences in Majors and Attitudes at a Catholic University. 31 *Psychology of Women Quarterly*, 282.

Karsh, E. 2002. *The Iran–Iraq War, 1980–1988*. Osprey Publishing.

Karst, K.L. 1991. The Pursuit of Manhood and the Desegregation of the Armed Forces. 38 *University of California Los Angeles Law Review* 3, 499.

Katzenstein, M.F. 1999. *Faithful and Fearless: Moving Feminist Protest Inside the Church and Military*. Princeton University Press.

Kaufman, M. 2001. Strategic Planning to End Men's Violence: The White Ribbon Campaign. 27 *Aggressive Behaviour* 3, 158.

Kay, H.H. 1985. Equality and Difference: The Case of Pregnancy. 1 *Berkeley Women's Law Journal*, 1.

Keegan, J. 1993. *A History of Warfare*. Alfred A. Knopf.

Kelley, R.D.G. 1993. 'We are Not what we Seem': Rethinking Black Working-class Opposition in the Jim Crow South. 80 *Journal of American History* 1, 75.

Kelly, K.A. 2003. *Domestic Violence and the Politics of Privacy*. Cornell University Press.

Kelly, L. 1996. When Does the Speaking Profit Us?: Reflections on the Challenges of Developing Feminist Perspectives on Abuse and Violence by Women, in

Women, Violence and Male Power: Feminist Activism, Research and Practice, edited by M. Hester. Sage.

Kelly, L. 2003. Disabusing the Definition of Domestic Abuse: How Women Batter Men and the Role of the Feminist State. 30 *Florida State University Law Review*, 791.

Kenedy, R.A. 2004. *Fathers for Justice: The Rise of a New Social Movement in Canada as a Case Study of Collective Identity Formation*. Caravan.

Kenning, C. 2005. Single Sex Schools: Jefferson County Officials Think Teaching Boys and Girls Separately at a Pair of Middle Schools would Reduce Distractions and Boost Achievement. *Courier-Journal*, 16 October.

Kerrigan v. Commissioner of Public Health [Conn. 2008] 957 A.2d 407.

Kessler, M. 1995. Lawyers and Social Change in the Postmodern World. 29 *Law & Society Review*, 769.

Khabar Online. 2009. Zaribafan: Khanevadeh Neda Agha Sultan Taht-e Poshesh Bonyad Shahid Gharar Migirad (Zaribafan: The Family of Neda Agha Sultan will be under the Cover of the Martyrs' Foundations), 7 October [online]. Available at: http://www.khabaronline.ir/news-20369.aspx [accessed: 7 January 2013].

Khalili, L. 2007. *Heroes and Martyrs of Palestine: The Politics of National Commemorations*. Cambridge University Press.

Khan, A. 2009. Single-sex Campus Aims to Divide and Conquer. *Los Angeles Times*, 30 November.

Khomeini, R. 1982. *Sahifa-yi Nur* (The Book of Light), Vol. 21. Vezarat-e Ershad Eslami.

Khosrokhavar, F. 2002. *Suicide Bombers Allah's New Martyrs*, translated by D. Macey. Pluto.

Kickbusch, I. 2006. The Health Society: The Need for Theory. 60 *Journal of Epidemiology and Community Health*, 561.

Kimmel, M.S. 1994. *Masculinity as Homophobia: Fear, Shame, and Silence in the Construction of Gender Identity, in Theorizing Masculinities*, edited by Harry Brod and Michael Kaufman. Sage.

Kimmel, M.S. 1997a. Integrating Men into the Curriculum. 4 *Duke Journal of Gender, Law, and Policy*, 181.

Kimmel, M.S. 1997b. Masculinity as Homophobia, in *Toward a New Psychology of Gender: A Reader*, edited by M.M. Gergen and S. Davis. Rutledge Press.

Kimmel, M.S. 2005a. *Manhood in America: A Cultural History*. Oxford University Press.

Kimmel, M.S. 2005b. *The Gender of Desire: Essays on Male Sexuality*. S.U.N.Y. Press.

Kimmel, M.S. 2006. *Manhood in America: A Cultural History*, 2nd edn. Oxford University Press.

Kimmel, M.S. 2010. *Misframing Men: The Politics of Contemporary Masculinities*. Rutgers University Press.

Kimmel, M. n.d. No Safe Place: Violence against Women. Interview [online]. Available at: www.pbs.org/kued/nosafeplace/interv/kimmel.html [accessed: 17 May 2013].

Kimmel, M. and Messner, M. 2010. *Men's Lives*, 8th edn. Allyn and Bacon.

Kimmel, M. and Plante, R., eds. 2004. *Sexualities: Identities, Behaviours, and Society*. Oxford University Press.

Kimmel, M.S. and Traver, A. 2005. Mentoring Masculinities: Race and Class in the (Re-) construction of Gender in the USA and the UK. 2 *Irish Journal of Sociology*, 213.

Kindlon, D. and Thomson, M. 1999. *Raising Cain: Protecting the Emotional Life of Boys*, 1st edn, with T. Barker. Ballantine Books.

Kingma, K. 2001. *Demobilisation and Reintegration of Ex-combatants in Post-war and Transition Countries: Trends and Challenges of External Support*. Bonn International Center for Conversion [online]. Available at: http://www.bicc.de/uploads/tx_bicctools/demobilisation.pdf [accessed: 3 January 2013].

Kingsbury, A. 2009. New Mental Health Policy Came Days before Fort Hood Shooting, *U.S. News & World Report*, 5 November. WLNR 22250115 [online]. Available via https://lawschool.westlaw.com/shared/signon10.asp?path=%2fDesktopDefault.aspx [accessed: 31 May 2013].

Kirby, P. 2006. *Vulnerability and Violence*. Pluto.

Kline, M. 1989. Race, Racism and Feminist Legal Theory. 12 *Harvard Women's Law Journal*, 115.

Kline, M., Johnston, J.R. and Tschann, J.M. 1991. The Long Shadow of Marital Conflict: A Model of Children's Postdivorce Adjustment. 53 *Journal of Marriage and the Family* 2, 297.

Kline, M. et al. 1989. Children's Adjustment in Joint and Sole Physical Custody Families. 25 *Developmental Psychology* 3, 430.

Knight, M. and Özerdem, A. 2004. Guns, Camps and Cash: Disarmament, Demobilization and Reinsertion of Former Combatants in Transitions from War to Peace. 41 *Journal of Peace Research* 4, 499.

Koplow, D.A. and Schrag, P.G. 1991. Carrying a Big Carrot: Linking Multilateral Disarmament and Development Assistance. 91 *Columbia Law Review* 5, 993.

Koppelman, A. 1994. Why Discrimination against Lesbians and Gay Men is Sex Discrimination. 69 *New York University Law Review* 2, 197.

Koth, M. 2005. To End a War: Demobilization and Reintegration of Paramilitaries in Colombia, Paper 43. Bonn International Center for Conversion.

Kreisberg, L. 2006. *Mothers in Poverty: A Study of Fatherless Families*. Aldine Publishing Company.

Krueger, A.B. and Maleková, J. 2003. Education, Poverty and Terrorism: Is There a Causal Connection? 17 *The Journal of Economic Perspectives* 4, 119.

Kruse, A. 1992. '… We Have Learnt Not Just to Sit Back, Twiddle Our Thumbs and Let Them Take Over.' Single-sex Settings and the Development of a Pedagogy for Girls and a Pedagogy for Boys in Danish Schools. 4 *Gender and Education*, 81.

Laird, J. et al. 2006. *Dropout Rates in the United States: 2002 and 2003*. National Centre for Education Statistics.

Lamb, M. 2000. The History of Research on Father Involvement: An Overview, in *Fatherhood: Research, Interventions, and Policies*, edited by H. Peters, R. Day et al. Hawthorne Press.

Laplante, L.J. and Theidon, K. 2006. Transitional Justice in Times of Conflict: Colombia's Ley de Justicia y Paz. 28 *Michigan Journal of International Law* 1, 49.

Laqueur, T. 1992. *Making Sex: Bodies and Gender from the Greeks to Freud*. Harvard University Press.

LaRossa, R. 1997. The Modernization of Fatherhood: A Social and Political History. 103 *The American Journal of Sociology* 4, 1158.

Lawrence v. Texas [2003] 539 U.S. 558.

Lawrence, D.H. 1968. Self-pity, in *Complete Poems*, edited by V. de Sola Pinto and W.F. Roberts. Penguin, 189.

Lawrence III, C.R. 1987. The Id, the Ego, and Equal Protection: Reckoning with Unconscious Racism. 39 *Stanford Law Review* 2, 317.

Law, S. 1988. Homosexuality and the Social Meaning of Gender. 1988 *Wisconsin Law Review* 2, 187.

The Laws of Jamaica. 1938. Vol. 5, Unnatural Offenses, § 66.

Leake, D.O. and Leake, B.L. 1992. Islands of Hope: Milwaukee's African American Immersion Schools. 61 *The Journal of Negro Education* 1, 24.

Lee, M.-Y. 2002. A Model of Children's Postdivorce Behavioral Adjustment in Maternal and Dual Resident Arrangements. 23 *Journal of Family Issues* 5, 672.

Lee III, J.W. 2006. Class Warfare 1988–2005 over Top Individual Income Tax Rates: Teeter-totter from Soak-the-rich to Robin-Hood-in-reverse. 2 *Hastings Business Law Journal* 47, 147.

Lesko, N. 2000a. Introduction, in *Masculinities at School*, edited by Nancy Lesko. Sage.

Lesko, N. 2000b. Preparing To ~~Teach~~ Coach: Tracking the Gendered Relations of Dominance On and Off the Football Field, in *Masculinities at School*, edited by Nancy Lesko. Sage.

Lessig, L. 1995. The Regulation of Social Meaning. 62 *University of Chicago Law Review*, 943.

Leszkay, B. 2003. Feminism on the Front Lines. 14 *Hastings Women's Law Journal*, 133.

Levit, N. 1996. Feminism for Men: Legal Ideology and the Construction of Maleness. 43 *University of California Los Angeles Law Review* 4, 1037.

Levit, N. 1999. Separating Equals: Educational Research and the Long-term Consequences of Sex Segregation. 67 *George Washington Law Review* 3, 451.

Levit, N. 2001. Male Prisoners: Privacy, Suffering, and the Legal Construction of Masculinity, in *Prison Masculinities*, edited by Don Sabo et al. Temple University Press.

Levit, N. 2005. Embracing Segregation: The Jurisprudence of Choice and Diversity in Race and Sex Separatism in Schools. 2 *University of Illinois Law Review*, 455.

Levit, N. 2010. Separate Silos: Marginalizing Men in Feminist Theory and Forgetting Females in Masculinities Studies. SSRN [online]. Available at: http://ssrn.com/abstract=1550365 [accessed: 21 May 2013].

Lewin, A.M. 2006. Can Boys Really Not Sit Still in School? *ABC News*, 26 January.

Lewis, J. 2005. Fathering Practices in Twenty-six Intact Families and the Implications for Child Contact. 1 *International Journal of Law in Context*, 81–99.

Libby, W. 2007. Single-sex Education Worthy of its Revival. *Columbia Tribune*, 15 April.

Linder, M. 2000. *Wars of Attrition: Vietnam, the Business Roundtable and the Decline of Construction Unions*, 2nd edn. Fanpihua Press.

Lister, R. 2006. Children (But Not Women) First: New Labour, Child Welfare and Gender. 26 *Critical Social Policy* 2, 315.

Littleton, C.A. 1987. Equality and Feminist Legal Theory. 48 *University of Pittsburgh Law Review*, 1043.

Llewellyn, K.N. 1930. A Realistic Jurisprudence: The Next Step. 30 *Columbia Law Review* 431, 455.

Llewellyn, K.N. 1945. Group Prejudice and Social Education, in *Civilization and Group Relationships*, edited by R.M. MacIver.

Local Uses of Funds, 20 U.S.C. § 7215(a)(23)(2006).

Lofton v. Kearney [S.D. Fla. 2001], 157 F. Supp. 2d 1372.

Lofton v. Secretary of Department of Children and Family Services [11th Cir. 2004], 358 F.3d 804.

Lorber, J. 1994. *Paradoxes of Gender*. Yale University Press.

Luepnitz, D.A. 1982. *Child Custody*. DC Heath and Company.

Lundin v. Lundin [La. Ct. App. 1990], 563 So.2d 1273.

Lupton, D. 1994. *Medicine as Culture: Illness, Disease and the Body in Western Societies*. Sage.

Lupton, D. 1995. *The Imperative of Health: Public Health and the Regulated Body*. Sage.

Luton, D. 2009. Buggery Laws Firm – PM Says Life or 15 Years for Same-sex Offence Breaches. *Jamaica Gleaner* [online]. Available at: http://www.jamaica-gleaner.com/gleaner/20090304/lead/lead1.html [accessed: 8 January 2013].

Lynch v Freeman [6th Cir. 1987] 817 F.2d 380.

M.J.P. v. J.G.P. [Okla. 1982], 640 P.2d 966.

Macaulay, S. 2005. The New Versus Old Realism: 'Things Ain't What They Used to Be.' 2005 *Wisconsin Law Review*, 365.

Macaulay, S., Friedman, L.M. and Mertz, E. 2007. *Law in Action: A Socio-legal Reader*. Foundation Press.

Maccoby, E.E. et al. 1993. Postdivorce Roles of Mothers and Fathers in the Lives of their Children. 7 *Journal of Family Psychology* 1, 24.
MacKinnon, C.A. 1979. *Sexual Harassment of Working Women: A Case of Sex Discrimination*. Yale University Press.
MacKinnon, C.A. 1983. Feminism, Marxism, Method, and the State: Toward a Feminist Jurisprudence. 8 *Signs: Journal of Women in Culture and Society* 4, 635.
MacKinnon, C.A. 1987. *Feminism Unmodified: Discourses on Life and Law*, 1st edn. Harvard University Press.
MacKinnon, C.A. 1988. Privacy v. Equality: Beyond *Roe v. Wade*, in *Feminism Unmodified: Discourses on Life and Law*. Harvard University Press.
MacKinnon, C.A. 1989. *Toward a Feminist Theory of the State*. Harvard University Press.
MacKinnon, C.A. 2004. The Road Not Taken: Sex Equality in *Lawrence v. Texas*. 65 *Ohio State Law Journal*, 1081.
Maclin, T. 1998. *Terry v. Ohio's* Fourth Amendment Legacy: Black Men and Police Discretion. 72 *Saint John's Law Review* 3–4, 1271.
Mael, F. et al. 2005. Single-sex versus Coeducational Schooling: A Systematic Review. Available at: www.ed.gov/rschstat/eval/other/single-sex/single-sex.pdf [accessed: 17 May 2013].
Maguire, A. 2009. 'Security Starts with the Law': The Role of International Law in the Protection of Women's Security Post-conflict, in *The Role of International Law in Rebuilding Societies after Conflict: Great Expectations*, edited by Brett Bowden et al. Cambridge University Press.
Mahoney, R. 2006. Boys, Girls Divide, Conquer Lessons. *Orlando Sentinel*, 20 June.
Maier, M. and Messerschmidt, J.W. 1998. Commonalities, Conflicts, and Contradiction in Organizational Masculinities: Exploring the Gendered Genesis of the Challenger Disaster. 35 *Canadian Review of Sociology and Anthropology* 3, 325.
Mallinder, L. 2008. *Amnesty, Human Rights and Political Transitions: Bridging the Peace and Justice Divide*. Hart.
Manchanda, R. 2001. Ambivalent Gains in South Asian Conflicts, in *The Aftermath: Women in Post-conflict Transformation*, edited by Sheila Meintjes et al. Zed Books.
Mandel, L. and Shakeshaft, C. 2000. Heterosexism in Middle Schools, in *Masculinities at School*, edited by Nancy Lesko. Sage.
Manochehr, D. 1997. Symbolic and Utilitarian Political Value of a Tradition: Martyrdom in the Iranian Political Culture. 59 *The Review of Politics* 3, *Non-Western Political Thought*, 489.
Marion, N. 1994. *A History of Federal Crime Control Initiatives 1960–1993*. Praeger.
Martin, P.Y. 2003. 'Said and Done' versus 'Saying and Doing': Gendering Practices, Practicing Gender at Work. 17 *Gender & Society* 3, 342.

Martin, S.E. 1999. Police Force or Police Service? Gender and Emotional Labor. 561 *Annals of the American Academy of Political and Social Science*, 111.

Maryland Medical Journal. 1894. Circumcision for the Correction of Sexual Crimes among the Negro Race. 30 *Maryland Medical Journal*, 345.

Mason, M.A. 1999. *The Custody Wars: Why Children Are Losing the Legal Battle, and What We Can Do About It*. Basic Books.

Mason, M.A. and Goulden, M. 2004a. Do Babies Matter (Part II)? Closing the Baby Gap. 90 *Academe* 6, 10.

Mason, M.A. and Goulden, M. 2004b. Marriage and Baby Blues: Re-defining Gender Equity. 596 *The Annals of the American Academy of Political and Social Science* 1, 86.

Mass, L. 1990. *Dialogues of the Sexual Revolution: Homosexuality and Sexuality—Volume I*. Harworth Press.

Masturbate-a-thon. 2010 [online]. Available at: www.masturbate-a-thon.co.uk [accessed: 31 October 2010].

Matsuda, M.J. 1992. When the First Quail Calls: Multiple Consciousness as Jurisprudential Method. 14 *Women's Rights Law Reporter*, 297.

May, E.T. 1999. *Homeward Bound: American Families in the Cold War Era*. Basic Books.

May, L., Strikwerda, R. and Hopkins, P. 1996. *Rethinking Masculinity: Philosophical Explorations in the Light of Feminism*. Rowman & Littlefield.

May, S. 2001. Child Custody and Visitation. 2 *Georgetown Journal of Gender and the Law* 2, 382.

Mayeri, S. 2006. The Strange Career of Jane Crow. 18 *Yale Journal of Law & the Humanities* 187, 272.

Mazur, D. 1999. A Call to Arms. 22 *Harvard Women's Law Journal*, 39.

McCall, L. 2005. The Complexity of Intersectionality. 30 *Signs: Journal of Women in Culture and Society* 3, 1771.

McCandless, J. and Sheldon, S. 2010. The Human Fertilisation and Embryology Act (2008) and the Tenacity of the Sexual Family Form. 73 *Modern Law Review* 2, 175.

McClain, C. 1988. Of Medicine, Race and American Law: The Bubonic Plague Outbreak of 1900. 13 *Law & Social Inquiry*, 447.

McCoy, S.I., Watts, C.H. and Padian, N.S. Preventing HIV Infection: Turning the Tide for Young Women. *The Lancet* [online]. Available via: http://www.thelancet.com/journals/lancet/article/PIIS0140-6736(10)61309-8/fulltext?_eventId=login [accessed: 17 May 2013].

McDonnell Douglas Corp v Green [1973] 411 U.S. 792.

McEnaney, L. 2000. Atomic Age Motherhood: Maternalism and Militarism in the 1950s, in *Women's America: Refocusing the Past*, edited by L.K. Kerber and J. Sherron De Hart. Oxford University Press.

McFadden, D. 2008. A First Amendment Analysis of Military Regulations Restricting the Wearing of Military Uniforms by Members of the Individual

Ready Reserve Who Participate in Politically Theme Theatrical Productions. 49 *Boston College Law Review*, 1153.
McGee, J.M. 1882. Genital Irritation as a Cause of Nervous Disorders. 2 *Mississippi Valley Medical Monthly*, 103.
McGinley, A.C. 1993. Credulous Courts and the Tortured Trilogy: The Improper Use of Summary Judgment in Title VII and ADEA Cases. 34 *Boston College Law Review* 2, 203.
McGinley A.C. 2004. Masculinities at Work. 83 *Oregon Law Review* 2, 359.
McGinley A.C. 2007a. Babes and Beefcake: Exclusive Hiring Arrangements and Sexy Dress Codes. 14 *Duke Journal of Gender, Law, and Policy*, 257.
McGinley, A.C. 2007b. Harassing 'Girls' at the Hard Rock: Masculinities in Sexualized Environments. 2007 *University of Illinois Law Review*, 1229.
McGinley, A.C. 2008. Creating Masculine Identities: Bullying and Harassment 'Because of Sex.' 79 *University of Colorado Law Review* 4, 1151.
McGinley, A.C. 2009a. Hillary Clinton, Sarah Palin and Michelle Obama: Performing Gender, Race, and Class on the Campaign Trail. 86 *Denver University Law Review* 3, 709.
McGinley, A.C. 2009b. Reproducing Gender on Law School Faculties. 1 *Brigham Young University Law Review*, 99.
McGinley, A.C. 2010. Ricci v. DeStefano: A Masculinities Theory Analysis. 33 *Harvard Journal of Law and Gender* 2, 581.
McKay, S. and Mazurana, D. 2004. *Where Are the Girls? Girls in Fighting Forces in Northern Uganda, Sierra Leone, and Mozambique: Their Lives during and after War*. International Centre for Human Rights and Democratic Development.
McNay, L. 1992. *Foucault and Feminism*. Polity.
McNeil, D.G. 2010. US Apologizes for Syphilis Tests in Guatemala. *The New York Times*, 1 October.
McVeigh, T. 2010. GPs Fail to Help Men Suffering Depression. *The Observer*, 2 May.
McWilliams, M. et al. 1995. *Tackling Domestic Violence: A Policy for Northern Ireland*. Department of Health and Social Services and the Northern Ireland Office.
MDRP [Multi-country Demobilization & Reintegration Program]. 2007. MDRP Launches Learning for Equality, Access and Peace Program, 4 December [online]. Available at: http://www.mdrp.org/PDFs/N&N_16_07.pdf [accessed: 3 January 2013].
MDRP. 2009. Regional Activities [online]. Available at: http://www.mdrp.org/regional_act_main.htm [accessed: 3 January 2013].
Mead, S. 2006. The Evidence Suggests Otherwise: The Truth about Boys and Girls. Education Sector [online]. Available at: http://www.educationsector.org/research/research_show.htm?doc_id=378705 [accessed: 11 February 2010].
Mehr News. 2004. Avalin Yegan Esteshhadi dar Iran Elaam Mojoodiat Kard (the First Martyred Union in Iran Proclaimed its Availability), 3

December [online]. Available at: http://www.mehrnews.com/fa/NewsDetail.aspx?NewsID=135818 [accessed: 7 January 2013].

Mehrnews. 2004. Bayani-e Setad-e Pasdasht Nehzat-e Jahani-e Islam dar Eteraz be Tagheer Naam-e Khiaybaan-e Khaled Eslamboli (The Declaration of the World Islamic Organization Headquarters for Remembering the Martyrs in Protest of the Change of Name of the Street Khaled Eslamoboli), 9 January [online]. Available at: http://www.mehrnews.com/fa/NewsDetail.aspx?NewsID=50848 [accessed: 7 January 2013].

Meintjes, S. et al. 2001. There Is No Aftermath for Women, in *The Aftermath: Women in Post-conflict Transformation*, edited by Sheila Meintjes et al. Zed Books.

MEMRI. 2002. *Wafa Idris: The Celebration of the First Female Palestinian Suicide Bomber*. Inquiry and Analysis, no. 83, 12 February [online]. Available at: http://www.memri.org/bin/articles.cgi?Area=palestinian&ID=IA8302#_edn12 [accessed: 7 January 2013].

Merton, R.K. 1967. *Social Theory and Social Structure*. Free Press.

Messerschmidt, J.W. 1993. *Masculinities and Crime: Critique and Reconceptualization of Theory*. Rowman & Littlefield.

Messerschmidt, J.W. 2000. Becoming 'Real Men': Adolescent Masculinity Challenges and Sexual Violence. 2 *Men and Masculinities* 3, 286.

Metzl, J.M. and Kirkland, A., eds. 2010. *Against Health: How Health Became the New Morality*. New York University Press.

Meyer v. Nebraska [1923] 262 U.S. 390.

Middleton, P. 1992. *The Inward Gaze: Masculinity and Subjectivity in Modern Culture*. Routledge.

Milbank, D. 2009. It Wasn't One for the Guinness Book. *Washington Post*, 31 July.

Miles, T.J. and Sunstein, C.R. 2008. The New Legal Realism. 75 *University of Chicago Law Review*, 831.

Military Selective Service Act of 1967. 50 U.S.C. app. § 453(a) (2006).

Millar, A. 2003. Men's Experience of Considering Counselling: 'Entering the Unknown'. 3 *Counselling and Psychotherapy Research* 1, 16.

Miller, G.P. 2001. Law, Self-pollution and the Management of Social Anxiety. 7 *Michigan Journal of Gender and Law*, 221.

Miller, G.P. 2002. Circumcision: Cultural–Legal Analysis. 9 *Virginia Journal of Social Policy and the Law*, 497.

Miller, J.A. et al. 2008. Circumcision Status and Risk of HIV and Sexually Transmitted Infections among Men who have Sex with Men: A Meta-analysis. 300 *Journal of the American Medical Association* 14, 1674.

Miller, L. 2001. Feminism and the Exclusion of Army Women from Combat, in *Women in the Military*, edited by R.J. Simon. Transaction Publishers.

Mills, M., Francis, B. and Skelton, C. 2009. Gender Policies in Australia and the United Kingdom: The Construction of 'New' Boys and Girls, in *The Problem with Boys' Education*, edited by W. Martino, M. Kehler and M.B. Weaver-Hightower. Routledge.

Mississippi University for Women v. Hogan [1982] 458 U.S. 718.

Mitchell, J. 1974. *Psychoanalysis and Feminism: A Radical Reassessment of Freudian Psychoanalysis*. Basic Books.

Mitchell, J. and Mishra, S.K. 2000. *Psychoanalysis and Feminism: A Radical Reassessment of Freudian Psychoanalysis*, rev. edn. Basic Books.

Mitchell, S. 2009. Gays in US Boycott Jamaica, *Jamaica Gleaner* [online]. Available at: http://www.jamaica-gleaner.com/gleaner/20090401/news/news2.html [accessed: 8 January 2013].

Mohammad, A.S., ed. 2005. Dokhtaran-e Zeytoon: Be Yad-e Zanan-e Shahdat Talab-e Felestini (Daughters of Olive: In the Memory of the Palestinian Women Martyrdom Seekers), 2nd edn. Sazman-e Farhangi-e Siyahatiy-e Kothar.

Mohammed, M.H. 2007. Martyrdom Mythology in Iraq: How Jihadists Frame Suicide Terrorism in Videos and Biographies. 19 *Terrorism and Political Violence* 1, 95.

Monteagudo, J. 2010. The Odyssey of Rev. Grant Lynn Ford. SouthFloridaGayNews.com [online]. Available at: http://www.southfloridagaynews.com/sfgn-columnists/columnists/jesses-journal/1578-the-odyssey-of-rev-grant-lynn-ford.html [accessed: 8 January 2013].

Montgomery v. Independent School District No. 709 [D. Minn. 2000] 109 F. Supp. 2d 1081.

Montgomery, J. 2007. Medicalizing Crime – Criminalizing Health? The Role of Law, in *The Criminal Justice System and Health Care*, edited by C. Erin and S. Ost. Oxford University Press.

Moran, L.J. 1996. *The Homosexual(ity) of Law*. Routledge.

Morgan, M.J. 2008. *The American Military after 9/11: Women in the Military*. Palgrave Macmillan.

Morrison, A. 2003. Queering Domestic Violence to 'Straighten Out' Criminal Law: What Might Happen When Queer Theory and Practice Meets Criminal Law's Conventional Responses to Domestic Violence. 13 *Southern California Review of Law and Women's Studies*, 81.

Moses, S. et al. 1994. The Association between Lack of Male Circumcision and the Risk of HIV Infection: A Review of the Epidemiological Data. 21 *Sexually Transmitted Disease* 4, 201.

Muňoz-Laboy, M.A. 2004. Beyond 'MSM': Sexual Desire among Bisexually-active Latino Men in New York City. 7 *Sexualities* 1, 55.

Murnane, L.S. 2007. Legal Impediments to Service: Women in the Military and the Rule of Law. 14 *Duke Journal of Gender Law and Policy*, 1064.

Mutua, A.D. 2006a. *Progressive Black Masculinities*. Routledge.

Mutua, A.D. 2006b. Theorizing Progressive Black Masculinities, in *Progressive Black Masculinities*, edited by A. Mutua. Routledge.

Mutua, A.D. 2012. The Multidimensional Turn: Revisiting Progressive Black Masculinities, in *Masculinities and the Law: A Multidimensional Approach*, edited by F.R. Cooper and A.C. McGinley. New York University Press.

Nagel, J. 2000. Sexualizing the Sociological: Queering and Querying the Intimate Substructure of Social Life. 41 *The Sociological Quarterly* 1, 1.

Naser, P. 2003. Amaliyat-e Esteshhadi dar Felestin (Tarikhche, Elal, Dastavarha) (Martyrdom Operations in Palestine (History, Reasons and Results)). *Hozoor*, no. 40 [online]. Available at: http://www.hawzah.net/Hawzah/Magazines/MagArt.aspx?MagazineNumberID=6120&id=64714_[accessed: 7 January 2013].

Nash, Jennifer. 2008. Re-thinking Intersectionality. 89 *Feminist Review*, 1.

National Center for Education Statistics. 2007. *The Condition of Education 2007*. U.S. Department of Education.

National Collegiate Athletic Association. 2007. *1981–82 – 2005–06: NCAA Sports Sponsorship and Participation Rates Report*. National Collegiate Athletic Association.

National Counterterrorism Center. 2007. A Fact Sheet from the Worldwide Incident Team. Document no. 20071212-06 [online]. Available at: http://www.fbiic.gov/public/2008/sept/NCTC%20Did%20you%20know%20the%20first%20suicide%20bombing%20may%20have%20occurred%20in%201881.pdf [accessed: 4 June 2013].

National Geographic. 2007. Reggae: National Geographic World Music [online]. Available at: http://worldmusic.nationalgeographic.com/view/page.basic/genre/content.genre/reggae_775 [accessed: 8 January 2013].

National Labor Relations Act [2006] 29 U.S.C. § 152(3).

National Public Radio. 2004. Dancehall Reggae Artists under Fire for Anti-gay Lyrics, 6 August [online]. Available at: http://www.npr.org/templates/story/story.php?%20storyId=3837073 [accessed: 8 January 2013].

Neal v. Board of Trustees of the California State Universities [9th Cir. 1999] 198 F. 3d 763.

Nelken, D. 1984. Law in Action or Living Law? Back to the Beginning Sociology of Law. 4 *Legal Studies*, 157.

Nelson, C.A. 2007. American Husbandry: Legal Norms Impacting the Production of (Re)productivity. 19 *Yale Journal of Law & Feminism*, 1.

Nelson, C.A. 2008. Lyrical Assault: Dancehall versus the Cultural Imperialism of the North-west. 17 *Southern California Interdisciplinary Law Journal*, 231.

Nelson, C.A. and Grossberg, L., eds. 1988. *Marxism and the Interpretation of Culture*. University of Illinois Press.

Nelson, T.S. 2002. *For Love of Country: Confronting Rape and Sexual Harassment in the U.S. Military*. The Haworth Press, Inc.

Neu, T. and Weinfeld, R. 2007. *Helping Boys Succeed in School: A Practical Guide for Parents and Teachers*. Prufrock Press Inc.

Newman, M. 2006. Comment, Barnes v. City of Cincinnati: Command Presence, Gender Bias, and Problems of Police Aggression. 29 *Harvard Journal Law and Gender* 2, 485.

Ní Aoláin, F. 2009. Women, Security and the Patriarchy of Internationalized Transitional Justice. 31 *Human Rights Quarterly* 4, 1055.

Ní Aoláin, F. and Turner, C. 2007. Gender, Truth, and Transition. 16 *UCLA Women's Law Journal* 2, 229.

Niemann, Y.F. 2001. Stereotypes about Chicanas and Chicanos: Implications for Counseling. 29 *The Counseling Psychologist* 1, 55.

Nissimov, M., Mansharof, Y. and Savyon, A. 2009. Iranian Women's Magazine Shut Down for Publishing Investigative Article on Martyrdom Movement. Middle East Media Research Institute (MEMRI) Inquiry & Analysis, no. 439, 2 May [online]. Available at: http://memri.org/ftp/publicdocs/Zanan_IA_sm.pdf [accessed: 10 August 2009].

Noguera, P. 1996. Responding to the Crisis Confronting California's Black Male Youth: Providing Support without Further Marginalization. 65 *The Journal of Negro Education* 2, 219.

Nondiscrimination in Federally Assisted Programs. 71 F.R. 206, 62530.

Northern Ireland Office. 1998. The Agreement [online]. Available at: http://www.nio.gov.uk/Publications/Article/The-Agreement [accessed: 3 January 2013].

Nourse, G.V. and Shaffer, G. 2009. Varieties of New Legal Realism: Can a New World Order Prompt a New Legal Theory? 95 *Cornell Law Review*, 61.

Nunn, K.B. 2002. The Child as Other: Race and Differential Treatment in the Juvenile Justice System. 51 *DePaul Law Review*, 679.

Nussbaum, M. 2004. *Hiding from Humanity: Disgust, Shame and the Law*. Princeton University Press.

O'Donovan, K. 1993. *Family Law Matters*. Pluto.

Offences Against the Person Act, § 76 and §77, L.N. 123/2011, available at http://www.moj.gov.jm/sites/default/files/laws/Offences%20Against%20the%20Person%20Act.pdf

Office for Civil Rights. 2001. R*evised Sexual Harassment Guidance: Harassment of Students by School Employees, Other Students, or Third Parties*. Department of Education.

Office of the Inspector General, U.S. Department of Defense. 2003. *The Tailhook Report: Official Inquiry into the Events of Tailhook '91*. St. Martin's Press.

Ogletree, C. 2009. Lawyer's Statement on the Arrest of Henry Luis Gates, Jr. *The Root* [online]. Available at: http://www.theroot.com/views/lawyers-statement-arrest-henry-luis-gates-jr [accessed: 5 December 2011].

Okwusoa, T.M., Guopa, V. and Goel, A. 2009. Male Circumcision for Prevention of HIV Transmission. 37 *Lancet*, 1497.

Ottoson, D. 2010. State-sponsored Homophobia: A World Survey of Laws Prohibiting Same Sex Activity between Consenting Adults, International Lesbian, Gay, Bisexual, Trans and Intersex Association [online]. Available at: http://ilga.org/historic/Statehomophobia/State_sponsored_homophobia_ILGA_07.pdf [accessed: 8 January 2013].

Paap, K. 2006. *Working Construction: Why White Working-class Men Put Themselves – and the Labor Movement – in Harm's Way*. Cornell University Press.

Padgett, T. 2006. The Most Homophobic Place on Earth? *Time*, 12 April [online]. Available at: http://www.time.com/time/world/article/0,8599,1182991,00.html [accessed: 8 January 2013].

Page, W.H. 1977. Professor Ehrlich's Czernowitz Seminar of Living Law. 4 *Northern Kentucky Law Review*, 37.

Parker, A. 1996. The Construction of Masculinity within Boys' Physical Education. 8 *Gender and Education*, 141.

Parker, K. 2004. Myth of Equality Aids the Enemy. *Kansas City Star*, 31 May.

Parks, S. 2008. Toward a Critical Race Realism. 17 *Cornell Journal of Law and Public Policy*, 683.

Parks, G.S. and Rachlinski, J. 2008. A Better Metric: The Role of Unconscious Race and Gender Bias in the 2008 Presidential Election, Cornell Legal Studies Research Paper no. 08-007 [online]. Available at: http://ssrn.com/abstract=1102704 [accessed: 31 May 2013].

Pascoe, C.J. 2007. *Dude, You're a Fag: Masculinity and Sexuality in High School*. University of California Press.

Patterson, C. 1992. Children of Lesbian and Gay Parents. 63 *Child Development* 5, 1025.

Patterson, O. 2001. The Roots of Conflict in Jamaica. *New York Times*, 23 July.

Peacebuild—The Canadian Peacebuilding Network. 2008. *Emerging Issues: Youth, Gender and the Changing Nature of Armed Conflict*, February [online]. Available at: http://www.peacebuild.ca/documents/Report-Youth-and-Gender-Conflict-FINAL-draft-EN-Feb-29_FINAL.pdf [accessed: 3 January 2013].

Peacey, V. and Hunt, J. 2008. *Problematic Contact after Separation and Divorce? A National Survey of Parents*. One Parent Families/Gingerbread.

Peltz, M. 1995. Second-parent Adoption: Overcoming Barriers to Lesbian Family Rights. 3 *Michigan Journal of Gender & Law* 1, 175.

Perrin, E. et al. 2002. Technical Report: Co-parent or Second-parent Adoption by Same-sex Parents. 109 *Pediatrics* 2, 341.

Perry v. Schwarzenegger [N.D. Cal. 2010], 704 F. Supp. 2d 921.

Peter, K. et al. 2005. *Gender Differences in Participation and Completion of Undergraduate Education and How They Have Changed over Time*. National Centre for Education Statistics,

Petersen, A. and Lupton, D. 1996. *The New Public Health and Self in the Age of Risk*. Allen and Unwin.

Peterson, S. and Runyan, A.S. 1999. *Global Gender Issues*, 2nd edn. Westview Press.

Petertatchell.net. 2007a. Buju Banton Says Boom Bye Bye To Homophobia [online]. Available at: http://www.petertatchell.net/pop_music/bujubanton byebyehomophobia.htm [accessed: 8 January 2013].

Petertatchell.net. 2007b. Reggae Stars Renounce Homophobia [online]. Available at: http://www.petertatchell.net/pop_music/reggaecompassiondeal.htm [accessed: 8 January 2013].

Philpott, A. 2004. The Female Condom and Sexual Pleasure: The Pleasure Project, Paper presented at XV International AIDS Conference, Bangkok, Thailand, 11–16 July [online]. Available via: www.the-pleasure-project.org [accessed: 31 May 2013].

Philpott, A. et al. 2006a. Pleasure and Prevention: When Good Sex is Safer Sex. 14 *Reproductive Health Matters* 28, 23.

Philpott, A. et al. 2006b. Promoting Protection and Pleasure: Amplifying the Effectiveness of Barriers against Sexually Transmitted Infections and Pregnancy. 368 *Lancet*, 2028.

Pierce v. Society of Sisters [1925], 268 U.S. 510, 534–5.

Pillard, C. 2007. Our Other Reproductive Choices: Equality in Sex Education, Contraceptive Access, and Work–Family Policy. 56 *Emory Law Journal*, 941.

Pillay, A. 2001. Violence against Women in the Aftermath, in *The Aftermath: Women in Post-Conflict Transformation*, edited by Sheila Meintjes et al. Zed Books.

Piot, P. 1998. Address to the VIIth Conference on Woman and AIDS, Dakar Senegal, 14–17 December.

Pitcher, L.M. 1998. 'The Divine Impatience': Ritual, Narrative, and Symbolization in the Practice of Martyrdom in Palestine. 12 *Medical Anthropology Quarterly* 1, 8.

Planas, A. 2007. Separating the Sexes, *Las Vegas Review Journal*, 8 January.

Pleasant v. Pleasant [Ill. App. Ct. 1993] 628 N.E.2d 633.

Pleck, E. 1987. *Domestic Tyranny: The Making of Social Policy against Domestic Violence from Colonial Times to the Present.* Oxford University Press.

Pleck, J. 1980. Men's Power with Women, Other Men, and Society: A Men's Movement Analysis, in *The American Man*, edited by J.H. Pleck and E.H. Pleck. Prentice Hall Trade.

Pleck, J. 1997. Parental Involvement: Levels, Sources and Consequences, in *The Role of the Father in Child Development*, edited by M. Lamb, 3rd edn. Wiley.

Pleck, J.H. 1987. American Fathering in Historical Perspective, in *Changing Men: New Directions in Research on Men and Masculinity*, edited by M. Kimmel. Sage.

Polikoff, N. 1986. Lesbian Mothers, Lesbian Families: Legal Obstacles, Legal Challenges. 14 *New York University Review of Law and Social Change* 4, 907.

Polikoff, N. 1990. This Child Does Have Two Mothers: Redefining Parenthood to Meet the Needs of Children in Lesbian-mother and Other Non-traditional Families. 78 *Georgetown Law Journal* 3, 459.

Polikoff, N. 1996. The Deliberate Construction of Families without Fathers: Is it an Option for Lesbian and Homosexual Mothers? 36 *Santa Clara Law Review* 2, 375.

Pollack, W. 1998. *Real Boys: Rescuing Our Sons from the Myths of Boyhood.* Owl Books.

Pound, R. 1910. Law in Books and Law in Action. 44 *American Law Review*, 12.

Pourhossein, N. 2003. Amaliyat-e Esteshhadi dar Felestin (Tarikhche, Elal, Dastavarha) (Martyrdom Operations in Palestine (History, Reasons and Results)). 40 *Hozoor* [online]. Available at: http://www.hawzah.net/Hawzah/Magazines/MagArt.aspx?MagazineNumberID=6120&id=64714_[accessed: 7 January 2013].

Powell, A. 2007. Sexual Pressure and Young People's Negotiation of Consent. *ACSSA (Australian Centre for the Study of Sexual Assault) Newsletter*, 14 (June).

Pribbenow, C.M. et al. 2010. The Tenure Process and Extending the Tenure Clock: The Experience of Faculty at One University. 23 *Higher Education Policy* 1, 17.

Price Waterhouse v. Hopkins [1989] 490 U.S. 228.

Prince v. Massachusetts [1944] 321 U.S. 158, 166 (1944).

Prokos, A. and Padavic, I. 2002. 'There oughtta be a law against bitches': Masculinities Lessons in Police Academy Training. 9 *Gender, Work & Organizations* 4, 439.

Prosecutor v. Thomas Lubanga Dvilo, Warrant of Arrest [2006] ICC Case No. ICC-01-02-01/06, 10 February [online]. Available at: http://www.icc-cpi.int/iccdocs/doc/doc236258.pdf [accessed: 3 January 2013].

Pyke, K.D. 1996. Class-based Masculinities: The Interdependence of Gender, Class, and Interpersonal Power. 10 *Gender & Society* 5, 527.

Quimby, B. 2006. Single Sex Learning: A Portland Elementary School Experiments with All-boy and All-girl Classrooms to See if it will Make Boys More Successful. *Portland Press Herald*, 9 October.

Rabourn, M. 2008. Organized Labor in Residential Construction. 33 *Labor Studies* 1, 9.

Race, K. 2008. The Use of Pleasure in Harm Reduction: Perspectives from *The History of Sexuality*. 19 *International Journal of Drug Policy* 5, 417.

Radford, J. and Stanko, E. 1996. Violence against Women and Children: The Contradictions of Crime Control under Patriarchy, in *Women, Violence and Male Power: Feminist Activism, Research and Practice*, edited by M. Hester. Sage.

Rajaee, F., ed. 2003. *The Iran–Iraq War: The Politics of Aggression*. The University Press of Florida.

Ralston, J.Y. 1998. Geishas, Gays and Grunts: What the Exploitation of Asian Pacific Women Reveals about Military Culture and the Legal Ban on Lesbian, Gay and Bisexual Service Members. 16 *Law and Inequality*, 666.

Rambo, K.S. 2008. *'Trivial Complaints': The Role of Privacy in Domestic Violence Law and Activism in the U.S.* Columbia University Press.

Ranson, G. 2001. Men at Work: Change – or No Change? – in the Era of the 'New Father'. 4 *Men and Masculinities* 1, 3.

Rau, K. 2008. Jamaica Boycott Called Off. *Xtra!* [online]. Available at: http://www.xtra.ca/public/viewstory.aspx?STORY_ID=4808&PUB_TEMPLATE_ID=9 [accessed: 8 January 2013].

Reece, H. 2003. *Divorcing Responsibly*. Hart.

Reece, H. 2009. The Degradation of Parental Responsibility, in *Responsible Parents and Parental Responsibility*, edited by R. Probert, S. Gilmore and J. Herring. Hart.

Reese, W. 2005. *America's Public Schools: From the Common School to 'No Child Left Behind.'* The Johns Hopkins University Press.

Reeser, T.W. 2010. *Masculinities in Theory*. Wiley-Blackwell.

Reichert, M. and Hawley, R. 2009. *Teaching Boys: A Global Study of Effective Practices*. International Boys' School Coalition [online]. Available at: http://teachingtoboys.wikispaces.com/file/view/Teaching+Boys,+A+Global+Study.pdf [accessed: 29 May 2013].

Remondino, P.C. 1891. *History of Circumcision from the Earliest Times to the Present: Moral and Physical Reasons for its Performance*. F.A. Davis.

Remondino, P.C. 1894. Questions of the Day: Negro Rapes and their Social Problems. 4 *National Popular Review*, 3.

Remy, J. 1990. Patriarchy and Fratriarchy as Forms of Androcracy, in *Men, Masculinities & Social Theory*, edited by Jeff Hearn and David Morgan. Unwin Hyman.

Renold, E. 2004. 'Other' Boys: Negotiating Non-hegemonic Masculinities in the Primary School. 16 *Gender & Education*, 247.

Renold, E. 2005. *Girls, Boys and Junior Sexualities: Exploring Children's Gender and Sexual Relations in the Primary School*. RoutledgeFalmer.

Re-public. 2008. Gendering Border Crossings [online]. Available via: www.re-public.gr/en [accessed: 31 October 2010].

Reskin, B.F. and Roos, P.A. 1990. *Gender Queues: Explaining Women's Inroads into Male Occupations*. Temple University Press.

Reverby, S.M., ed. 2000. *Tuskegee's Truth: Rethinking the Tuskegee Syphilis Study*. University of North Carolina Press.

Rhoades, H. 2002. The 'No Contact Mother' in the Era of the 'New Father'. 16 *International Journal of Law, Policy and the Family*, 71.

Rhode, D.L. 1989. *Justice and Gender: Sex Discrimination and the Law*. Harvard University Press.

Ricci v DeStefano [2009] 129 S. Ct. 2658.

Rich, A. 1986. Compulsory Heterosexuality and Lesbian Experience, in *Blood, Bread, and Poetry*. W. W. Norton & Co.

Richardson, D. 2001. Sexuality and Gender, in *International Encyclopaedia of the Social and Behavioural Sciences*. Elsevier [online]. Available via: www.iesbs.com [accessed: 17 May 2013].

Richardson, D. 2004. *Rethinking Sexuality*. Sage.

Richman, K. 2009. *Courting Change: Queer Parents, Judges, and the Transformation of American Family Law*. New York University Press.

Riggs, M. 1999. Black Macho Revisited: Reflections of a Snap! Queen, in *Black Men on Race, Gender, and Sexuality: A Critical Reader*, edited by D.W. Carbado. New York University Press.

Rimer, S. 1996. At Maryland Post, Talk is of Shame. *New York Times*, 23 November.
Risingstarstv.net. 2010. Here's a Copy of the Reggae Compassionate Act Allegedly Signed by Dee-Jay Vybz Kartel aka Adidja Palmer [online]. Available at: http://www.risingstarstv.net/profiles/blogs/heres-a-copy-of-the-reggae [accessed: 8 January 2013].
Ritzer, G. 2000. *The McDonaldization of Society*. Pine Forge Press.
Rivera, C. 2006. Single-sex Classes on a Forward Course: More Schools in L.A. and across the Nation Separate Boys and Girls. *Los Angeles Times*, 20 November.
Rivers, C. and Barnett, R.C. 2006. The Myth of 'The Boy Crisis'. *The Washington Post*, 9 April.
Roberts, A. and Kurst-Swanger, K. 2002. Police Response to Battered Women, in *Handbook of Domestic Violence Intervention Strategies: Policies, Programs, And Legal Remedies*, edited by Albert R. Roberts. Oxford University Press.
Roberts, D. 1997. *Killing the Black Body*. Vintage.
Robertson, S. 2007. *Understanding Men's Health: Masculinity, Identity and Well-being*. Open University Press.
Robinson-English, T. 2006. Saving Black Boys: Is Single-Sex Education the Answer? *Ebony*, December.
Robson, R. 1994. Third Parties and the Third Sex: Child Custody and Lesbian Legal Theory. 26 *Connecticut Law Review* 4, 1377.
Robson, R. 2000. Making Mothers: Lesbian Legal Theory and the Judicial Construction of Lesbian Mothers. 22 *Women's Rights Law Reporter* 1, 15.
Robson, R. 2002. Assimilation, Marriage, and Lesbian Liberation. 75 *Temple Law Review*, 709.
Roe v. Roe [Va. 1985] 324 S.E.2d 691.
Roediger, D. 2007. *The Wages of Whiteness: Race and the Making of the American Working Class*, rev. edn. Verso.
Rogers, W.A. 2005. Feminism and Public Health Ethics. 31 *Journal of Medical Ethics*, 351.
Romer v. Evans [1996] 517 U.S. 620.
Römkens, R. 2001. Law as a Trojan Horse: Unintended Consequences of Rights-based Interventions to Support Battered Women. 13 *Yale Journal of Law & Feminism*, 265.
Ronner, A. 1995. *Bottoms v. Bottoms*: The Lesbian Mother and the Judicial Perpetuation of Damaging Stereotypes. 7 *Yale Journal of Law & Feminism* 2, 341.
Rosenfeld, D. and Faircloth, C.A., eds. 2006. *Medicalized Masculinities*. Temple University Press.
Rosky, C.J. 2009. Like Father, Like Son: Homosexuality, Parenthood and the Gender of Homophobia. 20 *Yale Journal of Law and Feminism* 2, 257.
Ross, A. 1998. *Real Love: In Pursuit of Cultural Justice*. New York University Press.

Rubenstein, W. 1997. *Cases and Materials on Sexual Orientation and the Law*. West Publishing.

Rubin, A.J. 2009. How Baida Wanted to Die. *New York Times*, 12 August [online]. Available at: http://www.nytimes.com/2009/08/16/magazine/16suicide-t.html?pagewanted=all [accessed: 7 January 2013].

Rubin, E. 2005. Sex, Politics, and Morality. 47 *William and Mary Law Review* 1, 1.

Rubin, G. 1994. Sexual Traffic, interview with Judith Butler. 6 *differences: A Journal of Feminist Cultural Studies* 2–3, 62.

Rubio-Marin, R. 2009. The Gender of Reparations in Transitional Societies, in *The Gender of Reparations: Unsettling Sexual Hierarchies while Redressing Human Rights Violations*, edited by Ruth Rubio-Marin. Cambridge University Press.

Rush, S. 1993. Breaking with Tradition: Surrogacy and Gay Fathers, in *Kindred Matters: Rethinking the Philosophy of the Family*, edited by Diana Tietjens Meyers et al. Cornell University Press.

Ruskola, T. 1996. Minor Disregard: The Legal Construction of the Fantasy that Gay and Lesbian Youth do not Exist. 8 *Yale Journal of Law and Feminism* 2, 269.

Ryan Report. 2009. *Government of Ireland, Commission to Inquire into Child Abuse (Ryan Report)* [online]. Available at: http://www.childabusecommission.com [accessed: 6 September 2010].

Sabo, D. 2005. The Study of Masculinities and Men's Health, in *Handbook of Studies on Men and Masculinities*, edited by M. Kimmel, J. Hearn and R.W. Connell. Sage.

Sacchetti, M. 2006. Charter School Puts Hope in Same-sex Classes. *Boston Globe*, 27 November.

Sack, E.J. 2004. Battered Women and the State: The Struggle for the Future of Domestic Violence Policy. 2004 *Wisconsin Law Review*, 1657.

Sacramento State News, Chuck D to present his 'State of the Union' [online]. Available at: http://www.csus.edu/news/012004chuckD.stm [accessed: 7 April 2010].

Saeid A. 2005. Saheedaan Fahmide (Salrooz Shahadat Shahid Fahmideh). *Golbarg*, no. 56 [online]. Available at: http://www.hawzah.net/Hawzah/Magazines/MagArt.aspx?Id=34273&PageNum=1_[accessed: 7 January 2013].

Said, E. 1993. *Culture and Imperialism*. Alfred A. Knopf, Inc.

Saint-Aubin, A.F. 2002. A Grammar of Black Masculinity: A Body of Science. 10 *Journal of Men's Studies* 3, 247.

Saito, N. Taylor. 2000. From Slavery and Seminoles to AIDS in South Africa: An Essay on Race and Property in International Law. 45 *Villanova Law Review*, 1135.

Salewicz, C. and Boot, A. 2001. *Reggae Explosion: The Story of Jamaican Music*. Harry N. Abrams, Inc.

Salomone, R. 2003. *Same, Different, Equal*. Yale University Press.

Samadi, M.A., ed. 2005. *Dokhtaran-e Zeytoon: Be Yad-e Zana-e Shahdat Talab Felestini* (Daughters of Olive: In the Memory of the Palestinian Women Martyrdom Seekers), 2nd edn. Tehran: Sazman-e Farhangi-e Siyahatiy-e Kothar.

Sandals. 2011 [online]. Available at: http://www.sandals.com/general/included.cfm [accessed: 15 January 2011].

Sandberg, J.F. and Hofferth, S.L. 2001. Changes in Children's Time with Parents: United States, 1981–1997. 38 *Demography* 3, 423.

Sanford, K. and Blair, H. 2002. Engendering Public Education: Single-sex Schooling in Western Canada, in *Gender in Policy and Practice: Perspectives on Single-sex and Coeducational Schooling*, edited by Amanda Datnow and Lee Hubbard. RoutledgeFalmer.

Sarat, A. et al. 1998. *Crossing Boundaries: Traditions and Transformations in Law and Society Research*, 4th edn. Northwestern University Press.

Sarmaye. 2006. Goftegoo ba Firozeh Rajaifar, Dabirkol-e Esteshhadiyoon-e Iran, Farmandey-e Shahadat Talaban Iran. 303 *Sarmaye*, 21 October.

Saucedo, L.M. 2006. The Employer Preference for the Subservient Worker and the Making of the Brown Collar Workplace. 67 *Ohio State Law Journal* 5, 961.

Saucedo, L.M. 2008a. A New 'U': Organizing Victims and Protecting Immigrant Workers. 42 *Richmond Law Review* 4, 891.

Saucedo, L.M. 2008b. Addressing Segregation in the Brown Collar Workplace: Toward a Solution for the Inexorable 100%. 41 *University of Michigan Journal of Law Reform* 2, 447.

Saucedo, L.M. and Morales, M.C. 2010. Masculinities Narratives and Latino Immigrant Workers: A Case Study of the Las Vegas Residential Construction Trades. 33 *Harvard Journal of Law and Gender* 2, 625.

Saul, S. 1991. Equal Opportunity Combat? Rules Banning Women Could Be Rescinded. *Newsday*, 21 May.

Saunders, H. 2004. Twenty-nine Child Homicides: Lessons to be Learnt on Domestic Violence and Child Protection. Women's Aid.

Sax, L. 2005. The Promise and Peril of Single-sex Public Education. *Education Week*, 2 March.

Sax, L. 2006. *Why Gender Matters: What Parents and Teachers Need to Know about the Emerging Science of Sex Differences*. Doubleday.

Sayer, L.C., Bianchi, S.M. and Robinson, J.P. 2004. Are Parents Investing Less Time in Children? 110 *American Journal of Sociology* 1, 1.

Schafer, J. 1998. 'A Baby who does not Cry will not be Suckled': AMODEG and the Reintegration of Demobilised Soldiers. 24 *Journal of South African Studies* 1, 207.

Schechter, S. 1982. *Women and Male Violence*. South End Press.

Scherrer, C.P. 2002. *Genocide and Crisis in Central Africa: Conflict Roots, Mass Violence and Regional War*. Praeger Publishers.

Schmesser, A. 2007. Real Men may not Cry, but they are Victims of Domestic Violence: Bias in the Application of Domestic Violence Laws. 58 *Syracuse Law Review*, 171.

Schmidt, K.L. 1995. *Transforming Abuse: Nonviolent Resistance and Recovery*. New Society Publishers.

Schneider, E.M. 2002. *Battered Women and Feminist Lawmaking*. Yale University Press.

Schubotz, D. et al. 2004. Sexual Behaviour of Young People in Northern Ireland: First Sexual Experience. 14 *Critical Public Health* 2, 177.

Schultz, V. 1998. Reconceptualizing Sexual Harassment. 107 *Yale Law Journal*, 1683.

Schwartz, J. 2009. Slinging Ink and Solace. *Austin American-Statesman*, 13 December. WLNR 22250115. Available via: https://lawschool.westlaw.com/shared/signon10.asp?path=%2fDesktopDefault.aspx [accessed: 31 May 2013].

Schweitzer, Y. 2003. Female Suicide Bombers for God. 88 *Tel Aviv Notes*, 1.

Scott, J.F. 1970. Racial Group Membership, Role Orientation, and Police Conduct among Urban Policemen. 31 *Phylon* 1, 5.

Scott, S. and Jackson, S. 2007. *Theorising Sexuality*. Open University Press.

Scott-Sheldon, L.A. and Johnson, B.T. 2006. Eroticizing Creates Safer Sex: A Research Synthesis. 27 *Journal of Primary Prevention* 6, 619.

Scourfield, J. and Drakeford, M. 2002. New Labour and the 'Problem of Men'. 22 *Critical Social Policy*, 619.

Sedgwick, E. 1991. How to Bring Your Kids up Gay. 29 *Social Text*, 18.

Sedgwick, E.K. 1993. How to Bring your Kids up Gay: The War on Effeminate Boys, in *Tendencies*, edited by E.K. Sedgwick. Duke University Press.

Sedgwick, E.V. 1985. *Between Men: English Literature and Male Homosocial Desire*. Columbia University Press.

Segal, D.R. and Segal, M.W. 2004. Population Reference Bureau: America's Military Population. Population Bulletin [online]. Available at: http://www.prb.org/source/ACF1396.pdf [accessed: 22 March 2010].

Segal, M.W. 1998. Gender and the Propensity to Enlist in the U.S. Military, in *Women in the Military*, edited by R.J. Simon. Transaction Publishers.

Seidman, S. 1991. *Romantic Longings: Love in America, 1830–1980*. Routledge.

Seiner, J.A. and Gutman, B.N. 2010. Does *Ricci* Herald a New Disparate Impact? 90 *Boston University Law Review* 6, 2181.

Sella, C. 1991. When a Mother is a Legal Stranger to her Child: The Law's Challenge to the Lesbian Nonbiological Mother. 1 *UCLA Women's Law Journal* 1, 135.

Sellers, J. 2006. To Each, His or Her Own: More Schools Try Keeping Boys, Girls in Separate Classes. *Augusta Chronicle*, 11 August.

Shalhoub-Kevorkian, N. 2009. *Militarization and Violence against Women in Conflict Zones in the Middle East*. Cambridge University Press.

Sharma, S. 2003. Beyond 'Driving while Black' and 'Flying while Brown': Using Intersectionality to Uncover the Gendered Aspects of Racial Profiling. 12 *Columbia Journal of Gender and Law*, 275.

Shapiro, A. and Lambert, J.D. 1999. Longitudinal Effects of Divorce on the Quality of the Father–Child Relationship and on Fathers' Psychological Well-being. 61 *Journal of Marriage and the Family* 2, 397.

Sharp, L. 2006. Babes and Baboons: Jesica Santillan and Experimental Pediatric Transplant Research in America, in *A Death Retold: Jessica Santillan, the Bungled Transplant and the Paradoxes of Medical Citizenship*, edited by K. Wailoo et al. University of North Carolina Press.

Sharp, L. 2011. Imagining Transpecies Kinship in Xenotransplantation. 1 *Sites: A Journal of Social Anthropology and Cultural Studies* 8, 12.

Sheikhani, L. 2008. *Goftegoo ba Madar Shahidan Fahmideh* (Interview with the Mother of Martyrs Fahmideh). Sajed, Imposed War Official Website, 7 November [online]. Available at: http://www.sajed.ir/new/index.php?option=com_content&view=article&id=11277&catid=274:barrators&Itemid=184 [accessed: 7 January 2013].

Sheldon, S. 2009. From 'Absent Objects of Blame' to 'Fathers who Want to Take Responsibility': Reforming Birth Registration Law. 31 *Journal of Social Welfare and Family Law* 4, 373.

Shelton, D. and Berndt, D. 1974. Sex Discrimination in Vocational Education: Title IX and Other Remedies. 62 *California Law Review*, 1121.

SHEPP Toronto. 2010 [online]. Available at: www.shepptoronto.com [accessed: 31 October 2010].

Shilts, R. 2007. *And the Band Played On: Politics, People and the AIDS Epidemic*. St. Martin's Press.

SHine SA [Sexual Health Information Networking and Education]. 2003. *Report on the First Year of the SHARE Project*. SHine SA.

SHine SA. 2008. Sexual Health Statistics February 2008 [online]. Available at www.sexual_health_statistics_2008.pdf [accessed: 31 October 2010].

Showalter, E. 1987. *The Female Malady: Women, Madness and English Culture 1830–1980*. Virago.

Shrier, D.K. and Shrier, L.A. 2009. Psychosocial Aspects of Women's Lives: Work and Family/Personal Life and Life Cycle Issues. 36 *Obstetrics and Gynecology Clinics of North America* 4, 753.

Shugart, H.A. and Waggoner, C. 2008. *Making Camp: Rhetorics of Transgression in U.S. Popular Culture*. University of Alabama Press.

Sideris, T. 2001. Rape in War and Peace, in *The Aftermath: Women in Post-conflict Transformation*, edited by Sheila Meintjes et al. Zed Books.

Siegel, R. 2004. Equality Talk: Antisubordination and Anticlassification Values in Constitutional Struggles over Brown. 117 *Harvard Law Review*, 1470.

Sikwibele, A., Shonga C. and Baylies, C. 2000. AIDS in Kapulanga, Mongu: Poverty, Neglect and Gendered Patterns of Blame, in *AIDS, Sexuality and*

Gender in Africa: Collective Strategies and Struggles in Tanzania and Zambia, edited by C. Baylies and J. Bujra. Routledge.
Single-sex Classes and Schools: Guidelines on Title IX Requirements, 67 Fed. Reg. 31, 101–3, 8 May 2002.
Single-sex Classes Crop Up in Richmond Area. *Richmond Times Dispatch*, 16 October 2008.
Single-sex Education Spreads. *USA Today*, 13 October 2008.
Single-sex Final Rules Notice, 34 C.F.R pt. 106, at 62,530 (2006).
Sklansky, D.A. 2008. 'One train may hide another': Katz, Stonewall, and the Secret Subtext of Criminal Procedure. 41 *University of California Davis Law Review* 3, 875.
Smart, C. 1989. *Feminism and the Power of Law*. Routledge.
Smart, C. 2004. Equal Shares: Rights for Fathers or Recognition for Children? 24 *Critical Social Policy* 4, 484.
Smart, C. 2006a. Preface, in *Fathers Rights Activism and Legal Reform*, edited by R. Collier and S. Sheldon. Hart.
Smart, C. 2006b. The Ethic of Justice Strikes Back, in *Feminist Perspectives on Family Law*, edited by A. Diduck and K. O'Donovan. Routledge-Cavendish.
Smart, C. 2007. *Personal Life*. Polity.
Smart, C. and Neale, B. 1999. *Family Fragments*. Polity.
Smith, A. 2005. Beyond Pro-choice versus Pro-life. 17 *NWSA Journal*, 119.
Smith, A. et al./NSASS. 2003. Secondary Students and Sexual Health 2002: Results of the 3rd National Survey of Australian Secondary Students, HIV/AIDS and Sexual Health. Monograph series no. 47. Australian Research Centre in Sex, Health & Society.
Smith, P. 1996. Introduction, in *Boys: Masculinities in Contemporary Culture*, edited by P. Smith. Harper-Collins.
Smithers, A. and Robinson, P. 2006. *The Paradox of Single-sex and Co-educational Schooling*. Carmichael Press.
Socarides, C. 1978. *Homosexuality*. Jason Aronson, Inc.
Sommers, C.H. 2000. *The War against Boys: How Misguided Feminism is Harming Our Young Men*. Simon & Schuster.
Soulrebels.org. [n.d.]. The Reggae Compassionate Act [online]. Available at: http://www.soulrebels.org/dancehall/w_compassionate_001.htm [accessed: 8 January 2013].
Spalter-Roth, R. and Erskine, W. 2005. Beyond the Fear Factor: Work/Family Policies in Academia: Resources or Rewards? 37 *Change* 6, 19.
Sparks, A. 1997. Feminists Negotiate the Executive Branch: The Policing of Male Violence, in *Feminists Negotiate the State*, ed. Cynthia R. Daniels et al. University Press of America.
Spector-Mersel, G. 2006. Never Aging Stories: Western Hegemonic Masculinity Scripts. 15 *Journal of Gender Studies* 1, 67.
Spelman, E. 1988. *Inessential Woman: Problems of Exclusion in Feminist Thought*. Beacon Press.

Spitko, G. 2005. From Queer to Paternity: How Primary Gay Fathers are Changing Fatherhood and Gay Identity. 24 *St. Louis University Public Law Review* 1, 195.

Spivak, G. 2007. Can the Subaltern Speak?, in *Marxism and the Interpretation of Culture*, edited by C. Nelson and L. Grossberg. University of Illinois Press.

St. Louis Post-dispatch. 2009. Dividing Boys, Girls Grow Exponentially. 20 February.

St. Petersburg Times. 2008. Separating Sexes for Better Learning, 1 September.

Stabiner, K. 2002. *All Girls: Single-sex Education and Why it Matters*. Riverhead Books.

Stacey, J. and Biblarz, T. 2001. (How) Does the Sexual Orientation of Parents Matter? 66 *American Sociological Review* 2, 159.

Stahl, P.M. 1994. *Conducting Child Custody Evaluations: A Comprehensive Guide*. Sage.

Stanley v. Illinois [1972] 405 U.S. 645.

States News Service. 2009. More Mental Health Care Called for in Wake of Ft. Hood Shootings. *States News Service*, 11 December. WLNR 22250115 [online]. Available via https://lawschool.westlaw.com/shared/signon10.asp?path=%2fDesktopDefault.aspx [accessed: 31 May 2013].

Steckel, A. 1987. Psychosocial Development of Children of Lesbian Mothers, in *Gay and Lesbian Parents*, edited by F.W. Bozett. Praeger.

Steele, R. 1993. All Things Not Being Equal: The Case for Race Separate Schools. 43 *Case Western Reserve Law Review*, 591.

Stein, E. 2001. Evaluating the Sex Discrimination Argument for Lesbian and Gay Rights. 49 *UCLA Law Review* 2, 471.

Stemple, L. 2009. Male Rape and Human Rights. 60 *Hastings Law Journal*, 605.

Stockton, K. 2009. *The Queer Child, or Growing Sideways in the Twentieth Century*. Duke University Press.

Stolzoff, N.C. 2000. *Wake the Town and Tell the People: Dancehall Culture in Jamaica*. Duke University Press.

Stone, K.V.W. 2004. *From Widgets to Digits: Employment Regulation for the Changing Workplace*. Cambridge University Press.

Streitmatter, J.L. 1999. *For Girls Only*. State University of New York Press.

Strolovich, D. 2007. *Affirmative Advocacy*. University of Chicago Press.

Stychin, C.F. 1998. *A Nation by Rights: National Cultures, Sexual Identity Politics and the Discourse of Rights*. Temple University Press.

Suk, J. 2006. Criminal Law Comes Home, 12 *Yale Law Journal*, 2.

Suk, J. 2009. *At Home in the Law: How the Domestic Violence Revolution is Transforming Privacy*. Yale University Press.

Sullivan, N. 1997. Fleshing Out Pleasure: Canonization or Crucifixion? 12 *Australian Feminist Studies* 26, 283.

Swash, R. 2007. Beenie Man, Sizzla and Capleton Renounce Homophobia. *The Guardian*, 14 June [online]. Available at: http://www.guardian.co.uk/music/2007/jun/14/news.rosieswash [accessed: 8 January 2013].

Sweet, L. et al. 2009. Officer in Gates Flap Tried to Save Reggie. *Boston Herald*, 23 July.

Szabo, T. and Short, R.V. 2000. How does Male Circumcision Protect against HIV Infection? 85 *British Medical Journal* 1, 19.

Tasker, F. and Golombok, S. 1997. *Growing Up in a Lesbian Family*. Guilford.

Tatchell, P. 2007a. Hate v. Free Speech. *The Guardian* [online]. Available at: http://commentisfree.guardian.co.uk/peter_tatchell/2007/10/hate_speech_v_free_speech.html [accessed: 8 January 2013].

Tatchell, P. 2007b. Reggae Tips: Top Jamaican singers have Signed a Deal to Renounce Homophobic Hatred and Halt 'Murder Music' – but Do They Really Mean it? *The Guardian* [online]. Available at: http://www.guardian.co.uk/commentisfree/2007/aug/02/reggaetips [accessed: 8 January 2013].

Tehranian, J. 2007. Compulsory Whiteness: Towards a Middle-Eastern Legal Scholarship. 82 *Indian Law Journal* 1, 1.

The Medical Institute for Sexual Health. 2013 [online]. Available at: www.medinstitute.org [accessed: 17 May 2013].

The Power of Pleasure. 2010 [online]. Institute of Development Studies, University of Brighton. Available at: http://www.ids.ac.uk/ids/news/powerpleasure.html [accessed: 31 October 2010].

The Sambhavana Trust. 2010 [online]. Available at: www.samabhavana.org [accessed: 31 October 2010].

The Victoria Advocate. 1991. Combat Role for Women Debated, 19 June.

Theidon, K. 2007. Transitional Subjects: The Disarmament, Demobilization and Reintegration of Former Combatants in Colombia. 1 *International Journal of Transitional Justice* 1, 66.

Theidon, K. 2009. Reconstructing Masculinities: The Disarmament, Demobilization and Reintegration of Former Combatants in Colombia. 31 *Human Rights Quarterly* 1, 1.

Thomasson, D. 2006. Single-sex Education is Good Common Sense. *Deseret Morning News*, 31 October.

Thompson, A.C. 1999. Stopping the Usual Suspects: Race and the Fourth Amendment. 74 *New York University Law Review* 4, 956.

Thompson, K. and Thompson, C.W. 2009. Officer Tells his Side of the Story in Gates Arrest. *Washington Post*, 24 July.

Thomson, M. 2008. *Endowed: Regulating the Male Sexed Body*. Routledge.

Thorne, B. 1993. *Gender Play: Girls and Boys in School*. Rutgers University Press.

Thornton, M. 2004. Neoliberal Melancholia: The Case of Feminist Legal Scholarship. 20 *Australian Feminist Law Journal*, 7.

Thornton, S. 2005. Implementing Flexible Tenure Clock Policies. 130 *New Directions for Higher Education*, 81.

Tickner, J.A. 1992. *Gender in International Relations: Feminist Perspectives on Achieving Global Security*. Columbia University Press.

Tickner, J.A. 2001. *Gendering World Politics*. Columbia University Press.

Topping, A. 2007. Victory for Gay Rights Campaign as Reggae Star Agrees to Ditch Homophobic Lyrics. *The Guardian* [online]. Available at: http://www.guardian.co.uk/uk/2007/jul/23/musicnews.gayrights [accessed: 8 January 2013].

Tosh, J. 2004. Hegemonic Masculinity and the History of Gender, in *Masculinities in Politics and War*, edited by S. Dudink, K. Hagerman and J. Tosh. Manchester University Press.

Toth, C. 2005. Women and the Military, in *The Handbook of Women, Psychology, and the Law*, edited by A. Barnes. Jossey-Bass.

Transitional Justice Institute. 2008. Peace Agreement Database [online]. Available at: http://www.transitionaljustice.ulster.ac.uk/peace_agreements_database.html [accessed: 3 January 2013].

Trinder, L. and Kellett, J. 2007. *The Longer-term Outcomes of In-court Conciliation*. Ministry of Justice.

Trinder, L. et al. 2005. *A Profile of Applicants and Respondents in Contact Cases in Essex*. DCA.

Trinder, L. et al. 2006. *Making Contact Happen or Making Contact Work? The Process and Outcomes of In-court Conciliation*. DCA.

Turner, B.S. 2006. *Vulnerability and Human Rights*. Pennsylvania State University Press.

Tyack, D. and Hansot, E. 1990. *Learning Together: A History of Coeducation in American Public Schools*. Yale University Press.

Tyre, P. 2005. Boy Brains, Girl Brains; Are Separate Classrooms the Best Way to Teach Kids? *Newsweek*, 19 September.

Tyre, P. 2008. *The Trouble with Boys: A Surprising Report Card on our Sons, their Problems at School, and What Parents and Educators Must Do*. Three Rivers Press.

U.S. Department of Defense Directive No. 6400.1. Family Advocacy Program. 2009 [online]. Available at: http://www.dtic.mil/whs/directives/corres/pdf/640001p.pdf [accessed: 11 August 2009].

U.S. Department of Justice, Bureau of Justice Statistics, 2000. Extent, Nature, and Consequences of Intimate Partner Violence: Findings from the National Violence against Women Survey [online]. Available at: http://www.ojp.usdoj.gov/nij/pubs-sum/181867.htm [accessed: 13 September 2009].

U.S. v Silk [1947] 331 U.S. 704.

UNAIDS/WHO. 2009. AIDS Epidemic Update. December. UNAIDS/WHO.

UNDDRC [United Nations Disarmament, Demobilization and Reintegration Resource Centre]. 2006. *Integrated Disarmament, Demobilization and Reintegration Standard: 2.20 Post-conflict Stabilization, Peace-building and Recovery Frameworks*. UNDDR.

UNDDRC. 2009. Country Programmes [online]. Available at: http://www.un.org/en/peacekeeping/operations/ [accessed: 1 December 2009).

UNDPKO [United Nations Department of Peacekeeping Operations]. 2000. Disarmament, Demobilization and Reintegration of Ex-combatants in a

Peacekeeping Environment: Principles and Guidelines [online]. Available at: http://reliefweb.int/sites/reliefweb.int/files/resources/7ED78CD7FEFA5FEEC1256DC60049CE9E-dpko-ex-comb-dec99.pdf [accessed: 3 January 2013].

UNHCR [United Nations High Commissioner for Refugees]. 2009. The UN Refugee Agency [online]. Available at: http://www.unhcr.org [accessed: 1 December 2009].

UNIFEM [United Nations Development Fund for Women]. 2004. Getting it Right, Doing it Right: Gender and Disarmament, Demobilization and Reintegration [online]. Available at: http://www.iknowpolitics.org/files/Getting_it_Right__Doing_it_Right.pdf [accessed: 3 January 2013].

United Kingdom Human Rights Act. 1998. 42, sched. 1, pt. I, arts. 10, 12, 14 [online]. Available at: http://www.legislation.gov.uk/ukpga/1998/42/schedule/1/part/I [accessed: 8 January 2013].

United Nations. 2002. *Human Development Report 2002*. United Nations.

United Nations. 2006. Operational Guide to the Integrated Disarmament, Demobilization and Reintegration Standards, OG 5.10, Peacekeeping and Stability Operations Institute [online]. Available at: http://pksoi.army.mil/doctrine_concepts/documents/UN%20Guidelines/IDDRS.pdf [accessed: 3 January 2013].

United Nations Department for Disarmament Affairs and the Office of the Special Adviser on Gender Issues and the Advancement of Women. 2001. Gender Perspectives on Disarmament, Demobilization, and Reintegration (DDR) [online]. Available at: http://www.un.org/disarmament/HomePage/gender/docs/note4.pdf [accessed: 3 January 2013].

United States v Morrison [2000] 529 U.S. 598.

United States v Virginia [1996] 518 U.S. 515.

United States Senate. 1980. Senate Rep. no. 96–826, at 159.

University of Michigan Center for the Education of Women. 2007. Family Friendly Policies in Higher Education: A Five-year Report [online]. Available at: http://www.umich.edu/~cew/PDFs/Redux%20Brief%20Final%205-1.pdf [accessed: 28 April 2010].

UNOCHA [United Nations Office for the Coordination of Humanitarian Affairs]. 2008. The Nature, Scope and Motivation for Sexual Violence against Men and Boys in Armed Conflict, Discussion Paper 2, UN OCHA Research Meeting, 26 June [online]. Available at: http://ochaonline.un.org/OchaLinkClick.aspx?link=ocha&docId=1092305 [accessed: 3 January 2013].

UNODA [United Nations Office for Disarmament Affairs]. 2013 [online]. Available at: http://www.un.org/disarmament/ [accessed: 3 January 2013].

Valdes, F. 1995a. Queers, Sissies, Dykes, and Tom Boys: Deconstructing the Conflation of 'Sex,' 'Gender,' and 'Sex Orientation' in Euro-American Law and Society. 83 *University of California Law Review* 1, 33.

Valdes, F. 1995b. Sex and Race in Queer Legal Culture: Ruminations on Identities and Inter-connectivities. 5 *Southern California Review of Law and Women's Studies*, 25.

Valdes, F. 1998. Beyond Sexual Orientation in Queer Legal Theory: Majoritarianism, Multidimensionality and Responsibility in Social Justice Scholarship or Legal Scholars as Cultural Warriors. 75 *Denver University Law Review* 4, 1409.

Vale v. Louisiana [1970] 399 U.S. 30.

Vallance-Webb, G. 2008. Child Contact: Vengeful Mothers, Good Fathers and Vice Versa. *Family Law* 678.

Valocchi, S. 2005. Not Yet Queer Enough: The Lessons of Queer Theory for the Sociology of Gender and Sexuality. 19 *Gender & Society*, 750.

Vandavel, J.M., MD. 1889. Circumcision Enforced by Law. 5 *Daniel's Texas Medical Journal*, 7.

Varnum v. Brien [Iowa 2009] 763 N.W.2d 862.

Varona, A. and Monks, J. 2000. En/gendering Equality: Seeking Relief under Title VII against Employment Discrimination Based on Sexual Orientation. 7 *William & Mary Journal of Women and the Law*, 67.

Veliz v Rental Services Corp. USA, Inc. [M.D. Fla. 2003] 313 F. Supp. 2d 1317.

Velte, K. 2001. Towards Constitutional Recognition of the Lesbian-parented Family. 26 *New York University Review of Law & Social Change* 3, 245.

Vennochi, J. 2009. Machismo and the Gates Incident. *Boston Globe*, 23 July.

Victor, B. 2004. *Army of Roses: Inside the World of Palestinian Women Suicide Bombers*. Robinson.

Visit Jamaica. 2011 [online]. Available at: http://www.visitjamaica.com/ [accessed: 15 January 2011].

Vojdik, V.K. 2002. Gender Outlaws: Challenging Masculinity in Traditionally Male Institutions. 17 *Berkeley Women's Law Journal* 1, 68.

Vojdik, V. 2005a. Beyond Stereotyping in Equal Protection Doctrine: Reframing the Exclusion of Women from Combat. 57 *Alabama Law Review*, 303.

Vojdik, V. 2005b. Women and War: A Critical Discourse Panel Two – Women Warriors. 20 *Berkeley Journal of Gender Law and Justice*, 342.

Von Drehle, D. 2007. The Boys Are All Right. *Time*, 6 August.

Vorchheimer v. Sch. Dist. [1976] 532 F.2d 880, 881.

Vorchheimer v. Sch. Dist. [1977] 430 U.S. 703.

Waddoups, C.J. 2000. Unions and Wages in Nevada's Hotel-casino Industry. 21 *Journal of Labor Research* 2, 345.

Wailoo, K. et al., eds. 2006. *A Death Retold: Jessica Santillan, the Bungled Transplant and the Paradoxes of Medical Citizenship*. University of North Carolina Press.

Wald, M. 2006. Adults' Sexual Orientation and State Determinations regarding Placement of Children. 40 *Family Law Quarterly* 3, 381.

Waldby, C. 1996. *AIDS and the Body Politic: Biomedical and Sexual Difference*. Routledge.

Wallace, J.E. and Young, M.C. 2008. Parenthood and Productivity: A Study of Demands, Resources and Family-friendly Firms. 72 *Journal of Vocational Behavior* 1, 110.

Wallbank, J. 2005. Getting Tough on Mothers: Regulating Contact and Residence. 15 *Feminist Legal Studies* 2, 189.
Wallbank, J., Choudhry, S. and Herring, J., eds. 2009. *Rights, Gender and Family Law.* Routledge-Cavendish.
Waller, M.R. 2002. *My Baby's Father: Unmarried Parents and Paternal Responsibility*. Cornell University Press.
Walsh, M.R. 1977. *'Doctors Wanted: No Women Need Apply': Sexual Barriers in the Medical Profession, 1835–1975*. Yale University Press.
Wardle, L.D. 1997. The Potential Impact of Homosexual Parenting on Children. 1997 *University of Illinois Law Review*, 833.
Wards Cove Packing Company v Atonio [1989] 490 U.S. 642.
Warner, J. 2009. A Lot Said and Unsaid, about Race. *New York Times*, 26 July.
Wascoe, D. 2006. Lesson in Letting Boys Be Boys, Girls Be Girls: Schools Try Single-sex Classes to Close Gender Gaps in Education. *Star Tribune*, 15 May.
Washington, H. 2008. *Medical Apartheid: The Dark History of Medical Experimentation on Black Americans from Colonial Times to the Present.* Harlem Moon.
Watney, S. 1988. The Spectacle of AIDS, in *AIDS: Cultural Analysis/Cultural Activism*, edited by D. Crimp. MIT Press.
Watson v Forth Worth Bank & Trust [1988] 487 U.S. 977.
Wawer, M.J. et al. 2009. Circumcision in HIV-infected Men and its Effect on HIV Transmission to Female Partners in Rakai, Uganda: A Randomised Controlled Trial. 374 *Lancet*, 229.
Weaver, C.N. 2005. The Changing Image of Hispanic Americans. 27 *Hispanic Journal of Behavioral Sciences* 3, 337.
Weaver-Hightower, M. 2003. The 'Boy Turn' in Research on Gender and Education. 73 *Review of Educational Research* 4, 471.
Weaver-Hightower, M. 2008. *The Politics of Policy in Boys' Education: Getting Boys 'Right'*. Palgrave.
Weber, M.J. 1993. Immersed in an Educational Crisis: Alternative Programs for African–American Males. 45 *Stanford Law Review* 4, 1099.
Weil, E. 2008. Teaching to the Testosterone. *The New York Times Magazine*, 2 March.
Weiler, J.D. 2000. *Codes and Contradictions: Race, Gender Identity, and Schooling*. State University of New York Press.
Weinberg, M.S. and Williams, C.J. 1988. Black Sexuality: A Test of Two Theories. 25 *Journal of Sex Research* 2, 197.
Weisberg, D.K. 1993. *Feminist Legal Theory: Foundations*, 1st edn. Temple University Press.
Weisberg, D.S. et al. 2008. The Seductive Allure of Neuroscience Explanations. 20 *Journal of Cognitive Neuroscience* 3, 470.
Weiss v. United States [1994] 510 U.S. 163.

Wencelblat, P. 2004. Boys Will Be Boys? An Analysis of Male-on-male Heterosexual Sexual Violence. 38 *Columbia Journal of Law and Social Problems*, 61.

Wermers, J. 2004. A Return to Roots: Isolating Boys in Single-sex Programs Grows More Common. *Richmond Times Dispatch*, 4 May.

West, C. and Zimmerman, D.H. 2008. Doing Gender, in *Sex, Gender, and Sexuality*, edited by A.L. Ferber et al. Oxford University Press.

Whaley Eager, P. 2008. *From Freedom Fighters to Terrorists: Women and Political Violence*. Ashgate.

Wheeler, S. 2003. Men and Therapy – Are They Compatible? 3 *Counselling and Psychotherapy Research* 1, 2.

White, M. 2000. *Reflections on Narrative Practice*. Dulwich Centre Publications.

White, M. 2005. Children, Trauma and Subordinate Storyline Development. 3–4 *International Journal of Narrative Therapy and Community Work*, 10.

Whitehead, S. 2002. *Men and Masculinities: Key Themes and New Directions*. Polity.

WHO [World Health Organization]. 2002a. Sexual Health [online]. Available at: www.who.int/reproductive-health/gender/sexualhealth.html#2 [accessed: 31 October 2010].

WHO. 2002b. Sexuality [online]. Available at: www.who.int/reproductive-health/gender/sexual_health.html [accessed: 31 October 2010].

WHO/UNAIDS, 2007. New Data on Male Circumcision and HIV Prevention: Policy and Programme Implications [online]. Available at: http://data.unaids.org/pub/Report/2007/mc_recommendations_en.pdf [accessed: 21 January 2013].

Wiegman, R. 1993. The Anatomy of Lynching. 3 *Journal of the History of Sexuality* 3, 445.

Wiegman, R. 2002. The Progress of Gender: Whither 'Women'?, in *Women's Studies on its Own: A Next Wave Reader in Institutional Change*. Duke University Press.

Williams, G.I. and Williams, R.H. 1995. All We Want is Equality: Rhetorical Framing in the Fathers' Rights Movement, in *Images of Issues: Typifying Contemporary Social Problems*, edited by J. Best. Aldine De Gruyter.

Williams, J. 1989. Deconstructing Gender. 87 *Michigan Law Review*, 797.

Williams, J. 2000. *Unbending Gender: Why Family and Work Conflict and What to Do about it*. Oxford University Press.

Williams, J. 2009. Obama Parries, and Critics Pounce; GOP, Police Officials Decry his Critique. *Boston Globe*, 24 July.

Williams, J. and Segal, N. 2001. Beyond the Maternal Wall: Relief for Family Caregivers who are Discriminated against on the Job. 26 *Harvard Women's Law Journal*, 77.

Williams, R.M. 1998. Living at the Crossroads: Explorations in Race, Nationality, Sexuality, and Gender, in *The House that Race Built: Original Essays by Toni*

Morrison, Angela Y. Davis, Cornel West, and Others on Black Americans and Politics in America Today, edited by W. Lubiano. Vintage.

Williams, T. 2009. 80 Are Killed in 3 Suicide Bombings in Iraq. *New York Times*, 23 April [online]. Available at: http://www.nytimes.com/2009/04/24/world/middleeast/24iraq.html [accessed: 7 January 2013].

Williams, V. 2004. Reform or Retrenchment?: Single-sex Education and the Construction of Race and Gender. 2004 *Wisconsin Law Review*, 15.

Williams, W.W. 1982. The Equality Crisis: Some Reflections on Culture, Courts, and Feminism. 7 *Women's Rights Law Reporter*, 175.

Willis, P. 1979. Shop Floor Culture, Masculinity and the Wage Form, in *Working-class Culture: Studies in History and Theory*, edited by J. Clarke, C. Critcher and R. Johnson. Hutchinson.

Wilson, K.K. 1998. The Disparate Classification of Gender and Sexual Orientation in American Psychiatry, Paper presented at Annual Meeting of the American Psychiatric Association, 2 June.

Wilson, R. 2004. Northwestern University Concludes Investigation of Sex Researcher but Keeps Results Secret. *The Chronicle of Higher Education*, 1 December.

Wilson, R. 2005. The Laws of Physics. 52 *The Chronicle of Higher Education* 12, A10.

Wilson, R. 2008. More Colleges are Adding Family-friendly Benefits. 54 *The Chronicle of Higher Education* 45, B22.

Wilton, T. 1997. *Engendering AIDS: Deconstructing Sex, Text and Epidemic*. Sage.

Woan, S. 2008. White Sexual Imperialism: A Theory of Asian Feminist Jurisprudence. 14 *Washington and Lee Journal of Civil Rights and Social Justice*, 275.

Wolfinger, N.H., Mason, M.A. and Goulden, M. 2008. Problems in the Pipeline: Gender, Marriage, and Fertility in the Ivory Tower. 79 *Journal of Higher Education* 4, 388.

Wolfinger, N.H., Mason, M.A. and Goulden, M. 2009a. Alone in the Ivory Tower. 31 *Journal of Family Issues* 12, 1652.

Wolfinger, N.H., Mason, M.A. and Goulden, M. 2009b. Stay in the Game: Gender, Family Formation and Alternative Trajectories in the Academic Life Course. 87 *Social Forces* 3, 1591.

Women in Military Service for America Memorial Foundation, Inc. 2011. Statistics on Women in the Military [online]. Available at: http://www.womensmemorial.org/PDFs/StatsonWIM.pdf [accessed: 3 July 2013].

Women's Research Institute. 2003. Chronology of Significant Policy Changes Affecting Women in the Military: 1947–2003 [online]. Available at: http://www.wrei.org/Women%20in%20the%20Military/Women%20in%20the%20Military%20Chronology%20of%20Legal%20Policy.pdf [accessed: 22 March 2010].

Women's Worlds Congress. 2008. 10th International Interdisciplinary Congress on Women, Complutense University, Madrid (Spain), 3–9 July [online]. Available at: http://www.mmww08.org/index.cfm?nav_id=41 [accessed: 31 October 2010].

Woodall, K. and Woodall, N. 2007. *Putting Children First: A Handbook for Separated Parents*. Piaktus.

Woodhouse, B.B. 2008. Individualism and Early Childhood in the U.S.: How Culture and Tradition Have Impeded Evidence-based Reform. 8 *Journal of Korean Law*, 97.

Woodhouse, B.B. 2009. A World Fit for Children is a World Fit for Everyone: Ecogenerism, Feminism, and Vulnerability. 46 *Houston Law Review*, 817.

Woodruff v. Woodruff [N.C. Ct. App. 1979] 260 S.E.2d 775.

Wright, W.J. 1991–92. The Endangered Black Male Child. *Education Leadership*, December–January.

Wulf, H. 1992. *Disarmament as a Chance for Human Development: Is There a Peace Dividend?* Human Development Report Office, Occasional Paper no. 5. UNDP.

Wygant v Jackson Board of Education [1986] 476 U.S. 267.

Yoshino, K. 2002. Covering. 111 *Yale Law Journal* 4, 769.

Young, I.M. 1990. *Justice and the Politics of Difference*. Princeton University Press.

Younge, G. 2006. Troubled Island: In Jamaica, where Politicians are Openly Homophobic and Song Lyrics Incite Violence against Gay People, Coming Out can be Fatal. *The Guardian* [online]. Available at: http://www.guardian.co.uk/world/2006/apr/27/gayrights.comment [accessed: 8 January 2013].

Yuval-Davis, N. 1997. *Gender and Nation*. Sage.

Zarabadi, S. 2007. Koshte Mishavand ta Bokoshand (They Die in order to Kill). 140 *Zanan* [online]. No longer available.

Zheng v Liberty [2d Cir. 2003] 355 F. 3d 61.

Zinn, M.B. 1982. Chicano Men and Masculinity. 10 *Journal of Ethnic Studies* 2, 39.

Zucker, K. and Spitzer, R. 2005. Was the Gender Identity Disorder of Childhood Diagnosis Introduced into DSM-III as a Backdoor Maneuver to Replace Homosexuality? A Historical Note. 31 *Sex and Marital Therapy* 1, 31.

Index